D1557583

OXFORD HISTORICAL MONOGRAPHS

THE PROTESTANT CRUSADE IN GREAT BRITAIN

1829–1860

JOHN WOLFFE

CLARENDON PRESS · OXFORD
1991

Oxford University Press, Walton Street, Oxford OX2 6DP
Oxford New York Toronto
Delhi Bombay Calcutta Madras Karachi
Petaling Jaya Singapore Hong Kong Tokyo
Nairobi Dar es Salaam Cape Town
Melbourne Auckland

and associated companies in
Berlin Ibadan

Oxford is a trade mark of Oxford University Press

Published in the United States
by Oxford University Press, New York

British Library Cataloguing in Publication Data
Wolffe, John
The Protestant crusade in Great Britain, 1829–1860
1. Great Britain. Catholic Church. Persecution 1789 –
Protestant churches
I. Title
272. 9

ISBN 0–19–820199–0

Library of Congress Cataloging in Publication Data
Wolffe, John.
The Protestant Crusade in Great Britain, 1829–1860 / John Wolffe.
p. cm.—(Oxford historical monographs)
Includes bibliographical references and index.
1. Protestant churches—Great Britain—History—19th century.
2. Anti-Catholicism—Great Britain—History—19th century. 3. Great
Britain—Church history—19th century. I. Title. II. Series.
BX4838.W64 1991 305.6'2041'09034—dc20 90–47443
ISBN 0–19–820199–0

Typeset by Pentacor PLC, High Wycombe, Bucks
Printed and bound in
Great Britain by Bookcraft Ltd.,
Midsomer Norton, Bath

To the memory of my father

BERTRAM WOLFFE
(1922–1988)

PREFACE

To write the history of mid-nineteenth-century anti-Catholicism is to venture into a scholarly minefield. In order to circumscribe the dangers, four points must be made at the outset. Firstly, in approaching a subject of which polemic is the very essence, the ideal of scholarly historical detachment lies not in passing judgement on the protagonists but in seeking to understand them. In other words, the purpose of this book is not to consider whether anti-Catholic agitators were justified in their attacks, but to explain why they felt and acted as they did, and what consequences their campaigns had. Secondly, the topic is one with enormous ramifications in the history of the period: consequently, the definition of a basis and a limit for research has been a recurrent problem. In the attempt to steer a safe course between the Scylla of superficiality and the Charybdis of excessive detail, six central chapters primarily examining the development of the anti-Catholic societies and their impact will be framed by opening and concluding discussions of the wider context. Thirdly, the very language employed may seem to have a polemical implication, so it is necessary at the outset to define the usage of some key words. The hyphenated 'anti-Catholic' is adopted here as more neutral than 'anticatholic' or 'anti-Roman Catholic'. 'Protestant' is used more narrowly than is conventional, as a virtual synonym for 'anti-Catholic', and implying active support for movements against Catholicism. This reflects contemporary usage by the societies themselves, and conveys the flavour of the movement's perception of itself. As an indication of this specific usage, a capital 'P' will be employed. The word 'priest' is used exclusively of Roman Catholic clergy. With a capital 'E', 'Evangelical' refers to parties in the Established Churches; in lower case, 'evangelical' incorporates Dissenters as well. Finally, it will be clear that this book reflects a view of religion as, at its core, an irreducible historical force which, however much influenced by political, ideological, and socio-economic factors, cannot be explained solely in terms of them.

I have naturally incurred many debts both in the writing of this book and in completing the research for the thesis on which it is based. John Walsh originally suggested the subject and has maintained a strong

viii   *Preface*

interest in the progress of the work; John Prest was a painstaking and
generous supervisor, and Michael Brock has been a most helpful
editor. David Bebbington and Sheridan Gilley read large portions of
earlier drafts and made many helpful suggestions. I have also gained
much from comments made by Walter Arnstein, John Bossy, David
Hempton, Donal Kerr, Donald Lewis, Denis Paz, and Allen Warren,
and by numerous other friends, colleagues, and students in Oxford,
London, and York.

Current officers of the surviving Protestant societies have given
most generously of their time and assistance: I am especially indebted
to the Revd David Samuel of the Protestant Reformation Society and
Church Society, Mr Ernst Priefert of the National Club, the Revd
Clive Calver of the Evangelical Alliance, and the Revd A. Sinclair
Horne of the Scottish Reformation Society. I am pleased to thank the
following for allowing me access to documents: the Duke of Norfolk,
the Earl of Clarendon, the Earl of Derby, Lord Kenyon, Lord Blake,
G. Finch, Esq., the Dean and Chapter of Canterbury, the Society of
Jesus, the Trustees of the Broadlands Archives Trust (Shaftesbury)
Papers), and the National Trust (Disraeli Papers). I also acknowledge
my gratitude to the late Earl of Harrowby.

Financial support was gratefully received from the Department of
Education and Science, Exeter College, Oxford, The Twenty-Seven
Foundation, and the History Department of the University of York,
which also generously allowed me a sabbatical term to work on the
manuscript. Comparative work on the United States was supported by
fellowships at the American Antiquarian Society and the Newberry
Library. Several friends and relatives have been generous with their
hospitality to me when on research visits. This book also owes a great
deal to my parents: my mother typed some earlier drafts and has been a
never-failing source of encouragement; while the earliest and greatest
of my intellectual debts is recorded in the dedication.

JOHN WOLFFE

York
June 1989

CONTENTS

LIST OF FIGURES

LIST OF TABLES

LIST OF ABBREVIATIONS

AR	*Annual Report.*
Boase	Frederic Boase (ed.), *Modern English Biography* (Truro, 1892–1921).
BP	*British Protestant.*
DNB	L. Stephen and S. Lee (eds.), *The Dictionary of National Biography* (1885–1900).
EA	Evangelical Alliance.
2 *Hansard*	*Hansard's Parliamentary Debates*, 2nd series.
3 *Hansard*	*Hansard's Parliamentary Debates*, 3rd series.
NC	National Club.
PAll	Protestant Alliance.
PAss	Protestant Association.
PDC	Protestant Defence Committee.
PM	*Protestant Magazine.*
PP	*Parliamentary Papers.*
PPO	*Penny Protestant Operative.*
PRO	Public Record Office.
R	*Record.*
RS	British Society for Promoting the Religious Principles of the Reformation (1827–53); Protestant Reformation Society (1853–).
SRO	Scottish Record Office.
SRS	Scottish Reformation Society.
TCD	Trinity College, Dublin.
WPC	*Wellington Political Correspondence*, i (1975), ed. J. Brooke and J. Gandy; ii (1986), ed. R. J. Olney and J. Melvin.

I

THE ROOTS OF ANTI-CATHOLICISM

ON 13 April 1829 George IV grudgingly but irrevocably gave his assent to Catholic Emancipation. The Ultra-Tory Duke of Newcastle condemned the king's weakness and failure to abide by his coronation oath which, the duke believed, put a seal on the destruction of the constitution and left the country a prey to anarchy and discord.[1] On the other hand, Bishop Bramston, the Roman Catholic Vicar Apostolic of the London District, wrote of a new and most important era for British Catholics, now 'by the wisdom and bounty of the Legislature placed civilly and politically on a level with their fellow-subjects'.[2] These contemporary judgements have been echoed by a number of historians. G. I. T. Machin writes of Emancipation as 'one of the great liberal achievements of English statesmanship'; A. D. Gilbert sees it as symbolizing dramatically 'the failure of the old monopolistic conception of the Establishment'; and J. C. D. Clark suggests that George IV's 'betrayal' of the constitution defined the end of the *ancien régime* in England.[3]

Such judgements on Emancipation must not obscure the fact that its effect was, if anything, to strengthen active anti-Catholicism. Early in 1831 a Catholic writer complained of the polemical onslaught which was being waged against the faith, on platforms and in the press, associated with the gross misrepresentation of Catholic practices and principles.[4] There was a lull in Protestant activity in 1832 and 1833, but it revived in 1834, reached a peak in the summer of 1835, and remained at a high level until 1841. A new wave began with the anti-Maynooth agitation of 1845. This had by no means subsided when the creation of the Roman Catholic episcopal hierarchy in the autumn of

[1] Nottingham University Library, Newcastle MSS (4th duke), Diary, Ne2F2, 12 Apr., 31 Dec. 1829.
[2] Quoted by B. Ward, *The Eve of Catholic Emancipation* (1912), iii. 272
[3] G. I. T. Machin, *The Catholic Question in English Politics 1820 to 1830* (Oxford, 1964), 193; A. D. Gilbert, *Religion and Society in Industrial England* (1976), 125; J. C. D. Clark, *English Society 1688–1832* (Cambridge, 1985), 419.
[4] *Catholic Magazine*, 1 (1831), 2.

1850 was followed by widespread public indignation, raising 'No Popery' frenzy to its highest pitch since the Gordon Riots of 1780. Antagonism to Catholics continued very much in evidence during the 1850s, both in popular disturbances such as the Stockport riots of 1852 and in political campaigns for the repeal of the Maynooth grant and the regulation of convents. These had lost momentum by the end of the decade, but during the 1860s and 1870s anti-Catholic feeling was kept alive by the attack on Anglican ritualism and the inflammatory lectures of William Murphy. Victorian 'No Popery' never approached the savage intensity of the Gordon Riots, but there is strong support for the view that, as a whole, the half-century succeeding 1829 saw much more antagonism to Catholics than that which had preceded Emancipation.

Any attempt to understand nineteenth-century anti-Catholicism has to begin by coming to terms with the diversity and pervasiveness of the phenomenon. Hatred of Catholicism was associated with the popular culture of Guy Fawkes celebrations, the communal rivalries of Lancashire and Clydeside, the sexual attitudes of Victorian middle-class society, and the yearning of all groups for excitement and entertainment. On the plane of political theory, Protestantism was integral to much discussion of the nature of the constitution, the Establishment of the Church of England, and the maintenance of the Union with Ireland. Anti-Catholic sentiment was seldom far below the surface in parliamentary discussion of Irish and ecclesiastical issues, and the same motifs were readily rehearsed before a wide audience at election time. Evangelicals, fired by prophetic speculation about the impending fall of Babylon and frustration at the failure of their missionary efforts in Ireland, added very significantly to the ferment.

The most virulent anti-Catholicism was to be found in the areas of substantial Irish settlement, in Lancashire and the West of Scotland. London and Birmingham were also notable centres. Elsewhere in England antagonism towards Catholics tended to be just as strong in the cathedral cities, resorts, and country towns of the South as in the industrializing areas of Yorkshire and the North-East. Scotland, though quieter than England in the 1830s, began to catch up during the 1840s, and by the mid-1850s seemed to be setting the pace for anti-Catholic activity throughout Britain. North of the Border, militant Protestantism was centred on Edinburgh as well as Glasgow, and found active sympathizers in numerous other towns.

In 1851, when Protestant fervour was at its height, John Henry

Newman delivered a series of lectures which cogently addressed the question of

> why it is, that, in this intelligent nation, and in this rational nineteenth century, we Catholics are so despised and hated by our own countrymen, with whom we have lived all our lives, that they are prompt to believe any story, however extravagant, that is told to our disadvantage; as if beyond a doubt we were, every one of us, either brutishly deluded or preternaturally hypocritical . . . [5]

It is unfortunate that Newman's *Lectures on the Present Position of Catholics in England* have been remembered more for the libel action to which they gave occasion[6] than for their actual content. They were an interesting treatment of the problem of anti-Catholicism from an observer whose partisan commitment did not cause him to slide into mere polemic and who had the advantage of viewing the religious battlefield from both sides of the tortured no man's land of Littlemore. Newman maintained that the contemporary English Protestant view of the Roman Catholic Church was the result of ignorance of its true nature combined with a relentless refusal to listen seriously to anything that might be said in its defence.[7] Protestantism was based on 'immemorial unauthenticated tradition', embodied in the Crown at the Reformation, transmitted by the mechanisms of government and the law, perpetuated in literary and cultural life, and sustained by the clergy of the Anglican Establishment.[8] The tradition was fed by unverified allegations which had originally arisen from misunderstanding, wilful distortion, or sheer delusion. Accurate information about Catholicism was ignored because it appeared inconsistent with the ideas which were already held.[9] Naturally, Catholics were subject to human failings, but it was logically inconsistent that these lapses should be charged against their religion, when parallel, equally numerous, Protestant faults were not so regarded.[10] At the root of Protestant distortion of the reality of Catholicism was deeply ingrained prejudice which gave a hostile construction to all factual evidence.[11] There was a 'growing class' which sought to rise above such biased

---

[5] J. H. Newman, *Lectures on the Present Position of Catholics in England* (1892 edn.), 1.
[6] See below, pp. 124–5.   [7] Newman, *Lectures*, pp. 8–24, Lecture I.
[8] Ibid. 42–82, Lecture II.   [9] Ibid. 83–176, Lectures III and IV.
[10] Ibid. 177–222, Lecture V.   [11] Ibid. 223–70, Lecture VI.

judgements, but it too ultimately found itself hostile to Catholicism. This was because it differed from it on the level of first principles, as in the rejection of the possibility of miracles in post-apostolic times.[12] It was almost impossible for Catholics to answer arguments against their Church, because Protestants would refuse to listen, believing their adversaries to be irrevocably evil.[13] Catholics must respond by tactful, patient, and courageous involvement in local life, which ultimately should begin to reduce antagonism towards them.[14] Newman qualified his general thesis to the extent of admitting somewhat contemptuously that 'there are arguments of a different calibre . . . which weigh against Catholics with half-a-dozen members of a University',[15] but in general he was quite certain that anti-Catholicism was a product of psychological, historical, and cultural factors rather than of rational conviction.

Newman's account of the mental and social processes lying behind anti-Catholicism can be refined by reference to the work of modern social scientists, who have examined similar attitudes in twentieth-century America and contemporary Northern Ireland. Prejudice is a consequence of the inherent tendency of the human mind to generalize, and its capacity to form irrational categories quite as readily as rational ones. Once assumptions have been made, conflicting evidence is either ignored or merely admitted as an exception which does not affect the general principle.[16] A vicious circle forms whereby stereotypes are reinforced by ignorance, itself arising from the social separation caused by prejudice.[17] Genuine cultural differences and divergent value systems usually combine with elements of economic competition. In addition, Protestants display rational, if disproportionate, opposition to the tendency of Catholicism to involve itself in all aspects of the social order.[18] In Northern Ireland explicit anti-Catholicism also serves the function of uniting otherwise disparate elements in the Protestant community.[19]

For the historian, however, analysis of the mental and sociological processes which contribute to the development of anti-Catholicism can be no more than a starting-point. The diversity of the forms in

---

[12] Newman, *Lectures*, pp. 271–314, Lecture VII.   [13] Ibid. 315–61, Lecture VIII.
[14] Ibid. 363–403, Lecture IX.   [15] Ibid. 126, Lecture III.
[16] G. W. Allport, *The Nature of Prejudice* (Reading, Mass., 1954), 17–27.
[17] D. O. Moberg. *The Church as a Social Institution* (Englewood Cliffs, NJ, 1962), 313; R. Harris, *Prejudice and Tolerance in Ulster* (Manchester, 1972), 149.
[18] Moberg, *Church as a Social Institution*, pp. 311–16.
[19] Harris, *Prejudice and Tolerance*, pp. 156–65.

which antagonism to Rome was expressed means that theoretical generalizations have to be assessed with great care. More specifically, both Newman and modern social scientists, though for very different reasons, have tended to misunderstand the distinction between negative prejudice and positive religious belief. Furthermore, the relationship between aristocratic, middle-class, and working-class varieties of anti-Catholicism requires consideration not only as a means of isolating the causes of antagonism, but also in order to relate religious conflict to social class. It is also important to take note of the oscillations in 'No Popery' feeling, which suggest that Newman's view of a constantly transmitted tradition should be refined. In other words, broad judgements about the significance and nature of Victorian anti-Catholicism can be no substitute for detailed investigation of it.

Historical treatment of anti-Catholicism has naturally tended to focus on particular aspects of the problem, in the hope of bringing coherence to a diffuse subject. The pioneering but limited study of J. E. Handley considered anti-Catholicism as an aspect of the history of the Irish in Britain, an approach which has been developed in more recent work by other scholars.[20] In 1956 G. A. Cahill was the first to treat Protestantism as a political force, and his contribution has been followed by detailed narrative accounts from G. I. T. Machin.[21] Meanwhile, others have been approaching the problem from the perspective of religious history, whether as an aspect of evangelicalism or as the obverse of the history of Roman Catholicism itself.[22] E. R. Norman provided something of a cross-section of 'No Popery' activity through the analysis of some major outbursts, and W. Ralls explored the background to the outcry against the 'Papal Aggression' of 1850.[23] A recent book by W. L. Arnstein has used the career of the prominent back-bencher Charles Newdegate as a connecting theme.[24] Arnstein

[20] J. E. Handley, *The Irish in Modern Scotland* (Cork, 1947), 94–117; R. Swift and S. Gilley (eds.), *The Irish in the Victorian City* (1985), 6–8 and *passim*.

[21] G. A. Cahill, 'Irish Catholicism and English Toryism', *Review of Politics*, 19 (1956), 62–76; G. I. T. Machin, *Politics and the Churches in Great Britain, 1832–1868* (Oxford, 1977), 91–9, 169–80, 218–51; id., *Catholic Question*.

[22] I. S. Rennie, 'Evangelicalism and English Public Life', Ph.D. thesis (Toronto, 1962); P. Toon, *Evangelical Theology 1833–1856* (1979); E. R. Norman, *The English Catholic Church in the Nineteenth Century* (Oxford, 1984), 15–24.

[23] E. R. Norman, *Anti-Catholicism in Victorian England* (1968); W. Ralls, 'The Papal Aggression of 1850: A Study in Victorian Anti-Catholicism', *Church History*, 43 (1974), 242–56. Ralls's article has recently been reprinted in G. Parsons (ed.), *Religion in Victorian Britain*, iv. *Interpretations* (Manchester, 1988), 115–34.

[24] W. L. Arnstein, *Protestant versus Catholic in Mid-Victorian England* (Columbia, Mo., 1982).

developed the thesis that anti-Catholicism is better perceived as a symptom of rivalry between the Churches than as merely negative prejudice, a view that had already been advanced by Sheridan Gilley in his treatment of rival Protestant and Roman Catholic missions in the London slums.[25] The development of interest in popular culture has directed attention towards Guy Fawkes celebrations, but a seminal article by G. F. A. Best, written twenty years ago, still remains the most effective general treatment of popular Protestantism.[26]

The study of anti-Catholicism suffers particularly from the general methodological dilemma that a historian's conclusions are likely to a considerable extent to be predetermined by his initial terms of reference. Historians of the Irish see it as a product of communal tensions; students of politics relate it to party competition; while Church historians emphasize the primacy of theological and ecclesi-ological issues. This confusion is compounded by the fundamental difficulty of taking as a starting-point a concept which, however much vindicated by historical common sense, is not susceptible to precise definition and will inevitably tacitly be understood in different ways by different writers.

In the face of this problem, the organizational core of anti-Catholicism will be examined in this book as a means of achieving some objective historiographical coherence, while bridging the conventional subdisciplinary divides between political, social, and ecclesiastical history. Anti-Catholic agitations were pursued by a variety of societies and pressure groups, especially the British Society for Promoting the Religious Principles of the Reformation, founded in 1827, the Protestant Association (1835), the National Club (1845), the Scottish Reformation Society (1850), and the Protestant Alliance (1851).[27] None of these organizations ever numbered their member-

---

[25] S. Gilley, 'Protestant London, No-Popery and the Irish Poor, 1830–1860', *Recusant History*, 10 (1970), 210–21; 11 (1971), 21–38.

[26] R. D. Storch, 'Please to Remember the Fifth of November', in R. D. Storch (ed.), *Popular Culture and Custom in Nineteenth Century Britain* (1982), 71–99; G. F. A. Best, 'Popular Protestantism in Victorian Britain', in R. Robson (ed.), *Ideas and Institutions of Victorian Britain* (1967), 115–42. Since I completed the manuscript of this book, Professor Denis Paz has graciously sent me a copy of the text of his proposed book on 'Popular Anti-Catholicism in Mid-Victorian England'. This has come too late for me to take any specific account of it here, but it can be noted that it develops and updates Best's work in important ways, and should serve as a useful complement to my own work.

[27] For a full list of Protestant societies, see Appendix.

ship in more than thousands, and, even taken together, they cannot be regarded as a mass movement on anything approaching the level of Chartism or the Catholic Association in Ireland. Nevertheless, when consideration is given to the large audiences at many of their meetings, to the numerous visits carried out by their agents, and to the considerable literature which they published and circulated, it is clear that the Protestant societies, hitherto largely neglected by historians, merit careful investigation. Their concerns linked those aspects of anti-Catholicism which scholars have been prone to separate from each other: the articulation of Protestant ideology and theology; the stimulation of 'No Popery' feeling in the country; the evangelization of Roman Catholics; and the marshalling of political pressure. When the organizations are investigated from outside as well as from within, and it is recognized that their successes and failures were by no means synonymous with the strengths and weaknesses of anti-Catholicism in Britain, valuable insights are yielded into the motivation and objectives of those who espoused 'No Popery' sentiments. It is not pretended that this approach will provide a 'total' history of 'anti-Catholicism', any more than the prudent historian of the Whig–Liberal political structures in the same period would claim to have written a complete history of 'liberalism', but it should set the subject in a clearer framework than it has hitherto possessed.

A central theme of this book will be the relationship between anti-Catholicism and conflicts between Protestants, above all the onslaught of Dissent on the Establishment. The thesis will be developed that the strength of anti-Catholicism in the mid-nineteenth century was not, as Newman supposed, a simple result of the dominance of an Anglican religious tradition. It was due rather to the efforts of a beleaguered Established Church to defend itself from Nonconformist attack, and to the search of evangelicalism, both Anglican and Dissenting, for a defined identity, at a period when the enthusiasm and rapid expansion which had characterized the early nineteenth century was beginning to lose momentum.

Attention will be centred on the three decades following Emancipation, up to about 1860. The year 1829 hardly needs to be defended as a point of departure. Catholic Relief had a considerable psychological impact on Protestant and Catholic alike, and was symbolic of other important changes. It coincided with a period of ferment in evangelicalism and of new-found self-confidence among Roman

8   *The Roots of Anti-Catholicism*

Catholics, while the Irish influx was reaching a level which was forcing adaptation upon the Roman Church.[28] There is no such obvious watershed to serve as a terminal date, but 1860 has been chosen as representing a discernible lull and related change in the nature of the movement. In the political context, this was the mid-point of the Palmerston ascendancy which succeeded the instability of the central years of the century in which the Protestant societies, like other pressure groups, had enjoyed particular influence. Ireland, which was an otherwise almost constant stimulus to anti-Catholic feeling in Britain, was passing through one of the quietest periods of its history under the Union. In the religious sphere, Darwin, shortly to be joined by Colenso and the authors of *Essays and Reviews*, was providing a rival challenge to Protestant orthodoxy, while the Revival of 1859 was absorbing the energy of much of the evangelical constituency. Ritualism was certainly becoming an issue, but it was not to be systematically agitated until the formation of the Church Association in 1864. On a popular level, Irish immigration was passing its peak, and Guy Fawkes celebrations were shortly to begin to change their nature.[29] The discontinuity must not be exaggerated, but it was probably greater around 1860 than at any other date between 1829 and 1914.

In the remainder of this chapter the background to the early Victorian anti-Catholic movement will be analysed, beginning with a consideration of the transmission of the anti-Catholic tradition in Britain since the Reformation, and particularly since the eighteenth century. It will be suggested that the quarter-century after the Gordon Riots in 1780 saw a substantial receding of anti-Catholicism and that its nineteenth-century history needs to be viewed primarily as a revival rather than a continuation. Two reasons for this revival, the changing nature of Catholicism itself and the political controversy over Emancipation, will be considered at the end of this chapter, and a third factor, the influence of evangelicalism, which was the most immediate stimulus to the emergence of Protestant societies from the late 1820s onwards, will be explored in Chapter 2.

Anti-Catholicism can readily be traced back to the Reformation,

[28] J. Bossy, *The English Catholic Community 1570–1850* (1975), 427; C. Johnson, *Developments in the Roman Catholic Church in Scotland 1789–1829* (Edinburgh, 1983), 249.
[29] M. A. G. O'Tuathaigh, in Swift and Gilley, *Irish in the Victorian City*, p. 14; Storch, 'Fifth of November', pp. 92 ff.

but, although elements of continuity and similarity between its manifestations in different periods are striking, it is also clear that its strength and nature reflected prevailing social, political, and religious conditions.[30] The tradition had its origins in the Elizabethan period, formed by the memories of the Marian persecution disseminated and maintained by Foxe's *Book of Martyrs* and reinforced by Catholic plots against Elizabeth and the Spanish threat.[31]

During the next century the arrival of William of Orange at Torbay on the same date as that on which the Gunpowder Plot had been discovered eighty-three years before, assured anti-Catholicism of a clear place in the popular and liturgical calendar. Official celebrations of the Fifth of November were widespread in the eighteenth century.[32] Meanwhile, the unsettled years of the mid-seventeenth century had seen frequent localized panic fears of Catholics, who were believed to be responsible for all the country's woes.[33] Such alarms were resurrected on a national scale in 1678 by the agency of Titus Oates. During the Exclusion Crisis the Whigs kept alive the fervour of popular reaction to the 'Popish Plot' by means of pope-burning processions. The paranoid spirit of these years left its mark on the Monument, whose inscription alleged that the Great Fire of London had been the work of 'Popish' incendiaries.[34]

The reign of James II and the subsequent recurrent Jacobite threat seemed to give further political foundation to the charge that Catholicism was incompatible with British liberties. The Fifteen and the Forty-five rebellions were both accompanied by the extensive publication of anti-Catholic literature. This represented an exaggerated reaction to a genuine threat, but showed an inability to distinguish between Jacobite sympathizers and those who simply wanted to

---

[30] This statement would be platitudinous were it not for the tendency of scholars to make simplistic references to something they term 'anti-Catholic prejudice' as though it was somehow largely independent of its general historical context. Cf. O'Tuathaigh, in Swift and Gilley, *Irish in the Victorian City*, p. 27.

[31] W. Haller, *Foxe's Book of Martyrs and the Elect Nation* (1963); C. Z. Wiener, 'The Beleaguered Isle: A Study of Elizabethan and Early Jacobean Anticatholicism', *Past and Present*, 51 (1971), 27–62.

[32] Storch, 'Fifth of November', pp. 71–2.

[33] R. Clifton, 'The Popular Fear of Catholics during the English Revolution', *Past and Present*, 52 (1971), 23–55.

[34] J. P. Kenyon, *The Popish Plot* (1972); O. W. Furley, 'The Pope-Burning Processions of the Late Seventeenth Century'. *History*, 45 (1959), 16–23; *Guide to the Monument with an Account of the Great Fire of London of 1666 which it Commemorates* (1957), 8.

practise their religion undisturbed.[35] In Scotland anti-Catholicism was fuelled by continuing popular devotion to the tradition of the Covenants, while, as in England, new generations found fresh symbols of national identity defined in an essentially Protestant sense in the Revolution Settlement and the Act of Union.[36] During this period, too, the social and cultural antagonism stirred by Catholics was reflected in their legal status under the penal laws which restricted their worship and cut them off from the mainstream of political and national life.[37]

In practice, the institutionalization of anti-Catholicism began to weaken from the mid-eighteenth century onwards, a development which received some legislative legitimacy with the passing of the Relief Act of 1778. This was a modest measure passed primarily in response to the demands of war, in order to stimulate Catholic recruitment to the army and to strengthen the loyalty of Ireland and French Canada. It repealed legislation which was already virtually a dead letter: Catholics were now legally entitled to inherit property, and priests were relieved from the possibility of life imprisonment. The Act initially applied to England and Wales only, and although it was extended to Ireland in 1779, vigorous agitation thwarted for the present the passing of similar legislation for Scotland.[38]

The most important reason for this slight easing of hostility was probably the realization after the defeat of the Forty-five rebellion that Catholicism no longer presented any objective political threat to the Hanoverian dynasty. The eclipse of the associated ideology of Jacobitism was confirmed in the realignment of political life on the accession of George III.[39] Meanwhile, the seeming insignificance and passivity of the English Catholic community induced a sense that the case for repression was no longer valid. This was reinforced by signs of moderation in the Roman Church as a whole, instanced particularly by Clement XIV's dissolution of the Jesuits in 1773. The elder Pitt maintained that the time for penal laws had now passed and that the

[35] R. Blackey, 'A War of Words: The Significance of the Propaganda Conflict between English Catholics and Protestants, 1715–1745', *Catholic Historical Review*, 58 (1972–3), 535–55.

[36] I. A. Muirhead, 'Catholic Emancipation in Scotland: The Debate and the Aftermath', *Innes Review*, 24 (1973), 104.

[37] E. R. Norman, *Roman Catholicism in England* (Oxford, 1985), 38–41.

[38] R. B. Sher, *Church and University in the Scottish Enlightenment* (Edinburgh, 1985), 277–9; Norman, *Roman Catholicism*, p. 55.

[39] Clark, *English Society*, pp. 12–84, 196.

Catholics were 'men of principle' and 'valuable subjects to the state'.[40]

A relevant but more problematic factor was the influence of the Enlightenment. The conventional argument that the receding of religious zeal combined with the advance of toleration, deism, and scepticism to induce a less hostile attitude to Catholics is open to question on three grounds.[41] Firstly, recent scholarship on the Enlightenment has exposed the inadequacy of viewing the scepticism of the French *philosophes* as a normative basis for understanding this broad movement in European culture. In England, as in Germany, the Enlightenment 'throve . . . within piety', and in Scotland concentration on the figure of David Hume needs to be balanced by an awareness of the important contribution of the clergy of the Church of Scotland under the leadership of William Robertson.[42] Moreover, there is a strong case for viewing even John Wesley as a product of the Enlightenment rather than as a 'rebel' against it. Christianity was certainly changing in the eighteenth century, but this did not necessarily mean that Catholicism would be viewed more warmly. Indeed, to the extent that the Roman Church was perceived as perpetuating the obscurantism and bigotry of a past age, 'enlightened' thought may even have reinforced hostility towards it.[43]

Secondly, even on the purely political level there was an underlying ambiguity towards Roman Catholicism. It is worth quoting here a familiar passage from Locke's first *Letter Concerning Toleration* which served as a seminal articulation of attitudes on this point until well into the nineteenth century. Despite Locke's general defence of freedom of worship, he nevertheless made important qualifications with regard to those who would not keep faith with heretics:

These, therefore, and the like, who attribute unto the faithful religious and orthodox, that is, in plain terms, unto themselves, any peculiar privilege or power above other mortals, in civil concernments; or who upon pretence of religion do challenge any manner of authority over such as are not associated with them in their ecclesiastical communion, I say these have no right to be

---

[40] *Cursory Remarks on a Late Fanatical Publication Entitled a Full Detection of Popery etc.* (1783), 51.

[41] Cf. C. Haydon, 'Anti-Catholicism in Eighteenth-Century England *c.*1714–1780', D.Phil. thesis (Oxford, 1985), 20–3 and *passim*; Sher, *Church and University*, p. 277.

[42] R. Porter and M. Teich (eds.), *The Enlightenment in National Context* (Cambridge, 1981), 6 and *passim*; Sher, *Church and University*, *passim*.

[43] D. W. Bebbington, *Evangelicalism in Modern Britain: A History from the 1730s to the 1980s* (1989), 50–60; D. Hempton, *Methodism and Politics in British Society 1750–1850* (1984), 33–44.

tolerated by the magistrate; as neither those that will not own and teach the
duty of tolerating all men in matters of religion . . .

Again: That Church can have no right to be tolerated by the magistrate
which is constituted upon such a bottom that all those who enter into it do
thereby *ipso facto* deliver themselves up to the protection and service of another
prince.[44]

This was generally taken to refer to Catholics when it was written, but
was not so readily applied by 1778. However, it was circumstances
rather than principles that had changed. Indeed, when the Catholic
Joseph Berington published a defence of his religion in 1780, it was
clearly couched within this framework. Berington stressed that he was
a Catholic but not a 'Papist', that Catholics were no friends to arbitrary
power, and that the pope only held spiritual authority.[45] The danger
was that, if public perceptions were to point in a different direction, an
'enlightened' outlook in general and a Lockian one in particular still
gave legitimacy to attacks on Catholics.

Thirdly, the view that there was a divergence between élite
toleration and popular prejudice also seems questionable in the light of
Roy Porter's view that the English Enlightenment should not be seen
as purely a movement in high culture.[46] This general point is
important in viewing the background to the Gordon Riots, in which
anti-Catholic arguments were promoted as much by members of the
'élite' as by the populace. Even in Scotland popular 'No Popery' was
noticeably sluggish until stimulated into action from above, stirred in
1778 and 1779 by a curious assortment of malcontent Church of
Scotland clergy, Edinburgh tradesmen, and Episcopalians anxious to
demonstrate their own Protestant character.[47] Meanwhile, in England
Dissenters such as Richard Price had been notable for their anti-
Catholic pronouncements. These should be seen in the context of a
patriotic, radical tradition of opposition to the government in which
militant Protestantism played a major part.[48] Anti-Catholicism was thus

[44] J. Locke, *A Letter Concerning Toleration*, ed. C. L. Sherman (New York, 1979),
210–12.

[45] [J. Berington], *The State and Behaviour of English Catholics, from the Reformation to
the Year 1780 with a View of their Present Number, Wealth, Character &c.* (1780); Norman,
Roman Catholicism, p. 47.

[46] Porter and Teich, *Enlightenment*, p. 11.

[47] Sher, *Church and University*, pp. 281–2.

[48] L. Colley, 'Radical Patriotism in Eighteenth-Century England', in R. Samuel
(ed.), *Patriotism: The Making and Unmaking of British National Identity*, i. *History and
Politics* (1989), 171.

not solely, or even primarily, the property of the mob, but was also an aspect of the world-view of those who in other respects held advanced political and religious opinions.[49]

What, then, were the implications of the Gordon Riots? Undoubtedly these demonstrated the continuing potency of a popular 'No Popery' tradition. In London the 285 deaths and £100,000 worth of damage done to property made them the most serious outbreak of violence in Britain between the seventeenth century and the present. Furthermore, the unrest in the metropolis was echoed, albeit on a less spectacular level, both in Scotland and in the English provinces. The religious influence was clearly evident in Gordon's Protestant Association, whose demonstration on 2 June 1780 attracted 60,000 of 'the better sort of tradesmen', chanting hymns and psalms. Religion was linked with radical patriotic xenophobia in the face of the continuing war across the Atlantic, while there is evidence that the growing Irish presence in London was giving rise to antagonism. Rudé has discerned elements of social protest, but the riots can also be seen as an extreme manifestation of a semi-ritualized violent popular culture of an essentially conservative character. The scale of the disturbances can be attributed as much to the pusillanimity and even the passive collusion of the authorities as to the innate ferocity of the mob.[50]

The Gordon Riots precipitated a lasting reaction in favour of the Catholics and against active Protestantism. An anonymous pamphleteer judged in 1783 that 'the more sensible part of the public seem now sufficiently convinced of the danger of promoting or encouraging such dark-designing *Juntos* as the Protestant Association'. This was echoed from a longer perspective by Robert Southey, who wrote in 1807 of a 'sentiment of compassion' for Catholics being excited in the more respectable part of the community.[51] The events of 1780 made the 'No Popery' cry seem disreputable and intolerant, whereas at an earlier date it had been widely accepted as enlightened and patriotic. This frame of mind was still evident in the late 1830s, when Charles Dickens's fictional account of the Gordon Riots in *Barnaby Rudge*

[49] Sher, *Church and University*, p. 284.
[50] J. Stevenson, *Popular Disturbances in England 1700–1870* (1979), 76–90; G. F. E. Rudé, 'The Gordon Riots: A Study of the Rioters and their Victims', *Transactions of the Royal Historical Society*, 5th series, 6 (1956), 93–113; Haydon, 'Anti-Catholicism', pp. 254–80.
[51] *Cursory Remarks on a Late Fanatical Publication*, p. 13; R. Southey, *Letters from England*, ed. J. Simmonds (1984), 155.

carried an implicit but intentional moral in the light of the contemporary disorder and the activities of a new Protestant Association.[52]

Other factors operative in the last two decades of the century reinforced this trend. The French Revolution in particular presented a far more genuine and immediate peril to British religion and liberty than Roman Catholicism had become. Thus, in Edmund Burke the traditional Whig suspicion of Catholicism was entirely subordinated to the attack on the irreligion of the Revolution.[53] Similarly, Bishop Samuel Horsley allowed his outrage at the severing of the union of religion and civil government to overcome his dislike of Catholicism. This attitude, voiced in an influential sermon on 30 January 1793, was shared by many Anglican clergy, who warmly welcomed the émigré French priests.[54] On a theological level, the rise of 'infidelity'—not only in Paris but in the teaching of Tom Paine at home—led to a weakening of the traditional identification of the pope and Antichrist, as a new candidate for the title now seemed to be asserting itself.[55] By 1791 a Relief Act had already given legal status to registered Catholic places of worship in England and had admitted Catholics to the professions; in 1793 the Acts of 1778 and 1791 were extended to Scotland without any public outcry, and in Ireland the franchise was given to 40s. Catholic freeholders. In 1795 the Irish administration responded favourably to the Catholic bishops' concern that their students would be exposed 'to the contagion of sedition and infidelity' if they continued to be educated in France by giving an endowment for the launching of the Royal College of St Patrick at Maynooth.[56] Similar anxiety in Scotland led the government for a short period to give a grant to supplement the stipends of clergy and assist the new college at Aquhorties near Aberdeen.[57]

Among a wider public, too, present circumstances were a distraction from traditional antagonism. Loyalists enjoyed some success in appropriating the historic radical vocabulary, but the 'No Popery' cry had ambiguous implications now and they did not appear to use it much, concentrating instead on attacking Dissenters. Meanwhile, the

---

[52] C. Dickens, *Barnaby Rudge: A Tale of the Riots of 'Eighty*, ed. K. Tillotson (1954), pp. viii, xxiv.

[53] E. Burke, *Reflections on the Revolution in France*, ed. C. C. O'Brien (1969), 187 ff.

[54] D. Bellenger, 'The Émigré Clergy and the English Church, 1789–1815', *Journal of Ecclesiastical History*, 34 (1983), 393–8.

[55] Haydon, 'Anti-Catholicism', pp. 298–9.

[56] D. A. Kerr, *Peel, Priests and Politics* (Oxford, 1982), 226–7.

[57] Johnson, *Roman Catholic Church in Scotland*, pp. 119–29.

impact of the Revolution, Tom Paine, and the war combined to weaken the religious and anti-Catholic strand in radicalism.[58] Later, in the 1820s, William Cobbett's *History of the Protestant Reformation* suggested a redefinition of the patriotic radical tradition itself in a manner which rehabilitated Catholicism. It had a wide influence.[59]

The political reorientation brought about by the French Revolution has to be seen in conjunction with the social dislocation arising from industrialization. Anti-Catholicism in its eighteenth-century form was an integral part of a popular culture which was now being disrupted, at least in the North. In the South the Fifth of November continued to be celebrated in the traditional manner, but even there during the early nineteenth century the festival seems to have been declining and moving away from religious roots.[60] In religious terms, the period saw great Methodist revivalism and the rise of millenarian sects such as the Southcottians and the followers of Richard Brothers. Anti-Catholicism was implicit in these movements, but was obscured by their positive fervour. Meanwhile, the Evangelical reform movements led by William Wilberforce and Hannah More were gathering momentum and directing the energies of the faithful not against Rome but against the slave-trade overseas and the corruption of morals at home.[61]

Further evidence confirms the impression that the force of anti-Catholicism as a general cultural assumption was weaker by the turn of the century. The use of language was revealing: up to the 1790s the word 'Papist' was used indiscriminately by everyone, with a general disregard for the feelings of Catholics who resented its use. Thereafter, however, the label 'Roman Catholic' became increasingly common, and 'Papist' the property of those who used it with deliberate polemical intent.[62] The trend was noted by further contemporary observers: in 1807 *The Times* reported a belief that 'No Popery' was threatened with sinking into oblivion as an active force.[63] In 1812 the newly founded *Protestant Advocate* bemoaned the 'unaccountable

[58] H. Cunningham, 'The Language of Patriotism', *History Workshop Journal*, 12 (1981), 13–16; A. Booth, 'Popular Loyalism and Public Violence in the North-West of England, 1790–1800', *Social History*, 8 (1983), 295–313.

[59] A. Briggs, *William Cobbett* (Oxford, 1967), 52; G. D. H. Cole, *The Life of William Cobbett* (1924), 289.

[60] See below, pp. 145–6, *Western Times*, 8 Nov. 1834; cf. Storch, 'Fifth of November', pp. 70–4.

[61] E. M. Howse, *Saints in Politics* (1953); J. F. C. Harrison, *The Second Coming: Popular Millenarianism 1780–1850* (1979).

[62] J. A. Lesourd, *Sociologie du catholicisme anglais 1767–1851* (Nancy, 1981), 13–17.

[63] *The Times*, 28 Apr. 1807.

apathy [which] seems at present to reign in the bosoms of our countrymen'.[64]

In contending that the years between 1780 and 1800 saw a hiatus in the history of anti-Catholicism, it is not suggested that the stream of 'No Popery' dried up. It was, however, largely diverted underground for a period, particularly as a result of revulsion after 1780 and a sense of irrelevancy after 1789. Its flow had previously been strengthened by its capacity to assimilate aspects of Enlightenment cultural and political influence and by its association through Wesley with the stirrings of evangelical revival evident before 1780. When the stream resurfaced in the early nineteenth century, its flow still possessed considerable volume but it had been directed into a narrower and deeper channel. In other words, anti-Catholicism was not, except in a very diffuse sense, a general cultural assumption in the nineteenth century to the extent that it had been in the eighteenth, but it did attract a body of militant advocates who secured for it a significant continuing influence.

It is not improbable that the passing of the generation which had experienced the horror of the 'Riots of 'Eighty', and the general ebbing of the revolutionary tide in Europe, might eventually have resulted in at least a partial reversion to anti-Catholic positions, but the strength and persistence of that recovery is attributable to new factors operating from the early nineteenth century onwards. A key development underlying the nineteenth-century resurgence of anti-Catholicism was the steady growth in Catholic numbers at a rate substantially in excess of the general population increase. It has been estimated that there were 80,000 Catholics in England and Wales in 1770, 208,000 in 1815, and 460,000 in 1840, at which date there were also 90,000 Catholics in Scotland.[65] The greatest concentrations were in Lancashire and London, although there was also a significant Catholic presence in the North-East and in parts of the West Midlands. Elsewhere, particularly in the East Midlands and the West Country, Catholicism was very thin on the ground. Until the commencement of the Irish settlement in Glamorgan it was virtually non-existent in Wales.[66] The overall growth of the Catholic community between 1770

[64] *Protestant Advocate*, 1 (1812), 6.
[65] Bossy, *English Catholic Community*, p. 185; J. A. Lesourd, 'Les Catholiques dans la société anglaise, 1765–1865', Ph.D. thesis (Lille, 1973), iv. 258, 303.
[66] Bossy, *English Catholic Community*, pp. 408–13; Lesourd, 'Les Catholiques', iv. 258.

and 1829 did not significantly affect its regional distribution in England.[67] In Scotland, however, the half-century before Emancipation saw a significant shift in the geographical areas of Catholic presence. Up to the late eighteenth century the Catholic population in the South was very limited and the Church was centred in two main areas, Banffshire and western Inverness-shire. While the former stronghold remained, the latter weakened seriously due to the general economic decline of the Highlands leading to considerable emigration to Canada and, within Scotland, a move southwards to Clydeside.[68]

With the spectacular exception of the Gordon Riots, late eighteenth-century British Catholics do not appear to have experienced particular hostility from their Protestant neighbours. Their position was assisted by a moral teaching which enjoined charity towards their fellow-countrymen and upheld the existing constitution, despite its exclusion of Catholics from public life.[69] Bishop Geddes, Vicar Apostolic of the Lowland District, was able to mix freely in Edinburgh society during the 1780s, and, on a humbler level, a number of Lancashire Catholics were able actively to share in the growing prosperity of Manchester and Salford.[70] There were occasions when Scottish Catholic workmen complained of discrimination from their employers, but this arose in part from practical problems, such as their absences on holy days and their insistence on alternative diets on fast days, rather than from *odium theologicum*. Significantly, until the 1820s the inclination of lay Catholics was towards compromise rather than confrontation.[71]

John Bossy has shown that, from the 1770s onwards, English Catholicism was expanding and changing at a rate which remained quite independent of the readjustment necessitated by the numbers of Irish. He quotes figures of 19,200 English and 31,800 Irish for four sample Lancashire towns in 1834. The English were thus substantially outnumbered but they were not yet overwhelmed. Their own numbers had increased five-fold from a total of only about 4,000 in 1767.[72] Catholics, concentrated in those areas of the country that were

---

[67] Bossy, *English Catholic Community*, p. 413.
[68] Johnson, *Roman Catholic Church in Scotland*, pp. 1–2.
[69] Bossy, *English Catholic Community*, p. 380.
[70] Johnson, *Roman Catholic Church in Scotland*, pp. 24–5; G. Connolly, 'The Transubstantiation of Myth: Towards a New Popular History of Roman Catholicism in England', *Journal of Ecclesiastical History*, 30 (1984), 81–4.
[71] Johnson, *Roman Catholic Church in Scotland*, p. 171.
[72] Bossy, *English Catholic Community*, pp. 303–8.

undergoing rapid economic change, tended to move particularly quickly into non-agricultural occupations and urban settlements.[73] This facilitated a shift in the leadership of the community from the old Catholic gentry to the priests. Clerical ascendancy, however, was not achieved without a substantial amount of tension within the community. This arose not only between priests and middle-class laity trying unsuccessfully to assert congregational influence, but also between regular and secular clergy.[74] In England Catholics could be found at all levels of society, but there was a natural drift towards 'respectability', and except perhaps in Lancashire, few were readily definable as 'working class'. Despite the decline of the Catholic gentry, about 200 landed families remained, notably the Talbot Earls of Shrewsbury in Staffordshire, the Welds and the Cliffords in the West Country, and the Stonors in Oxfordshire. The Howard Dukes of Norfolk had conformed to the Church of England on various occasions during the seventeenth and eighteenth centuries, but the twelfth duke, who succeeded in 1815, was a Catholic.[75]

Irish immigration transformed the social profile of British Catholicism, and the Protestant arrivals played a significant part in 'No Popery' campaigns. There had been a slow but steady flow of Irish into Britain during the eighteenth century, but this escalated from 1815 onwards. In the 1841 census 289,404 Irish-born were recorded as living in England, of whom about 75,000 were in London, 105,916 in Lancashire, 126,321 in Scotland, and 3,531 in Wales.[76] Obviously, the number of ethnic Irish was actually larger, because of those born in Britain who cannot be readily identified from the census records. The Irish who came to Britain were generally of low economic status, lacking money for the fare to America, although the poorest of all remained behind. They entered by three main routes. Firstly, there was a stream from Munster and southern Leinster to South Wales, Bristol, and on to London. These immigrants, reflecting the areas from which they came, were almost entirely Catholic. In London they settled initially in St Giles, Whitechapel, Southwark, and Bermondsey, but gradually they began to disperse throughout the metropolis. The

---

[73] Bossy, *English Catholic Community*, p. 299.

[74] Ibid. 338–54; Norman, *Roman Catholicism*; J. Champ, 'Assimilation and Separation: The Catholic Revival in Birmingham, *c.*1650–1850', Ph.D. thesis (Birmingham, 1985), 142–207.

[75] Bossy, *English Catholic Community*, pp. 151, 307–13, 325–7.

[76] L. H. Lees, *Exiles of Erin* (Manchester, 1979), 42, 45; O'Tuathaigh, in Swift and Gilley, *Irish in the Victorian City*, p. 14.

only Protestants among them were people of a superior social class who came to London and Bristol for professional and social reasons and settled in English neighbourhoods. Secondly, from Leinster and eastern Connaught migrants moved directly east to Liverpool. Most stayed in Lancashire, but a minority went on into Yorkshire. This group was predominantly Catholic but had a significant Protestant presence. Finally, from Ulster and parts of northern Connaught and Leinster the Irish crossed to South-West Scotland. While the majority stayed on in the Glasgow region, others moved on to Dundee and Edinburgh, which had both acquired significant Irish communities by the middle of the century. In Scotland the proportions of Catholics and Protestants among the Irish were much more evenly balanced than in England, although the Protestants tended to remain in the West.[77] This pattern of settlement serves to explain the weakness of Orangeism in London and Edinburgh relative to the North of England and the West of Scotland, as this was a distinctively Irish and working-class form of Protestant organization. On the other hand, the presence of middle-class and upper-class Irish Protestants in the English capital strengthened the resources of leadership and finance available to native anti-Catholics.[78]

The Catholic Irish were separated from the majority of their British co-religionists by ethnic origin as well as social status.[79] At the same time, their tendency to link Catholicism with Irish nationalism and popular superstition served, however undeservedly, to discredit the Church in Protestant eyes. Their numbers placed a severe strain on the Church's manpower and resources. The ratio of priests to Catholics decreased from 1 : 190 in 1773 to 1 : 466 in 1803, and 1 : 780 in 1837. Furthermore, the low level of Irish attendance at Mass obliged the priests to adopt a 'missionary' approach in order to translate the general sense of Catholic identity felt by most of the non-Protestant immigrants into active participation in religious observance.[80]

The growth of the native Catholic community combined with the Irish influx to present an alarming impression to hostile observers. While it is probable that most of the increase in Catholic numbers can

[77] Lees, *Exiles of Erin*, pp. 43–4, 53–8; O'Tuathaigh, in Swift and Gilley, *Irish in the Victorian City*, p. 15; Johnson, *Roman Catholic Church in Scotland*, pp. 249–52.

[78] See below, Chap. 3, pp. 74–5; Chap. 5 *passim*.

[79] Bossy, *English Catholic Community*, pp. 307–10; D. McRoberts (ed.), *Modern Scottish Catholicism 1878–1978* (Glasgow, 1979), 23.

[80] Bossy, *English Catholic Community*, pp. 313–16; Connolly, 'Transubstantiation of Myth', pp. 87–91; Lees, *Exiles of Erin*, pp. 172–89; Lesourd, 'Les Catholiques', iv. 360.

be attributed to the natural growth of the community, there were instances in which nominal Protestants were won over to Catholicism by an enterprising priest operating in an area where other religious provision was weak.[81] As Anglicans, during the 1820s, acquired a greater consciousness of the extent to which their own Church was failing to keep up with population growth, they became aware of the quiet Catholic expansion which had been continuing for decades. Uninformed as to the already considerable scale of Irish immigration, they exaggerated the extent to which this was being achieved by conversion of the English. At the same time, their own efforts to reclaim the unchurched brought them increasingly into contact and conflict with Roman Catholic clergy engaged on a similar mission.[82]

There were other aspects of the development of Catholicism which, by the 1820s, were both a potential source of provocation to Protestants while pre-conditioning Catholics to react strongly to attacks on their religion. Firstly, the international context of the Bourbon restoration in France, linked with a revivalist Ultramontanism evident elsewhere in Europe, reawakened suspicions of authoritarian papalism with absolutist political implications.[83] Secondly, the clericalization of the Roman Church began to lead to an increasingly rigid and dogmatic spirit in the maintenance of orthodoxy, and a shift away from the charitable view of Protestantism which had been in the ascendant up to the turn of the century. This development can be associated with the influence of John Milner, Vicar Apostolic of the Midland District from 1803 until his death in 1826, and the most dominant English Catholic of his generation. Milner endeavoured to secure uniformity in liturgical practice; he campaigned for unqualified Emancipation and sought to secure the restoration of the Jesuits to England.[84] Milner's published statement of the Catholic position, aimed at Protestants, was *The End of Religious Controversy* (1818), and this showed a noticeable difference in tone from Berington's work of forty years before. Milner devoted part of his work to tearing off the 'hideous mask' that had been placed over the Catholic Church, but he also took the offensive with arguments that private judgement could

[81] Bossy, *English Catholic Community*, pp. 316–22. Lesourd ('Les Catholiques', iv. 258) estimates that between 1800 and 1815, while the population as a whole increased by 21.4%, Catholic numbers increased by 75%.

[82] RS, *1st AR* (1828), 18–19; *3rd AR* (1830), 15–16; *4th AR* (1831), Map of Roman Catholic Chapels and Seminaries; Gilley, 'Protestant London', *passim*.

[83] Cf. J. Droz, *Europe between Revolutions* (1967), 190–214.

[84] Bossy, *English Catholic Community*, pp. 334–7, 383–5.

The Roots of Anti-Catholicism

not be an unerring rule for interpreting Scripture; that there was only
one holy catholic and apostolic Church, and that Protestants were
hopelessly divided.[85] A more extreme, although localized, example of
the new spirit in Roman Catholicism was provided by the activities of
the Revd Joseph Curr, who in January 1821 launched an attack on the
Bible Society in Manchester and Salford. Thus began what Gerard
Connolly has described as 'quite the worst religious feud in the twin
towns since the seventeenth century'. Curr also engaged in the revision
of Challoner's *Garden of the Soul*, changing this classic of quiet
eighteenth-century devotion into a statement of more militant
Catholicism.[86] Thirdly, the growing tensions within the Catholic
community—between Irish and English, seculars and regulars, clergy
and laity—meant that the heightening of Protestant antagonism could
be welcomed as a means of unifying the diverse elements of
Catholicism. The vigour with which the priests reacted to the attacks
of the Reformation Society in the late 1820s arose from their anxiety to
assert their ascendancy in their own Church.[87]

Parallel with the increasing assertiveness and numerical strength of
the Roman Catholic Church itself, the aftermath of the Union with
Ireland brought the position of Catholics to the centre of the political
agenda. It is important to note that the roots of the Emancipation
struggle lay more in debates over the nature of the constitution and the
best means of governing Ireland than in any clear-cut argument over
religious toleration.[88] In 1812 the *Protestant Advocate*, while opposing
Emancipation, claimed that it sought to serve the 'sacred cause of
religious liberty' and bemoaned the 'melancholy fact, that many people
cannot distinguish between religious liberty and the impartition of the
civil power'.[89] For the anti-Emancipationists the distinction was
fundamental: they agreed that Catholics should be allowed freedom of

[85] Connolly, 'Transubstantiation of Myth', pp. 95–7.
[86] J. Milner, *The End of Religious Controversy, in a Friendly Controversy between a
Religious Society of Protestants and a Roman Catholic Divine* (1819 edn,), 191–5.
[87] Champ, 'Assimilation and Separation', *passim*; Bossy, *English Catholic Community*, pp. 341–9, 359–60; see below, pp. 46–9.
[88] J. C. D. Clark's view (*English Society*, p. 354) of the defence of the Protestant
constitution between 1800 and 1829 as an 'Indian summer' of political theology in the
eighteenth-century sense is valid in some respects, but underestimates the significance
of the events of 1780–1800, particularly those in Ireland. Reference should be made to
Clark and to Machin, *Catholic Question*, for detailed discussion of events up to 1829. The
account which follows here aims only to isolate the matters most relevant to the
discussion of anti-Catholicism after 1829.
[89] *Protestant Advocate*, 1 (1812), 2–4.

worship, but thought it dangerous and illogical to allow them to sit in Parliament.

Pitt had envisaged Emancipation as a natural corollary of Union with Ireland: the Protestant minority in Ireland would no longer have cause to fear political domination by the Catholic majority as they would be secured by the Protestant majority in Britain. However, Pitt was thwarted by the conscientious opposition of George III and by the lack of sufficient resolve in his own Cabinet for him to be able to pressurize the king into submission.[90] Thus, in its early stages the debate about Emancipation was linked to a continuation of eighteenth-century controversy over the use of royal power. This dimension was more prominent than the Catholic question itself in the general election of 1806.[91] After the resignation of the ministry of 'All the Talents' in March 1807 because of the king's refusal to countenance their proposal that Catholics be admitted to staff appointments in the army, the incoming ministers decided to go to the country again. The Cabinet rejected Spencer Perceval's anti-Catholic draft for the king's speech proroguing Parliament and chose instead to have George emphasize his anxiety for his people to 'support him in every exercise of the prerogatives of his Crown'.[92]

The issue of the royal prerogative receded later, although it by no means disappeared, but the Emancipation problem continued to be seen in a wider constitutional context. In his classic speech on 9 May 1817 Peel presented the matter as one of fundamental principle, involving the alteration of the Protestant constitution created at the Revolution of 1688. Concession would lead to 'a wild and irreconcilable contradiction of principles'.[93] Such views found their fullest development among the Ultra-Tories, who emerged as a distinct group from 1824 onwards. Their beliefs, which can be seen as an archaic brand of Whiggery,[94] encompassed a sense of Protestantism as the fundamental essence of the British constitution, which had already reached its most perfect conceivable form. Any change would therefore be synonymous with decline. Society was believed to be essentially stable and to be safeguarded by the maintenance of the

[90] J. C. Beckett, *The Making of Modern Ireland 1603–1923* (1966), 288.

[91] *The Times*, Nov. 1806, *passim*.

[92] Ibid. 28 Apr. 1807; D. Gray, *Spencer Perceval: The Evangelical Prime Minister 1762–1812* (Manchester, 1963), 103.

[93] N. Gash, *Mr Secretary Peel* (1961), pp. 207–9.

[94] D. G. S. Simes, 'The Ultra Tories in British Politics, 1824–1834', D.Phil. thesis (Oxford, 1975), 66–70, 152.

existing political order. The increasing social and political tensions evident since 1789 were thus regarded as temporary aberrations which, if courageously responded to, would prove to be only passing clouds in an otherwise clear sky. To make concessions in response to such disorders would be a cowardly loss of nerve, undermining the order and stability of the whole constitutional and social structure. The Ultras therefore opposed all but the most limited proposals for parliamentary reform, but to many the continued exclusion of Catholics from political life was an equally—indeed, perhaps more— important matter. Their admission to Parliament would remove a logical corner-stone of the structure set up in 1688. Furthermore, the close association between the State and a Protestant Established Church meant that it would be an absurdity to admit Catholics to Parliament, where they would legislate for the Church of England.[95] In addition, it was consistently alleged that Catholics had a divided allegiance, owing temporal as well as spiritual loyalty to the pope, and feeling no obligation to keep faith with heretics. Catholic denials of the charges could thus be dismissed as merely equivocation and deception.[96]

The doyen of the Ultras was John Scott, Earl of Eldon (1751–1838), lord chancellor until Liverpool's retirement in 1827. Frederick Augustus, Duke of York, and Ernest Augustus, Duke of Cumberland (1771–1851), were prominent supporters and provided a useful avenue to George IV, who was sympathetic to the Ultras, but York died in 1827, while Cumberland's unscrupulousness and dubious morals made him widely unpopular.[97] Henry Pelham-Clinton, fourth Duke of Newcastle (1785–1851), was a manic-depressive, prone in periods of euphoria to see himself as the saviour of his country and to take impetuous initiatives only subsequently to lapse into long periods of despondency and inaction.[98] George Finch-Hatton, Earl of Winchilsea and Nottingham (1791–1858), possessed a similarly excitable temperament, being described by Newcastle as 'an honest and excellent fellow', but possessing 'the *tête montée* and all the chivalry of a Don Quixote'.[99] Winchilsea was a splendid orator and displayed

---

[95] G. F. A. Best, 'The Protestant Constitution and its Supporters, 1800–29', *Transactions of the Royal Historical Society*, 5th series, 8 (1958), 105–27.
[96] Machin, *Catholic Question*, pp. 15–17.
[97] Ibid. 167; Simes, 'Ultra Tories in British Politics', pp. 159–61.
[98] J. Martineau, *The Life of Henry Pelham, Fifth Duke of Newcastle* (1908), 4; *Newcastle Diary*, *passim*.
[99] *Newcastle Diary*, Ne2F3, 26 Oct. 1828, 10 Feb. 1829.

considerable drive and determination. With this hard core of resistance, the Lords consistently rejected Emancipation measures sent up to them prior to 1829 by the Commons, where the Ultras lacked any clear group until the final stages of the struggle and the anti-Catholic cause relied on the moderate leadership provided by Peel.

Ultra-Toryism also found active supporters among the clergy. In the days before the Oxford Movement, High-Churchmen were among the strongest opponents of Rome, linking theological objections to transubstantiation, the sacrificial role of the priesthood, the veneration of saints, and other Catholic beliefs with exaltation of the royal supremacy in the Church and attacks on divided allegiance. One of the ablest exponents of such views was Dr Henry Phillpotts (1778–1869), a canon of Durham who was to become Bishop of Exeter in 1830. In his *Letters to Charles Butler*, published in 1825, Phillpotts argued that Roman doctrines were not innocent and harmless, as their apologists maintained, but were in reality a serious departure from the beliefs of the early Church and differed fundamentally from those of the Church of England. The leading episcopal Ultra-Tories were William Van Mildert (1765–1836), Bishop of Llandaff from 1819 to 1826, when he was translated to Durham, and Thomas Burgess, Bishop of St Davids from 1803 to 1825 and of Salisbury until his death in 1837.[100]

The range of political, constitutional, and theological considerations related to the Emancipation question received a further crucial dimension from Ireland. Irish Protestants, concerned to preserve their ascendancy, found ready supporters among the British Ultras, who now came to view the Act of Union as itself part of the sacrosanct constitutional order defining a Protestant 'empire' extending across the Irish Sea, in which Catholics, while allowed freedom of worship, could not expect political equality. Thus the original Pittite conception of the relationship between Union and Emancipation was totally reversed, and it was felt that concession would undermine the Union.[101]

The opponents of Emancipation raised the stakes and broadened the issues to the extent that, while arguments against Catholicism itself were not neglected, they only formed one strand in a debate which was

[100] Best, 'Protestant Constitution', p. 113; G. C. B. Davies, *Henry Phillpotts, Bishop of Exeter, 1778–1869* (1954), 43–51; H. Phillpotts, *Letters to Charles Butler, Esq. on the Theological Parts of His Book of the Roman Catholic Chuch* (1825).

[101] Machin, *Catholic Question*, p. 3; Fourth Duke of Newcastle, *Thoughts in Times Past, Tested by Subsequent Events* (1837), 85–90.

extended to encompass the whole nature of the constitution, the Union, and the role of the Church. This reflected a continuing consciousness arising from the memory of the Gordon Riots that anti-Catholicism could only appear 'respectable' if it transcended rabble-rousing bigotry.[102] There were two important consequences for anti-Catholicism after 1829 which may be noted now, although they will be considered in more detail below. Firstly, it confirmed the continuance of modes of thinking whereby the relationship between government and Catholics was seen as central to the texture of political and social life. Hence, objectively minor adjustments of that relationship encountered vigorous resistance in the early Victorian period. Secondly, as they built so much upon resistance to the single issue of Emancipation, anti-Catholics found that the eventual passing of that measure forced them to reconstruct their ideology on changed premises, a process which was associated with a shift in the nature and leadership of the organized 'No Popery' movement.

The relationship between political anti-Catholicism and public opinion before 1829 can be explored by reference to the two general elections in which the 'No Popery' cry was most conspicuously heard, those of 1807 and 1826, and by a consideration of early attempts to organize an anti-Catholic movement, the Orange Order and the Protestant Union. The consensus of historical comment on the 1807 general election is that it was fought on the Catholic issue.[103] This is a judgement which needs to be refined. As has been shown above, the government concentrated more on the general issue of the royal prerogative, although under the circumstances this could not be separated from the 'No Popery' cry. There were clearly efforts by the ministerialists to stir anti-Catholicism for party purposes, but Whigs generally attributed their defeat to electoral corruption, while William Roscoe at Liverpool felt that he had suffered particularly owing to his part in the abolition of the slave-trade.[104] Furthermore, when the 'No Popery' cry was raised, it sometimes, as in Yorkshire and Middlesex, appears to have done the government more harm than good.[105] The *Annual Register* saw the most striking characteristic of the election as the independence of a public opinion which had shown no confidence in such factional cries.[106]

[102] Protestant Union, *Paper I* (1813), 10.
[103] Gray, *Spencer Perceval*, p. 106; Haydon, 'Anti-Catholicism', p. 303.
[104] Gray, *Spencer Perceval*, pp. 107–8; *The Times*, 8 May 1807.
[105] *The Times*, 15, 17 June 1807.
[106] *Annual Register* (1807), 235.

There was a similar superficiality about the role of anti-Catholicism in the 1826 general election. In December 1825 Wellington described the electorate as apathetic, believing that it would not 'be very easy to revive a public feeling in this country upon the Roman Catholic question, which would enable those inclined to oppose themselves to the Roman Catholic claims to resist them effectively'.[107] The *Annual Register* attributed such Protestant reaction as there was to resentment at the proceedings of the Catholic Association in Ireland, and observed that 'Emancipation, or resistance to Emancipation was not indeed proposed to candidates as a test or generally or loudly.'[108] The assessments of the 1826 election by Hexter and Machin serve to confirm contemporary judgements: in eighty-four contested elections in Great Britain the net gain of the anti-Catholics was only eight members, and their advantage was even more marginal in seats which were relatively free from influence. The electorate was concerned about Catholicism, but by no means to the exclusion of other considerations.[109]

The impression derived from the elections that the 'No Popery' cry was of a somewhat limited and ephemeral appeal is confirmed by a consideration of anti-Catholic organizations. The Protestant Union for the Defence and Support of the Protestant Religion and the British Constitution was formed at the house of Joseph Butterworth, a Methodist MP, in January 1813. Other leading figures included Thomas Allan, another prominent Methodist, and Granville Sharp, a veteran anti-slavery campaigner, who became chairman,[110] thus illustrating the connection made in the evangelical mind between the physical slavery of the West Indies and the 'spiritual slavery' of Rome. The Protestant Union confined itself to issuing a series of papers on the constitutional and religious aspects of the Catholic question. Its publications provide no evidence of any further activity.[111] It claimed that it had contributed to the defeat of the Emancipation movement of 1812–13, but in reality the collapse of this initially promising initiative by Canning and Grattan was attributable largely to differences

[107] Second Duke of Wellington (ed.), *Despatches, Correspondence and Memoranda of the Duke of Wellington*, ii (1867), 594.

[108] *Annual Register* (1826), 171.

[109] Machin, *Catholic Question*, pp. 64–87; J. H. Hexter, 'The Protestant Revival and the Catholic Question in England, 1778–1829', *Journal of Modern History*, 8 (1936), 312–13.

[110] Hempton, *Methodism and Politics*, pp. 127–8.

[111] Protestant Union, *Papers I–II* (1813–14).

between the English and Irish Catholics themselves over the proposed government veto on episcopal appointments.[112] By November 1814 the Protestant Union was £280 in debt and had clearly found Sharp's death in July 1813 a personal loss it could ill afford. An underlying problem, which anticipated the difficulties of the Protestant societies in the mid-nineteenth century, was an inability to retain lasting support from Dissenters. The organization folded at the end of 1814.[113]

Orangeism was initially brought into Britain at the turn of the century by soldiers returning from service in Ireland and by Protestant emigrants. It is probable that the Order's membership perceived its function as primarily a social one. It took several years to become established, and a British grand lodge was not founded until 1808. Even then it found it hard to establish a foothold outside Lancashire and the army. The London lodge hid its numerical weakness behind grandiose pretensions, and, while the Duke of York was briefly recruited as grand master in February 1821, he resigned in June having been advised that the lodges were illegal. Orangeism gave rise to a number of outbreaks of sectarian violence in the North-West, but it is clear that it remained a small and somewhat exotic movement.[114]

The historian of nineteenth-century anti-Catholicism is faced with the task not of chronicling a continuous tradition but of analysing a process of change and revival under influences which arose from contemporary historical circumstances. Popular prejudice and folk memory provided, in some cases at least, receptive soil for the seed sown by Protestant agitators, but they were not the prime motive forces. Nevertheless, the stimulus for a recovery and reorientation of anti-Catholicism was already present before 1829. Before the reasons for this can be appreciated, the present discussion of the impact of the growth in the Roman Catholic Church and the political struggle over Emancipation needs to be supplemented by examination of a crucial third factor, the change in the nature of Anglican Evangelicalism during the 1820s, which forms the immediate background to the formation of the British Reformation Society in 1827.

This chapter began with the observation that Emancipation served more to initiate anti-Catholicism than to terminate it. In this respect it can be viewed as a mirror image of the Gordon Riots fifty years earlier. Whereas the Gordon Riots revealed the depths of antagonism to

[112] Machin, *Catholic Question*, pp. 14–15.
[113] Protestant Union, *Paper II* (1814), 133; *Protestant Advocate*, 4 (1815–16), 134.
[114] H. Senior, *Orangeism in Ireland and Britain 1795–1836* (1966), 151–76.

Catholics still present in British society, Emancipation demonstrated the existence of more accommodating attitudes. On the other hand, while the sequel to the Gordon Riots had been a reaction against bigotry, Emancipation was to be followed by sustained efforts to show that toleration still had its limits.

2

REFORMATION AND EVANGELICALISM

THE purpose of this chapter is to consider the emergence of a new form of organized anti-Catholicism in the shape of the British Reformation Society at the end of the 1820s. It will be shown that this was not so much a direct reaction to Emancipation, as a result of internal developments in Evangelicalism and a response to the religious situation in Ireland. The fortunes of the Reformation Society in the years after 1829 will then be considered. These relate to the continuing conflicts among Evangelicals, to which militant Protestantism was intimately related. Detailed consideration of the political implications of anti-Catholicism after 1829 will be postponed to Chapter 3.

The mainstream of Anglican Evangelicalism emerged from the Calvinistic controversies of the late eighteenth century with an ambiguous theological stance but a confident attitude to the world. Charles Simeon, who influenced the ideas of generations of Cambridge undergraduates, disliked theological systems and was increasingly explicit in rejecting Calvinism.[1] William Wilberforce, in his *Practical View of the Prevailing Religious System of Professed Christians*, published in 1797, expressed a vision that Christians would sanctify existing society by their influence rather than escape from it into a subculture of the elect. Evangelicals had a sense of being called by God to co-operate with him in his purpose of winning the world for Christ. Thus the early nineteenth century was a period of great enthusiasm for missionary societies, reflecting a confident expectation that evil and paganism would gradually disappear in the growing light of the coming millennium.[2] This was a mood stimulated by the French Revolution and the wars that followed it, both in engendering a sense

---

[1] H. C. G. Moule, *Charles Simeon* (1965 edn.), 77; D. W. Bebbington, *Evangelicalism in Modern Britain* (1989), 58, 78.

[2] W. J. C. Ervine, 'Doctrine and Diplomacy: Some Aspects of the Life and Thought of the Anglican Evangelical Clergy, 1797–1837', Ph.D. thesis (Cambridge, 1979), 14–15, 34–5; S. C. Orchard, 'English Evangelical Eschatology, 1790–1850', Ph.D. thesis (Cambridge, 1968), 32–57.

that Catholicism was no longer a serious challenge and in encouraging a sense of crusading fervour which reached its height in 1815.[3]

During the 1820s this confident triumphalism was called into question. The social and political turmoil of the post-war years suggested that earlier optimism had been naïve and premature, and stimulated a desire for the security of a clearer doctrinal framework. Some found this in the traditions of the Church, and moved away from Evangelicalism altogether into High-Churchmanship or even Roman Catholicism.[4] However, others responded to increasing uncertainty by adopting a more fundamentalist attitude to Scripture and a sharp dualism, viewing the world as under God's judgement and heading for imminent catastrophe. The only hope of salvation came through the redemptive power of Christ rescuing the elect from the destruction awaiting those around them. This new outlook also reflected the cultural impact of a Romantic yearning for more intense spiritual experience, but this was blended with a transmuted legacy of Enlightenment rationality in the construction of grand theological and exegetical schemes in an attempt to make sense of the action of God in history in the face of the disorder of contemporary events. The world might seem irrational, but God, whose purposes were revealed in the inspired word of Scripture, was not.[5]

Early nineteenth-century Evangelicals had tended to be moderate in their anti-Catholicism, believing that Catholics would gradually be won from error, and the Roman Church would progressively fade away. However, a more dogmatic millennial nationalist Protestantism came increasingly to the surface in the 1820s, expressed particularly by two Scots. Robert Haldane (1764–1842) attacked current missionary policies on the Continent, feeling that too many compromises were being made with the Catholics. He founded the Calvinist-dominated

---

[3] N. U. Murray, 'The Influence of the French Revolution on the Church of England and its Rivals, 1789–1802', D. Phil. thesis (Oxford, 1975), 279; W. H. Oliver, *Prophets and Millennialists* (Auckland, 1978), 64–7.

[4] Cf. D. Newsome, *The Parting of Friends* (1966).

[5] Cf. H. Willmer, 'Evangelicalism, 1785–1835', Hulsean prize essay (Cambridge, 1962); Bebbington, *Evangelicalism*, pp. 80–1. I differ here from Bebbington in suggesting that the 'new' Evangelicalism combined Enlightenment and Romantic influences. There may, however, be a useful distinction to be drawn between Irving and the Catholic Apostolic Church, who can be seen as 'pure' evangelical Romantics, and men such as McNeile, who denounced the seceders for their 'diverse excesses of extravagant excitement' (Oliver, *Prophets and Millennialists*, p. 131). McNeile and his associates adhered to a view of a rational and ordered world in which the intervention of God was predictable on the basis of Scripture.

Continental Society as a vehicle for the application of his views.[6] Edward Irving (1792–1834) became minister of the National Scottish Church in London in 1822, and quickly established himself as a vigorous critic of compromise by Evangelicals. In 1826 he addressed the Continental Society on the subject of 'Babylon foredoomed', arguing that, although the Roman Church would be destroyed by Christ at the second coming, in the meantime it would grow in strength. Protestants had a responsibility to cry out against Rome and to be instruments in God's hands for saving an elect remnant.[7]

A series of conferences of students of biblical prophecy held between 1826 and 1830 at Albury Park in Surrey were a seminal influence on the development of a changed approach to eschatology which stirred stronger anti-Catholicism. The host at these gatherings was Henry Drummond (1786–1860), a banker and ex-Tory MP, who was a co-founder of the Continental Society and later of the Catholic Apostolic Church. The moderator was Hugh McNeile (1795–1879), an Ulsterman and graduate of Trinity College, Dublin, presented by Drummond to the living of Albury in 1822. He was later to become a prominent leader of Evangelical anti-Catholicism. Irving was also a major participant in the Albury gatherings.[8] Thus, although the new movement in Evangelicalism took place on English soil, it is noteworthy that much of its leadership came from men of Scottish and Irish origins.

Moderate Evangelicals generally adopted the optimistic post-millennial doctrine that a period of universal peace and knowledge of God could be achieved through human means and that only after this would Christ return. However, the Albury group were pre-millennialists who believed that the state of the world would continue to deteriorate until the second coming, which they thought was imminent, and the subsequent salvation of the elect and destruction of the powers of sin and evil.[9] They also tended to treat as axiomatic

[6] Ervine, 'Doctrine and Diplomacy', p. 266; T. Stunt, 'Geneva and British Evangelicals in the Early Nineteenth Century', *Journal of Ecclesiastical History*, 32 (1981), 35–46.

[7] E. Irving, *Babylon and Infidelity Foredoomed of God* (Glasgow, 1826), 430–44; I. S. Rennie, 'Evangelicalism and English Public Life', Ph.D. thesis (Toronto, 1962), 57. On Irving, see M. O. W. Oliphant, *The Life of Edward Irving*, 2 vols. (1862).

[8] *DNB*, xvi. 28, on Drummond; xxxi. 246, on McNeile; J. A. Wardle, 'The Life and Times of the Rev. Dr Hugh M'Neile, DD, 1795–1875', MA thesis (Manchester, 1981), 1–9, 30–44; Oliphant, *Irving*, i. 389 ff.; Rennie, 'Evangelicalism', p. 55.

[9] Some, like Irving, saw infidelity as another fundamental power of evil, but continued to place stress on Rome as the root of sin. See E. R. Sandeen, *The Roots of Fundamentalism* (Chicago, 1970), 17.

identifications between Rome and the mystic Babylon and between
Antichrist and the papacy, whereas prophetic writings between 1789
and 1815 had seriously explored the possibility of a revolutionary or
Napoleonic Antichrist. The precise mental mechanism by which anti-
Catholicism became a key part of prophetic schemes remains
somewhat unclear, but once the connection had been made, it served
to give powerful reinforcement to Evangelical Protestant feeling.[10]

From the late 1820s onwards this increasingly hardline approach
found expression in the pages of the *Record* newspaper, which had
commenced publication on 1 January 1828. Robert Haldane's nephew
Alexander, who attended several of the Albury conferences,[11] was the
proprietor and dominant influence on the editorial policy of the paper
from shortly after its foundation until his death more than half a
century later. Alexander Haldane was to recall his view of the situation
in the Evangelical world at this time in an article in the *Record* in 1853:
'we have no hesitation in avowing the belief, that when the *Record*
commenced its labours, a widespread spirit of wordly wisdom and
sinful compromise had come over a considerable portion of the
Evangelical party in the Church'.[12] From the outset the new journal
left its readers in no doubt about its attitude towards Rome. The leader
in the first issue stated the aim of upholding Christian principles in
politics, and went on to express a desire to exclude religious
disputation from its columns; but it warned that 'We shall . . . feel no
obligation to extend similar forbearance to that antichristian Hierarchy, which, under the pretence of keeping, has taken away, the key of
knowledge, and which systematically teaches, for the doctrines of God,
the commandments of men.'[13]

Such views had been greatly intensified by the hardening of

[10] Oliver, *Prophets and Millennialists*, pp. 57–64; D. N. Hempton, 'Evangelicalism and
Eschatology'. *Journal of Ecclesiastical History*, 31 (1980), 184–5.
[11] Alexander Haldane was commissioned as an intermediary by Drummond in
September 1827, in an unsuccessful attempt to secure Thomas Chalmers's attendance
at Albury (New College, Edinburgh, Chalmers MSS 4.75.22, Haldane to Chalmers,
8 Sept. 1827).
[12] Haldane died in 1882. *R*, 28 July 1882; A. H. Corsbie, *Alexander Haldane:
A Biographical Sketch* (1882), 12. The precise sequence of events in the early history of
the *Record* is rather confused. Ervine ('Doctrine and Diplomacy', p. 297) states that
Drummond and Lord Mandeville were also involved, but this appears to be based on a
misreading of Oliphant (*Irving*, ii. 45). However, the important role played by Haldane
seems to be clearly established. Cf. Orchard, 'English Evangelical Eschatology', p. 76;
J. L. Altholz, 'Alexander Haldane, the *Record* and Religious Journalism', *Victorian
Periodicals Review*, 20 (1987), 28–31.
[13] *R*, 1 Jan. 1828.

religious conflict in Ireland. In south Ulster in the early years of the century Methodist revivalism and sectarian tensions reinforced each other, while missionary concern for Ireland stimulated anti-Catholicism among British Wesleyans.[14] Anglicans, too, began to acquire significant interests in Ireland, becoming involved in a growing range of societies concerned with promoting the development of education and the circulation of the Bible, including the Hibernian Bible Society (1808), the Hibernian Sunday School Society (1809), and the London Hibernian Society.[15] This movement was not initially associated with direct proselytism, and commanded widespread support, even being viewed sympathetically in government circles. Lord Liverpool wrote in October 1823 that he was 'perfectly convinced that the most effectual means of improving morals and promoting the happiness of the lower classes in Ireland, will be found in the extension of the benefit of Education and in the circulation of the Holy Scriptures'.[16]

During the 1820s Protestant efforts, dubbed the 'Second Reformation', became more vigorous and extreme, partially as a result of increasing self-confidence among Irish Evangelicals and partially due to a growing consciousness that it was unrealistic to hope that Catholicism would simply die away as a result of education and social progress. Rather, it had to be directly confronted. The Irish Society, founded in 1818, and the Scripture Readers' Society (1822) were more geared towards explicit evangelism than earlier organizations had been. In October 1822 Archbishop Magee of Dublin delivered a notorious Charge in which he spoke of Catholics as 'blindly enslaved to a supposed infallible ecclesiastical authority', provoking an infuriated reaction from Roman Catholic leaders.[17] At the same time, Protestant denominational rivalries continued very much in evidence: Magee denounced Nonconformity in almost the same breath as he attacked Catholicism, and Anglican Evangelicals continued to be profoundly suspicious of the Methodists.[18] Their fears were shared by

[14] D. N. Hempton, 'The Methodist Crusade in Ireland, 1795–1845', *Irish Historical Studies*, 22 (1980–1), 33–48; id., 'Methodism in Irish Society, 1770–1830', *Transactions of the Royal Historical Society*, 5th series, 36 (1986), 132, 138–9.

[15] A. R. Acheson, 'The Evangelicals in the Church of Ireland, 1784–1859', Ph.D. thesis (Belfast, 1967), 230–3; M. Hill, 'Evangelicalism and the Churches in Ulster Society, 1770–1850', Ph.D. thesis (Belfast, 1987), 147–84. I am indebted to David Hempton for the latter reference.

[16] Liverpool Papers, BL Add. MS 38297, f. 13, Liverpool to J. E. Gordon, 3 Oct. 1823.

[17] Acheson, 'Evangelicals in the Church of Ireland', pp. 233–7; D. Bowen, *The Protestant Crusade in Ireland* (Dublin, 1978), 88–96.

[18] Acheson, 'Evangelicals in the Church of Ireland', pp. 136–7.

a Sligo Independent minister who felt that, in respect of their radical implications, 'popery' and Methodism had much in common.[19] An anxiety not to be outflanked by Protestant competitors probably contributed to efforts to proselytize among the Roman Catholics.

However, the most important development of the 1820s was increased Catholic militancy. In part this was a direct reaction to Protestant attacks and an expression of resistance to the distribution of the Protestant Bible, but it also had internal causes. Priests were becoming more self-assured and numerous: there was a 52 per cent increase in the number of Catholic clergy in Ulster between 1800 and 1835.[20] Popular hostility to Protestantism was fuelled in 1823 and 1824 by the circulation of the Pastorini prophecies, foretelling that Protestants would be overthrown three centuries after the Reformation, dated ominously to 1525. Above all, there was the political campaign of Daniel O'Connell and the Catholic Association, drawing strength from religious tensions but in the long term itself giving greater force to them. For example, the education issue was shrewdly used to involve the priests in the movement, thus giving sectarian and political significance to an issue with religious roots.[21]

It was against this background that James Edward Gordon, the founder of the Reformation Society, developed his ideas. He was a Scot, born around 1790, who had occupied himself with charitable and religious work since his retirement from the Royal Navy at the end of the Napoleonic wars. He had contacts with the Clapham Sect and with Thomas Chalmers. Initially Gordon's energies were employed in naval charities, but by 1820 he had turned his attention to the task of educating and converting the Irish Roman Catholic peasantry.[22] Extensive study of the Irish school system led him to conclude that the Roman Catholic religion was the root of all the problems of Ireland and that economic, social, and political remedies would never bear fruit until the country had undergone 'a species of exorcism', carried out by the application of 'the *Christianity* of Protestantism . . . through

[19] Dr Williams Library, London, Blackburn MSS, L 53/3/5, William Newick to Blackburn, 4 May 1824.
[20] Hill, 'Evangelicalism in Ulster Society', pp. 173–5.
[21] Blackburn MSS, L 53/3/5, Newick to Blackburn, 4 May 1824; F. O'Ferrall, *Catholic Emancipation: Daniel O'Connell and the Birth of Irish Democracy* (Dublin, 1985), 37–63.
[22] A. Lewis, *George Maxwell Gordon, The Pilgrim Missionary of the Punjab* (1889), 1–7; A. Moody Stewart, *The Life and Letters of Elizabeth, Last Duchess of Gordon*, 3rd edn. (1865), 146–7; *R*, 2 May 1864; Chalmers MSS 4.8.7, 4.15.36, Gordon to Chalmers, 10 Jan. 1818, 17 July 1820.

the organs of the Bible, the Pulpit and the School'.[23] He noticed that there was widespread anticlericalism in rural Irish society, and hoped that this might be exploited to turn the people against the Catholic Church.[24]

In the autumn of 1824 a tour by Gordon and the Hon. Baptist Noel[25] on behalf of the Hibernian Bible Society coincided with the initial surge of support for the Catholic Association. On 9 September Sheil and O'Connell spoke up at a meeting in Cork of the ladies' auxiliary to the Munster School Society, acknowledging that reading the Bible was subversive of the Roman Catholic Church, arguing that it would make the people 'Muggletonians', and accusing the Society of proselytism. Public discussions involving several priests ensued.[26] Pro-Catholics alleged in the Commons in February 1825 that Evangelical meetings had given rise to great excitement among Catholics, who suspected a systematic plan to put down their religion. They claimed that almost the whole of southern Ireland had been converted into a 'scene of outrage and disorder', giving rise to a rapid growth in support for the Catholic Association.[27] Gordon wrote to Peel to claim that O'Connell and Sheil had started the trouble by intruding upon a 'strictly private' meeting concerned with education not the distribution of the Scriptures. His opponents, however, argued that, whilst Gordon and Noel 'had education in their mouths, they had proselytism in their hearts'.[28] Clearly, Evangelical activities had been provocative, but it was equally apparent that the Catholic Association was endeavouring to extract the maximum possible political capital from them.

Gordon was sufficiently perceptive to appreciate that political nationalism was inextricably bound up with loyalty to the Irish Roman Catholic Church. This served to strengthen his conviction of the

[23] Liverpool Papers, BL Add. MS 38295, f. 165, 38299, f. 296, Gordon to Liverpool, 11 July 1823, 7 Jan. 1825.
[24] Liverpool Papers, BL. Add. MS 38380, ff. 280–1, Gordon to Liverpool, 23 Sept. 1823. Cf. S. J. Connolly, *Priests and People in Pre-Famine Ireland* (Dublin, 1982), 239–55.
[25] Baptist Wriothesley Noel (1798–1873) was to be minister of the proprietary chapel of St John's, Bedford Row from 1827 to 1848, when he caused a major sensation by leaving the Church of England to become a Baptist (cf. *DNB*, xii. 89; D. W. Bebbington, 'The Life of Baptist Noel', *Baptist Quarterly*, 24 (1972), 390–401).
[26] *A Report of the Proceedings of Three Public Meetings in the City of Cork* (Dublin, 1825), 19–20, 40–5, 73–5.
[27] 2 *Hansard*, xii. 216–17, 281–3, 10, 11 Feb. 1825.
[28] Peel Papers, BL Add. MS 40373, ff. 240–1, Gordon to Peel, 25 Feb. 1825; 2 *Hansard*, xii. 281, 11 Feb. 1825.

inherent evil of 'Popery' and the necessity of strenuous opposition to it; like many of his contemporaries, he believed that O'Connell was the tool of the priests, rather than the other way round.[29] A belief that the struggle was intensifying led Gordon to feel that education on its own was not sufficient to win Ireland for Protestantism, because the education societies 'were pledged to the strictest neutrality upon the subjects of creeds and Churches'. He felt that there was a need openly to propagate Protestant doctrine and refute Catholic 'errors'.[30]

The development of such hardline views led to tensions within the London Hibernian Society, culminating in a split in the spring of 1827, when the British Society for Promoting the Religious Principles of the Reformation was formed at a meeting in Freemasons' Hall on 27 May. McNeile was among Gordon's supporters, declaring that in the newly formed organization 'at least we may speak out our whole minds on the case of Ireland'.[31] The objectives of the Society—the circulation of books and tracts, the holding of meetings for religious discussion, the collection of information relating to the 'progress of the Reformation', and the promotion of education for Roman Catholics— added up to an attempt to secure the wholesale conversion of Ireland to Protestantism, and the elimination of Romanism from the British Isles.[32]

The Reformation Society had direct links with the Albury group as well as with Irish Evangelicalism. McNeile and Drummond were both active supporters, and the Society's first president, Viscount Mandeville (1799–1855), son of the Duke of Manchester, and Tory MP for Huntingdonshire, had also been a regular attender at Albury. Nevertheless, it was Ireland rather than prophecy that primarily determined the character and programme of the Society in its early years. Neither Gordon nor his two most important lieutenants, Captain F. E. Vernon (1790–1883), a son of the Archbishop of York,

---

[29] Liverpool Papers, BL Add. MS 38295, f. 164, 38299, f. 241, Gordon to Liverpool, 11 July 1823, 22 Dec. 1824.

[30] RS, *1st AR* (1828), 5 (Bod. Lib. copy). This was almost certainly written by Gordon.

[31] Ervine, 'Doctrine and Diplomacy', p. 269. In 1853 the Society changed its name to the even more cumbersome 'Protestant Society for Promoting the Religious Principles of the Reformation and for Special Missions to Roman Catholics in Great Britain', but in practice it became known as the 'Protestant Reformation Society' (*British Protestant*, 9 (1853), 85). For convenience it will generally be referred to in this book simply as the 'Reformation Society'.

[32] RS minutes (in the custody of the current general secretary), 21 May 1827.

and George Finch (1794–1870), a natural son of the ninth Earl of Winchilsea, had attended any of the Albury meetings.[33] Conversely, Edward Irving took no active role in the Reformation Society. Mandeville's family were substantial Irish landowners, and there were several Irish peers among the vice-presidents, most notably Robert Jocelyn, third Earl of Roden (1788–1870), a committed Evangelical.

The Society explicitly distanced itself from the political resistance to Catholic Emancipation, resolving 'That the Society now formed disclaim all connection with politics, and that it hold forth no secular inducements to proselytism.'[34] This reflected a conviction that the problems of Ireland were of a spiritual rather than political or material character, and that the apparent security offered by the institutions of the Protestant Ascendancy was hence illusory.[35] Although Ultra-Tories such as the Earl of Winchilsea and the Bishop of Salisbury were to be found among the vice-presidents, the regular administration of the Society was carried on by a committee of twenty-five relatively obscure laymen, dominated by Gordon. Had the Ultras seen the Society as relevant to their purposes, one would have expected them to be more extensively involved in it.[36]

In the later 1820s the Reformation Society pursued its programme with considerable energy. About ten members of the committee met regularly to receive and answer correspondence, make arrangements for the publication and circulation of tracts, organize meetings, and review the finances. During the first two years of the Society's existence the committee met about once a week, but during 1829 this dropped to three times a month. In June 1828 W. G. Rhind, yet another former naval officer, was appointed secretary at a salary of £200 per annum, and a travelling agent was recruited to carry out preparatory work for visits by deputations. From an early date the salaried staff also included a collector and an assistant secretary to carry out the routine office-work.[37] A publications subcommittee, set up in July 1827, produced short tracts for mass circulation and also more substantial works intended to fortify clergy and educated laymen

---

[33] Vernon later attained the rank of vice-admiral, and took the additional surname of Harcourt in 1831. Finch was a distant cousin of the 10th (current) Earl of Winchilsea: *Burke's Peerage and Baronetage*, 105th edn. (1980), 2708; *Burke's Landed Gentry*, 17th edn. (1852), 783; Boase, ii. 75; Orchard, 'English Evangelical Eschatology'. p. 98 n. 55.

[34] RS minutes, 21 May 1827.

[35] R. J. M'Ghee, *Truth and Error Contrasted* (1830), 251–9.

[36] RS minutes, *passim*.

[37] RS minutes, 18 Apr., 28 May, 17 June 1828.

with arguments against Rome. These ranged from pamphlets giving the text of speeches at Reformation meetings to a two-volume anthology of extracts from Catholic works, compiled by Finch.[38]

The major focus of this activity was proselytism. In the second half of 1827 Gordon and Vernon held a series of eighteen meetings in different parts of Ireland, aiming to 'attract popular attention to the errors of the Romish creed' and, if possible, to establish local auxiliary societies. They were undeterred by Protestant criticism of their activities as 'offensively aggressive' and unrealistic in their avoidance of politics. The 'no politics' rule was rigorously adhered to, and paid dividends in enabling the Society to hold surprisingly orderly meetings.[39] In December 1827 there was a crowded inaugural meeting of the Dublin Metropolitan Auxiliary, chaired by Archbishop Magee and attended by numbers of 'respectable' Roman Catholics headed by Mr Curran, a barrister, who debated at length with the Protestant speakers.[40] In all, there were twelve occasions on which Roman Catholics offered opposition to the proceedings. Initially this came exclusively from laymen, but subsequently the priests, clearly anxious to assert their leadership, became involved. Another tour of Ireland was made by Gordon and Finch in 1828. The priests kept a watchful eye on the proceedings but did not participate as they had done in the previous year. The Society endeavoured to maintain more permanent operations in Ireland by appointing Scripture readers in response to local initiatives and by making grants for the circulation of tracts. Fourteen Scripture readers were working in Ireland in connection with the Society by May 1828.[41]

The Reformation Society commenced operations at a time when the wider 'Second Reformation' movement was meeting with some success. This was described by John Jebb, the Bishop of Limerick, in a letter to the Evangelical politician Sir Robert Inglis in April 1827. Jebb admitted that he had initially been sceptical about the claims of extensive success, but went on:

Within these last few weeks, my opinion has undergone a considerable change. I have learned from various trust-worthy quarters, that in almost every part of Ireland, inquiry, and thirst for knowledge, and even, in some instances, a degree of religious anxiety, are gaining ground among the Roman Catholics.

[38] RS minutes, 11 July 1827, 9 Mar. 1831; G. Finch, *A Sketch of the Romish Controversy* (1830).

[39] RS, *1st AR* (1828), 22–5, 27–36 (BL copy).

[40] RS, *Quarterly Extracts*, 2 (Jan. 1828), 10–14.

[41] RS, *1st AR* (1828), 13 (Bod. Lib. copy); *2nd AR* (1829), 31–9.

Numbers, I am well informed, in neighbourhoods predominantly popish, are thinking, and inquiring, and reading the Scriptures, who have not as yet proposed to conform.

In September 1827 it was noted that there had been 2,357 converts. As Jebb had observed, a substantial proportion of these occurred on the single estate of Lord Farnham, who had promoted systematic proselytism among his dependents in County Cavan, but the bishop was also aware of cases in his own diocese where conversions had occurred without there having been a concerted Protestant campaign.[42]

Jebb's letter provides an interesting background to consideration of the local Catholic population's response to the Reformation Society's activities, which was variable but initially not wholly hostile. At Kilkenny in November 1827 it was claimed that 500 to 600 Roman Catholics came to listen to their advocates debating with the Protestant champions.[43] At Maryborough in 1828 a large Roman Catholic contingent attended in spite of efforts by the priests to keep them away, and at Ennis, recently the scene of the tumult of the Clare election, the Society claimed that it had held a peaceful meeting, attracting a substantial Catholic attendance. This led Gordon to conclude that, however potent the influence of the priests might be in stirring political excitement, 'it was incapable of deterring a body of the same people from listening to information which struck at the very roots of their own existence'. On the other hand, in 1827 at Waterford Catholics who were alleged to be intent on causing a riot had to be excluded from the meeting, and at Londonderry and Downpatrick in 1827 the Catholics prevented the formation of local auxiliaries and engaged in lengthy public discussions. In the next year in Londonderry a riot forced the postponement of the Society's meeting. It seems that positive Catholic interest was greater in these areas where Protestantism was a less credible threat to the dominance of Catholicism in the community: it was in the North that the most vigorous Catholic opposition was encountered.[44]

[42] Canterbury Cathedral Library, Inglis MSS, Jebb to Inglis, 7 Apr. 1827; RS, *Quarterly Extracts*, 2 (Jan. 1828), 16. O'Ferrall (*Catholic Emancipation*, p. 165) notes that there were also converts in the opposite direction. See also Hill, 'Evangelicalism in Ulster Society', pp. 273–85, 302. John Jebb (1775–1833), a precursor of the Oxford Movement, was Bishop of Limerick from 1822 to 1833 (*DNB*, xxix. 259). On Inglis, see below. Chap. 3 n. 14.

[43] RS, *Quarterly Extracts*, 2 (Jan. 1828), 10–14.

[44] RS, *1st AR* (1828), 11–13 (Bod. Lib. copy), 33–6 (BL copy); RS, *2nd AR* (1829), 31–9; RS, *Quarterly Extracts*, 2 (Jan. 1828), 12. Cf. Hill, 'Evangelicalism in Ulster Society', pp. 281–3.

The Reformation Society had never attracted general Protestant support, even among Evangelicals, and its methods in Ireland led to much criticism. Jebb was firmly opposed to the promotion of public doctrinal controversy,[45] and an explicit attack on the Society was made by the Tory High-Churchman Samuel O'Sullivan in *Blackwood's* in July 1829. He argued that the key to the amelioration of Ireland's situation lay in her material condition rather than her religion, an argument which other *Blackwood's* writers used to attack proposals for Emancipation on the grounds that it would solve nothing. O'Sullivan went on to describe the Reformation meetings:

> In general, the speakers on the Protestant side exhibit more zeal than either discretion or ability; and their adversaries, amidst a profusion of vulgarity, ignorance, and misrepresentation, sometimes display ingenuity worthy of a better cause. But as far as we have had an opportunity of observing, these meetings are always more calculated to exasperate the feelings than to win the affections, or inform the judgements, of those for whose edification they are especially got up; and who, when they do attend them, attend them more from an idle curiosity than any real anxiety upon the subject of their salvation.[46]

In private correspondence with William Blackwood, O'Sullivan noted that although the Society had received extensive enthusiastic support at first, its subsequent failures, and evidence that its activity was proving counter-productive, were turning Evangelicals against it. Even Gordon was willing to admit by 1831 that his initial hopes of what would be achieved in Ireland had been over-sanguine.[47] Moderate Evangelical periodicals were indeed very critical of the Reformation Society: the *Christian Observer* thought that the progress of reformation had been impeded 'in no slight degree',[48] and a few years later the *Christian Guardian* was to maintain that 'there is much truth in the proposition, that the most severe check ever given to Scriptural education in Ireland, arose from the injudicious conduct of the founders and early advocates of that Society'.[49]

In attempting to offer an objective analysis of the impact of the

[45] Inglis MSS, Jebb to Inglis, 7 Apr. 1827.
[46] 'Modern Reformation in Ireland', *Blackwood's Edinburgh Magazine*, 26 (1829), 84–96. On O'Sullivan, see *DNB*, xlii. 320. The *Blackwood's* critique of Emancipation is discussed by J. M. Milne, 'The Politics of *Blackwood's*, 1817–1846', Ph.D. thesis (Newcastle, 1984), 202–48.
[47] National Library of Scotland, Blackwood Papers, MS 4031, ff. 8–18, O'Sullivan to Blackwood, 20, 29 Oct., 4 Nov., 6, 29 Dec. 1831.
[48] *Christian Observer*, 31 (1831), 447.
[49] *Christian Guardian*, 1840, p. 107.

Reformation Society in Ireland, it is essential to recognize that contemporary accounts inevitably linked their assessments with more fundamental criticism of the approach to Ireland and evangelism which the Society represented as a key focus of the 'new' Evangelicalism. Evangelical proselytism undoubtedly contributed to the mobilization of popular support behind the Catholic Association, but evidence that the reception accorded to the Reformation Society was frequently one of critical curiosity rather than automatic hostility implies that much depended on the ability of O'Connell and Sheil to exploit the situation. This they did very effectively by identifying themselves with the spiritual cause of the Catholic Church, participating on occasion in theological controversies. They exploited the priests' fears for the religious condition of the people by harnessing clerical energies to the political endeavours of the Association.[50] In the early 1830s the tithe war extended the political and material confrontation of Protestant and Catholic throughout the South, and the cause of purely 'religious' Protestantism, always fragile, thus became for a time hopeless. In relation to this development, the Reformation Society was probably as much victim as villain: although witnesses to parliamentary committees sometimes cited the 'Second Reformation' as productive of increased Catholic unrest, generally more stress was laid on wider social and economic factors.[51] The Catholics, however, continued to find that Evangelical activity was a useful scapegoat: in February 1834 William Finn commented in the Commons that such operations 'had done more mischief, and excited more dissension, and . . . done more to destroy the Irish Church than any Irish orators had ever done'.[52]

The Reformation Society's operations in Britain were initially intended to be subsidiary to their Irish activities, but they quickly acquired a momentum of their own. In the autumn of 1827 a provisional local committee was formed for the London slum district of St Giles, already the object of Evangelical concern. A series of fortnightly lectures were held in Tavistock Chapel, Drury Lane 'on the points in controversy between Roman Catholics and Protestants', attended on occasions by up to 200 Irish Catholics. By May 1828 over

[50] O'Ferrall, *Catholic Emancipation*, p. 166.
[51] *PP* 1831–2, xvi (677), 3–9; P. O'Donaghue, 'Causes of the Opposition to Tithes, 1830–8', *Studia Hibernica*, 5 (1965), 11–13.
[52] Finn was Daniel O'Connell's brother-in-law, a barrister and repealer, MP for Co. Kilkenny, 1832–7 (M. Stenton, *Who's Who of British Members of Parliament* (1976), i. 140); 3 *Hansard*, xxi. 417, 17 Feb. 1834.

30,000 tracts had been distributed and four Irish-speaking Scripture readers appointed. During the first few months of its operation the St Giles auxiliary claimed twelve conversions to Protestantism, although one would suspect, in view of the fact that the inhabitants of St Giles were 'without knowledge even of the peculiar doctrines their church teaches', that these were nominal rather than practising Catholics.[53] Three meetings intended formally to inaugurate the St Giles society were held at Freemasons' Hall during February and March 1828, during which there was spirited opposition from Catholics. These meetings were notable for the introduction into England of polemical discussion on the Irish pattern. The committee tried unsuccessfully to enforce rules regulating the procedure to be followed in debate, and the final meeting degenerated into a state of chaos.[54]

Further auxiliary societies were formed for Long Acre Episcopal Chapel, the county of Kent, and Southwark, the first two apparently as a result of local initiatives.[55] At St Giles by May 1829 a fifth Scripture reader was being employed and a school had been formed for the instruction of Catholics. Support for the work was stengthened by the commencement of a ladies' branch society.[56] From the summer of 1828 efforts were made to expand operations to other parts of England by means of a deputation of Gordon, Finch, and Rhind which toured the Midlands and the West during July and August, holding a series of meetings in which Roman Catholic speakers participated in debates, most notably at Birmingham and Bristol.[57] Meanwhile, interest was developing in a range of other centres, especially in the North. In its 1829 *Annual Report* the Society claimed to have some form of organization in a total of sixteen provincial centres, ranging from Newcastle in the north to Bristol in the south, and repositories of tracts in five other towns.[58]

This early expansion clearly has to be understood against the

---

[53] *Lectures on the Points in Controversy between Romanists and Protestants* (1828); *Report of the Proceedings of the Auxiliary Reformation Society for St Giles* (1828); cf. S. Gilley, 'Protestant London', *Recusant History*, 10 (1970), 217; L. H. Lees, *Exiles of Erin* (Manchester, 1979), 85–6.

[54] *R*, 15, 22 Feb., 21 Mar. 1828; RS, *1st AR* (1828), 7–8 (Bod. Lib. copy); RS minutes, 15 Mar. 1828.

[55] RS, *1st AR* (1828), 7 (Bod. Lib. copy); *R*, 4 July 1828.

[56] RS, *2nd AR* (1829), 23–4, 62–3. I can find no evidence for Gilley's assertion ('Protestant London', pp. 217–18) that there were working-class operative auxiliaries in St Giles and Southwark at this period.

[57] RS minutes, 11 June 1828; see below, pp. 46–7.

[58] RS, *2nd AR* (1829), 15–20.

background of political conflict over Emancipation, but the Reformation Society kept out of explicit involvement in this struggle. The rigour with which the 'no politics' rule was implemented is illustrated by a committee minute of July 1827. A grant of £5 was made to a Revd Mr Storey to enable him to buy tracts, but it was stipulated that his attention be called 'to the fundamental rule of the Society which disclaims *all* political views, in order that he may avoid in the selection of such tracts all which can be considered in the slightest degree to have a political tendency'.[59] At the Society's first annual meeting in May 1828 the Earl of Winchilsea also alluded to this policy in his speech from the chair: a 'feature which he admired in this Society's character was the exclusion of all political topics from its discussions. The Society's exertions were solely occupied about rescuing our fellow-creatures from superstitious ignorance and the power of sin . . .'[60] The rule was evidently implemented with almost unbroken consistency, as there is scarcely any allusion to Emancipation in the very full minute-books surviving from this period.

There were several reasons for this in addition to Irish considerations. Above all, Anglican Evangelicals were sharply divided in their attitude to Emancipation.[61] 'Saints' and Whig Evangelicals supported concession on the grounds of charity and a belief that Catholics would be won over most effectively by conciliation and tolerance, but conflicting attitudes towards Emancipation were evident even among the predominantly Tory supporters of the Reformation Society. Although most of its members with seats in the Lords or Commons voted against Emancipation, a significant minority, including Henry Drummond, John H. Calcraft, and Henry Ryder, the Bishop of Lichfield, supported the measure.[62] Lord Barham, another vice-president, although he did not vote in the final division in the Lords, was also in favour of Emancipation.[63] The Hon. G. D. Ryder, an active committee member, would have been in Parliament at this time were it not that the corporation of Tiverton had refused to elect him, in spite

[59] RS minutes, 11 July 1827.

[60] *R*, 30 May 1828.

[61] I. C. Bradley, 'The Politics of Godliness: Evangelicals in Parliament 1784–1832', D. Phil. thesis (Oxford, 1974), 178 ff.; J. H. Hexter, 'The Protestant Revival and the Catholic Question in England, 1778–1829', *Journal of Modern History*, 8 (1936), 307–8; Rennie, 'Evangelicalism', pp. 115–16.

[62] 2 *Hansard*, xx. 1633–8, 30 Mar. 1829; xxi. 394–7, 4 Apr. 1829.

[63] Northamptonshire Record Office, Winchilsea MSS 4598, Barham to Winchilsea, 2 Sept. 1828.

of considerable pressure from the Ryder family, precisely because of his support for Emancipation.[64] The different Evangelical opinions on Emancipation were also represented in the pages of the *Record*, which between September 1828 and February 1829 published various letters on both sides of the question, admitted Evangelicals were divided, and felt that it could not presume to judge between them.[65]

Reluctance to take sides on Emancipation was also a consequence of the Society's desire to retain a genuinely interdenominational character at a period when the mood of evangelical co-operation evident during the early decades of the century was beginning to decline.[66] The Reformation Society was anxious to attract Dissenting ministers, who were given the right to ex-officio membership of the committee on the same basis as Anglican clergy. It endeavoured to find two secretaries, one of whom was to be an Anglican and the other a Nonconformist.[67] In August 1827 there was even an attempt to suspend the introduction of Churchmen to the committee, presumably in order to enable Dissenters to gain an increased stake in the running of its affairs.[68] In general, however, Dissenters were not prominent in the central organization of the Society, although there was a marked presence of members of the Scottish and Irish Establishments. Nevertheless, there were occasions, notably at Bristol and Bradford in 1828, when they took an active part on a local level. In this, as in most other respects, it is important to distinguish between Methodists, who sometimes allowed their chapels to be used for the Society's early meetings, and the mainstream of older Nonconformity, which was generally less fully involved. In the face of Dissenting sympathy for toleration, and Methodist abstention from politics, a more active political stance by the Society would have alienated even this limited non-Anglican support.[69]

---

[64] Sandon Hall, Stafford, Harrowby MSS. lxi. 464–6, G. D. Ryder to Viscount Ebrington, 29 Dec. 1827.

[65] *R*, 26 Sept., 14, 31 Oct., 4, 11, 20 Nov., 4, 8, 11, 18, 22 Dec. 1828, 22 Jan., 19, 23 Feb. 1829.

[66] R. H. Martin, *Evangelicals United: Ecumenical Stirrings in Pre-Victorian Britain, 1795–1830* (Metuchen, NJ, 1983), 194–203.

[67] RS minutes, 21 May, 18, 30 July, 19, 26 Sept. 1827; *R*, 14, 30 May 1828.

[68] RS minutes, 15 Aug. 1827.

[69] *R*, 15 Aug. 1828; *Report of a Public Discussion held at Eastbrook Chapel in Bradford* (Bradford, 1829), p. iv. A Wesleyan chapel at Hartlepool was used as late as 1840 (*Full Report of the Proceedings of a Public Meeting held at the Wesleyan Chapel, Hartlepool* (Sunderland, 1840)). Cf. D. N. Hempton, *Methodism and Politics in British Society 1750–1850* (1984), 134–6.

Furthermore, the new temper of Evangelicalism emerging at this period implied something of a withdrawal from the concerns of secular politics. Evangelicals had always been cautious about political involvement and were especially keen to dissociate themselves from party ties. However, whereas the group of 'Saints' around Wilberforce saw political activity as a means of bringing Christian influence to bear in improving morals and the condition of society, the 'Recordites' saw involvement in Parliament rather as a vehicle for making uncompromising public testimony to the sinfulness of the nation and the impending judgement of God.[70] Political activity was only justified in so far as it served this purpose and was thus confined to 'religious' issues. Discussion therefore centred on the question of whether a particular matter was 'religious' or not, a problem of definition that was especially acute in relation to Emancipation. Some Evangelicals with very strong anti-Catholic views and Tory political loyalties supported Emancipation because they believed that it was a purely 'political' matter and that the exclusion of Catholics from Parliament was an illegitimate and even counter-productive way of combating their errors, especially in giving rise to increased religious conflict in Ireland. This view received influential endorsement from Thomas Chalmers, who argued in the face of the dominant anti-Emancipationism of the Kirk that exclusion on the grounds of difference of religion was not justified if danger to the State had ceased. Truth, he maintained, would prevail without the need for support from civil authority.[71] The alternative position was that it was right to resist Emancipation because the admission of Catholics to political power would compromise the State and nation in the eyes of God by placing it in alliance with anti-Christian apostasy. It would also disastrously weaken the 'religious' as well as the 'political' prospects of Protestantism in Ireland. This standpoint was quite close to that of the High-Church Ultras, although the Evangelicals placed greater emphasis on the idea of national responsibility and less on the sanctity of the Protestant constitution.[72]

Nevertheless, the advocates of such opinions studiously avoided giving voice to them on Reformation Society platforms. Instead, in Britain, as in Ireland, their oratory focused on theological denunciation

---

[70] Bradley, 'Politics of Godliness', pp. 1–68, 251–69.

[71] I. A. Muirhead, 'Catholic Emancipation in Scotland: The Debate and the Aftermath', *Innes Review*, 24 (1973), 111–13.

[72] *R*, 24 Oct. 1828; Rennie, 'Evangelicalism', pp. 115–16, 120–3.

of the Roman Catholic Church, which was attacked fundamentally for being unscriptural in its beliefs and practices, notably with regard to purgatory and the veneration of saints. The influence of eschatological speculation was evident in the frequent equation of Rome and the biblical Babylon. Much use was made of selective quotation in giving distorted impressions of Catholic beliefs, an approach that enjoyed considerable success with partisan audiences. From the outset, however, the Society was willing to engage in public debate with Roman Catholics, who were initially very ready to rise to the challenge. They regularly claimed that their beliefs were being misrepresented, and at Freemasons' Hall in February 1828 the Revd Mr Spooner, a convert from Protestantism, alleged that the Society's attempts to proselytize were 'a *direct* and positive *invasion* of that right of *private judgement* which forms the fundamental principle of the Protestant Reformation'.[73]

During the latter part of 1828 the Catholics developed a sustained response, clearly realizing that presenting themselves as suffering unjust persecution could only assist the cause of Emancipation. Their leader was the Revd Thomas Michael McDonnell (1792–1869). He had been ordained in 1817, and, after serving at Worksop, moved in 1824 to the charge of St Peter's Chapel in Birmingham. He was a vigorous parish priest who made many converts, including Ambrose Phillips de Lisle. At Birmingham McDonnell endeavoured to bring the Catholic community out of the ghetto and to establish it as a force in local society, with an affinity to militant Dissent. He campaigned actively for a variety of liberal causes, including parliamentary reform and the abolition of church-rates, formed a local branch of the Catholic Association, and linked its cause with 'universal Emancipation'. He was a close friend of Daniel O'Connell, and wrote and spoke much on Emancipation.[74]

McDonnell placed the Catholic cause on the broad ground of religious liberty. At the Reformation Society's meeting in Birmingham in July 1828 he complained that 'when the bonds of peace were

[73] *R*, 22 Feb. 1828; *Catholic Magazine*, 1 (1831), 70–5, 129–36, 257–68.

[74] J. Gillow, *A Literary and Biographical History of the English Catholics*, 5 vols. (1885–1903), iv. 372–84; F. C. Husenbeth, *Sermon Preached at the Funeral of the Very Rev. Thomas Michael McDonnell* (1869); *Report of the Proceedings of the Midland Catholic Association at their Annual Meeting* (1826), 13; J. Champ, 'Priesthood and Politics in the Nineteenth Century: The Turbulent Career of Thomas McDonnell', *Recusant History*, 18 (1987), 289–303; ead., 'Assimilation and Separation: The Catholic Revival in Birmingham, c.1650–1850', Ph.D. thesis (Birmingham, 1985), *passim*.

scarcely cemented between Roman Catholics and Protestants, there
were a number of emissaries sent among them from a distant Society,
for the purpose of exciting and exasperating feelings between them'.[75]
At Bristol on 4 August a local priest, the Revd F. Edgeworth, sought to
drive wedges between his opponents. He asked Dissenters whether
they were ready to see Roman Catholics converted to the Established
Church, and, alleging that the respectable Anglican clergy of the city
were conspicuous by their absence from the meeting, claimed that the
Society's proceedings were inconsistent with Church order. He
concluded with the charge that, as Scripture could be interpreted in a
wide range of different ways, advocating reliance on it would give a
triumph to infidelity. McDonnell developed this theme by maintaining
that Gordon's speech on behalf of the Society evaded the question of
what the 'principles of the Reformation' actually were.[76] Such tactics
enjoyed some success. On several occasions the Reformation Society
observed that its speakers were opposed by Protestants as well as by
the Catholics themselves, and at both Birmingham and Bristol
McDonnell and his colleagues succeeded in causing considerable
disruption to the meetings even though the Catholics were in a small
minority.[77] The charge that the Reformation Society was united only
by its hatred of Rome was taken up at length by O'Sullivan in his
Blackwood's article in July 1829. He urged that the only sure basis for
anti-Catholic activity lay in exclusively Church of England principles.[78]

Sometimes Roman Catholics took the initiative themselves. At
Banbury on 12 August 1828 Mr Hefferman, the Earl of Shrewsbury's
chaplain, began a series of lectures 'on the doctrines and evidences of
the Catholic Religion'. They were well argued and attuned to
Protestant sensibilities. For example, Hefferman denied that Catholics
worshipped images and saints, but defended asking for their prayers by
reference to St Paul's requests for the prayers of fellow-Christians.[79]
At Bradford Catholic interference with a meeting of the local Bible
Society resulted in the formation of a local auxiliary to the Reformation
Society, led by the Revd G. S. Bull, later to play a prominent role in
the Ten Hours agitation. A large meeting of the Reformation Society

[75] *R*, 22 July 1828.
[76] *R*, 15 Aug. 1828.
[77] RS, *1st AR* (1828), 16 (Bod. Lib. copy); *3rd AR* (1830), 16–19.
[78] *Blackwood's*, 26 (1829), 89.
[79] Bod. Lib., St Edmund Hall MS 67/7, John Hill Diary, 12 Aug. 1828; *R*, 17 Nov.
1828.

was held in a Wesleyan chapel in the town in early December.[80] Nine priests were present, and, on the Protestant side, some thirty-five ministers, clearly from a range of denominations, and 'many laymen of great influence and respectability'.[81] In the debate McDonnell was supported by priests from Blackburn and Manchester as well as by a Mr Spence, described as a 'rock-grown Irishman' who alleged that Protestantism at the present time was coherent in nothing but its hatred of 'popery'. His opponents included a brace of Baptist ministers as well as a number of Anglican clergy, some of whom had come a considerable distance. The discussion was acrimonious throughout and ended when all but one of the priests walked out. As he left, McDonnell claimed that six individuals at the previous day's meeting were now showing a positive interest in the Catholic Church, and that after the Bristol debate twelve people had done so. The Society attempted to hold a further discussion in April 1829, but the priests failed to turn up.[82] Meanwhile, the Bradford discussions attracted considerable attention in York, where the local Reformation Society became involved in a pamphlet war with a Catholic Defence Society which had been set up in April 1828 and was now strengthened by a deputation from the Catholic Association.[83]

Consideration of the Reformation Society's activities and the Catholic involvement in them in the latter part of 1828 suggests some insights into the apparent paradox of the failure of the political opponents of Emancipation to mobilize sufficient popular support to prevent the carrying of the measure in spite of the broad anti-Catholic sentiment of the country. The avoidance of explicit political allusion in these discussions—at the very time that the Brunswick Club movement against Catholic Relief was gaining momentum else-where—is striking and underlines the fact that, in the evangelical milieu, Emancipation was at this stage seldom seen as the real issue. It was possible to be vehemently anti-Catholic while being neutral on Emancipation, a conclusion supported by the absence of any recogniz-able organized Evangelical as opposed to Ultra resistance to Emancipation at a parliamentary level.

The sophisticated role played by the Catholics also had significant

[80] RS minutes, 21, 29 Oct., 19 Nov. 1828; *R*, 24 Oct. 1828; *Public Discussion at Bradford*, p. iii; J. C. Gill, *Parson Bull of Byerley* (1963).
[81] *Public Discussion at Bradford*, pp. iv–v.
[82] Ibid. 83; RS, *2nd AR* (1829), 18.
[83] RS minutes, 17 Dec. 1828; *R*, 15 Dec. 1828; *Yorkshire Gazette*, 27 Dec. 1828, 3 Jan. 1829.

implications. An increased self-confidence was evident in their readiness to confront their critics rather than ignore them, but they did not fall into the trap of allowing debates to proceed on Protestant ground and thus to confirm popular prejudices and stereotypes. Rather, they counter-attacked. When the rules of the game were drawn in such a manner at Bradford as to make this difficult, they posed as the injured party and withdrew. Such tactics further stirred the ire of the hard core of the Reformation Society's supporters, because they clearly had an impact in extending sympathy for the Catholic cause.

In the first two years of the existence of the Reformation Society there had been an important change in its character. It had been founded with grandiose visions of proselytism in Ireland, but by 1829 it was faced with stalemate in this chosen theatre of operations and was being forced on to the defensive at home. While these Irish origins are fundamental to an understanding of the nature of the Society, it was none the less clear that its future activity was to be centred in Britain.

A minor anti-climax followed the passing of Emancipation, reflected in the Reformation Society's income, which, having risen from £1,889 in 1827–8 to £2,663 in 1828–9, fell back to £1,967 in 1829–30.[84] However, given their lack of direct concern with the political issue, the set-back was only a limited one. Indeed, the *Record's* response to the prospect of Catholics sitting in Parliament was to express the hope that none would be elected: 'The nation is now put upon its trial: Protestantism has quitted the vantage ground of privilege and power, to descend into the arena of equal contest. If the spirit which animated the first Reformers is still alive, we entertain no fear for the issue of the contest.'[85] The Reformation Society, too, although continuing to avoid entanglement in political issues, rose enthusiastically to the challenge on the 'religious' front.

It was envisaged in 1828 that a network of local auxiliaries would be set up to raise money but also to 'act as watchmen for the district in which they are placed; and by the establishment of lectures on Romanism, and the distribution of Tracts, endeavour . . . to check the progress of those errors which are now so widely disseminated'.[86] The establishment of such associations was the primary objective of deputation tours in Britain, and, superficially at least, it appears to have

---

[84] RS, *1st AR* (1828), 49 (BL copy); *2nd AR* (1829), 68; *3rd AR* (1830), 88–9.
[85] *R*, 16 Apr. 1829.
[86] *R*, 17 Nov. 1828.

met with considerable success. By May 1831 there was a total of thirty-
nine local societies spread fairly evenly over the country and extending
from Launceston (Cornwall) to Aberdeen, a number that had
increased to fifty-three by May 1834.[87] In most cases the initiative for
their formation came from London, but sometimes, as at Bradford in
1828 and Aberdeen in 1831, organizations were established on a local
level and the parent society was merely asked to endorse a *fait
accompli*.[88] Figure 1 indicates the places in which, between 1827 and
1831, the Reformation Society held at least one meeting or formed an
auxiliary, demonstrating that the greater part of the country outside
Wales was touched by its activities during these years.[89] The Society
did not directly attempt to construct the machinery of a mass
movement, but to stimulate others into action.[90] Particular importance
was thus attached to the establishment in 1830 of auxiliaries at both
Oxford and Cambridge, because of their potential for influencing the
education of the clergy. In the event, the assistance of John Hill, the
Evangelical vice-principal of St Edmund Hall, ensured the survival of
the Oxford branch for some years, but that at Cambridge proved
short-lived.[91]

Subscription lists such as that for 1828–9, analysed in Table 1,
indicate that support came overwhelmingly from a professional, gentry,
and aristocratic constituency, with a substantial clerical and female
element. In the late 1820s the Society was supported by a substantial
minority of the Evangelical parliamentarians, but the membership lists
confirm the impression that support from them was far from
universal.[92] It is also worth noting the significant numbers of military
and naval officers, whose role in voluntary organizations after 1815
seems worthy of greater historical attention than it has hitherto
received. In addition to those whose names appear on the main
subscription list, approximately 300 people were members of local
auxiliaries. Their social composition varied significantly in accordance

[87] RS, *4th AR* (1831), 52–61; *7th AR* (1834).

[88] *Report of the Proceedings of the Aberdeen Auxiliary Reformation Society* (Aberdeen, 1831).

[89] RS, *Annual Reports*, RS minutes, the *Record*.

[90] *Protestant Journal*, 1 (1831), 112.

[91] RS, *4th AR* (1831), 14; *R*, 3 June 1830; St Edmund Hall MS 67/8, John Hill Diary, 24–30 May 1830 and *passim*. John Hill (1787–1855) was vice-principal of St Edmund Hall and a key Evangelical figure in Oxford (Boase, i. 1472; J. S. Reynolds, *The Evangelicals at Oxford 1735–1871* (Oxford, 1953), *passim*).

[92] Bradley, 'Politics of Godliness', p. 178, counts 49 Evangelicals in the Commons in the period 1812–29.

Figure 1. Centres of Reformation Society activity, 1827–1831

TABLE I. *Reformation Society subscribers, 1828–1829*

	No.	%
Bishops (Lichfield, Salisbury)	2	0.4
Lay peers	13	2.4
Other titled laymen	5	0.9
MPs	16	3.0
Clergy	119	22.3
Naval and military officers	30	5.6
Laymen styled 'Esq.', 'Hon.', 'Dr'	153	28.7
Laymen styled 'Mr'	36	6.7
Women	134	25.1
Anonymous	26	4.9
TOTAL	534	

Source: RS, *2nd AR* (1829).

with the character of different areas: for example, in 1828–9 the Bradford branch included 4 clergy, 10 women, 22 'Misters', and 1 doctor among its 38 members, but not a single 'Esquire'. Conversely, at Bath the membership of 27 included 3 women, 6 clergy, 13 'Esquires', and 4 'Misters'. At Holywell there were 15 clergy in a membership of 22, but such overwhelming clerical domination was exceptional.[93] The minimal extent of working-class support at this stage is confirmed by membership lists, both of the London branch and of its auxiliaries. Although all donations appear to have been recorded, there were few of less than half a guinea: some small contributions were no doubt made in the collections at meetings, but reports of these attest their generally 'respectable' character.

Catholics continued their opposition to the Society. When a Protestant deputation visited Liverpool in July 1829, they found a local Catholic Defence Society already organized and ready to resist them. The Reformation Society's speakers were frequently interrupted, but the Catholics were partially appeased when their spokesman was allowed to address the meeting. The debate was continued at a second meeting.[94] In February 1830 meetings at Walsall and Wolverhampton aroused the ire of the local priest, who advertised three sermons of his own, challenging the Protestants to answer them.[95] At Derby a

[93] At both Bradford and Bath there was 1 anonymous subscriber.
[94] *R*, 16 July 1829, 17 May 1830.
[95] *R*, 22, 25 Feb. 1830; W. Dalton, *A Brief Memoir of a Beloved Wife* (Wolverhampton, 1862), 25.

Catholic pamphlet attacked 'the devotees of that godly thing the Deformation—I humbly ask pardon—the Reformation', and alleged that the Society was motivated purely by mercenary motives. Ex-army and -naval officers, cheated of a real battle, were spoiling for a fight with the Catholics.[96]

Activity reached a peak in the latter half of 1830 with a series of lengthy debates between Catholics and the Reformation Society. At Cheltenham in August McDonnell and another priest interrupted the local annual meeting to complain about '*ex parte* statements affecting the character of the Church of Rome being set forth to the public without contradiction'. Gordon was becoming increasingly intolerant of Catholic complaints, but he did offer to arrange a meeting for discussion on 'The Creed of Pope Pius IV'. He refused to allow the Thirty-nine Articles to be discussed, as the Reformation Society wanted to keep the Catholics on the defensive, but suggested that if McDonnell wanted to take the offensive, he should arrange his own meeting in order to do so.[97]

The discussion lasted five days. Local interest increased as it proceeded, and both sides agreed in estimating the audience as reaching up to 4,000 people. The debate terminated when the Protestants took exception to the argument that fundamental Christian doctrines could not be proved from Scripture alone, and the priests consequently withdrew. Placards advertising another Protestant meeting were torn down or defaced, and the Catholics took no part in further meetings in the town. Both sides claimed victory. The Protestants argued that the Catholic attack on the supremacy of Scripture was intended to distract attention from their own indefensible position, while the Catholics maintained that Protestant refusal to countenance their line of argument was a tacit admission that it was unanswerable.[98]

Similar discussions occurred at Birmingham, Walsall, and Liverpool, where the proceedings lasted for eleven days, while at Nottingham Catholic opposition forced the dissolution of a meeting

---

[96] *A Letter to the Inhabitants of Derby*, by a Catholic (Wirksworth, 1830).

[97] *R*, 16 Aug. 1830.

[98] *R*, 26 Aug., 2, 9, 16 Sept. 1830; *Protestant Journal*, 1 (1831), 112; *Catholic Magazine*, 1 (1831), 134–5. Francis Close, the prominent Evangelical incumbent of Cheltenham (on whom, see M. Hennell, *Sons of the Prophets* (1979), 104–21) does not appear to have taken any part in these debates, a significant indicator of the divided attitude to the Reformation Society even among hardline Evangelicals (cf. RS minutes, 26 Apr. 1841).

called to form a local Reformation Society.[99] In the following March a meeting at Newcastle upon Tyne led to a further Catholic pamphlet, in which the Reformation Society was strongly attacked and accused of systematically attempting to discredit its opponents. The writer alleged that the Society was motivated by a cynical desire to safeguard the material wealth of the Protestant Establishment in Ireland. This pamphlet sold 500 copies in four days. The Reformation Society responded by arranging a second meeting in June. At the invitation of the local Catholic Defence Society, Mr Falvey, an itinerant speaker who had also played a prominent role at Cheltenham, came to represent the Catholics in a discussion with the Protestant deputation.[100] Local feelings ran high in the face of extreme speeches by the Reformation Society's representatives, and they left behind them on Tyneside a lasting distaste for their methods.[101]

Protestant operations were extended to Scotland in 1830, when Gordon toured north of the Border, and auxiliaries were formed at Greenock, Glasgow, and Edinburgh and a student society at Glasgow University.[102] He returned the next year with Nicholas Armstrong,[103] and visited Aberdeen, Dundee, and Perth as well. Generally Gordon appeared quite satisfied with his reception, but in Edinburgh, where pro-Emancipation opinion headed by Chalmers had been unusually conspicuous in 1829, the Society's cause did not prove popular.[104] There was a noticeable difference between the Scottish and English Catholic reaction: the priests in Scotland less frequently rose to the bait to participate in public discussions, presumably feeling that in the more staunchly Protestant climate they were less likely to be able to turn such encounters to their own advantage.[105]

In February 1831 McDonnell and a group of priests began to publish the *Catholic Magazine*. A series of articles during 1831 vigorously attacked the Reformation Society, accusing it of inconsistency, misrepresentation, and unfair management of meetings, which

[99] *R*, 11, 14, 28 Oct., 15 Nov. 1830.

[100] C. Larkin, *A Vindication of the Catholic Religion* (Newcastle upon Tyne, 1831); *Catholic Magazine*, 1 (1831), 622.

[101] *Protestant Journal*, 5 (1835), 53–5.

[102] RS, *3rd AR* (1830), 23–4.

[103] Nicholas Armstrong (?1801–79) had Irish origins. He was an ordained clergyman employed as a 'missionary' by the Reformation Society from August 1830 (RS minutes, 20 Oct. 1830). He later became an apostle in the Catholic Apostolic Church (P. E. Shaw, *The Catholic Apostolic Church* (New York, 1946), 82; Boase, i. 85).

[104] Chalmers MSS 4.159.38–9, Gordon to Chalmers, n.d. 1831.

[105] RS, *ARs, passim; Protestant Journal*, 3 (1833), 202–3.

invariably produced ill feeling between Protestants and Catholics where, it was claimed, none had existed before. Roman Catholics disagreed among themselves as to whether it was wise to participate in debates with the Reformation Society. The *Catholic Magazine* held that they should continue to do so because these meetings provided an opportunity to impress the Catholic position upon the open-minded and were even a means of making converts to Catholicism. It was claimed that there had been five such converts at Cheltenham.[106]

The Protestants responded in kind, immediately announcing the commencement of their own periodical, to be called the *Protestant Catholic Journal*.[107] This was not directly under the control of the Reformation Society but was taken over by it in 1834, and throughout its existence, which continued until 1837, the magazine gave considerable space to the Society's activities.[108] It responded to the *Catholic Magazine*'s attacks with further forceful denunciations of 'Popery', which its adversary disdained to answer.[109]

The energetic activity of Gordon and his colleagues concealed underlying weaknesses in the Reformation Society. Finance was a recurrent problem: income did not expand sufficiently to match the ambitious scale of operations and was only maintained by continual tapping of the initial Protestant enthusiasm of new areas of the country. The committee was perplexed by this, and commented in 1830:

When [they] . . . compare the meagerness [*sic*] of their financial resources, with the deep-felt interest in . . . the Society's objects by a large and influential class of the public, they are utterly at a loss to reconcile the consistency of fond and enthusiastic profession with the almost nothingness of actual performance, and they cannot but advert with pain to the unnatural contrast which is exhibited between the income of this religiously Protestant Institution, and the liberality of Protestantism when a mere political object is the object of the appeal.[110]

The Reformation Society fell between two stools. Its explicit disavowal of political intentions rendered it unattractive to Ultra-Tories and those concerned to defend material Irish Protestant interests. On the

---

[106] *Catholic Magazine*, 1 (1831), 70–5, 129–36, 257–68.

[107] *R*, 30 Dec. 1830; *Protestant Journal*, 1 (1831), 1. The full title of the periodical was intended as a protest against what was seen as arrogant appropriation by the Roman Church of the description 'Catholic'.

[108] RS, *7th AR*, (1834), 77.

[109] *Protestant Magazine, passim.*

[110] RS, *3rd AR* (1830), 26.

other hand, its extreme methods and its association with the 'Recordite' party increasingly alienated that moderate Evangelical constituency which was prepared to give massive sums to overseas missionary societies during this same period. Charles Simeon considered that its methods were useless in England, although they might do some good in Ireland.[111] The *Christian Guardian*, reviewing in March 1840 a sermon by W. F. Hook which alleged that meetings of the Reformation Society always led to twenty or more converts to Rome, clearly considered such High-Church criticism overstated, but still felt that the Irish origins of the Society had caused its advocates to make descriptions of Catholic practice which appeared exaggerated in a British context.[112]

The success of the Society's meetings in terms of attendance and press interest was due in general to the elements of spectacle and novelty which they offered rather than to conscientious hardline Evangelical religious conviction. The essential shallowness of this response meant that long-term financial support remained very uncertain. There was seldom sufficient local support consistently to maintain auxiliary societies. When these did prove viable, it was attributable either to a conspicuous individual, such as Hill at Oxford or Bull at Bradford, or to a strong local Catholic presence, as at Bath and York. However, the Society does not seem to have gained much of a foothold in Lancashire at this period, probably because of its non-political character.[113]

During the early 1830s internal tensions were also evident, both over the Society's attitude to Dissenters and over Irvingite ideas. In 1830 an unsuccessful attempt was made to exclude Dissenting ministers from their ex-officio committee seats, and, as an MP, Gordon's utterances left little doubt that he at least had very little sympathy for Nonconformity. He saw it as a potentially revolutionary force, and came close to equating it with Catholicism.[114] Nevertheless, the committee as a whole continued to express a desire to attack Rome on the basis of broad Protestant principle rather than Anglican

---

[111] A. N. Brown, *Recollections of the Conversation Parties of the Revd Charles Simeon, MA* (1863), 293.

[112] *Christian Guardian*, 1840, pp. 106–7.

[113] RS, *ARs, passim*.

[114] RS minutes, 17, 28 Mar. 1830; 3 *Hansard*, iv. 1201, 13 July 1831. On Gordon's political activities, see below, Chap. 3. Ironically, Gordon's own ecclesiastical status, as a Scottish adherent to the Church of England, was somewhat ambiguous (cf. 3 *Hansard*, v. 24, 823, 19 July, 5 Aug. 1831).

exclusiveness. In July 1832 it welcomed a proposal from some Yorkshire Independent ministers that they should unite their anti-Catholic activities with those of the Society. This was seen as 'an opening in providence towards that intimate and general connexion with the Dissenting body in the prosecution of the great object in which the Society is engaged—which was contemplated at its formation, and has never been lost sight of in the progress of its operations'.[115] However, manifestations of such an attitude were rare after the early 1830s, and in 1834 it was explicitly stated that the Society's secretaries should be clergymen of the Established Church of England or Scotland.[116] The problem of Protestant rivalries was especially acute in Scotland, where after 1833 the Society's agents frequently found that its potential supporters were too preoccupied with taking sides over Voluntaryism and Non-Intrusionism to be able to spare much energy for attacking Rome.[117]

The move towards establishmentarian exclusiveness had considerable significance for the future, but a more serious short-term crisis arose as a result of the extreme views of the Society's missionary, Nicholas Armstrong. In May 1831, at a meeting unconnected with the Reformation Society, convened in London to discuss ways of relieving famine and distress in Ireland, Armstrong caused uproar by attributing the famine to God's judgement on Romish apostasy, to the outrage of the many Catholics present. Armstrong was supported by William Dalton, the Reformation Society's former clerical secretary. However, the Hon. and Revd Gerard Noel, himself a supporter of the Society, while agreeing with their views on Roman Catholicism, 'considered the time, and the place, and occasion, wholly foreign for such discussion, and [that] they owed an apology to their Catholic brethren for this uncalled-for attack upon them [*Applause*]'.[118] The *Record* wholeheartedly agreed, arguing that it was unfair to trap Catholics into a theological argument on this occasion, but when *The Times* vigorously attacked Armstrong, Evangelical solidarity caused the *Record* to rally to his defence. Although Armstrong had been tactless, it was 'an error arising from those views of things, spiritual and eternal, of which the

---

[115] RS minutes, 4 July 1832.
[116] Ibid. 14 May 1834.
[117] *The Protestant Journal*, 4 (1834), 692, 695.
[118] *R*, 30 May 1831. On Dalton, later the leading Evangelical clergyman in Wolverhampton for much of the early Victorian period, see J. D. Walters, 'The Impact of Anglican Evangelicalism on the Religious Life of Wolverhampton and its Locality', M.Phil. thesis (CNAA, Wolverhampton Polytechnic, 1983).

writers of the *Times* have not the feeblest imagination—which led
Ridley and Latimer in triumph to the stake, secured the religious and
civil emancipation of Britain, and lies at the foundation of the
unexampled prosperity and glory which this country has so long
enjoyed'.[119] This article was hardly calculated to gain the *Record* or the
Reformation Society the sympathy of the public as a whole, but it did
something to restore the fragile fabric of Evangelical unity.

A further crisis arose within a few months, as a focus of the more
general conflict within the Evangelical world over Irving's doctrines
and practices. His powerful emphasis on the Incarnation, and his
belief that Christ, though sinless in virtue of the indwelling of the
Spirit, had taken upon himself fallen human nature, led to allegations
that he was heretically teaching 'the sinfulness of Christ's human
nature'.[120] In 1830 there were manifestations of tongues in the West of
Scotland, and in the spring of 1831 these spread to Irving's church in
London. After investigation, Irving himself sanctioned this development. His views were shared by Armstrong, who believed that 'the
baptism of the Holy Ghost is for the Church now as well as in ancient
times'.[121] During the autumn of 1831 complaints were made that
Armstrong had been promulgating Irvingite views while speaking on
behalf of the Reformation Society. When challenged, he admitted the
charge and refused to suppress his opinions, holding that they were
very relevant to the discussion of questions between Roman Catholics
and Protestants, because the outpouring of the Spirit formed part of
that same millennial scheme which led him to anticipate imminent
divine judgement on Rome.[122] At a meeting on 16 November the
committee found itself to be hopelessly divided on the issue. They
could only agree on a non-committal resolution which was seen as a
victory for Irvingism and led to a number of resignations from the
committee, including those of Vernon Harcourt and Finch. The *Record*
strongly supported their stand and asserted that nine-tenths of the
membership of the Society were opposed to Armstrong's doctrines.[123]
The dispute was thus brought into the open, and the Society suffered a
rapid loss of support. On 1 December there was reluctant agreement

[119] *R*, 9 June 1831.
[120] A. L. Drummond, *Edward Irving and his Circle* (1937), 112–13; C. G. Strachan,
The Pentecostal Theology of Edward Irving (1973), 30–1; Bebbington, *Evangelicalism*, p. 93.
[121] Drummond, *Irving and his Circle*, pp. 136–60; RS minutes, 16 Nov. 1831.
[122] RS minutes, 16 Nov. 1831; Rennie, 'Evangelicalism', p. 73.
[123] *R*, 21, 28 Nov. 1831.

to dismiss Armstrong, but attempts to proscribe Irvingite opinions were defeated. A similar attempt failed in early 1832.[124]

The Society was now close to total collapse, but in April Gordon led a recovery by the orthodox party. Harcourt and Finch were re-elected to the committee and, significantly, Drummond withdrew from the Society. On 13 April, in order to 'obviate anything in the form of a misconception respecting their principles and sentiments', the committee disclaimed 'in the most explicit manner all connexion and identity with . . . [Irvingite] doctrines and opinions'. The text of this resolution was inserted in a number of newspapers.[125] Nevertheless, serious damage had already been done. The 1832 *Annual Report* announced that the Society was £600 in debt. A considerable proportion of the auxiliaries appear to have collapsed during this period, and the *Catholic Magazine* claimed that even some of those which survived had scarcely any support.[126]

The 1831–2 crisis also served as the final nail in the coffin of the Society's Irish operations. Gordon and Finch had made a further tour between October 1829 and February 1830, holding sixty-five meetings in Munster, but thereafter visits by deputations were not repeated, as they were clearly proving fruitless in the face of the disturbed condition of the country.[127] However, the Society continued to maintain an Irish office and a number of Scripture readers until March 1832, when the financial situation forced a complete withdrawal. In 1833 an agent made vigorous efforts to revive operations, but achieved nothing. The London committee recorded that it was grieved, but not surprised, by this failure.[128]

The two years after 1832 nevertheless saw something of a recovery in the Society's British operations, under the leadership of an energetic new secretary, Edward Tottenham, an Irishman who had previously been secretary of the now defunct Dublin Reformation Society.[129] A meeting in Oxford in June 1832 led to the establishment of a Protestant Theological Society in the University, which survived for some years, and there were extensive tours by deputations in the

---

[124] RS minutes, 1, 8 Dec. 1831, 20 Jan., 1 Feb. 1832.
[125] Ibid. 4, 13 Apr. 1832.
[126] RS, *5th AR* (1832), 31; *Catholic Magazine*, 5 (1834), 696–7.
[127] RS, *3rd AR* (1830), 20; *4th AR* (1831), 22.
[128] RS minutes, 14 Mar. 1832, 22 May, 25 Oct., 22 Nov. 1833.
[129] *R*, 23 June 1853; W. C. Magee, *Remains of Edward Tottenham*, BD (1855), pp. xxii ff.

South of England.[130] It was also decided to appoint a number of clerical missionaries. The Revd Robert Shanks became missionary for Scotland in November 1833, under the supervision of the Glasgow auxiliary. In England a number of men were prepared to work for the Society on a short-term basis, but no permanent appointment was made until the job was given to Tottenham, who was ordained in 1833.[132]

Although some meetings of the Reformation Society were very poorly attended, as at Leicester in August 1833, others still attracted very large audiences, as at Chatham in September 1832 and at Portsea in the autumn of 1833. Roman Catholics continued to debate with the representatives of the Society, although rather less frequently than hitherto.[132] The feeling that Protestants were better ignored than confronted was gaining ground in Catholic circles, and this was reflected in an almost complete silence on the subject of the Reformation Society in the pages of the *Catholic Magazine* throughout 1832 and 1833.

In February and March 1834 a higher profile was achieved when Downside Abbey (near Bath) became the setting for a large-scale theological discussion, the first time such an event had been held in a Catholic building. The main speakers were Tottenham and Mc-Donnell. The debate attracted considerable local interest and was conducted in a more charitable spirit than had previously distinguished the Society's activities.[133] The respect thus established proved to be brittle and short-lived, however, and an acrimonious dispute soon developed over the publication of the speeches.[134] In July a Catholic was refused a hearing at a Protestant meeting in Hackney, and the organizers tried to get the police to arrest him.[135] Protestant criticism of the Reformation Society's activities continued, stemming partly from a distaste for division and controversy. In May 1834 Finch also suggested that the Society's avoidance of politics was losing it support and that its readiness to accept Dissenters alienated those primarily concerned to defend the Establishment. Similar reservations probably

---

[130] St Edmund Hall MS 67/9, John Hill Diary, 15, 16 June 1832, 6 June 1834; RS minutes, 26 June 1833; RS, *6th AR* (1833), 18–26.

[131] RS minutes, 16 May, 7 Nov. 1832, 20 Nov., 11 Dec. 1833.

[132] *R*, 13 Sept. 1832; RS, *6th AR* (1833), 17–27; *7th AR* (1834), 56–73; *Catholic Magazine*, 4 (1833), 184.

[133] *Catholic Magazine*, 5 (1834), 68–9; *Protestant Journal*, 4 (1834), 261.

[134] *Protestant Journal*, 4 (1834), 316–27; *Catholic Magazine*, 5 (1834), 83, 402–3.

[135] *Catholic Magazine*, 5 (1834), 461–3.

lay behind an evident decline in Gordon's enthusiasm for the Society.[136]

The development of the Reformation Society during the first seven years of its history provides important insights into the nature of the changes and conflicts taking place in the Evangelical world. Uncompromising anti-Catholicism was a natural and central strand in a world-view that could admit no shades of grey in the struggle of truth and error. In relation to Ireland in the late 1820s, such an interpretation in terms of a conflict of elemental forces had a credibility which enabled the Society to serve as an important focus for those Evangelicals who yearned for a more crusading spirit. The transference of this approach to Britian was more incongruous, and meant that moderate sympathy was lost and the tendency, evident at the outset, for the Reformation Society to serve as a focus for extremism was accentuated. This development reached its culmination in Armstrong's tainting of the Society with Irvingism in 1831. However, the ultimate success of the relative moderates in the ensuing conflict was part of a process by which 'Recordite' Evangelicalism was defining its own boundaries and demonstrating that the process of radicalization that had proceeded since the mid-1820s could not advance indefinitely unchecked. The secession of the extremists to form the Catholic Apostolic Church, while depriving the 'new' Evangelicalism of some of its most dynamic elements, assured it of a respectability which increasingly enabled it to determine the tone of the Evangelical world as a whole.[137]

The hardening of conflict over the status of the Established Churches was a further important development of these years. In the face of the radical attack on the Church of England and Whig reform of the Church of Ireland, efforts to co-operate with Dissenters even on matters of purely 'religious' character were subject to considerable suspicion. Indeed, taken in conjunction with the evident continued politicization of Irish Catholicism, the recognition that the status of the Church was now a major parliamentary issue made the maintenance of the non-political character of Evangelical anti-Catholicism an increasingly difficult task. Emancipation, far from freeing religion from politics, as some of its advocates had hoped, had had exactly the reverse effect.

---

[136] *R*, 1, 5 May 1834.
[137] *Edinburgh Review*, 200 (1853), 283–4.

Thus, by 1834 several of the major themes in the history of mid-nineteenth-century anti-Catholicism had already emerged. There was a tendency towards fragmentation and internal conflict, especially in the face of the problem of the Church Establishment. Questions were continually being asked about the relationship of 'religious' and 'political' activity, and there was a lively propaganda battle with the Catholics themselves. This conclusion has important implications for understanding two key developments of the mid-1830s, the recovery of Conservatism and the Tractarian movement. The former will be discussed in the next chapter, but the latter requires some initial consideration at this point.

In October and November 1833 the *Record* published a series of letters signed by 'A Churchman', concerned with the revival of Church discipline.[138] The writer was none other than J. H. Newman. It is easy to dismiss his success in getting his writing inserted into an extreme Evangelical publication as being a testimony to his own disingenuousness and Haldane's naïvety.[139] However, there was more common ground between 'Recordites' and High-Churchmen at this stage than might appear at first sight. Pre-Tractarian High-Churchmen generally held strong anti-Roman views, and some were willing to agree with the Evangelicals' identification of Rome as Antichrist. Newman himself had held this view at an earlier date, although he had moved away from it by 1833.[140] However, it was as recently as 1830 that he had parted company with the Evangelicals in the Church Missionary Society in Oxford, and this was due more to differences with the radical wing represented by H. B. Bulteel than to general antagonism to Evangelicalism.[141] By 1833, now that the secession of the Irvingites had rendered the 'Recordites' more moderate than a few years before, it was not unreasonable for Newman to explore the possibility of co-operation. He professed himself able to go 'a great way with the peculiars',[142] and in a letter to Haldane in December 1833 he urged him to think carefully before opposing the Oxford tracts:

[138] *The Letters and Diaries of John Henry Newman*, ed. I. Ker and T. Gornall (1980), iv. 63–103, *passim*. Cf. P. Toon, *Evangelical Theology 1833–1856: A Response to Tractarianism* (1979), 16–23.

[139] Altholz, 'Alexander Haldane', p. 25.

[140] P. B. Nockles, 'Continuity and Change in Anglican High Churchmanship in Britain, 1792–1850', D.Phil. thesis (Oxford, 1982), 175–84; S. Gilley, 'Newman and Prophecy, Evangelical and Catholic', *Journal of the United Reformed Church History Society*, 3 (1985), 160–88. Cf. Bebbington, *Evangelicalism*, p. 97.

[141] T. C. F. Stunt, 'John Henry Newman and the Evangelicals', *Journal of Ecclesiastical History*, 21 (1970), 65–74.

[142] Ker and Gornall, *Newman*, iv. 337, Newman to Jasmine Newman, 2 Oct. 1834.

You have them on your side in their horror and abjuration of liberalism, in their reverence for inspired Scripture and their willingness to stand or fall by it, in their exact and zealous orthodoxy on the doctrines of the Trinity and the Incarnation, in their belief in the Atonement, in the influences of grace and the necessity of a spiritual change in the heart of every individual in order to salvation, in their earnest desire that no alterations should be made in our Articles and Liturgy, and in their abomination of Popery properly so called.[143]

Newman's strong views on this last point formed the subject of the last of his five letters to the *Record*, which expressed concern at the recent strengthening of Catholicism in England. Although he went on to criticize extreme responses, his comments implied objections to the means rather than the ends, and were reminiscent of those of moderate Evangelicals: 'These Protestants have had nothing definite to appeal to or point at, either in creed or polity; they have necessarily aimed more at weakening attachment to Rome, than at supplying some other guide in its place; at unsettling than instructing; at disabusing than converting the mind and hearts.' The real solution, Newman maintained, lay in restoring the discipline of the Church of England, thus making her a truly effective bulwark against Rome.[144]

Given the polemical contours of the 'Recordite' mind, it was inevitable that it would tend to polarize the issues in a manner that left little room for Newman's views. The initial parting of the ways came over the best means of restoring Church order, when the *Record* in December 1833 forcefully denounced the tracts' emphasis on the apostolic succession. However, this was more because it was liable to divide the Church of England and hence play into the hands of its attackers than because it was 'Popish' *per se*.[145] Although a sustained Evangelical attack on Tractarianism did not develop for several years,[146] the *Record*'s repulse of Newman's approaches may well have had a significant impact on his development, in that it demonstrated that his hopes of building on common ground with Evangelicals in the defence of the Church were misplaced. He thus moved initially to his explicit attempt to construct a *via media*, but then, as this seemed impossible to sustain, reluctantly and painfully to Rome itself.

The subtitle of Peter Toon's study of Evangelical theology in the period after 1833 implies that it was primarily a 'response to

---

[143] Ibid. 130, Newman to the editor of the *Record*, 3 Dec. 1833.
[144] Ibid. 102; *R*, 14 Nov. 1833.
[145] *R*, 5, 9, 12 Dec. 1833; D. Rosman, *Evangelicals and Culture* (1984), 34.
[146] Toon, *Evangelical Theology*, p. 23.

Tractarianism'. However, when later developments are set in the context of the years preceding 1833, the relationship appears to have been much more of a two-way one. In their Victorian forms, both movements had a common root in their desire for a more uncompromisingly spiritual response to the problems of the late 1820s and early 1830s, but, as this chapter has shown, militantly anti-Catholic Evangelicalism had already emerged before 1833, the product of theological questioning from within the movement, the intensification of religious conflict in Ireland, and the understandable, but still unexpectedly belligerent, response of Roman Catholics in England to Protestant attacks. It is now time to consider the political implications of this development.

3

PROTESTANTISM AND CONSERVATISM
1829–1841

PROTESTANTISM during the 1830s was brought to bear on political life by two initially distinct groups: Ultra-Tories struggling to come to terms with an era in which Catholics were now able to play a full part in political life; and Anglican Evangelicals finding that their religiously based concern to maintain Reformation principles had inescapable political implications. These were evoked particularly in relation to education and in the bearing of a prophetic witness to the parlous spiritual state of the nation. Ireland was a crucial catalyst in both these movements, and the point at which they made contact with each other. Protestantism was a political force with a life of its own, but the circumstances of the later 1830s meant that its renewed vitality was almost entirely channelled into support for the Conservative party.

Before considering the development of political Protestantism after 1829, some preliminary comment on the failure of the opposition to Emancipation is required. Evangelicals' reluctance to be directly involved was attributable not only to their own concerns, discussed in the previous chapter, but also to the extent to which the conduct of the Ultras disturbed their sensibilities. Newcastle's inflexible conservatism and his use of religion to support a political position repelled the *Record*. Winchilsea also damaged his prestige in that quarter by a slanderous attack on Wellington which resulted in a duel.[1]

The difficulties of the Ultras were compounded by their lack of effective leadership, especially in the Commons, and by their own constitutional assumptions. They were very cautious about inciting what they saw as 'party spirit' which might destroy the unity of the constitutional fabric. A number of the replies received by Winchilsea in response to a circular to the Kentish nobility urging resistance to Emancipation expressed opposition to concessions to the Catholics, but suggested that Protestant organization to resist them would be

[1] *R*, 26 Sept. 1828; G. I. T. Machin, *The Catholic Question in English Politics 1820 to 1830* (Oxford, 1964), 175; RS, *2nd AR* (1829), 40–2.

unconstitutional.[2] Newcastle initially believed that agitation would be wrong. When a Protestant Club was formed in July 1828, 'it was urged in the first instance that a committee should be appointed, this I objected to on the grounds of its impropriety, organisation, correspondence and incitement could not suit us, we blame it in our opponents, we ought not . . . to adopt it ourselves'.[3] Subsequently, increasing desperation drove him to think more favourably of such measures, but Ultra-Tories continued to be painfully aware of the anomaly of resorting to them.

The passing of the Relief Act left the Ultras seriously disorientated. Emancipation had now acquired constitutional legitimacy, and the possibility of repealing it was never seriously envisaged at this stage. Newcastle lapsed into a state of deep depression,[4] but other anti-Emancipationists displayed a certain sense of relief that the matter had at least been settled. Winchilsea said in November 1829: 'whatever opinion prevailed upon the great question on which they had differed, they were bound now to give obedience to the law against which they had heretofore contended'.[5] He hoped his fears about the consequences of passing the measure would prove to be unjustified. Another instance of this state of mind was provided by the behaviour of the corporation of Tiverton, which in 1827 had refused to allow their anti-Emancipationist MP, Richard Ryder, to retire in favour of his pro-Emancipationist nephew Granville Ryder. In 1830, however, they gave entirely unsolicited assurances that their objection to the change was removed by the final settlement of the question.[6]

The Ultra challenges to Wellington in 1829 and 1830 thus lacked ideological coherence. They stemmed essentially from anxiety for revenge on the duke and Peel for their political apostasy, and a desire for power legitimized by the conviction that they alone had the requisite virtue to salvage something from the wreckage. Agricultural distress did much to keep their discontent alive, but it was an insufficiently clear rallying-point to prevent Wellington weakening them by winning individuals back to the government, especially after

    [2] Machin, *Catholic Question*, pp. 135–6.
    [3] Nottingham University Library, Newcastle MSS, Diary Ne2F3, 12 Nov. 1828.
    [4] Ibid. 23 May, 26 May, 24 June 1829.
    [5] *R*, 16 Nov. 1829.
    [6] Sandon Hall, Stafford, Harrowby MSS, lxi. 464–6, G. D. Ryder to Viscount Ebrington, 29 Dec. 1827; mclxxvi. 43a, Richard Ryder to Mayor of Tiverton, 3 July 1830.

their hopes of power were finally shattered by the death of George IV on 26 June 1830. By November 1830 they had come to the conclusion that there was little more that they could do as an independent body.[7]

However, having abandoned their own ambitions, some Ultras were still sore enough to feel that there was nothing to choose between Wellington and the Whigs. On 15 November thirty-four Tory rebels joined the opposition in defeating the government in the Commons. The Duke of Richmond even accepted office under Grey, while Winchilsea pledged support for the incoming administration, an act which he later justified as follows:

He would honestly say, that after the passing of those two great measures—the repeal of the Test and Corporation Acts, and of the Roman disabilities—he had thought that all distinctions of Whig and Tory had ceased to exist, and that both parties having pledged themselves anxious for the maintenance of the Constitution, they were now thoroughly united in their desire to support it.[8]

Newcastle, although feeling that Richmond had gone too far and suspicious of some members of the new government, also believed that there was little of significance separating himself from Grey.[9]

While the Ultras floundered, Evangelical reluctance to raise the stakes too high in relation to Emancipation began to pay off. In Parliament, as in the country, legislative concession fuelled their Protestant ardour. On 22 May 1829 Mandeville rose in the Commons to protest against the parliamentary grant to the Roman Catholic seminary at Maynooth, given initially by the Irish Parliament in 1795 and continued on an annual basis by the united Parliament after 1800. Mandeville argued that the grant was in direct opposition to the principle on which Emancipation had been granted, namely, that there should be no connections between the Roman Catholic Church and the State. He felt that the continuance of the grant would lead to divine judgement, and claimed that Lord Liverpool had believed it to be 'the most unchristian grant that a Christian country could make'.[10]

During the two years immediately succeeding Catholic Emancipation Evangelicals took up the case of two officers, Captain Atchison and Lieutenant Dawson, who had been cashiered from the army for

---

[7] Cf. B. T. Bradfield, 'Sir Richard Vyvyan and Tory Politics', Ph.D. thesis (London, 1965), 67–83; R. Stewart, *The Foundation of the Conservative Party 1830–1867* (1978), 50–5; Newcastle Diary, Ne2F3, 31 Oct., 2 Nov. 1830.

[8] 3 *Hansard*, iv. 108, 21 June 1831.

[9] Newcastle Diary, Ne2F3, 31 Oct., 20 Nov. 1830.

[10] 2 *Hansard*, xxi. 1554–6, 22 May 1829.

refusing to obey an order to fire salutes in honour of a Roman Catholic religious ceremony in Malta. On 12 June 1829 Sir Robert Inglis, who had triumphed over Peel at the Oxford University election in the previous February, presented a petition on the matter urging that the officers should be reinstated. Sir Henry Hardinge, the secretary at war, was unsympathetic.[11] The *Record* published a series of articles considering the case and concluded that 'we are labouring under the weight of a national crime, for which, if unrepented of, we may be assured that, sooner or later, the righteous vengeance of God will overtake this country'.[12] When Winchilsea raised the matter in the Lords in May 1830, Wellington reiterated the government's refusal to concede. During June Inglis twice presented petitions in the Commons, receiving the unlikely support of Daniel O'Connell, who felt that existing military practice was a violation of the general principle of religious liberty.[13]

Mandeville and Inglis both had strong roots in the Evangelical world,[14] but at this stage their attempts to assert Protestantism, although they had considerable moral support from the *Record*, were low-key and did not represent the efforts of any organized Evangelical group. However, on 12 July 1830 the *Record* published an address 'To the Christian Proprietors and Freeholders of Great Britain'. The anonymous author maintained that 'Christianity in its scriptural and Protestant form' held the nation together, criticized the Christians in Parliament for being too accommodating, and urged electors to unite at the forthcoming general election to return MPs who would support the Protestant interest.[15] The general elections of 1830 and 1831 did indeed see the return of a number of hardline Evangelicals to

---

[11] 2 *Hansard*, xxi. 1772–3, 12 June 1829.

[12] *R*, 18, 22, 25 June 1829.

[13] *R*, 7, 22, 28 Jan., 1 Feb., 26 Apr. 1830; 2 *Hansard*, xxiv. 918–19, 21 May 1830; xxv. 351–2, 421–4, 15, 17 June 1830.

[14] Sir Robert Harry Inglis (1786–1855), 2nd baronet, MP for Dundalk, 1824–6, Ripon, 1828–9, Oxford University, 1829–54 (*DNB*, xxix. 6). Inglis's Evangelicalism has been questioned by some, but is clearly substantiated by J. C. Colquhoun, *William Wilberforce: His Friends and his Times* (1966), 342 ff. The confusion arises from his very strong support for Establishment which caused him to talk at times like an old-style High-Churchman, and his political and religious independence, which meant that he very seldom aligned himself explicitly with Evangelical institutions. Boyd Hilton (*The Age of Atonement* (Oxford, 1988), 212) errs, however, in associating him with the 'Recordites': as will emerge below, he always kept his distance from them, and is better regarded as one of the last of the Clapham Sect.

[15] *R*, 12 July 1830.

Parliament, including Granville Ryder at Tiverton, Andrew Johnston[16] at St Andrews, and, most significantly, Captain James E. Gordon of the Reformation Society, who was returned in 1831 for the Earl of Roden's pocket borough of Dundalk.[17]

It remains unclear to what extent the small group of Evangelicals in Parliament in the early 1830s co-ordinated their activities. They represented a cross-section of party loyalties, including firm Tories such as Gordon, Ryder, and Spencer Perceval,[18] but also Whigs, notably Johnston and Sir George Sinclair.[19] A prayer-meeting was held regularly in Johnston's rooms,[20] but it does not necessarily follow that this would have been an occasion for co-ordinating action in Parliament, as its objectives might well have been purely devotional in character. While Evangelical interventions in debates clearly show a commitment to common ideals, it is difficult to discern evidence of a planned campaign of parliamentary action, at least not in relation to specifically Protestant matters.[21] Whatever political force their anti-Catholicism possessed, came rather from their close links with extra-parliamentary agitation as represented by the *Record* and the Reformation Society. At a time when the political horizons of most people were filled by the Reform Bill, the Evangelical response to the troubled state of the country was to urge a reassertion of Christian Protestant principles in the face of liberalism and infidelity.

Parliamentary action in 1831 was foreshadowed by a public meeting in Freemasons' Tavern on 19 March to promote a petition against the Maynooth grant. George Finch took the chair, and Gordon delivered

[16] Andrew Johnston (1798–1862), MP for St Andrews, 1831–7, and an associate of Thomas Chalmers (M. Stenton, *Who's Who of British Members of Parliament* (1976), i. 213; New College, Edinburgh, Chalmers MSS 4.161.42–5, Johnston to Chalmers, 14 June, 6 Sept. 1831).

[17] See I. S. Rennie, 'Evangelicalism and English Public Life', Ph.D. thesis (Toronto, 1962), I. C. Bradley, 'The Politics of Godliness: Evangelicals in Parliament 1784–1832', D.Phil. thesis (Oxford, 1974), 255, for full lists of Evangelical MPs in Parliament.

[18] Spencer Perceval (1795–1859), eldest son of the former prime minister, MP for Newport (IOW), 1827–31, and for Tiverton, 1831–2. Perceval participated in the Albury conferences and was later an apostle in the Catholic Apostolic Church (Boase, ii. 1462; P. E. Shaw, *The Catholic Apostolic Church* (New York, 1946), 80).

[19] Sir George Sinclair (1790–1868), 2nd baronet, MP for Caithness 1811–41, with a few intervals. He had strongly supported Catholic Emancipation and, like Johnston, the anti-slavery cause (*DNB*, lii. 295).

[20] J. Bridges, *Memoir of Sir Andrew Agnew of Lochnaw, Bt.* (Edinburgh, 1849), 7–8.

[21] I disagree with Rennie's assertion ('Evangelicalism', p. 147) that in the Maynooth debate on 26 September 1831 members had 'clearly' been briefed on the parts they were to take.

an impassioned speech calling for 'a bold and determined effort to wipe out the foul stain resting on British Protestants'.[22] On 23 June Mandeville rose in the Commons to present several anti-Maynooth petitions, provoking the comment from O'Connell that there was 'no little ingenuity requisite to make out the position that the evils of Ireland were attributable to the £9,000 or £11,000 a year granted to the College of Maynooth'.[23] O'Connell subsequently complained to the House about the anti-Catholic language of these petitions and of one presented by Gordon some weeks later. A motion that this latter petition should not be received was withdrawn as being inconsistent with free speech, but Gordon's proposal that the petition should be printed was negatived without a division, as MPs felt that sentiments so offensive to a section of the population should not be circulated at public expense. The *Record* saw this outcome as proof that 'modern liberalism has eaten out all the Protestantism of the nation'.[24]

During July, August, and September 1831 Gordon repeatedly clashed in the Commons with the Irish Catholic members. On 5 August O'Connell alluded to Gordon's participation in polemical religious discussions and expressed the hope that he would not make the House of Commons an arena for such debates.[25] However, the proposals, which Stanley introduced on 9 September, to end the grant for education in Ireland to the Kildare Place Society, and to create a board for national education in its place, inevitably reopened the battle that Gordon and O'Connell had fought on Irish platforms in the 1820s, but with the stakes substantially increased. Gordon defended the record of the protestant educational societies and condemned Catholic educational provision as subversive and unscriptural. His speech was described by O'Connell as 'marked . . . by bigotry, intolerance and ignorance, which were new to many hon. Members, but not to him [O'Connell] recollecting the quarter from which they came'. Gordon then rose to bemoan the fact that he 'was not a match for the hon. member for Kerry in the language of the fish-market'. To cries of 'Order!', O'Connell appealed to the chairman, who felt that he had heard so much strong language during the evening that he was at a loss to decide what was in order and what was not. Overstatement of

[22] *R*, 21 Mar., 4 Apr. 1831; cf. Rennie, 'Evangelicalism', p. 139.
[23] 3 *Hansard*, iv. 267, 23 June 1831.
[24] Ibid. v. 16–28, 19 July 1831; *R*, 21 July 1831.
[25] 3 *Hansard*, v. 822, 5 Aug. 1831.

the Protestant case was clearly doing it little service, and the House passed the government proposals.[26]

In September Spencer Perceval proposed the discontinuation of the Maynooth grant after the present year, maintaining that the vote of money to such purposes was inconsistent with the Protestant spirit of the constitution, which, he held, had not been compromised by Emancipation. Granville Ryder supported him, declaring himself an advocate of Protestant Ascendancy, not in a party-political sense but rather as applying the supremacy of Protestant religious principles derived from the Bible. Stanley, speaking for the government, maintained that Maynooth was a political not a religious question. The grant, he pointed out, had been supported by Pitt, Fox, and Grattan, and withdrawing it now would greatly alienate the Irish Catholics. However, speakers against the grant felt that a double standard was being applied now that the allocation of money to the Kildare Place Society had been discontinued. On a division, 47 members voted against the Maynooth grant, but 148 were in favour of it.[27]

In committee O'Connell immediately took the offensive, reminding the House of the extensive support which Irish Catholics were forced to give to the Established Church. Perceval denied the charge that his objections were uncharitable, saying that he did not wish to make any personal attacks, but simply maintained that if 'Protestantism be truth, then Popery is falsehood'. This was the cue for Gordon to make a rambling speech asserting that the Roman Catholic religion taught politically subversive doctrines and that the priests trained at Maynooth would 'direct the hostility of the population against the Government and against the Protestantism of the empire'. Once again Gordon had overplayed his hand and alienated moderate Protestant support. Thomas Lefroy,[28] an Irish Evangelical, opposed the grant, but commented that 'he saw no reason why the subject might not be discussed without the necessity of hon. Members wounding feelings of one another'. Only Andrew Johnston was prepared explicitly to associate himself with the arguments expressed by Gordon.[29]

---

[26] Ibid. vi. 1249–1305, 9 Sept. 1831.

[27] Ibid. vii. 606–21, 26 Sept. 1831.

[28] Thomas Langlois Lefroy (1776–1869), MP for the University of Dublin, 1830–41; later lord chief justice of Queen's Bench (Ireland), 1852–66 (*DNB*, xxxii. 404; A. R. Acheson, 'The Evangelicals in the Church of Ireland, 1784–1859', Ph.D. thesis (Belfast, 1967), 192.

[29] 3 *Hansard*, vii. 621–45, 26 Sept. 1831.

The dogmatic, hardline position adopted by some Evangelicals, especially Gordon, in the parliamentary session of 1831 was attributable to their sense that political involvement was only justifiable if it offered an explicitly Christian challenge to perceived religious indifference in national life. Hence they took little active part in the struggles over the Reform Bill, although they were concerned about its implications for Protestant interests in Ireland. Clearly Gordon saw his parliamentary activities as a development of his Reformation Society deputation work. Similar tensions were evident in the political side of the movement as were displayed in relation to its religious aspect. The moderate *Christian Observer* followed criticism of the Reformation Society with an attack on the political extremism of Gordon and the *Record*.[30] The Irvingite problem also compromised the Evangelicals in Parliament early in 1832, when Spencer Perceval, who had fallen under their influence, first excited ridicule by moving for a general fast, and then, amidst scenes of considerable confusion, used a speech on the Reform Bill to prophesy God's judgement on the nation.[31] Thus, in 1832 the Evangelical voice in Parliament was less united and effective than it had been in the previous year. Despite Gordon's vigorous efforts, only seventeen votes were cast against the national education scheme, and the Maynooth grant was carried with only eight opposing votes in a poorly attended House at two o'clock in the morning.[32] The *Catholic Magazine* thus appeared vindicated in its gloating over the discomfiture of its opponents, whom it described as 'the expiring family of the saints'.[33]

Nevertheless, despite the parliamentary failure of Gordon's campaign in 1831–2, it had an important impact on the future development of anti-Catholicism. During 1831 there was very little sign of independent action by the Ultras on Protestant issues. They were preoccupied with the Reform question, having been driven into a scramble for reconciliation with Wellington and Peel when they recognized that their former leaders provided the best focus for resistance to government measures which went far further than they had anticipated.[34] The Reform struggle was frequently seen in

[30] *Christian Observer*, 31 (1831), 447 ff.; *R*, 4 Aug. 1831.

[31] 3 *Hansard*, ix. 895–903, 26 Jan. 1832; xi. 577–87, 20 Mar. 1832; Chalmers MSS 4.182.14, Johnston to Chalmers, 14 Feb. 1832.

[32] 3 *Hansard*, xii. 651–69, 23 July 1832; xiv. 890–6, 27 July 1832.

[33] *Catholic Magazine*, 2 (1832), 183.

[34] B. T. Bradfield, 'Sir Richard Vyvyan and the Country Gentlemen', *English Historical Review*, 83 (1968), 734; J. R. Wolffe, 'Protestant Societies and Anti-Catholic Agitation in Great Britain, 1829–1860', D.Phil. thesis (Oxford, 1984), 48–9.

religious terms, but in England this usually implied the conflict of Church and Dissent rather than Protestant and Catholic. Newcastle, however, had a nightmare vision of cosmic conflict, with the constitution, order, Protestantism, and the Church facing the united horrors of revolution, disorder, Catholicism, and Dissent.[35] Winchilsea came closest to seeing Protestantism as the key rallying-point in politics. When he annnounced in June 1831 that he was withdrawing his support from the government, he said that he did not differ from them over the principle of parliamentary reform, although he thought that the proposed measure went too far, but considered that 'The great distinction which prevailed between the parties was, that a large portion of those now in power had not set a true value on sound Protestant principles.'[36]

Thus anti-Catholic feeling among the Ultras continued to be strong, but lacked a distinct focus. Moreover, Winchilsea's intervention over the Atchison and Dawson case in May 1830 had already shown that an Evangelical campaign was capable of evoking support from Tory peers. This process had clearly advanced further when a large public meeting on Irish education was held at Exeter Hall on 8 February 1832. It was chaired by Viscount Lorton, and the speakers included Lord Kenyon in addition to Gordon, Mandeville, and a number of Evangelical clergy. The meeting was adjourned to 15 February, when the speakers at a very crowded gathering included the prominent Tories Sir Robert Bateson and Lord Redesdale as well as numerous Evangelical worthies. A similar trend was evident in some of the provincial meetings that followed.[37] In the Lords the most prominent critics of Stanley's plan were Roden and Winchilsea, but they received enthusiastic support from, among others, Kenyon, Bishop Phillpotts, and Lord Londonderry, who said that further concessions were causing him almost to regret the pro-Emancipation stance he had taken in 1829.[38]

The combination of Tories and Evangelicals on the education question did not go uncriticized. Johnston feared that the February Exeter Hall meetings had 'a political tendency, being chiefly got up by Irish Protestant Anti-Reformers'. Significantly, the second meeting was disrupted by agitators. Lord King commented in the Lords on 15 May that

[35] Fourth Duke of Newcastle, *An Address to all Classes and Conditions of Englishmen* (1832), 42.
[36] 3 *Hansard*, iv. 107–9, 21 June 1831.
[37] *R*, 9, 16, 20 Feb., 5, 15 Mar., 19, 26 Apr., 3, 7, 28 May 1832.
[38] 3 *Hansard* xi. 583–633, 25 Mar. 1832; xii. 495–9, 16 Apr. 1832.

somehow or other it was a curious phenomenon in the proceedings of the 'saints' that though their spiritual visions were, it must be presumed, ever fixed upon the 'kingdom come', they seemed also to have an eye fixed upon this 'sublunary world below'. In opposing what the noble Earl [Roden] designated the anti-Christian education system of the Whigs, they contrived to make the opposition auxiliary . . . to the restoration of the Tories.[39]

Winchilsea and Roden strenuously denied such charges. Clearly, however, they themselves represented a middle ground in which religious and political motives were inextricably associated. It was a sign of the times that such connections, widely held as axiomatic before 1829, were now being openly questioned by both liberals and Evangelicals.[40]

Thus, despite the points of personal contact and limited co-operation between the two wings of the Protestant movement, they still represented very different emphases and preoccupations. This was accentuated by the Ultras' attempt from 1831 onwards to revive the Orange Order, which had become almost defunct in Britain in the wake of Emancipation. Mandeville and Winchilsea were Orangeman, but the central figures were the Duke of Cumberland and Lords Kenyon and Wynford, together with the deputy grand secretary, Colonel William Blennerhasset Fairman, who in 1832 went on an extensive tour of Britain to restore regularity in the institution and to found new lodges.[41] These efforts were part of an endeavour to establish the Orange Order as the backbone of a revived Tory party. An 'Appeal to the Conservatives of Great Britain' emphasized the value of Orangeism as a check on sedition as well as 'Popery', while an 'Address to the Carlton Club' issued in 1834 spoke of the need for extra-parliamentary Orange action to support the institutions of the country and cement relations between upper and lower classes.[42] The charge that Orangeism was merely an expression of religious bigotry was denied:

This is, exclusively, a Protestant Association: yet detesting an intolerant spirit,

---

[39] F. Holmes, *Henry Cooke* (Belfast, 1981), 100; Chalmers MSS 4.182.14, Johnston to Chalmers, 14 Feb. 1832; 3 *Hansard*, xii. 981.

[40] 3 *Hansard*, xi. 1076, 29 Mar. 1832; xii. 980–1, 15 May 1832.

[41] *PP* 1835, xvii (605), Report from the Select Committee on Orange Institutions in Great Britain and the Colonies, Appendix 2, pp. 28, 32–3. George Kenyon (1776–1853), 2nd baron, a barrister, had been associated with the Orange Order since 1815 (Boase, ii. 206–7; F. Neal, *Sectarian Violence: The Liverpool Experience, 1819–1914* (Manchester, 1988), 23).

[42] *PP* 1835, xvii (605), Appendix 5, pp. 92–3; Appendix 9, pp. 98–100.

it admits no person into its brotherhood who is not well known to be incapable of persecuting, injuring or upbraiding anyone on account of his religious opinions: its principle is, to aid and assist loyal subjects of every religious persuasion, by protecting them from violence and oppression.[43]

The high claims that the Orangemen made for themselves have misled both contemporaries and historians, but they bore little relationship to reality. Orangeism continued to be concentrated in Lancashire and the West of Scotland, and gained little foothold outside these areas. Although the Order claimed to have up to 150,000 members in Britain, a reasonable estimate of their numbers is only 6,000.[44] Moreover, the ideals advanced by the leaders did not receive general acceptance among the membership. In February 1834 the grand committee complained: 'That spirit of radical turbulence which displays itself in acts of insubordination to the constituted authorities in church and state, has found but too easy an admission into some parts of the ranks of the institution.' The minute went on to note the expulsion of a member for engaging in 'clandestine correspondence tending to foment dissatisfaction and insubordination throughout the institution'.[45] There were also a number of outbreaks of violence associated with Orangemen, notably at Girvan in Ayrshire in July 1831, when a procession led to riots in which a constable was killed and several people seriously injured. At Manchester in July 1834 Catholics attacked an Orange procession and were repulsed, with casualties.[46]

The 1832 general-election campaign further revealed the lack of unity among Protestants. Gordon was deprived of his seat at Dundalk by the Irish Reform Act, and proceeded to stand for Trinity College, Dublin. A committee was formed in London to support his candidature. British Evangelicals had only limited enthusiasm for his cause, and the amount subscribed towards meeting his election expenses was disappointing.[47] Irish Tories were even more unhappy with him, and induced Frederick Shaw,[48] a more moderate Evangelical, to stand against him. Shaw's supporters included Lord Roden, Gordon's

[43] Ibid. Appendix 3, p. 85
[44] H. Senior, *Orangeism in Ireland and Britain, 1795–1836* (1966), 230–1, 271–2.
[45] *PP* 1835, xvii (605), Appendix 2, pp. 50–1. No details were given.
[46] 3 *Hansard*, iv. 1415–16, 18 July 1831; *The Times*, 16 July 1834; G. I. T. Machin, *Politics and the Churches in Great Britain 1832–1868* (Oxford, 1977), 93.
[47] *R*, 27 Aug., 8, 11 Oct. 1832; Rennie, 'Evangelicalism', pp. 151–3.
[48] Frederick Shaw (1799–1876), MP for Dublin, 1830–2; for Dublin University, 1832–45 (*DNB*, li. 435).

former patron. Arbitrators were appointed; they came to the conclusion that, even if Shaw had not stood, there would have been no
reasonable prospect of Gordon being returned. Gordon's supporters
were far more likely to vote for Shaw than the reverse.[49] Gordon
accordingly withdrew from the contest and accepted an invitation to
stand for Nottingham. Although he received nearly a thousand votes,
he was still bottom of the poll in this Radical stronghold. His absence
from Parliament was deplored by the *Record*, but it meant that the
Evangelical parliamentary crusade had a less raucous character and
hence could attract more broadly based support.[50]

Evangelicals first returned at the 1832 election still showed a variety
of party allegiances. They included John Campbell Colquhoun[51]
(Radical, Dumbartonshire), George Finch (Tory, Stamford), John
Hardy (Whig, Bradford), and John Pemberton Plumptre[52] (Whig, East
Kent). However, the Irish Church issue tended severely to strain the
loyalties of Whig Evangelicals. In April 1833 Andrew Johnston
accused the Catholic MPs of being in breach of their parliamentary
oaths by taking part in the debates on the question. Both he and
Plumptre subsequently voted against the government. In May 1834 the
seceding 'Derby Dilly' included several Evangelicals, notably Plumptre
and Sinclair.[53] Thereafter it was unusual for 'Recordites' to support
the Whigs. Although members of the government, notably Charles
Grant, Sir George Grey, and Lord Althorp, demonstrated some
affinities with moderate Evangelicalism, they were very far removed
from the militant anti-Catholics.[54]

At the same time, Tories who had not been among the die-hards of
1829 found that their anti-Roman fears were being reawakened by the
education and Irish Church questions. With reference to the Irish
education issue, Phillpotts wrote in July 1832:

[49] *R*, 12, 19 Nov. 1832.

[50] *R*, 17, 20 Dec. 1832; Rennie, 'Evangelicalism', p. 153.

[51] John Campbell Colquhoun (1803–70), Radical MP for Dumbartonshire, 1832–5;
Tory MP for Kilmarnock, 1837–41, Newcastle under Lyme, 1842–7. Colquhoun was
also an active parliamentary representative of the Evangelical party in the Church of
Scotland (*DNB*, xi. 403; S. J. Brown, *Thomas Chalmers* (Oxford, 1982), 234).

[52] John Pemberton Plumptre (1791–1864), MP for East Kent, 1832–52, sat as a
Whig from 1832–5 and as a Conservative thereafter (*Burke's Landed Gentry* (1972), iii.
723–4; Stenton, *British Members of Parliament*, i. 314; H. James and E. Howe, *Two
Sermons Preached in the Parish Church of Nonington, Kent, January 17 1864* (1864)).

[53] 3 *Hansard*, xvi. 1348–52, 1 Apr. 1833; Rennie, 'Evangelicalism', pp. 154–9.

[54] Cf. R. Brent, *Liberal Anglican Politics* (Oxford, 1987), 127–9, 133, 273. Brent's
understanding of Evangelicalism is an unduly diffuse one.

The Protestant feeling of England ought, I think, to be aroused on this subject. In this County [Devon] I have endeavoured, and shall continue to endeavour, calmly but firmly to rouse it. Certainly, the experience of every day proves more strongly the mischievous operation of the Act of 1829. I am one of those, who thought it less dangerous to concede, *on wise securities*, than to continue to resist. My mind is changed, and I hesitate not to own it.[55]

In opposing the Irish Church Bill the following year, he maintained that its passage would suggest that the Protestant religion had lost the favour of the legislature.[56] Wellington himself, while still believing that he had been right to grant Emancipation, declared that he would oppose any further concessions. In the Commons Goulburn stressed his own conviction 'that the happiness and prosperity of Ireland mainly depended on the spread of the reformed Protestant faith in that country'.[57]

Indeed, in the context of a general revival of religious concerns in politics, it was clear that the Protestant position was beginning to acquire greater support both inside and outside Parliament. O'Connell commented in February 1833 that Emancipation would not have been carried by the present Parliament, and later deplored the growing tendency of MPs to think of Irish issues in religious terms.[58] In March 1834 Major Cumming Bruce expressed his fear of the consequences of further concessions to the Catholics. He believed that anti-Catholic feeling in Scotland was very far from being extinct, and in support of this claim he mentioned two recent well-attended meetings of the Reformation Society in Inverness.[59]

Events in Ireland in the second half of 1834, especially the continuing anti-tithe agitation and evidence that the government was considering appropriation, served as the catalyst which provided a common cause for all the strands of Protestantism and hence gave them increased force and coherence. Roden, who represented a human bridge between Evangelical, Ultra, and Irish interests, played a crucial role in this development. At the end of May 1834 he wrote to Wellington urging the House of Lords to offer firm resistance to 'the progress of destruction' and expressing his intention to build up his

[55] Bod. Lib. Burgess MSS, Eng.Lett.c.158, f. 7, Phillpotts to Burgess (Bishop of Salisbury), 18 July 1832.

[56] 3 *Hansard*, xix. 818–55, 18 July 1833.

[57] *WPC*, i. 269–70, Wellington to the Earl of Elgin, 27 July 1833; 416, Wellington to the Marquis of Londonderry, 14 Jan. 1834; 3 *Hansard*, xvii. 1148, 13 May 1833.

[58] 3 *Hansard*, xv. 483, 11 Feb. 1833; xxi. 421–2, 17 Feb. 1834.

[59] Ibid. xxii. 102–3, 12 Mar. 1834.

own base of support in Ireland.[60] A few days later the Conservative
committee in Dublin resolved on taking 'immediate steps . . . to elicit
the sentiments of our Protestant fellow-countrymen on the impending
dangers now threatened against the Protestant Church in Ireland, and
to awaken their most determined energies against any attempt to
establish Popish Supremacy on the ruins of Protestantism'.[61] There
was a large Protestant meeting in Dublin on 14 August which
successfully linked urban Tories with country gentry, nobility, and
parliamentarians. It impressed a number of English Ultras, notably
Cumberland, Newcastle, and Winchilsea, who was present at the
meeting and proved the most active sympathizer.[62] He issued an
address to the people of England, calling on them to rally to the
defence of the Established Church, but his efforts enjoyed scant
success. Although able to arrange some Conservative dinners, he
complained of the apathy and indifference of those who, while
professing attachment to the cause of Protestantism, made no exertion
themselves.[63]

Thus, had British sympathy for the Irish Protestants been confined
to the Ultras, it is unlikely that they would have achieved very much.
However, Roden's Evangelical associates were also ready to give their
sympathy and support. George Sinclair ruefully hinted that Whig
Evangelicals like himself and Andrew Johnston would before long be
forced into the arms of the Orangemen.[64] The *Record* called for the
'rousing up from its slumber with all possible expedition, the Christian
and Protestant feeling of the British nation', to bring pressure to bear
on a government that claimed to listen to the voice of the people. Not
only would the fate of the Irish Church be settled on British soil, but
the English and Scottish Establishments were themselves under
threat.[65]

Alarm for the Church and the Union also prompted Wellington to
encourage and guide the efforts of the Irish Protestants. On 19 August

---

[60] Public Record Office of Northern Ireland, Belfast, Roden MSS (microfilm),
MIC 147/5, Letter-Book, pp. 52, 177, MS biographical information; *WPC*, i. 547,
Roden to Wellington, 31 May 1834.

[61] Roden MSS, MIC 147/5, xi. 575, Sheehan to Roden, 8 June 1834.

[62] Ibid. MIC 147/7, xiv. 99–101, Cumberland to Roden, 21 Aug. 1834; Newcastle
Diary Ne2F4, 25 Aug. 1834; cf. K. T. Hoppen, *Elections, Politics and Society in Ireland,
1832–1885* (Oxford, 1984), 280, 304, 309.

[63] Roden MSS, MIC 147/7, xiv. 47–9, 58, 283–6, 345–6, 581–4. Winchilsea to
Roden, 18 Aug., 3, 16 Sept., 19 Oct. 1834, and notes by Roden.

[64] Ibid. 129, Sinclair to Roden, 25 Aug. 1834.

[65] *R*, 1, 4, 8, 15 Sept. 1834.

he wrote to Roden suggesting the formation of an association of Protestant gentlemen who would make a pledge of mutual protection and undertake to defend the Church of Ireland.[66] In subsequent letters, while assuring Roden of his desire 'to create for you a feeling in this country [England]', he warned that the Irish gentry did not at present command much sympathy in Britain, because they were thought to support the Church from selfish motives while coveting the tithes themselves. They should therefore form an association on the basis of the defence of the Protestant faith and of the 'rights and property of all'. Above all, the Orangemen, who were thoroughly unpopular in England, must be kept out of sight.[67] Roden concurred in these arguments, although he feared that it would be a difficult matter to keep the Orangemen quiet.[68] Wellington and Roden met at Walmer Castle on 19 September to co-ordinate action, and during the next few weeks they continued to correspond regularly.[69]

Bishop Phillpotts also took a close interest in developments in Ireland. On 29 August he wrote to Roden:

It is of inestimable importance to enlighten the English people on the real state of religious feeling, and the momentous persecution of Protestantism in the Popish parts of Ireland. A numerous deputation of able and discrite [*sic*] men—lay and clerical, might with incalculable effect pervade every important part of England, and rouse the dormant, but, I trust in God, the not extinct spirit of Protestantism amongst us.[70]

While anxious that he should not publicly appear as an agitator, Phillpotts was presumably calculating that the 'No Popery' cry might strengthen the position of the Church of England against the Dissenters, as well as that of the Church of Ireland against the Catholics. Subsequently he encouraged the Revd Charles Boyton of the Dublin Conservative Society to arrange a deputation to England. Boyton took further heart from a letter he had received from the Ripon Clerical Association which offered to collect subscriptions for the support of the Irish Protestants and expressed the view that 'in Ireland Protestantism is more persecuted now than it was in Queen Mary's day in England'.[71]

[66] *WPC*, i. 636–7.
[67] Ibid. 651, 657–9, 29 Aug., 1 Sept. 1834. Even Winchilsea agreed that the Orangemen were best kept inconspicuous (Roden MSS, MIC 147/7, xiv. 47–9).
[68] *WPC*, i. 671–3, Roden to Wellington, 11 Sept. 1834.
[69] Ibid. 677, 698–9, 706–7.
[70] Roden MSS, MIC 147/7, xiv. 411–12.
[71] Ibid. 389–94, Boyton to Roden, 27 Sept. 1834.

Meanwhile, in mid-September George Hamilton,[72] a leader of the Dublin Conservative Society, went to Bath, already established as a centre of Protestant activity, in order to investigate means of exciting sympathy for the Irish cause in that part of England. He reported that leading Conservatives anticipated 'some general organization of the friends of the Constitution and of the Protestant Religion throughout the Empire', with the Duke of Wellington at its head. Hamilton now began to make detailed plans to organize concentrated and permanent British support for Irish Protestantism.[73]

The Protestant campaign opened on 30 October with a mass meeting at Hillsborough in County Down, carefully planned with a view to British public opinion. Roden was able to persuade Henry Cooke,[74] a major figure in Ulster Presbyterianism, to attend, thus giving an impression of Protestant unity in the face of Catholic persecution. However, Cooke's decision to participate was widely criticized in his own denomination.[75] Following the Hillsborough meeting, a deputation set out for England. It consisted of Boyton and Mortimer O'Sullivan[76] (brother of Samuel), rector of Killyman, County Armagh. Both men, especially Boyton, were closer to conservative High-Churchmanship than to Evangelicalism, but the use of clerics was presumably intended to appeal to Evangelical Anglicans and, if possible, to Dissenters, suggesting that the movement had a primarily religious character.[77] However, shortly before the deputation made its first appearance on an English platform, William IV, himself an anxious observer of developments in Ireland, dismissed Lord Melbourne's ministry, and, in the consequently excited state of public

[72] George Alexander Hamilton (1802–71) was MP for Dublin from 1836 and for Dublin University from 1843–59. He was to serve as financial secretary to the Treasury in the 1852 and 1858 Conservative governments (*DNB*, xxiv. 158).

[73] Roden MSS, MIC 147/7, xiv. 341–4, 407–8, Hamilton to Roden, 13, 25 Sept. 1834. Hamilton sent suggestions for Protestant organizations in Britain, but this paper does not survive.

[74] Henry Cooke (1788–1868) established his prominence in Ulster Presbyterianism by leading the orthodox party in the Arian controversy of the 1820s. He was minister of May Street Chapel, Belfast, 1829–67. (*DNB*, xii. 67; Holmes, *Henry Cooke*).

[75] *WPC*, i. 698–9, 706–7, Roden to Wellington, 24, 31 Oct. 1834; Roden MSS, MIC 147/7, xiv. 635–41, Cooke to Roden, 25 Oct. 1834; Holmes, *Henry Cooke*, p. 113.

[76] Mortimer O'Sullivan (?1791–1859) came from a Catholic family but, like his brother, was converted to Protestantism at school. Initially he was relatively conciliatory in his attitude to Roman Catholicism, but by 1834 he had moved to a much more militantly Protestant position (*DNB*, xlii. 319; D. Bowen, *The Protestant Crusade in Ireland* (Dublin, 1978), 117–22; J. C. Colquhoun, *Memorials of H. M. C.* (1870), 69–80).

[77] P. B. Nockles, 'Continuity and Change in Anglican High Churchmanship in Britain, 1792–1830', D.Phil. thesis (Oxford, 1982), 405–6; Colquhoun, *Memorials*, p. 71.

opinion, the meetings assumed a greater importance and more ostensibly political character than had originally been expected.

The first meeting was sponsored by the South Lancashire Conservative Association, chaired by Lord Kenyon, and took place at Liverpool on 22 November with an attendance estimated at 4,000.[78] It showed that the evangelical and Ultra strands of Protestantism were now becoming quite closely associated. Boyton was taken ill and could not proceed with his speech, but O'Sullivan took over with a most effective and powerful piece of oratory.[79] He alleged that there was a conspiracy in Ireland to extirpate Protestantism and to separate the country from Great Britain. The present attacks on the Church of Ireland, far from being a penalty for negligence and corruption, were being made at the instigation of the Catholic hierarchy in order to counter renewed Protestant spiritual vitality. Hugh NcNeile, who had recently been appointed to the living of St Jude's, Liverpool, also took a prominent part in the proceedings, arguing that political efforts against Catholicism must proceed collaterally with religious endeavours to awaken Protestants to a real knowledge of 'Popery'. All the speakers made frequent allusions to the recent change of ministry and the importance of securing the return to Parliament of men committed to the interests of the Church. Kenyon wrote: 'I never saw an audience so worked up from mere attention and by good disposition to the utmost degree of zeal for a good cause in all my life.'[80]

A similar meeting was held at Bristol on 26 November. The *Record* emphasized the large attendance and the enthusiastic reception accorded to Boyton and O'Sullivan.[81] Boyton later retired from the deputation, but O'Sullivan went on to a meeting at Bath on 6 December called by the Church of England Lay Association, presided over by the Bishop of Bath and Wells, and attended by about a thousand people.[82] He subsequently spoke at meetings in Birmingham, Stamford, and Leicester and also spent some time staying with George Finch at Burley-on-the-Hill in Rutland, assisting him with his election campaign at Stamford. O'Sullivan made a very favourable impression on his British Evangelical Conservative associates, who

---

[78] *R*, 27 Nov. 1834.

[79] Colquhoun, *Memorials*, pp. 74–5.

[80] *R*, 27 Nov. 1834; Gredington, Clwyd, Kenyon MSS, Lord Kenyon to the Hon. Lloyd Kenyon, 22 Nov. 1834.

[81] *R*, 27 Nov., 1 Dec. 1834.

[82] *Standard*, 13 Dec. 1834; *Blackwood's Edinburgh Magazine*, 37 (1835), 216.

readily co-operated with him in seeking to give the maximum publicity to the cause of Protestantism in Ireland.[83]

An examination of letters written by Lord Kenyon and Captain Gordon in early December 1834 confirms the impression that there was very little difference between the Evangelical and Tory strands of Protestantism at this point. Kenyon issued an address to the Protestants of Great Britain, representing the crisis as a religious one and calling on the electorate to exert themselves to secure protection in Parliament for their Irish brethren, following the lead courageously taken by the king. Alluding to Cooke's participation in the Hillsborough meeting, he maintained that the question concerned all Protestants, not just the Established Church.[84] Meanwhile, Gordon, 'at the private but earnest solicitation, of one or two very influential supporters of the Govmt', addressed his observations on the situation to Wellington himself in a personal letter. He later sent a copy to Peel, with a covering note to the effect that his views were shared by the great majority of Evangelicals. He began by telling Wellington that he stood at a 'moral Thermopylae' in resisting the progress of revolution. His task would be hopeless unless he availed himself of the influence of 'religiously Protestant feeling', which was 'the moral cement of the constitutional structure'. Gordon believed that the State was suffering from the onslaught of the confederated forces of infidelity, Socinianism, and Romanism, finding their common ground in hostility to Protestant theological principles. Protestant Dissenters had thus been duped into collaborating with a movement which was really opposed to their fundamental interests. By replacing the cry of 'Church in danger', with that of 'Protestantism in danger', the Conservatives would gain the support of Irish Presbyterians, English Dissenters, the General Assembly of the Church of Scotland, and even political Whigs with Protestant sympathies. Warming to his theme, Gordon continued:

There is still . . . a potency in the term Protestantism which few who have not had intimate access to the popular feeling in this country would be willing to believe . . . The term is understood by tens of thousands who are ignorant of the distinction between the creeds of Whigs and Tories and by hundreds of thousands who have either transposed or misinterpreted the true significance of purely political designations.

[83] Ayston Hall, Rutland, Finch MSS (transcripts shown to me by Mr G. S. Finch: the originals were either lost or unavailable), George Finch to Lady Louisa Finch, 20, 22 Dec. 1834, and n.d.; Colquhoun, *Memorials*, pp. 71 ff.; *Standard*, 29 Dec. 1834; *Blackwood's*, 37, (1835), 217.
[84] *R*, 8 Dec. 1834.

Many who despised Toryism were deeply attached to Protestantism, identified in religious terms with 'the Christianity of the Reformation', and in political terms with the Revolution Settlement of 1688. The spirit of the Whigs of that era had now migrated into the Tory Party. Gordon believed that the Established Churches of England and Scotland had the potential to be the agents of national Protestant regeneration, and he concluded his letter by stressing how important it was to reform and extend them in order to render them efficient for this purpose.[85]

The general election of January 1835 marked the culmination of a process by which Protestantism returned to the status of a central issue in politics after the hiatus following Emancipation. Religious issues were very prominently agitated in the campaign, serving as a means of defining party loyalties. The situation of the Irish Protestants attracted widespread and emotive attention.[86] To emphasize this aspect of public opinion is to complement, but not to contradict, conventional attention to the Tamworth Manifesto and moderate Conservatism.[87] It was, after all, the Irish Church question that had led to the 'Derby Dilly' parting company with the Whigs and had provided Peel with the incentive to buy their support by a reformist stance on other matters. Militant anti-Catholicism was by this date very far from implying a general inflexible reactionary stance, even in religious matters. Gordon had written of the importance of Church reform, and Cooke had struck a similar note at Hillsborough.[88] Kenyon realized that 'It is vain to hope that Govt. can effectually oppose every objectionable measure that will be proposed, or avoid itself proposing some that are undesirable . . . '[89] Indeed, the greatest difficulty that Peel encountered from die-hard Toryism in the early days of his ministry arose not from Protestant ardour but from the self-importance of the agriculturalist lobby as represented by Buckingham and Chandos.[90]

---

[85] Peel Papers, BL Add. MS 40413, ff. 140–1, Gordon to Peel, 4 Feb. 1835; ff. 142–8, Gordon to Wellington (copy), 3 Dec. 1834.

[86] D. H. Close, 'The General Elections of 1835 and 1837 in England and Wales', D.Phil. thesis (Oxford, 1966), 75, 141–52.

[87] Cf. N. Gash, *Reaction and Reconstruction in English Politics, 1822–1852* (Oxford, 1966), 141–2.

[88] Holmes, *Henry Cooke*, p. 115.

[89] Peel Papers, BL Add. MS 40316, ff. 110–12, Kenyon to Lyndhurst, 15 Dec. 1834; R. W. Davis, 'Toryism to Tamworth: The Triumph of Reform, 1827–1835', *Albion*, 12 (1980), 144–5.

[90] Durham County Record Office, Durham, Londonderry MSS, D/Lo/C81(44), Buckingham to Londonderry, 15 Dec. 1834; N. Gash, *Sir Robert Peel* (1972), 90–2.

Between 1829 and 1834 Protestantism had gone through a similar process of metamorphosis to that experienced by the Tory party as a whole: the points of continuity were very evident, but with a new ideological framework provided by Evangelicalism, and a new cause provided by the Irish Church, it had become a dynamic and flexible movement that was not an atavistic relic of the past but an essential strand in the emergent Victorian political fabric.

Nevertheless, the appeal of Protestantism was limited by the concurrent struggle over the position of the Established Church, to which Evangelicals were ever more firmly committed. December 1834 saw the re-emergence of the Christian Candidates Committee which had supported Gordon's unsuccessful attempts to obtain re-election after the passing of the Reform Act. Its primary aim was to secure Gordon's return, but any surplus subscriptions were to be used for the support of other men who acknowledged similar principles. An appeal to Christian electors appeared in both the *Record* and the *Standard*, calling for the return of men who would 'openly, honestly and fearlessly' represent Protestant principles, evidently entailing the maintenance of the Church Establishment.[91] Kenyon had thought that gatherings such as that at Liverpool would have a great effect on the electorate and be particularly important in winning over Protestant Dissenters to the support of the Conservatives.[92] However, the majority of Nonconformists, preoccupied with their own grievances, were not so easily attracted. With the exception of a sizeable proportion of Wesleyan Methodists, they persevered in their allegiance to the Whigs.[93]

The extent to which the new Conservative government continued to appear to identify itself with Protestantism gave an opening to its adversaries. Peel offered the post of lord steward of the household to Roden, who, although declining it, sought to extract the maximum possible political capital from the endorsement thus given to his earlier activities.[94] The appointment of the two staunchly Protestant MPs for Dublin University as privy councillors was also not lost on the opposition. O'Connell and Russell alleged that the administration was countenancing Orangeism, and, in the hope of discrediting the

---

[91] *R*, 1 Jan. 1835; *Standard*, 2 Jan. 1835.

[92] *WPC*, ii. 119, Kenyon to Wellington, 28 Nov. 1834.

[93] Close, 'General Elections of 1835 and 1837', pp. 141–4; Machin, *Politics and the Churches*, pp. 49–50.

[94] Peel Papers, BL Add. MS 40407, f. 210, 40408, ff. 171–2, 40409, f. 40, Roden to Peel, 24, 31 Dec. 1834, 1 Jan 1835.

government, a systematic campaign was begun which led on 23 March to the appointment of a select committee to enquire into the Order's Irish operations.[95]

Peel and Wellington were well aware of this danger, and, although the duke at least avowed that he had taken office with the sole aim of saving the Irish Church, in practice they sought to distance themselves from militant Protestantism. Peel refused Roden's request that Church preferment be given to Robert M'Ghee,[96] an anti-Catholic polemicist, while the duke restrained Roden from presenting the petition from the Hillsborough meeting of the previous October and from pressing the Irish education issue.[97] This latter point was of particular significance, given the extent to which Evangelical political involvement had arisen from concern over education. Hence Protestants began to feel disappointed by the Conservative government. After it fell, Gordon complained to Roden: 'Conservatism, or in other words Peelism, is literally burking the Protestantism of the country, and until Protestants free themselves from the trammelling influence of political expediency and "red Tapists", that *third* party in the State, on whom, under God, the Salvation of the country must depend, will never be permitted to arise.'[98]

Nevertheless, the circumstances leading to the fall of Peel's administration at the beginning of April 1835 served to obscure such tensions. Following the Lichfield House compact between Whigs, Radicals, and Repealers, Russell proceeded, on 27 March, to give notice of his intention to move for a committee of the whole House to consider applying surplus revenues of the Irish Church to 'the religious and moral instruction of all classes of the community'. Many Protestants saw this as a blatant move to transfer Protestant funds to Roman Catholic uses.[99] Although the opposition generally professed

[95] 3 *Hansard*, xxvi. 604, 651, 6 Mar. 1835; xxvii. 135, 23 Mar. 1835; Senior, *Orangeism*, p. 267.

[96] Robert James M'Ghee (1789–1872), minister of Harold's Cross Church, Dublin, *c.*1838–46, rector of Holywell, Hunts., 1846–72. A prolific writer, M'Ghee had taken a leading role in the formation of a theological society at TCD in 1830 to promote the study of 'polemical divinity', and had defended the Reformation Society from Samuel O'Sullivan's attack (R. J. M'Ghee, *Truth and Error Contrasted* (1830); see above, p. 40; Bowen, *Protestant Crusade*, pp. 113–14; Boase, vi. 116; Venn, *Alumni Cantabrigienses*, ii. *1752–1900*, 6 vols. (1951), iv. 264; Acheson, 'Evangelicals in the Church of Ireland', p. 238.

[97] *WPC*, ii. 549, Wellington to Roden, 20 Mar. 1835; Peel Papers, BL Add. MS 40412, ff. 216–19, Roden to Peel, 30 Jan. 1835; f. 220, Peel to Roden, 4 Feb. 1835.

[98] Roden MSS, MIC 147/6, xii. 25–8, Gordon to Roden, 5 May 1835.

[99] 3 *Hansard*, xxvii. 313–14, 387, 522, 27, 30, 31 Mar. 1835.

to view the prospect of a renewed 'No Popery' cry with contempt, Andrew Johnston's continuing conflict of political and religious loyalties was evident in his abstention when Russell's motion was put to the vote on 2 April.[100]

Protestants forgot their dissatisfaction with the Conservatives in the attempt to keep out the far greater evil of the Whigs and O'Connell. On 29th March a panic-stricken Newcastle urged Peel to stay in office. He admitted that they had had their differences, but he would now give him wholehearted support as he was all that stood between the country and revolution.[101] On 6 April the *Record*, representing the issue as a pitched battle between 'Popery' and Protestantism, took a similar line.[102] Thus, Peel's resignation on 8 April was seen as a triumph for 'Popery', and Russell was represented as a puppet in the hands of O'Connell. The role played by the Irish Roman Catholic members in securing the fall of the government appeared to vindicate the worst fears of those who had opposed Emancipation in 1829. O'Connell and his colleagues were attacked as perjurors on the grounds that their parliamentary oath should have precluded them from participating in outright assault on the Church of Ireland. Lord John was portrayed as, at best, an unprincipled opportunist and, at worst, secretly in collusion with the Vatican.[103]

The 'No Popery' cry was a conspicuous feature of the by-election campaigns that followed the appointment of the second Melbourne ministry. In South Devon Russell found himself confronted by a determined Conservative campaign which had the support of Bishop Phillpotts and the local Anglican clergy, who attacked Lord John from their pulpits as an enemy to the Protestant religion.[104] Conservative election addresses showed an overwhelming preoccupation with the Catholic question, and in one case reduced the issues to the single query: 'Do you desire the overthrow of Protestantism and the re-establishment of Popery in these realms?' The London press focused considerable attention on the contest, and the Tory *Standard* implied that Russell was a more serious threat to Protestant England than Philip II or James II had been.[105] Russell lost the election by a margin

[100] 3 *Hansard*, xxvii. 794–5, 3 Apr. 1835.
[101] Peel Papers, BL Add. MS 40418, ff. 279–81.
[102] *R*, 6 Apr. 1835.
[103] *R*, 13 Apr. 1835; *Standard*, 13, 15, 21 Apr. 1835; *The Times*, 29 Apr. 1835.
[104] *PP* 1835, viii (547), Report from the Select Committee on Bribery at Elections, p. 165.
[105] *Standard*, 23, 24, 30 Apr., 2, 9 May 1835.

of 3,755 votes to 3,128 to an otherwise unknown country gentleman,[106] a result which Phillpotts reported to Roden as a 'most encouraging . . . display of Protestant feeling'.[107] However, evidence to a select committee suggested that the Catholic issue had only influenced 150–200 of the 'more ignorant' electors and that the main reason for the result had been Tory registration efforts. The liberal press, for its part, alleged that intimidation had been responsible. It thus seems that, while the Protestant cry had been a significant factor in the election, it did not win over any extensive Dissenting support to the Conservatives.[108]

In Essex the Whig candidate was defeated after a campaign in which the Protestant cry had been prominent, although not as much so as in Devon. At Inverness anti-Catholicism combined with dissatisfaction at Whig handling of the Scottish Church question to lead to the return of the Tory candidate, who fought the campaign entirely on religious issues.[109] On the other hand, Russell himself was quickly and smoothly returned unopposed for Stroud, and in the West Riding Morpeth, who was also closely associated with the policy of appropriation, obtained a comfortable majority. This was attributed by the *Record* to the continuing readiness of Dissenters in the constituency to make common cause with the Catholics.[110] The vigorous clerical use of the 'No Popery' cry, which had been so prominent a feature of the South Devon election, was not repeated on a similar level in any other constituency.

Meanwhile, the select committee on Orange lodges was providing a further forum for Protestant attack on the government. On 13 April Mortimer O'Sullivan began an effective testimony in the Orange interest, acknowledging that he had initially had prejudices against the Order himself, which he thought could only be justified as a reply to the Catholic efforts to destroy Protestantism in Ireland. He claimed that persecution was sanctioned by the Roman Church to the extent of punishing heretics with death, and that, through the confessional and

[106] At the general election in January Russell had been returned unopposed in company with the Conservative Sir J. B. Y. Buller (F. W. S. Craig, *British Parliamentary Election Results 1832–1885* (1977), 378).

[107] Roden MSS, MIC 147/6, xiii. 171–2, Phillpotts to Roden, 5 May 1835.

[108] *Standard*, 6, 12 Aug. 1835; *R*, 7 May 1835; *PP* 1835, viii (547), 163–6.

[109] *Standard*, 6 May 1835; *R*, 1 June 1835; I. A. Muirhead, 'Catholic Emancipation: Scottish Reactions in 1829', *Innes Review*, 24 (1973), 35; I. G. C. Hutchison, *A Political History of Scotland 1832–1924* (Edinburgh, 1986), 18.

[110] *R*, 11 May 1835; F. M. L. Thompson, 'Whigs and Liberals in the West Riding, 1830–1860', *English Historical Review*, 74 (1959), 214–39.

the sacrament of penance, the priests were able to exercise an overwhelming influence over the people of Ireland. The Church's subversive teaching was thus carried into the daily actions of the mass of the Irish people, and led to extensive violence against Protestants. Such arguments were sufficient to convince and mobilize those already predisposed to believe them. Phillpotts judged O'Sullivan's evidence to be a triumphant success and a powerful counter-attack on O'Connell and his faction.[111]

During the summer and autumn of 1835 Evangelical and Tory elements joined in an extensive campaign of Protestant agitation. Some still pinned their hopes on the Conservative party and its leaders: on 18 May the rising Lancashire Evangelical, Hugh Stowell,[112] wrote to the *Record* suggesting that those who had regrets about their support for Emancipation in 1829 should declare their change of heart. He called on Wellington himself to move its repeal.[113] Winchilsea called on Conservative Associations to 'put forth that they were working for the maintenance and defence of the religious doctrines of the Reformation and the political principles of the glorious revolution of 1688'.[114] Captain Gordon, on the other hand, thought that Conservative Associations, while useful, were too closely linked to political shibboleths, and he sought assistance from Ireland with a view to establishing an independent organization to serve as an agent for Protestant regeneration in Britain and ultimately to obtain the repeal of Catholic Emancipation.[115] It is significant that it was only in 1835 that the possibility of actually reversing the concession of 1829, as opposed simply to regretting that it had been made, began to be envisaged by Protestant advocates. They had been swayed by what they perceived as a practical demonstration of the evils of Catholic power in causing the fall of the Peel administration.

At the beginning of June an advertisement appeared in a number of newspapers, addressed 'To the Protestants of Great Britain and Ireland' and signed by nineteen Irish clergy, including O'Sullivan,

---

[111] *PP* 1835, xv (377), Report of the Select Committee [on] . . . Orange Lodges . . . in Ireland, pp. 31, 37, 44, 51, 65–71, 77–82, 179, 181; Bod. Lib., Giffard MSS, Eng.Lett.c.56, f. 228, Phillpotts to Giffard, 3 June 1835.

[112] Hugh Stowell (1799–1865), incumbent of Christ Church, Salford from 1831, and a major figure in the religious and political life of Manchester and Salford (*DNB*, lv. 7; J. B. Marsden, *Memoirs of the Life and Labours of the Rev. Hugh Stowell, MA* (1868)).

[113] *R*, 18 May 1835.

[114] *R*, 21 May 1835.

[115] Roden MSS, MIC 147/6, xii. 289, Gordon to Roden, 6 May 1835.

M'Ghee, and Cooke, bringing together High-Churchmen, Evangelicals and Presbyterians. The advertisers claimed that it had been established 'by authentic and unquestionable documents' that the principles adopted by the contemporary Roman Catholic Church in Ireland were 'of the same intolerant and persecuting nature at this day that are well known to have characterised their Church in former times'. It was announced that the documents alluded to would be submitted to a meeting at Exeter Hall on 20 June, and Daniel Murray,[116] the Catholic Archbishop of Dublin, was invited to attend in order to answer the charges. M'Ghee also sent an open letter to O'Connell inviting him to participate.[117]

The promise of sensational revelations attracted a packed audience. The chair was taken by Lord Kenyon, and the platform party included twenty-five MPs, among whom Evangelicals and Irish Tories predominated. The meeting was also attended by Gladstone, James MacKenzie, a Whig who sat for Ross and Cromarty, a constituency with a strong Evangelical presence, and Ralph Sheldon, a Radical whose presence appears more anomalous. Lord Ashley's presence was also noteworthy as marking the beginning of his long involvement with Protestant movements.[118] The majority of the clergy present were Anglicans, but Henry Cooke was prominent among the speakers. While making it clear that he did not speak for the Synod of Ulster, he pleaded the cause for co-operation between Presbyterians and Anglicans against the common foe. The proceedings mainly consisted of protracted denunciation of the Roman Catholic Church by Cooke, M'Ghee, and O'Sullivan on the basis of the allegedly subversive and immoral teaching contained in the *Theologia Moralis et Dogmatica* of Peter Dens, a mid-eighteenth-century Belgian scholar, which, it was claimed, was extensively used by the Irish Catholic clergy. At the end of the meeting Gordon announced the formation of the Protestant Association. Neither Murray nor O'Connell had been provoked into attending, and Catholics who attempted to address the meeting were

---

[116] Daniel Murray (1768–1852), Archbishop of Dublin, 1823–52. Trained at Salamanca, Murray was one of the last survivors of the generation of Irish bishops educated on the Continent before the French Revolution. Within the Roman Catholic Church he was a force for moderation, advocating a degree of co-operation with the British government (*DNB*, xxxix, 352; D. A. Kerr, *Peel, Priests and Politics* (Oxford, 1982), 16–21).

[117] M. O'Sullivan and R. J. M'Ghee, *Romanism as it Rules in Ireland* (1840), i. 1–4.

[118] Ibid. 5–6; Stenton, *British Members of Parliament*, i, *passim*.

refused a hearing on the grounds that they had not been given the requisite authority by the Irish bishops.[119]

A second meeting was held at Exeter Hall on 11 July and attracted a similarly large audience. The platform party was again predominantly Conservative, and Cooke did not participate, but two further junior members of the Peel administration, Lord Lincoln[120] and Sir George Clerk, were present among the thirty MPs.[121] Bishop Phillpotts did not attend, but on 16 July he repeated in the Lords the charge that the priests were instigators of sectarian violence. He received a sympathetic hearing and support not only from Irish Protestant peers but also from Wellington, who urged the government to adopt measures for the protection of the Irish Protestants, and the Archbishop of Canterbury (Howley), who thought that the objectionable passages ought to have been expunged from Dens's *Theologia*, and that the Catholic bishops should take effective action to control the political action of their clergy.[122]

Subsequent meetings were held at Worcester, Hereford, Glasgow, Paisley, and Airdrie in September; Edinburgh, Greenock, Perth, Aberdeen, Forres, Inverness, and Liverpool in October; Birmingham and Exeter in November; Brighton and Croydon in December; and during 1836 there were further meetings at Exeter Hall, Glasgow, Edinburgh, and Hereford.[123] Celebrations in October 1835 to mark the tercentenary of the English Reformation gave a further stimulus to Protestant feeling.[124] The relatively large number of meetings in Scotland provides an interesting contrast with the earlier relative lack of enthusiasm for the Reformation Society north of the Border. It would seem that the more political stance of the Protestant Association attracted those concerned about the Church question and ready to have their fears turned in an anti-Catholic direction, especially in the face of a rival speaking-tour in Scotland by O'Connell.[125] The English

---

[119] O'Sullivan and M'Ghee, *Romanism*, i. 5–74, esp. p. 41.

[120] Henry Pelham Fiennes Pelham-Clinton (1811–64), eldest son of the 4th Duke of Newcastle. Lincoln's later career showed a decisive rejection of his father's position (*DNB*, xi. 98; F. Darrell Munsell, *The Unfortunate Duke: Henry Pelham, Fifth Duke of Newcastle 1811–1864* (1985)).

[121] O'Sullivan and M'Ghee, *Romanism*, i. 86.

[122] 3 *Hansard*, xxix. 603–33, 16 July 1835.

[123] O'Sullivan and M'Ghee, *Romanism*, *passim*.

[124] *Protestant Journal*, 5 (1835), 720. See below, Chap. 4.

[125] O'Sullivan and M'Ghee, *Romanism*, i. 280; *Mr O'Connell's Political Tour to Manchester, Newcastle, Edinburgh and Other Towns in the North of England and Scotland* (Cork, 1835).

meetings were in locations which suggest a plan to derive the maximum possible effect from a short campaign: strong local interest was assured at Birmingham and Liverpool, while Brighton and Croydon were well-placed to make an impression on the Court and the Archbishop of Canterbury respectively. All the meetings except those at Glasgow and Edinburgh were dominated by one or more of the trio of O'Sullivan, M'Ghee, and Gordon, while local participants, mostly clergy, usually gave relatively short speeches. There was extensive press coverage, particularly in *The Times*, the *Standard*, and the *Record*, and the itinerant speakers showed an awareness of the value of this wider audience by introducing new material on each occasion in order to sustain interest. Invariably, Protestant sources claimed that the meetings were attended by very large audiences, usually estimated at over a thousand.[126]

In singling out Archbishop Murray for attack, Gordon, M'Ghee, and O'Sullivan made a significant error of judgement. Murray's mild and conciliatory manner contrasted strongly with the image of political rabble-rousing clergy presented by the Protestant Association. He wisely ignored the challenge to defend himself in person, but published an open letter to Lord Melbourne maintaining that persecuting doctrines were now yielding to 'mutual forbearance', except in Exeter Hall. Dens's *Theologia* was certainly still in use in Ireland, but some of its contents were now regarded as obsolete and it served as a basis for discussion rather than an authoritative guide. Murray's opponents represented this as dissimulation, but the archbishop addressed a further letter 'To the Protestants of Great Britain', appealing to their sense of justice and concern for truth.[127]

Murray's dignified response clearly had an impact on public opinion, but criticism of the Protestant Association focused rather on the charge that its activities really stemmed from a desire to promote the interests of the Established Church and the Tory party. An anonymous pamphlet, published in Hereford, attacked 'the new scheme of the Tories, who arrogate the character of pre-eminent godliness', and alleged that to all intents and purposes the Protestant Association was simply the Orange Order under another name.[128] Radicals maintained that O'Sullivan was receiving a substantial

[126] *Catholic Magazine*, 6 (1835), 246, strongly disputed such a claim in relation to a meeting at Worcester.

[127] O'Sullivan and M'Ghee, *Romanism*, i. 84, 514; Kerr, *Peel, Priests and Politics*, p. 21.

[128] *Protestant or Orange Associations*, by an English Protestant (Hereford, 1835), p. iii.

retainer from Conservative funds.[129] The *Eclectic Review* commented that 'the cry of "No Popery" has ever proceeded from a party the nearest akin to the Papists in their ecclesiastical polity', and surmised that Catholicism was really objected to as Dissent rather than as error.[130] The *Baptist Magazine* observed: 'Unhappily the date of these efforts is such, as to throw no inconsiderable suspicion around their designs . . . These zealous endeavours appear to excite but very little sympathy, where, perhaps, it was calculated that they would have produced surprising effects.'[131] However, some Nonconformist opinion was more sympathetic: the *Congregational Magazine* regretted the manner in which the Establishment issue was preventing Dissenters and Evangelical Anglicans from co-operating against 'Popery', and the *Wesleyan Methodist Magazine* welcomed the revelations made at Exeter Hall.[132]

Speakers at Protestant meetings were alive to Dissenting and Radical attacks. At the meeting at Glasgow on 7 October, chaired by the Evangelical former Radical J. C. Colquhoun, a speaker seized on the sentiment recently expressed in the *Voluntary Church Magazine* that 'Popery is no longer Popery when it declares on the side of Voluntaryism', and maintained that in Ireland Roman Catholics persecuted all Protestants irrespective of denomination. At the same meeting it was stressed that the chairman and a number of the platform party were not Conservatives, and this was hailed as 'a sufficient guarantee that this is no Tory job'. Colquhoun himself dissociated the movement from party politics.[133] At Liverpool the Dissenters were warned that the best reward they could expect for their alleged services to Popery was that of Polyphemus, that of being the last to be devoured.[134]

The brunt of the Radical and Catholic counter-attack was borne not by the Protestant Association but by the Orangemen. Disturbances in July 1835 at Airdrie, Port Glasgow, and Liverpool, together with fears about the disruptive effect of Orange lodges in the army, provided sufficient grounds for extending the select committee's brief to cover Britain as well as Ireland. However, on the division, the Orangemen

[129] O'Sullivan and M'Ghee, *Romanism*, i. 677, 680, 707.

[130] *Eclectic Review*, 3rd series, 14 (1835), 21.

[131] *Baptist Magazine*, 17 (1835), 380.

[132] *Congregational Magazine*, 2nd series, 11 (1835), 422–4; *Wesleyan Methodist Magazine*, 58 (1835), 565.

[133] O'Sullivan and M'Ghee, *Romanism*, i. 389, 411, 425.

[134] Ibid. 587.

still had forty supporters, including many of the MPs who had been present at the Protestant Association's meetings.[135] The committee confirmed the unauthorized existence of lodges in the army, and the king agreed to 'discourage and prevent any attempt to introduce secret societies into the ranks'.[136] Cumberland promptly rescinded the warrants for military lodges, and the commander-in-chief, Lord Hill, announced that any soldier participating in an Orange lodge would be court-martialled.[137]

The Orange Order might have weathered the storm caused by concern at sectarian violence and the existence of military lodges were it not for further, more dramatic, allegations which began to circulate in the autumn of 1835. On 21 October Joseph Haywood, who had recently been expelled from the Order, published a statement accusing Fairman of using his tours of inspection to sound out Orange opinion on a plan to depose William IV and replace him with the Duke of Cumberland. The grand lodge promptly instituted a libel action on Fairman's behalf, but Haywood died shortly before the case could come to court. However, Joseph Hume repeated the allegation in the Commons on 23 February 1836, adducing evidence which he claimed implicated Kenyon and Wynford.[138] The documents purporting to provide evidence of an Orange plot were published in the *London and Westminster Review* in April 1836. They show that in 1832 Fairman believed that the country was on the verge of revolution, and thought that a strong assertion of government authority was essential. He had a very low opinion of William IV, but was even more fearful of the consequences of his death being followed by a minority.[139] Although the evidence is almost entirely circumstantial, it thus seems possible that Fairman envisaged the installation of Cumberland as regent or even king after the death of William. The impression that he had something to hide was strengthened by his obstinate refusal to hand over his letter-book to the select committee in August 1835.[140] However, it is inherently unlikely that Cumberland and his associates in the grand lodge would ever formally have sanctioned such a plan, and, if it

[135] *PP* 1835, xvii (605), 141–4; *The Times*, 15 July 1835; 3 *Hansard*, xxx. 266–312, 10 Aug. 1835.
[136] Ibid. 559, 15 Aug. 1835.
[137] Kenyon MSS, Orange Institution Box; *PP* 1835, xvii (605), p. iii.
[138] 3 *Hansard*, xxxi. 779–810; Senior, *Orangeism*, p. 269.
[139] *London and Westminster Review*, 3 and 25 (1836), 181–220 (esp. pp. 185, 195, 201–4).
[140] 3 *Hansard*, xxx. 675–97, 19 Aug. 1834.

existed at all, it was probably only a vague scheme in Fairman's own mind. The published correspondence suggests that the conduct of the Orange peers was imprudent rather than treasonable.

However, sufficient mud stuck to the Orange Order for its fate to become certain. No English MP was prepared to argue against suppression. Frederick Shaw urged the Irish Orangemen not to divide the House, because of the danger of splitting the Tories. This advice was heeded and an address to the king was carried, asking him to take measures to discourage Orange lodges and all secret societies.[141] Such sympathy as the Orangemen received was a result of wider reflection on the implications of their suppression and was not voiced publicly: Newcastle was worried about the effects of their disgrace on the Protestant cause in Ireland, while Winchilsea, concerned to protect the independence of the House of Lords, wanted to ensure that the issue was properly debated there. Wellington, however, clearly thought that the Protestant cause could only benefit from the suppression of Orangeism, and felt that the Commons was acting within its rights.[142] Cumberland complied with parliamentary and royal wishes and dissolved the lodges in Britain and Ireland. Even Kenyon privately expressed 'great relief' at being 'delivered from a useless and occasionally mischievous Society conducted as it was'.[143]

The disgrace of the Orange Order considerably weakened the Protestant Association. A meeting on 11 May 1836 was thinly attended: although the platform party still included Sinclair, Gladstone, and others representing a variety of strands in the Conservative party, the total attendance of MPs was only nine, suggesting that the movement was no longer seen as having the same political potential as in the previous year. Gordon denied that the Association was simply a continuation of Orangeism in another form, claiming that it was a more broadly based movement. In fact, it was fast becoming little more than an Evangelical society. Newcastle, who spoke at the meeting, felt that he had 'got into the wrong body'. Clearly the Association's efforts to free itself from any imputation of Orangeism had their corollary in an inability to retain the active support of Orange and Ultra sympathizers.[144] At the next meeting on 14 July the number of MPs

[141] 3 *Hansard*, xxxi. 858, 23 Feb. 1836.
[142] Newcastle Diary, Ne2F5, 6, 7 Mar. 1836; Southampton University Library, Wellington MSS 2/33/83, Winchilsea to Wellington, 29 Feb. 1836; 2/33/85, Wellington to Winchilsea, 2 Mar. 1836.
[143] Kenyon MSS, Kenyon to the Hon. Lloyd Kenyon, 25, 26 Feb. 1836.
[144] *R*, 16 May 1836; Newcastle Diary, Ne2F5, 11 May 1836.

had declined to six, among whom Evangelicals predominated.[145] Thus the Protestant Association was very far from being a resurrection of the Orange Order. Its large, flamboyant public meetings contrasted with the secret masonic world of the lodges, and the backbone of its support came from an Evangelical constituency that insisted that at least lip-service be paid to a political neutrality wholly at variance with the Orange approach.[146]

Having restricted its appeal in the hope of attracting moderate Evangelical and Dissenting opinion, the Association was then discredited by the indiscretion of its agents. M'Ghee unearthed further 'revelations' about the persecuting and subversive character of Rome, and entertained sympathetic audiences with considerable showmanship.[147] However, this was clearly insufficient to win over the uncommitted, and the Catholics responded in a manner calculated to divide the Protestant Association from its less fanatical supporters. During Advent 1835 and Lent 1836 Nicholas Wiseman gave courses of lectures aimed specifically at attracting non-Catholics. The second series was delivered to a crowded audience in the large chapel of St Mary's, Moorfields. The lectures were a reasoned defence of principal Catholic doctrines and were apologetic rather than polemical in tone. A similar course was adopted by the *Dublin Review*, founded in London in 1836 by O'Connell and Michael Quin, with Wiseman serving as editor on religious matters. The new periodical avoided the harsh tones which had made the *Catholic Magazine* such a fitting sparring partner for the *Protestant Journal*.[148] Meanwhile, O'Connell continued to allege that the Association's motive was party-political advantage: 'Resolve away as fast and as long as you please, I care not; . . . your resolutions can harm only yourselves . . . Nobody ought to interfere in any way to prevent you. I am quite sure I will not. Your resolutions, therefore, for aught I care, may be reproba-tory, or

[145] O'Sullivan and M'Ghee, *Romanism*, ii. 159.

[146] G. A. Cahill's arguments for continuity between the two institutions were advanced in his 'The Protestant Association and the Anti-Maynooth Agitation of 1845', *Catholic Historical Review*, 43 (1957), 277–8, and 'Irish Catholicism and English Toryism', Ph.D. thesis (Iowa, 1954), 10/–15. Especially in relation to his claim that both bodies shared a similar 'hierarchical' structure, his argument rests on an impossibly strained interpretation of the evidence.

[147] Wolffe, 'Protestant Societies and Anti-Catholic Agitation', pp. 120–1.

[148] N. Wiseman, *Lectures on the Principal Doctrines and Practices of the Catholic Church* (1836); W. R. Ward, *The Life and Times of Cardinal Wiseman* (1897), i. 234–6, 249; D. Gywnn, *Cardinal Wiseman* (Dublin, 1950), 40–2.

approba-tory, lauda-tory, or explana-tory, or any other tory you please.'[149]

O'Connell clearly believed that the Protestant Association was compromising its public standing without any assistance from him. He was vindicated by M'Ghee's conduct during July 1836. On the eve of a Protestant meeting on 14 July M'Ghee was given a pamphlet purporting to be a translation of a Bull published by the present pope, Gregory XVI, in 1832. Under this document, the Irish Roman Catholic bishops were supposedly given permission to conceal aspects of Catholic belief in order not to alienate their supporters in Parliament. In reality, the pamphlet was a satire on the government's Irish education policy, intended to show that it was playing directly into the hands of the Catholics, and was written by James Henthorn Todd (1805–69), a fellow of Trinity College, Dublin and a leading High-Churchman. However, M'Ghee quoted from it at Exeter Hall as an authentic Bull. There can be little doubt that the mistake was an honest one, and reflected on M'Ghee's judgement not his integrity. On 16 July he realized that the Bull was not genuine and immediately wrote to the *Standard* to explain his error, but he compounded his mistake by suggesting that Todd's pamphlet was worthy of attention as 'an ingenious device . . . [for] bringing most important truths before the Protestants of this empire'.[150] This implied sanction for satire and fiction as legitimate polemical weapons brought down on M'Ghee the almost united condemnation of the press. The *Scotsman* exulted in prophesying the end of his career as 'an apostle of party and sectarian animosity'. Evangelicals, too, had harsh words to say: even the *Record* described M'Ghee's conduct as 'unchristian and indefensible', and the Protestant Association sought to salvage something of its own reputation by dissociating itself from M'Ghee's behaviour.[151] Meanwhile, Todd tried to exonerate himself in a manner hardly soothing to the hapless orator by claiming that no educated man could read the pamphlet and mistake its real nature. M'Ghee subsequently regained a modicum of credibility among Evangelicals, but his standing with more critical audiences was permanently undermined. Two years later he

[149] O'Sullivan and M'Ghee, *Romanism*, ii. 151.

[150] Ibid. 156–7, 195, 201; *Sanctissimi Domini Nostra Gregorii Papae XVI Epistola ad Archiepiscopos et Episcopos Hiberniae . . . Translated from the Original Latin and Now First Published* (1836); Nockles, 'Anglican High Churchmanship', pp. 350 ff.; *DNB*, lvi. 430.

[151] O'Sullivan and M'Ghee, *Romanism*, ii. 201–4; *R*, 18 July 1836; J. McHugh, *The Real Character of the Rev. Robert M'Ghee* (Dublin, 1836), pp. iii, x.

was still being heckled with cries of 'Where is the forgery?' and 'That's an ingenious device.'[152]

This farcical episode led to an increased sense of vulnerability to criticism and hence to even greater intolerance of opposition. Both at the meeting on 14 July and at a subsequent one on 2 August Catholics attempted to respond to the Association's charges, but their challenges to discussion were not taken up.[153] In Glasgow in October 1836 a considerable number of Catholics attended the Protestant meeting and were infuriated by a description of Maynooth students as wallowing 'like so many serpents amidst the impurities of Dens'. Colquhoun, who was in the chair, restored order with some difficulty and was only enabled to maintain it by the assistance of the police. There was no sign of any willingness to give the Catholics a fair hearing.[154] Indeed, the Protestant Association was now consolidating the organization of its 'public' meetings with a view to excluding those who might prove to be unsympathetic. McNeile now believed that, 'while public meetings are admirable mediums for giving an impulse to already willing minds, they are altogether unsuitable places for theological discussions'.[155]

Thus, by the end of 1836 organized political Protestantism had been substantially discredited, partly because of the indiscretions of the movement itself, partly because of the effectiveness of the campaign against it. However, during the previous two years it had played a central role in establishing the Conservative party on a convincing basis of public support, and, while the hiatus of 1836 was a significant one, anti-Catholicism remained a notable influence in the continuing Conservative revival in the years up to 1841. Indeed, Professor G. A. Cahill argued that the anti-Catholic campaign was the major reason for the eventual Tory triumph.[156] He failed to take account of the setback suffered in 1836 and of the numerous other factors at work, but his hypothesis still merits careful exploration. It is placed in a wider context by I. D. C. Newbould, who sees Protestantism as one strand in an essentially reactionary Toryism based on the Corn Laws, the Church, opposition to the New Poor Law, and support for factory

---

[152] *R*, 28 July 1836; O'Sullivan and M'Ghee, *Romanism*, ii. 204–72; *Christian Observer*, 37 (1837), 732; J. Murch, *The Trial of Maynooth* (Bath, 1838), 21.

[153] *Dublin Review*, 1 (1836), 501–2; O'Sullivan and M'Ghee, *Romanism*, ii. 220, 225.

[154] O'Sullivan and M'Ghee, *Romanism*, ii. 335, 342.

[155] *R*, 18 July 1836 (advertisement); O'Sullivan and M'Ghee, *Romanism*, ii. 461.

[156] G. A. Cahill, 'Irish Catholicism and English Toryism', *Review of Politics*, 19 (1956), 62–76.

reform that carried Peel to power in 1841.[157] In the remainder of this chapter the importance of the 'No Popery' motif in the politics of the later 1830s will accordingly be evaluated. Consideration will first be given to the hard core of the movement as represented by the Protestant Association and its sympathizers, and the extent to which anti-Catholicism was reflected in the actions and utterances of the Conservatives as a whole will then be examined.

Save perhaps in the first year of its existence, the Protestant Association was never a mass movement, and its paid-up membership was numbered in hundreds rather than thousands. It faced considerable financial problems, and in many places the Association had difficulty in maintaining its branches. It failed to attract any significant support from Dissenters, apart from Wesleyans.[158] Its capacity for direct electoral influence was further limited by its ambiguous attitude to pledges and parties. At the 1837 general election an address was issued urging united action for the defence of Protestantism but not advocating any specific measures. Although it vigorously attacked the government, the Protestant cause was not explicitly linked with the Tories.[159] In the 1841 election campaign the Protestant Association again issued an address, calling on electors to pause before they voted 'for *anyone* who directly or indirectly favours Popery or infidelity'. They specifically disavowed support for any particular party, although, under the circumstances, it was scarcely conceivable that anyone seeking to follow their advice would not vote for the Conservatives. Stowell published his own address urging that pressure be brought to bear on candidates, but not to the extent of exacting pledges, as these were 'the cobwebs which petty tyrants weave to entangle pliant knaves'.[160] Thus on the one hand the Protestant Association acknowledged that the return of sympathetic MPs was a *sine qua non* for successful parliamentary activity, but on the other they fought shy of direct organization to secure this end.

An important local exception to this pattern was the case of Liverpool. On 6 July 1836 the reformed town corporation decided to introduce an educational system based on the Irish national model of

[157] I. D. C. Newbould, 'Sir Robert Peel and the Conservative Party 1832–1841: A Study in Failure', *English Historical Review*, 98 (1983), 529–51.

[158] See below, Chap. 4, pp. 134–7.

[159] *R*, 10 July 1837.

[160] *Protestant Magazine*, 3 (1841), 190; *Address of the Protestant Association to the Electors of Great Britain* (Bath, 1841); H. Stowell, *A Letter to the Protestant Electors of Great Britain on Their Duty at the Present Crisis*, 2nd edn. (Manchester, 1841), 5.

interdenominational religious instruction. On 13 July, the eve of the Protestant Association meeting in London at which M'Ghee referred to the 'false Bull', a major public meeting in Liverpool inaugurated a sustained campaign against the plan. It was headed by McNeile. Thus, local personalities and issues prevented the anti-Catholic cause in Liverpool from suffering the loss of momentum which affected the Protestant Association nationally at this point. During the next few years McNeile was adept at stimulating popular sectarianism and channelling it into an organized Protestant campaign which culminated in Conservative victory at the municipal elections in 1841 and the end of the controversial education scheme. The campaign also had an impact on parliamentary elections, in which, from 1837 onwards, two Conservatives were returned.[161]

Elsewhere, examination of the electoral fortunes of the Association's active supporters suggests that their efforts were, if anything, counter-productive. The 1837 general election saw the defeat of two prominent anti-Catholics, John Hardy at Bradford and Sir Andrew Agnew at Wigtown, while George Finch, who had been obliged to retire from the representation of Stamford so that the Duke of Rutland could place his son in this pocket borough, was unable to find another seat.[162] The balance was redressed to some extent by the return for Kilmarnock of Colquhoun, who had undergone a political conversion to Conservatism since 1835, but in 1841, in the face of general Tory triumph, he lost the seat again.[163] In 1841, too, although Protestants were able to rejoice at Hardy's return for Bradford, Sir George Sinclair was defeated at Halifax, and it is striking that Bath, Derby, Finsbury, Glasgow, Hereford, Manchester, Marylebone, and Sheffield, in all of which locations the Protestant Association was active, each returned two liberals. If anti-Catholicism had any significant influence in these boroughs, it would appear to have been a negative one. In fact, Conservative victory was due to gains in counties and small boroughs where the Corn Law issue was important and where

[161] J. Murphy, *The Religious Problem in English Education* (Liverpool, 1959); Neal, *Sectarian Violence* pp. 43–60; J. A. Wardle, 'The Life and Times of the Rev. Dr Hugh M'Neile, DD, 1795–1875', MA thesis (Manchester, 1981), 104–8. There is an interesting parallel to be drawn with the political effects of the campaigns over the Bible in the schools in the United States (cf. R. A. Billington, *The Protestant Crusade* (New York, 1938) 142–56). McNeile's relationship to popular sectarianism will be discussed below in Chap. 5.

[162] *R*, 20 July, 3 Aug. 1837; Craig, *Election Results*, pp. 57, 563.

[163] *R*, 3 Aug. 1837; *Protestant Magazine*, 3 (1841), 251; Craig, *Election Results*, pp. 141, 552, 578.

the Protestant Association was seldom strong.[164] The Association's parliamentary supporters themselves sat for seats of this nature. In 1839, of nine MPs who were subscribers, three sat for small boroughs (Christchurch, Kilmarnock, and Wallingford), three for counties (Glamorgan, Kent, and Selkirk) and three for Ulster constituencies (County Armagh, County Cavan, and County Fermanagh).[165]

The Association exercised a more significant, though still modest, influence on politics in its attempts to secure the cessation of the Maynooth grant. From 1839 onwards there were systematic efforts to collect signatures to petitions, yielding a gradually rising tide of support.[166] In 1838, 39 petitions with 11,000 signatures were presented; in 1839, 199 with 51,202 signatures; in 1840, 458 petitions with 95,108 signatures; and in the truncated session of 1841, 211 petitions with 69,177 signatures. The low average number of signatures on petitions indicates that these were generally the product of individual effort or the protest of a particular congregation, among which Wesleyan chapels figured prominently, rather than a reflection of the views of large communities.[167]

In the Commons the opponents of the grant insisted, except in 1838, on registering their protest in the lobbies. They were rewarded with an increase in the anti-Maynooth vote from 11 in 1836 to 44 in 1840. However, this still fell short of the level attained in 1831, thus suggesting that, after the excesses of 1835–6, the hard core of anti-Catholic feeling in Parliament was, if anything, smaller than it had been in the early 1830s. On the other hand, between 1836 and 1841 66 individuals cast at least one vote against Maynooth, so there was certainly a significant body of concern about the grant. Increasing participation on the pro-Maynooth side also suggested that the issue was seen as assuming greater importance: there were 53 votes in favour of the grant in 1836, and 123 in 1840.[168]

The anti-Maynooth campaign in Parliament was only loosely co-ordinated. There were differences over tactics both between the Protestant Association and its parliamentary sympathizers, and also among the MPs themselves. In particular, there was disagreement as

[164] *R*, 1 July 1841; Craig, *Election Results, passim*; Newbould, 'Peel and the Conservative Party', pp. 533–4, 556–7.
[165] PAss, *3rd AR* (1839); *Dod's Parliamentary Companion* (1839).
[166] PAss, *3rd AR* (1839), 13–14; *PM*, 2 (1840), 24, 134.
[167] Reports of the Select Committee on Public Petitions; *Journals of the House of Commons, passim*; Wolffe, 'Protestant Societies and Anti-Catholic Agitation', pp. 161–2.
[168] 3 *Hansard, passim*.

to whether Maynooth should be attacked on principle because it compromised the Protestant character of the State, the view taken by Gladstone, or on pragmatic grounds because of its undesirable influence in Ireland.[169] A third view was that, however repulsive the grant might be, it was sanctioned by established usage, and abolishing it would produce a Catholic backlash. This opinion was held by a number of moderate Evangelicals, including Lord Sandon.[170] Up to 1841 a similar attitude restrained Colquhoun from taking an active part in opposition to the grant, but he then, to the irritation of Sir Robert Inglis, took up the issue without consulting those who had been voting against it in previous years.[171] The Protestant Association was unable to impose its insistence on uncompromising anti-Catholic principle on these diverse elements. Its supporters formed a nucleus of the opposition to the grant, but it is significant that a number of staunch Protestants, notably Ashley, Inglis, Shaw, and Sibthorp,[172] were not members.

Nevertheless, the Maynooth issue did serve as an irritant to the government, and a sign that hardline Protestant feeling was gaining some ground on the Conservative back-benches between 1838 and 1841. By contrast, the campaign for the repeal of Emancipation never appeared politically viable. Even at the peak of petitioning activity in 1840, there were only 46 petitions advocating this step, with 5,525 signatures in all. When, in June 1840, Plumptre presented two parallel petitions from 'the members and friends of the Protestant Association', out of 1,423 people who asked for the cessation of the Maynooth grant, only 617 urged the repeal of Emancipation.[173] Clearly, even among strong anti-Catholics, the possibility was regarded as hopeless or absurd, and the matter was hardly discussed at all in the Commons.

In the Lords, where Maynooth as a financial matter was not normally debated, there was more discussion of Emancipation. On 28 November 1837 Newcastle presented a petition which had been drawn up at the Protestant Association's meeting in June, although not before

---

[169] *PM*, 3 (1841), 97–100; 3 *Hansard*, xliv. 817, 30 July 1838.

[170] Dudley Ryder (1798–1882), styled Viscount Sandon until 1847, when he succeeded his father as second Earl of Harrowby. He was MP for Tiverton, 1819–31, and for Liverpool, 1831–47 (*DNB*, l. 44).

[171] 3 *Hansard*, xxxviii. 1628, 27 June 1837; lvi. 1223, 2 Mar. 1841; lxv. 388, 20 July 1842; Canterbury Cathedral Library, Inglis MSS, diary entry for 2 Mar. 1841.

[172] Charles de Laet Waldo Sibthorp (1783–1855), MP for Lincoln, 1826–55, and eccentric Tory (*DNB*, lii. 188).

[173] Report of the Select Committee on Public Petitions, 1840.

he had postponed doing so because of Roden's fear that discussion on the issue would interfere with a motion on the state of Ireland due to take place on 27 November. Lorton and Winchilsea supported Newcastle, but Brougham spoke of the impossibility of turning back the 'tide of progress', and Melbourne struck at the heart of the Ultra dilemma: 'The noble duke was an advocate of what was [*sic*] denominated Conservative principles . . . But he could do nothing more at variance with those principles than now to attempt to disturb a measure of such importance, which had so recently been determined upon.' This argument does not appear to have troubled Newcastle or the *Record*, which welcomed this 'initiatory act of very great importance'.[174] The dawn proved to be a false one. Phillpotts kept the issue alive during the 1838 session by raising the related question of Roman Catholic oaths, and in June 1839 Winchilsea revived the subject of Emancipation itself, but thereafter, even in the Lords, the matter was allowed to rest.[175]

However, it would be severely misleading to base a general evaluation of the extent of the influence of anti-Catholicism on the politics of the later 1830s solely on a consideration of the direct impact of the Protestant Association. While this body itself operated primarily among a limited Evangelical constituency and confined its agitation to a few issues, the more broadly based Protestant campaign of 1834–6 had left its mark on public opinion. The issues were kept to the fore in Parliament and the press, and by continuing national interest in the conflict in Liverpool. Parliamentary debates on Irish tithes and municipal corporations took on a strongly Protestant flavour, while Phillpotts committed his considerable energy and oratory to the education question.[176]

Furthermore, although the high Tory peers continued to give Wellington and Peel considerable difficulties in their endeavour to maintain a moderate course and not to precipitate the premature fall of the government, the leaders themselves were quite prepared at times to take a strongly Protestant stance. The duke continued to encourage Roden in his efforts to gain English support for the Irish Protestant

---

[174] 3 *Hansard*, xxxix. 339–54, 28 Nov. 1837; Newcastle Diary, Ne2F5, 25, 28 Nov. 1837; *R*, 4 Dec. 1837.
[175] 3 *Hansard*, xli. 1293–1312, 27 Mar. 1838; xlviii. 692–701, 21 June 1839.
[176] 3 *Hansard*, *passim*; Wellington MSS, 2/38/46, 2/38/54, Phillpotts to Wellington, 15, 17 Feb. 1836; G. C. B. Davies, *Henry Phillpotts, Bishop of Exeter, 1778–1869* (1954), 334–6; Murphy, *Religious Problem*, p. 62.

cause.[177] He also in 1838 gave strong support to Phillpotts over Irish education; in 1840 he successfully moved an amendment to the address on the queen's engagement to include an explicit statement confirming her future consort's status as a Protestant, and in 1841 he again supported Phillpotts when the bishop attacked the incorporation and state endowment of the Roman Catholic seminary at St Sulpice in Montreal. Wellington's European interests gave him further grounds for distrusting the Roman Church, as he thought that on the Continent Catholicism and radicalism were in alliance.[178]

For his part, Peel's major speeches in May 1835 and in 1838 spoke of the importance of standing by the Protestant religion. Addressing a Scottish deputation in March 1838, he said that it was impossible 'to look at the progress Popery is now making, without anxiety and alarm'. He thought that before long there would be a struggle for ascendancy in Britain between Protestantism and Catholicism. In January 1839 he expressed similar views in a letter to Ashley.[179] In the Commons he was more circumspect, but in 1846, with a bitterness derived from hindsight, Ashley graphically reflected on his conduct: 'All the changes that could be rung on the bells of Popery, O'Connell, Protestant Church, are performed by his friends; he stands by, and, though, he guards himself against any precise and indisputable statements, which may rise ghost-like, out of Hansard, he leaves everyone to suppose that he shares the sentiments and approves the policy.'[180] In reality, Peel's position was rather less disingenuous than Ashley thought: there was a genuine conflict of conscience between Protestant instincts and conciliatory attitudes in relation to Ireland which had certainly not been rendered any less painful by the role he had played in 1829.[181]

The Protestant concerns of the Conservatives were both stimulated and mediated to a wider public by the newspaper and periodical press described by Professor Cahill.[182] It was this rather than the direct agitation of the Protestant Association that ensured that anti-Catholic

---

[177] Wellington MSS, 2/52/79, Wellington to M'Ghee, n.d.; 2/43/110, Wellington to Roden, 31 Dec. 1836.

[178] 3 *Hansard*, xliii. 258–61, 25 May 1838; li, 11–14, 26 Jan. 1840; lvi. 1334–6, 4 Mar. 1841; Wellington MSS, 2/55/40–2, Wellington to Phillpotts, 12 Dec. 1838; 2/55/57, Wellington to Aberdeen, 19 Dec. 1838.

[179] 3 *Hansard*, lxxix. 1406–9, 28 Apr. 1845; E. Hodder, *The Life and Work of the Seventh Earl of Shaftesbury, KG* 3 vols. (1887), i. 242, quoting letter from Peel to Ashley of 11 Jan. 1839.

[180] Hodder, *Shaftesbury*, ii. 138–9, quoting Ashley's diary for 11 May 1846.

[181] Wolffe, 'Protestant Societies and Anti-Catholic Agitation', p. 174.

[182] Cahill, 'Irish Catholicism', pp. 68–70.

rhetoric was a frequent feature of elections between 1836 and 1841. Anti-Catholicism was now frequently explicitly linked with the cry of 'Church in danger', which shows that it had been recognized that there was little prospect of winning over the Dissenters. Contemporaries thought that such tactics were not unsuccessful. In July 1839 O'Connell complained that a 'stupid Tory' (Sir T. J. Cochrane) had been victorious in a by-election at Ipswich on the strength of the 'bigotry' of the constituency, and in June 1840 it was alleged in the Commons that 'many' Conservative MPs owed their seats to their opposition to Maynooth.[183] In Liverpool in 1841 the success of the Conservatives was squarely attributed to 'Protestant feeling', and the *Berkshire Chronicle* maintained that 'the most powerful instrument in changing the tone of political feeling is the subservience of the executive government to the sordid and mendicant papist'.[184]

Thus there was a paradoxical but revealing contrast between the prominence of anti-Catholic motifs in the parliamentary and electoral politics of the late 1830s, and the limited success achieved by the Protestant Association as an institution. In part this is explained by its obtrusively Evangelical character and the lasting discredit brought by the 'false Bull' affair. It also restricted its influence by taking up the fringe issues of Maynooth and Emancipation rather than seeking to play a direct role in the central political questions of the Irish Church and education. However, to a considerable extent Evangelicals in the late 1830s had become victims of their own success in making anti-Catholicism a central force in politics again: the Conservative party as a whole was so strongly Protestant in its outlook and propaganda during these years that there seemed to be little role for specific independent Protestant organization, and those who supported the Association were seen as engaging in a work of fanatical supereroga-tion whose extremism might compromise the wider cause.

This conclusion is confirmed by examination of the attitudes of militant anti-Catholics towards the Conservative party. Irish and former Ultra-Tory elements cherished the idea that the party would now be faithful to its Protestant soul and thus become an agent of national regeneration. Newcastle was still mistrustful of Peel and Stanley, but by 1840 he was ready to hope that they could be kept in line and that good, as he saw it, would ultimately triumph.[185]

---

[183] Stewart, *Foundation of the Conservative Party*, p. 158; Close, 'General Elections of 1835 and 1837', pp. 401–4; Newbould, 'Peel and the Conservative Party', pp. 552–4.
[184] Cited Newbould, 'Peel and the Conservative Party', pp. 553–4.
[185] Newcastle Diary, Ne2F6, 2, 3 July 1840.

Evangelicals were privately more pessimistic about Peel, but still felt that action independent of him was not a viable possibility. In June 1837 MPs pointedly absented themselves from a meeting called to petititon for the repeal of Emancipation, because they considered it inexpedient to agitate this issue at present.[186] Pleas for a separate Evangelical party were made, but by Churchmen not politicians. Stowell wrote of the need for 'an independent, united and powerful Protestant party', while Chalmers longed 'for a Wilberforce party in Parliament, consisting of men who would make it the polar star of their public and parliamentary conduct, to adopt such measures as were best for the moral and religious well-being of the population'.[187] He thought that Colquhoun would be the obvious man to lead such a party, but the latter had already rejected the possibility: 'We did not feel that we could then face the obloquy, the painful severance from party, the position of isolation, as it would seem of presumption which we should assume.'[188] In the context of the late 1830s, little was to be gained except a personal purity beloved of clergymen but elusive for politicians, and there would be much to be lost by embarrassing Peel and depriving themselves of the opportunity to exert their influence within the Conservative party to keep it on a Protestant course. A laconic comment on Peel in Sir Robert Inglis's diary for April 1839 summed up the mood: 'we must take him as we find him'.[189]

Attempts to understand the Conservative party of the 1830s in terms of rival 'Tamworthian' and 'reactionary' elements are helpful up to a point, but are liable to force the formation of categories that are ultimately simplistic and anachronistic. The picture has to be refined by the recognition that the new features of the decade were not only 'progressive' ones. Boyd Hilton has shown that many of Peel's reforming ideas which came to fruition in the great ministry of 1841–6 had their origins in the 1820s and earlier;[190] conversely, the political anti-Catholicism of the 1830s was not so much a continuation of the anti-Emancipationism of the 1820s as a new movement stimulated by Evangelicalism and by the circumstances in Ireland in the years immediately after Emancipation. Erstwhile Ultras such as Newcastle, Kenyon, and Cumberland were certainly still prominent in Protestant

[186] *R*, 12 June 1837.
[187] Stowell, *Letter to Protestant Electors*, p. 6; Comrie, Perthshire, Colquhoun MSS, Chalmers to Mrs Colquhoun, 26 June 1841.
[188] *A Report of the Speeches Delivered at the Dinner of the Members and Friends of the National Club, May 12 1847* (1847), 7.
[189] Inglis Diary, 15 Apr. 1839.
[190] B. Hilton, 'Peel: A Reappraisal', *Historical Journal*, 22 (1979), 585–614.

activity, but their efforts to continue agitation on the pre-1829 pattern were conspicuously unsuccessful, as demonstrated by the collapse of their independent political action in 1830-1 and in the disgrace of the Orange Order in 1835-6. Nevertheless, their conception of the intimate interrelationship of politics and religion was gaining a new lease of life in a wider context. Much of the support for Emancipation in 1829 had reflected not favour to Catholicism but a belief that religion and politics were separate. This state of mind reached its height in the critical reception accorded to the 'Recordites' in Parliament in 1831-2. By 1835, however, religious issues were again being perceived as the staple of political life. This fuelled anti-Catholicism and support for the Church, but also strengthened loyalties to Dissent and Catholicism itself. Evangelicals still hankered for a higher degree of religious integrity than the political world permitted them, but the framework of opinion had shifted sufficiently in their direction to enable them, at least for the present, to work within the existing structures rather than to proclaim divine judgement upon them from outside. This development was facilitated by the moderating of their own attitudes in the aftermath of the Irvingite secession. Thus, while Emancipation was a crucial event in that it brought to an end an era in which anti-Catholicism represented the national and constitutional consensus, its medium-term effect was to make religion more rather than less significant in political life, and, in shattering the ideological structure of the old Tory party, to lay a corner-stone of its eventual reconstruction in a modified but still recognizable form.

4

THE ANTI-CATHOLIC FRAME OF MIND

THE origins of the Victorian anti-Catholic movement have been surveyed in the preceding two chapters. This is therefore an appropriate point at which to analyse the components of the world-view associated with militant 'No Popery' feeling. The current chapter will be concerned primarily with the ideology of literary, clerical, and middle-class Protestantism, providing the background for Chapter 5, in which the nature of popular anti-Catholicism and its relationship to the activities of the Protestant societies will be explored. It will be argued below that educated opposition to Rome had strong roots in a wider religious consciousness and was in many respects a rational, if extreme, response to contemporary circumstances, a response which needs to be understood quite as much in terms of a positive Protestantism as of a negative anti-Catholicism. The analysis will begin with consideration of the theological and spiritual outlook of Anglican Evangelicals, who, as we have seen, made up the core of the Protestant movement. The social and political implications of their beliefs, reinforced by the events of the 1830s and 1840s, will then be studied. These related particularly to the social and political condition of Ireland, to Roman Catholic regulation of sexuality, and to an understanding of the nature of 'liberty'. In the final part of the chapter the theoretical ambiguities of anti-Catholicism will be linked to its lack of institutional coherence. The Protestant Association in particular did not succeed in overcoming the caution towards political action voiced by a substantial body of militant anti-Catholics. Above all, it failed to appeal to Dissenters. A more successful route to a broader anti-Catholic alignment proved to be the religious and spiritual one pursued by the Evangelical Alliance, but even there the differences in outlook could only be very partially overcome.

The Evangelical anti-Catholic position was developed in speeches and sermons, in the pages of the *Record*, in the serial and occasional publications of the Protestant societies, and in a variety of other published media, ranging from short tracts to multi-volume works. Its exponents generally can be identified with extreme 'Recordite' Evangelicalism.[1] A number of those who have already featured in this book contributed substantially to this material, notably James E. Gordon and Hugh McNeile. However, this is an appropriate point at which to introduce five other individuals. Edward Bickersteth (1786–1850) spent the first part of his ordained life working for the Church Missionary Society, culminating in six years as secretary from 1824 to 1830, when he retired to become rector of Watton, Hertfordshire. The social and political crisis of the early 1830s precipitated his conversion to pre-millennialism and intense anti-Catholicism. During the later years of his life Bickersteth was a central force in Evangelicalism, revered for his writing on theology and spirituality. He was also a close associate of Lord Ashley from 1835 onwards.[2] Robert Bickersteth (1816–84) was Edward's nephew, rector of St Giles, London from 1851 and Bishop of Ripon from 1857.[3] While the Bickersteths represented English Evangelicalism, the three other figures to be noted here indicated the strength of the Irish and Scottish connections of anti-Catholicism. Charlotte Elizabeth Tonna (1790–1846), the daughter of a clergyman, contracted an unhappy marriage to Captain George Phelan, who took her first to Canada and then to Ireland. She was converted to 'vital religion', and, living on the borders of County Tipperary in the disturbed early 1820s, she became convinced that 'Popery' was the root cause of all the problems of Ireland.[4] Returning to England in 1824, she set about popularizing her views through numerous novels, poems, short stories, and tracts, and, from 1834, through the medium of her *Christian Ladies' Magazine*. From 1841 to 1844 she was editor of the Protestant Association's monthly *Protestant Magazine*.[5] John Cumming (1807–81) was minister of the National Scottish Church at Crown Court, Covent Garden from 1832. He was a strong supporter of religious Establishments and identified closely

---

[1] The distinction between 'moderate' and 'extreme' evangelicalism is explored by B. Hilton, *The Age of Atonement* (Oxford, 1988), 7–26, and D. W. Bebbington, *Evangelicalism in Modern Britain: A History from the 1730s to the 1980s* (1989), 75–104.

[2] *DNB*, v. 3; M. Hennell, *Sons of the Prophets: Evangelical Leaders of the Victorian Church* (1979), 29–49; T. R. Birks, *Memoir of the Rev. Edward Bickersteth*, 2 vols. (1851).

[3] *DNB*, v. 6; D. N. Hempton, 'Bickersteth, Bishop of Ripon: The Episcopate of a mid-Victorian Evangelical', *Northern History*, 17 (1981), 183–202; M. C. Bickersteth, *A Sketch of the Life and Episcopate of the Rt. Rev. Robert Bickersteth, DD* (1887).

[4] *Memoir of Charlotte Elizabeth* (Bristol, 1852); C. L. Balfour, *A Sketch of Charlotte Elizabeth* (1854).

[5] Her first husband died in 1837 and she married Mr L. H. Tonna in 1840, acquiring the surname by which she is generally known. She died of cancer in July 1846.

with Anglicans in the Reformation Society, in which he became a dominant figure in the late 1830s. A successful popular preacher and lecturer on prophecy, Cumming was the focus of a sparkling attack by George Eliot in 1855.[6] Finally, Richard Paul Blakeney (1820–84), an Anglo-Irish graduate of Trinity College, Dublin, was initially a curate and then incumbent in Nottingham, but in 1852 he moved to Christ Church, Claughton, Birkenhead. He was also very active in the Reformation Society from the late 1840s onwards.[7]

At the core of Evangelical hostility to Rome were theological issues which formed the basis for the debates between the Reformation Society and its Catholic opponents.[8] The central question was that of authority. For Evangelicals, the supremacy of Scripture was axiomatic, and it was during this period that the doctrine of verbal inspiration took shape. Thus, in arguing against Roman doctrines, it was often felt sufficient to show that they were inconsistent with a Protestant interpretation of the Bible. An evangelical doctrine of Scripture was not clearly articulated in debates, but there was angry reaction to Catholic suggestions that the judgement of the Church was necessary in relation to difficult passages. When the Revd Mr Browne presented the Catholic case on such lines at Cheltenham in 1830, commenting that the Devil quoted Scripture, the *Record* judged that 'Popery would rather league herself with Infidelity against the Bible, than surrender her spiritual tyranny over the souls of men'.[9] Protestants attacked tradition as unreliable, and ridiculed the proposition that infallibility resided in the pope or in the Church as a whole, because the precise locus of infallibility remained undefined and the believer was thus left floating on a sea of uncertainty. Furthermore, by allegedly keeping the

---

[6] *DNB*, xiii. 297; R. B. Knox, 'Dr John Cumming and Crown Court Church, London', *Records of the Scottish Church History Society*, 22 (1984), 57–84; C. G. Cameron, *The Scots Kirk in London* (Oxford, 1979); G. Eliot, 'Evangelical Teaching: Dr Cumming', *Westminster Review*, 64 (Oct. 1855), reprinted in *Essays of George Eliot*, ed. T. Pinney (1963), 158–89.

[7] *DNB*, v. 186; RS minutes, *passim*. Blakeney's intense anti-Catholicism appears in part at least to have stemmed from some imperfectly documented personal tragedy, relating to his wife, for which he held the Roman Catholic Church responsible (SRO, Edinburgh, John Hope MSS (GD 253) 32/5/52, 32/6/11, 32/6/34, Blakeney to Hope, 24 May, 4, 19 June 1851).

[8] The Evangelical theological critique of Roman Catholicism is a vast subject in its own right, which needs further research from the perspective of historical theology and can only be treated in broad outline in this book. In so far as a response to Tractarianism was a motive force, the subject has been explored by Peter Toon in *Evangelical Theology 1832–1856* (1979), but more work on the treatment of Roman Catholicism is required.

[9] *R*, 26 Aug. 1830; Bebbington, *Evangelicalism*, pp. 85–91.

Bible from the laity, the Roman Church kept them in superstitious ignorance.[10]

The other main area of attack was centred on the means of grace and the Mass. Roman Catholic views on sacramental grace, confession, and penance seemed to undermine the principle of justification through faith alone. Forgiveness of sins was made dependent on the priest rather than Christ, and the Mass, by purporting to multiply the flesh of Christ, detracted from the supreme merit of his one perfect sacrifice on Calvary.[11] It was alleged that the Roman Church's invocation of saints and angels was idolatrous and insulting to the majesty of God. Robert Bickersteth believed that 'the Papacy was the gigantic lie which attempts to stand between the soul and Christ. He thought the whole system dishonouring to our Blessed Lord as the one Mediator between God and Man.'[12] All the areas of controversy were covered in a discussion which took place at Hammersmith between John Cumming and Daniel French, a Roman Catholic barrister, and which extended over eleven evenings during April and May 1838. Two evenings were spent debating transubstantiation, two on the sacrifice of the Mass, two on the invocation of saints and angels, one on purgatory, and the final four on the rule of faith. The published report covered 650 closely printed pages.[13]

Such debates were a reflection of the points of genuine theological difference between Roman Catholics and Protestants, but the problems were always approached in a polemical frame of mind rather than one that would admit scope for dialogue. Extreme manifestations of Catholic tendencies were represented as typical; for example, the frequent claims that superstitious popular Irish peasant beliefs were expressions of Catholic orthodoxy. Anti-Catholic polemicists, however, exposed real ambiguities in the Catholic response to popular religion, at a period when ecclesiastical authority was struggling to assimulate the uneducated without compromising official orthodoxy.[14] Their attack on tradition and infallibility also indicated an inherent difficulty in the Catholic system: to move away from supposedly

---

[10] *R*, 22 Feb. 1828, 16 May 1836, 7 May 1842.

[11] E. Bickersteth, *The Testimony of the Reformers* (1836), introductory remarks on the 'Progress of Popery', pp. xi–xix.

[12] M. C. Bickersteth, *Robert Bickersteth*, p. 48.

[13] C. M. Arthur, *Authenticated Report of the Controversial Discussion between the Rev. John Cumming, AM and Daniel French, Esq.* (1841).

[14] *R*, 4 July 1828 and *passim*; S. Connolly, *Religion and Society in Nineteenth-Century Ireland* (Dundalk, 1985), 47–54.

authoritative past statements without explicitly repudiating them. For Protestants, whose literalistic attitude of mind was evident in their attitude to Scripture, the intellectual processes thus involved were genuinely obscure and redolent of casuistry. Above all, the Protestants remained deeply convinced of Rome's antipathy to all that they held to be crucial to true Christian belief: this led them to be blind to conflicting evidence. The experience of polemical debate on specific theological issues undoubtedly hardened this attitude, but its origins need to be understood in a wider context.

To some extent this was provided by consciousness of the past. This was stirred particularly on 4 October 1835, when, in response to a pamphlet by the biblical scholar Thomas Hartwell Horne, many clergy preached commemorative sermons to mark the tercentenary of the publication of Coverdale's English Bible. It is significant that, in the face of considerable contemporaneous agitation over Dens's *Theologia* and the Irish Church, emphasis was generally placed on the Reformation as a spiritual movement based on the vernacular Bible, rather than on its political dimensions. For instance, at his church near Oxford John Hill chose as his text Psalm 19: 7–10, 'The law of the Lord is perfect, reviving the soul . . .'.[15]

Evangelicals of the early and mid-nineteenth century derived their knowledge of the past primarily from Joseph and Isaac Milner's *History of the Church of Christ*, published in the 1790s. This work sought to highlight instances of proto-evangelicalism in the medieval Church, and reached its climax with a discussion of Luther which emphasized the religious character of the Reformation and its common ground with eighteenth-century Evangelicalism.[16] Another extensively read book was J. H. Merle d'Aubigné's *Histoire de la Réformation*, published in Geneva in 1835 and translated into English from 1838. Both works reflected a concern with contemporary controversies and, insensitive to historical problems of context and change, encouraged their readers to see their situation as directly comparable with that of the sixteenth century. Their view of history thus reinforced their attitude to Scripture in leading to a sense of intense conflict with Rome.[17]

[15] T. H. Horne, *A Protestant Memorial for the Commemoration of the Fourth Day of October 1835* (1835); *Protestant Journal*, 5 (1835), 563–4, 720–1; Bod. Lib., St Edmund Hall MS 67/10, John Hill Diary, 4 Oct. 1835.
[16] J. D. Walsh, 'Joseph Milner's Evangelical Church History', *Journal of Ecclesiastical History*, 10 (1959), 174–87; W. J. Baker, 'The Attitudes of English Churchmen, 1800–1850, towards the Reformation', Ph.D. thesis (Cambridge, 1966), 17–20.
[17] Baker, 'Attitudes of English Churchmen', pp. 47–8; J. H. Merle d'Aubigné, *History of the Reformation*, trans. W. K. Kelly (1842?), 4–6.

The republication of the Protestant literature of past ages reflected this belief that the struggle with Rome was timeless. Two major new editions of Foxe's *Book of Martyrs* appeared in the late 1830s. Michael Hobart Seymour, the secretary of the Reformation Society, produced a two-volume version in 1838, explaining in his preface that the recent energies of the Church of Rome had prompted the republication of a work with which her influence had formerly been countered. Seymour's edition was aimed at a 'family' audience, and to that end all 'coarseness of expression' in the original was suppressed. It was frequently reprinted and had a wide circulation during the Victorian period.[18] A more scholarly edition was produced between 1838 and 1841 by Stephen Cattley, running to eight volumes and including a 400-page introduction by George Townsend, an old-style Durham High-Churchman, giving an historical account of Foxe's life and defending him against his critics, from Archbishop Laud to S. R. Maitland.[19] There were several abridged editions, including *A History of Protestant Martyrdom* published in 1839, which was compressed into 250 pages and little more than pocket-sized. The preface expressed the hope that it would be within reach of all classes of society.[20] Most nineteenth-century editions of Foxe were copiously illustrated with dramatic woodcuts in which the beatific expressions of the martyrs contrast strikingly with the violence and activity around them. The *Book of Martyrs* served to highlight the persecuting nature of Rome, while providing a sense of the spiritual legitimacy of Protestantism, born in heroism, suffering, and holy fervour, and linked closely to the development of English national identity.

The Parker Society, formed in 1840 to republish the works of the English Reformers, provided a more theological approach. Evangelicals were prominent in the organization, but a number of other Churchmen were also active as members of the council and as editors, an indication that by this stage Tractarianism was leading to a desire to reassert the Reformation which went beyond Evangelical circles. Fifty-four volumes were published by 1855.[21] A more exclusively Evangelical initiative was the Reformation Society's decision in June 1847 to republish the *Preservative against Popery* compiled by Edmund Gibson,

---

[18] J. Foxe, *The Acts and Monuments of the Church*, ed. M. H. Seymour, 2 vols. (1838), i, pp. i–ix; W. W. Wooden, *John Foxe* (Boston, Mass., 1983), 103.

[19] *The Acts and Monuments of John Foxe*, ed. S. R. Cattley, 8 vols. (1837–41).

[20] *A History of Protestant Martyrdom* (1839), p. ix.

[21] Toon, *Evangelical Theology*, pp. 43–4.

Bishop of London, during the first half of the eighteenth century. This was a collection of Protestant polemical works dating mainly from the reign of James II. It was claimed that it contained 'all that can be said on the Protestant and Romish controversies. From it, as from a vast arsenal, modern controversialists have drawn their weapons . . . '.[22] Gibson's compilation, which ran to eighteen octavo volumes in the Reformation Society's reprint edited by John Cumming, contained completely unabridged texts, because, Gibson had pointed out, detailed knowledge of the controversy was necessary to clergy engaged in 'close combat'. The tracts included vindications of the Reformation, attacks on papal supremacy, Roman Catholic worship and sacramental doctrines, and broadsides against Mariolatry.[23] The reprint attracted 600 subscribers, and, although this compared poorly with the Parker Society membership of 4,000, it provided adequate encouragement for the publication of a supplement running to a further eight volumes, containing works from the earlier part of the seventeenth century.[24] In addition to editing Gibson's *Preservative*, Cumming also brought out a new edition of Willet's *Synopsis Papismi*, and the period also saw several republications of other classic Protestant works such as Chillingworth's *Religion of Protestants*.[25]

A further wider ideological factor was the maintenance of the link between anti-Catholicism and apocalyptic expectation evident in the origins of the Reformation Society. Initially the purging of Irvingism combined with the relatively calm European political conditions of the later 1830s to render the eschatological strand in anti-Catholicism more subdued in the years immediately after 1832. The *Record* itself reverted to the more optimistic and less strident post-millennial position.[26] However, Edward Bickersteth emerged as a major exponent of the historicist pre-millennialist application of biblical prophecy, predicated on the assumption that the prophetic books provided an account of contemporary events in coded form. In 1836 Bickersteth explicitly identified Rome with 'the man of sin' of 2

[22] RS minutes, 14 June 1847; *BP*, 3 (1847), 133–4.
[23] *A Preservative against Popery . . . collected by the Rt. Rev. Edmund Gibson, DD*, ed. J. Cumming, 18 vols. (1848–9), i, p. v and *passim*.
[24] *Supplement to Gibson's Preservative from Popery*, ed. R. P. Blakeney, J. Cumming, and M. W. Foye, 8 vols. (1849–50); Toon, *Evangelical Theology*, p. 44.
[25] A. Willet, *Synopsis Papismi*, ed. J. Cumming (1852); W. Chillingworth, *The Religion of Protestants a Sure Way to Salvation* (Oxford, 1838; London 1846).
[26] D. M. Lewis, *Lighten Their Darkness: The Evangelical Mission to Working-Class London 1828–1860* (Westport, Conn., 1986), 101.

Thessalonians and the 'Babylon' of Revelation, and in 1842 he argued that the present was the time of the application of the sixth vial of Revelation 16: 13. 'The unclean spirit out of the mouth of the beast' represented Chartism and the Anti-Corn Law League, and 'the unclean spirit out of the mouth of the false prophet' was equated with Popery. The world was currently enjoying a season of divine long-suffering and grace, but apostasy was growing and time was rapidly running out, although there was still opportunity for repentance.[27]

In 1847 and 1848 John Cumming, also a historicist, who had been influenced by the work of E. B. Elliott, delivered a series of twenty-six lectures at Exeter Hall. Cumming took his audience on a breathless survey of world history from the writing of Revelation to the present time, identifying the seven seals with the period up to Constantine, the seven trumpets with the centuries from then to the Reformation, and the seven vials with the events since the French Revolution. Like Bickersteth, he thought that the sixth vial was currently being poured out, but he differed somewhat in his interpretation of the three evil spirits, whom he identified with 'Infidelity', 'Popery', and Tractarianism respectively. Cumming, thinking that he could discern signs of the seventh and last vial in the Irish famine and the current influenza and cholera epidemics, urged continual preparedness for the coming of Christ, as the present dispensation had only twenty more years to run.[28] As George Eliot was to observe, Cumming's glib style made him a most effective popularizer. His confident predictions of the unknowable clearly struck a chord in the evangelical imagination, and the dramatic events of 1848 in Europe served, for a time at least, to enhance his credibility.[29]

Anyone who accepted such views on the fulfilment of prophecy would naturally also imbibe related convictions regarding the nature of Rome. The strength of the identification between Rome and biblical prophecy is well illustrated by a lecture delivered by Robert Bickersteth in 1853. He professed not to prejudge the issue as to whether 'Romanism' was the apostasy foretold in 2 Thessalonians, but he then proceeded to develop his argument, whether consciously or not, in a manner which led inexorably to the conclusion that it was. He

[27] E. Bickersteth, *The Testimony of the Reformers* (1836), p. iv; id., *The Divine Warning to the Church* (1842), 4–16.
[28] J. Cumming, *Apocalyptic Sketches*, 9th edn. (1849), 505–29.
[29] Pinney, *Essays of George Eliot*, pp. 159–62; [W. J. Conybeare], 'Church Parties', *Edinburgh Review*, 200 (Oct. 1853), 196–7; *R*, 14 May 1849.

did not seriously consider other possible candidates—historical, contemporary, or future—for the designation of the 'mystery of iniquity', and some of his biblical exegesis appears somewhat strained.[30] However, writers on prophecy themselves were generally at pains to distinguish hatred of Roman Catholicism from hatred of Roman Catholics, who were protrayed as unfortunate victims of their religious system. Speakers at Reformation Society meetings argued that Protestants should denounce Roman Catholic doctrines precisely because they loved Catholics and sought to save them from God's impending judgement.[31]

The role of eschatology in both stimulating and confirming anti-Catholic views thus seems clear. In particular, the growth of pre-millennialism in the 1830s and 1840s served to harden positions. It is true that as late as 1845 the *Record* described post-millennialism as the dominant Evangelical view, but this situation was quickly changing.[32] However, the movement was troubled by differences of opinion over eschatology, which had been evident in the dispute over Irvingism in 1831–2. A few years later, at the 1840 annual meeting of the Reformation Society, Finch complained that the Society's work was being hampered by the prevalence of 'novel opinions' regarding the fulfilment of prophecy. The allusion was not further explained, but it would seem probable that Finch was referring to the emergence of futurist pre-millennialism, which, through arguing that biblical prophecy was not to be related to contemporary events but rather to the last days themselves, served to weaken the stimulus to regard scriptural denunciation of Babylon as relevant to the present position of Rome.[33] Similarly, in the course of the 1852 annual meeting the Revd H. H. Beamish asserted that the Church of Rome was merely 'the Antichristianity of the day', provoking Richard Blakeney to emphasize his own view that the 'Bishop of Rome' was a personal Antichrist. He believed that Beamish's view was a departure from the principles of the Reformation, which Blakeney regarded as being defined by opposition

---

[30] R. Bickersteth, *Romanism in Relation to the Second Coming of Christ* (1854).

[31] *R*, 7 May 1842, 16 May 1846, and *passim*. George Eliot's comment on this state of mind is worth noting: 'who that is in the slightest degree acquainted with the action of the human mind, will believe that any genuine and large charity can grow out of an exercise of love which is always to have an *arrière-pensée* of hatred? Of what quality would be the conjugal love of a husband who loved his spouse as a wife, but hated her as a woman?' (Pinney, *Essays of George Eliot*, p. 180.)

[32] *R*, 22 Dec. 1845; Lewis, *Lighten their Darkness*, pp. 32–3.

[33] *R*, 25 May 1840.

to Rome.[34] Nevertheless, the lines were by no means clearly drawn on this issue: Hugh McNeile, who was a futurist, could hardly be charged with lukewarmness in his anti-Catholicism.[35]

Prophetic speculation had an impact beyond the bounds of Evangelicalism. For example, the Duke of Newcastle shared an increasingly strong sense of apocalyptic expectation. In October 1842, in the face of economic and social distress, he noted: 'the events are wonderful and questionless are signs of the times and in fulfillment [*sic*] of Prophecy'. In November 1843 he thought the 'Latter Days' to be near at hand, and at the end of December 1848, mindful particularly of the pope's flight from Rome, he thought that 'the rapid fulfillment of prophecy is most marked and indubitable'.[36]

This theological background serves to explain the intensity of the Protestant reaction to Catholic advance in Britain. As a result of Irish immigration and population growth, there was a very substantial increase in the number of Roman Catholics, and associated rapid building of chapels.[37] The Reformation Society acknowledged that there were demographic reasons for this, but consistently believed that a significant proportion of the increase was due to conversions from Protestantism.[38] The Catholics themselves freely adopted the same myth, which strengthened their own morale.[39] Meanwhile, Protestants noted with alarm the growing expenditure of Propaganda Fide in Britain, discovered prayers for the conversion of England in Roman Catholic books, and were horrified at the circulation of tracts by the Catholic Institute. Stepping over the boundary between exaggerated fact and sheer fantasy, Cumming claimed that a copy of St Peter's in Rome was to be constructed in Bath, and others discerned sinister Catholic influences in the press and in the education system. It was alleged in 1845 that only half of the students at Maynooth became priests: the others were secretly at work as Jesuits.[40]

Roman spiritual and ideological influence was readily linked with

[34] *R*, 18 May 1852; Hope MSS 33/5/16, Blakeney to Hope, 22 May 1852.

[35] Lewis, *Lighten their Darkness*, p. 102.

[36] Nottingham University Library, Newcastle MSS, Diary, Ne2F6, 4 Oct. 1842; Ne2F7, 7 Oct. 1843; Ne2F8, 31 Dec. 1848.

[37] A. D. Gilbert, *Religion and Society in Industrial England* (1976), 45–7; J. Bossy, *The English Catholic Community 1570–1850* (1975), 302–7.

[38] *R*, 16 May 1831, 10 May 1841, 4 May 1860; Bickersteth, *Testimony of the Reformers*, p. v.

[39] G. Connolly, 'The Transubstantiation of Myth', *Journal of Ecclesiastical History*, 30 (1984), 79, 93–4, 98.

[40] *R*, 14 May 1835, 17 May 1845, and *passim*.

both 'Infidelity' and Tractarianism. Evangelicals used the word 'Infidelity' as a blanket term for a wide range of attitudes, ranging from active atheism through passive irreligion to the questioning of aspects of orthodox doctrine by those who saw themselves as adhering to a Christian stance. As with Catholicism itself, the eschatological framework in which they worked caused Protestants to see 'Infidelity' as a more coherent and active spiritual force than was commensurate with reality. Perceptions of the nature of its relationship with 'Popery' varied. The view that 'Infidelity' would overthrow and replace Rome was prevalent in the late 1820s, notably in the writing of Edward Irving and Charlotte Elizabeth,[41] but at a later date a sense that the two were merging together in a monstrous coalition against the truth was evident: Cumming asserted in May 1840 that 'Infidelity' was the 'germ and principle of Popery', being an honest and undisguised evil, whereas Rome had cloaked its real character.[42] Suggestions that 'Popery' and 'Infidelity' were linked gained ground because they appeared to be coexisting in Europe and within the amorphous connections of English and Irish radicalism. Fears of spiritual evil and theological unorthodoxy were associated here with dread of political subversion.[43]

Tractarianism, too, fitted admirably into the anti-Catholic outlook. The early tracts were criticized for taking their spiritual weapons from Rome, and the *Record* observed that the apostolic succession had provided no security for the Papacy against heresy and apostasy.[44] It must be reiterated, however, that in the early stages of the Oxford Movement the Protestant societies and press were only incidentally concerned with opposing it, and continued to direct the main force of their attack against Rome. For example, on 30 July 1835 the *Record* referred to the tracts as paving the way towards a restoration of 'Popery', but in the context of a wider discussion of the devious operations of Rome which was directed more against Dissent than against Oxford. Similarly, Edward Bickersteth only gave the Tractarians a short passage in his discussion of 'The Progress of Popery' published in 1836 and running to over seventy pages.

Only after the publication of Tract 90 in February 1841 did

---

[41] E. Irving, *Babylon and Infidelity Foredoomed of God* (Glasgow, 1826), i. 173, 305; *R*, 2, 9 Sept. 1830.
[42] *R*, 15 May 1840.
[43] *R*, 25 Aug. 1834, 20 May 1851.
[44] *R*, 2, 5, 9 Dec. 1833.

Tractarianism come to the forefront of anti-Catholic concerns. In 1842 the Reformation Society's committee unanimously resolved to take up the spread of 'Popish principles' within the Church of England as well as outside it.[45] Tractarians and Roman Catholics were regarded as standing on precisely the same ground; indeed, the former were more dangerous than the latter, because they were subverting the Church from within.[46] However, this does not appear to have implied a diversion of attention from Rome to Oxford, but rather a consciousness that a new front had to be opened. In the event, there was little connection, except in terms of broad sympathy, between the anti-Catholic movement that had developed since 1827 and the drama that played itself out in Oxford in the early 1840s. The latter was undoubtedly significant in polarizing forces within the Church of England, rendering moderate Evangelicals and old-style High-Churchmen more sympathetic to active anti-Catholicism than they had been in the 1830s. However, it was initially a secondary rather than a formative influence on the development of Protestant attitudes.[47]

The Evangelicals' antagonism towards the Tractarians reflected their wider sense that Catholicism, both Anglican and Roman, substituted forms for true spirituality and encouraged a reliance on the institutional Church, avoiding the self-abasement and upheaval required by conversion and justification by faith alone.[48] The superficially attractive nature of Catholic worship, with its music and display, seduced the senses, leading astray 'the unthinking, the disorientated, the lovers of pomp and lies in spiritual matters'.[49] 'Popery' was thus a spiritual cancer, a religion of nature attractive to the weaker side of humanity. McNeile asserted in 1830 that there was as much 'Popery' in an evangelical organization as in a Catholic 'mass-house'. Blakeney believed that 'Popery' was inherent in all ecclesiastical bodies, and professed to discern this in the unlikely environment of the Free Church of Scotland.[50] In 1836 Edward Bickersteth wrote to one of his children:

I am now full of work, with a tract against Popery which has taken longer than I

[45] RS, *15th AR* (1842), 9.
[46] *R*, 7 May 1841, 22 May 1844.
[47] For this reason the controversy at Oxford is not considered in detail here. A full account is given in Toon, *Evangelical Theology*, pp. 13–78. On conservative High-Church opposition to Rome in the later 1840s, see Chap. 6, below.
[48] *R*, 30 May 1828.
[49] *R*, 3 Nov. 1834, 16 May 1836.
[50] *R*, 17 May 1830; Hope MSS 34/11/97, Blakeney to Hope, 30 Nov. 1853.

expected, as I felt it an important opportunity to disclose Protestant Popery, of which there is a great abundance,—first in every carnal heart, and therefore in our own,—and then in all religious writings. Popery is, to be looking to ourselves and our own doings for salvation. Real Protestantism is, to be looking simply to Jesus for salvation . . . Now you will see my dear, how you and I, though we hate the Pope, may have plenty of self-popery.[51]

This passage is central to an understanding of the paradox of men like Edward Bickersteth who, possessing great personal and spiritual qualities, could, to the unsympathetic, appear thoroughly bigoted in their hostility to Rome. In their own minds, their shunning of 'Popery' was not negative but a positive quest for holiness. This 'dark' side of Victorian Evangelicals like Bickersteth, Shaftesbury, Stowell, and many others was the essential concomitant of their more attractive qualities. Anti-Catholicism provided them with a psychologically and theologically satisfying explanation for many of the tensions in their spiritual lives, and a central strand in their wider scheme of belief.[52]

The prolific writings of Charlotte Elizabeth were of seminal importance in translating this sense of 'Popery' as an insidious elemental force for evil from the spiritual into the social and political sphere. In her novel *The Rockite*, published in 1829, she offered her diagnosis and prescription for Ireland. Maurice, the hero, is a member of a Catholic agrarian secret society who progressively sees the error of his ways. After numerous adventures he is converted to Protestantism, but he is then captured by his former comrades and executed to the accompaniment of the ringing anathemas of a Catholic fanatic. The picture given has some subtlety: the author is aware of the tensions between priests and people in Ireland; she hints at the extent to which Protestant persecution has given force to Catholic resentment, and emphasizes the strength of sectarian loyalties, especially as she explores the struggles in Maurice's mind as he begins to turn from his former life. However, in the final analysis, all the complexities are related to her underlying sense of the deviousness and power of 'Popery'. She clearly feels that the social problems of the country are a consequence of Catholic influence rather than an independent root cause of unrest, and concludes with an exhortation to her readers to pour into the wounds of Ireland that vital healing balm, 'the oil and wine of Christian instruction'.[53]

[51] Birks, *Bickersteth*, ii. 89.
[52] Cf. Pinney, *Essays of George Eliot*, p. 162.
[53] *The Rockite: An Irish Story* (1829), see particularly pp. 27, 83, 162, 186–7, 252–5,

Arguments of a similar kind were advanced on numerous occasions in the pages of the *Record*, although here the emphasis was more on the general social and political backwardness associated with 'Popery' than on the specific issue of sectarian violence. In September 1828 an editorial argued that 'Popery' was in essence a system of slavery, debasing and enthralling its votaries in Austria, Italy, Spain, Portugal, and Ireland. The assumption that 'Romanism' was the same everywhere meant that radical Catholicism in Ireland was unquestioningly identified with conservative Catholicism in Europe. The destruction of the Roman Catholic religion was seen as essential for the progress of liberty and reform.[54] In its response to the announcement that Emancipation was to be granted, the *Record* explicitly linked the spiritual and temporal consequences of 'Popery':

Popery, as opposing itself to the nature, perfections and truth of the deity, must necessarily exclude all the positive principles of legislation from the bosoms of its votaries, and render them invariably hostile to every Protestant Government, in the degree to which it approaches the only mode of perfection—the Government of God himself . . . As a necessary consequence the human mind . . . under the baneful influence of Popery must be incapable of comprehending the nature, and appreciating the worth of liberty, civil, political or religious, invariably confounding it more or less with tyranny, with slavery and with licentiousness.

Ireland's social conditions were also attributable to her religion:

as long as Popery (necessarily to preserve its own existence) keeps the Irish peasantry in ignorance and idleness, in crime and wretchedness, the spirit of commercial enterprise and agricultural improvement cannot even breathe among them, while the best friends of their unhappy country will ever have presented to their view the most heart-rending of all spectacles, *a corrupt religion preying on the human body as well as on the human soul, and murdering at once the blessings of time and the bliss of eternity.*[55]

Attacks on the social consequences of Roman Catholicism were extensively developed during the two decades after 1829. In 1852 Blakeney published a synthesis of many of the arguments advanced under the title of *Popery in its Social Aspect*, exploring alleged Roman

286. Cf. J. S. Donnelly, 'Pastorini and Captain Rock: Millenarians and Sectarianism in the Rockite Movement of 1821–4', in S. Clark and J. S. Donnelly (eds.), *Irish Peasants, Violence and Political Unrest 1780–1914* (Manchester, 1983), 102–39.

[54] *R*, 23 Sept. 1828.
[55] *R*, 12 Feb. 1829.

hostility to 'peace, property, truth, morality and liberty'. He began by charging Rome with encouraging dissimulation, equivocation, and outright dishonesty and forgery; she was intolerant in principle, and engaged in vicious persecution whenever opportunity allowed. 'Popery' was opposed to the Bible and to knowledge. Most dangerous of all were the underground intrigues of the Jesuits against liberty and the Protestant Church and throne. Meanwhile, the confessional reinforced the power of the priest, disseminated sexual impurity, and generally undermined morality. The conventual system was unnatural and oppressive, and 'Popery' was wholly inimical to national greatness and independence.[56]

Three strands in the social polemic against Rome can be selected for more detailed comment. Catholicism was perceived as hostile to social progress, to personal morality, especially in sexual matters, and to political liberty. Firstly, there was the charge that it was a check on economic and social progress. Attention was drawn to the contrast between the backwardness of Ireland, despite its supposedly superior natural resources, and the prosperity of Scotland, and, within Ireland itself, to the difference between Protestant Ulster and the Catholic south. The *Record* was in no doubt that such distinctions had religious roots.[57] The point was made most frequently in relation to Ireland, but was readily applied to Britain. Commercial success was seen as inversely proportional to the extent to which Catholicism had a hold over the country.[58]

There was some ambiguity as to whether the baleful social consequences of 'Popery' stemmed from its generally spiritually and morally corrupting influence or whether they were to be attributed to the direct providential intervention of God.[59] The latter view was rarer, but surfaced on a number of occasions, especially at moments of particular crisis. William Dalton argued, in defending his own and Armstrong's controversial speeches at the meeting to discuss famine relief in Ireland in 1831: 'The failure of a potatoe crop has nothing to

[56] R. P. Blakeney, *Popery in its Social Aspect* (Edinburgh, 1852); Hope MSS 32/4/35, Blakeney to Hope, 12 Apr. 1851.
[57] *R*, 5 July 1832, 18 Feb. 1833.
[58] *R*, 14 May 1835.
[59] In this respect, as in others, anti-Catholicism cut across Boyd Hilton's division between moderate Evangelicals who believed in 'general' providence and 'extremists' with an interventionist conception of divine action (B. Hilton, 'The role of Providence in Evangelical Social Thought', in D. Beales and G. F. A. Best (eds.), *History, Society and the Churches* (Cambridge, 1985), 224–5).

do with absenteeism, or the want of poor laws; but in a Christian mind there is a close connection between this distress and the providence of God. The hand of God is stretched out in the way of solemn and appalling judgement, and the man who cannot see it must have read his Bible to little purpose.'[60] Such views surfaced again in response to the Great Famine in 1847, notably in a sermon by Hugh McNeile in which he asserted that 'plagues, pestilences, famines, wars, are national punishments for sin'. They were not arbitrary in their occurrence, but had a clear spiritual purpose of calling a sinning nation to repentance. McNeile gave a long list of sins, both religious and social, that had contributed to divine wrath, but most prominent among them was the encouragement of 'Romanism'.[61] His view that the famine was 'the Rod of God' did not stop him engaging in energetic activity to raise money to relieve the starving, but a rather more despairingly complacent attitude is evident in a hymn written for the Stockport Sunday School:

> Vainly men of every station
> Strove to save them from the rod
> But to save a stricken nation
> Mocks the power of all but God.[62]

In relating discussion of the social and economic aspects of anti-Catholicism to the wider development of Evangelical thought, it is helpful to bear in mind Boyd Hilton's distinction between 'moderate' Evangelicals, notably Thomas Chalmers, who were paternalists in morality but *laissez-faire* economists in material matters, and 'extremists', who believed moral improvement was the prerogative of God, but that paternalist intervention in the material conditions of human life was justified by analogy with the divine governance of the world by 'special' providences.[63] However, anti-Catholicism, although promoted more by the extremists than the moderates, can be seen as an example of moral paternalism, in that resistance to 'Popery' and the conversion of Roman Catholics were seen as central means to social improvement. The implication was that in Ireland and elsewhere economic panaceas were secondary, and *laissez-faire* attitudes could be

---

[60] *R*, 2 June 1831; see above, Chap. 2, pp. 57–8.
[61] H. McNeile, *The Famine the Rod of God* (1847), 16, 21–30.
[62] Ibid. Appendix; *Hymns Composed for the Use of . . . the Stockport Sunday School* (Manchester, 1848), 31, for the Annual Sermon, 17 Oct. 1847.
[63] Hilton, *Age of Atonement*, pp. 85–114.

endorsed.[64] Moreover, faced with the tragedy of the Irish famine, Chalmers himself was forced to acknowledge that a special providence had occurred in this case.[65] Study of anti-Catholicism thus suggests that Hilton's categories cannot be rigidly maintained and that the effect of the events of the 1840s was to produce a convergence between the two. A corollary of this is that anti-Catholicism became a key part of the ideological and theological system of both 'schools' of Evangelicalism in the late 1840s, a development further reinforced by reaction to Tractarianism among the moderates.

Secondly, from the mid-1830s onwards, the alleged sexual corruption of Rome attracted considerable attention. Concern was initially stirred by Dens's *Theologia*, which, like most Roman Catholic manuals of moral theology, contained sections on sexual sins and confessional practice with respect to them. The leader-writer of *The Times* perused these and found 'three pages of more systematic and disgusting obscenity than ever the Society for the Suppression of Vice had to deal with in their war against the filthy panders of this metropolis'.[66] The passage most strongly objected to was more analogous to a biology textbook than to a pornographic magazine. It was a discussion of sexual sins which could be committed within marriage, particularly *coitus interruptus*. It was suggested that if the confessor suspected that this was occurring, he should press for further details regarding the sexual behaviour of the couple.[67] Protestants do not appear to have been interested in contemporary Catholic debates over contraception, but they believed that inquisitions on these points would be a gross intrusion of privacy, and likely to be corrupting both for the confessor and the penitent. Similarly, it was feared that adolescents would have undesirable thoughts stirred by questioning regarding their emotions and impulses. Fears for sexual purity blended with concern that the authority of husbands and fathers should not be intruded upon by priests.[68] Anti-Catholics failed to appreciate that this learned discussion of fine points of moral theology, robed in the decency of ecclesiastical Latin, was not necessarily a reflection of regular confessional practice. The Protestant societies could only find very limited evidence of Catholics themselves feeling that they were

---

[64] Ibid. 213.
[65] Ibid. 108–14.
[66] *The Times*, 9 July 1835.
[67] P. Dens, *Theologia Moralis et Dogmatica* (Dublin, 1832), vii. 169.
[68] M. O'Sullivan and R. J. M'Ghee, *Romanism as it Rules in Ireland* (1840), i. 578.

subjected to undue inquisitions on intimate matters in the confession. In the absence of knowledge of the practice of English Catholic priests on this point, it is hard to be sure how far Protestant fears had any basis in fact, but contemporary French evidence suggests that, while there was concern about contraception, it was felt unwise to subject penitents to close inquisition on the matter.[69]

Choice extracts from Dens were published anonymously in Dublin in pamphlet form in 1836, with the Latin original set alongside a somewhat highly coloured English translation.[70] This pamphlet was republished on a number of occasions during the subsequent three decades, and in the 1860s acquired particular notoriety under the title of *The Confessional Unmasked*.[71] Another pamphlet of a similar character was compiled by the Tory MP Sir George Smyth and circulated by the Protestant Association in 1841 and 1842 as part of its anti-Maynooth campaign. Smyth gave an account of some of the teaching on sexual matters contained in textbooks used at the College, including definitions of homosexuality and of impotence that appeared particularly to shock him. Smyth was concerned that this material was being studied by celibates who ought to know nothing 'of the matters with which they are made so precociously conversant'. Christian self-denial required that they should put away such thoughts rather than risk temptation: the result of studying them would be either hypocrisy or an unnatural inurement to sexual sin.[72] Celibacy, however, was seen as having the further consequence that the priest would have no interests except in his Church, whose sinister power was thus further reinforced.[73]

The Newman–Achilli case in 1852 seemed to provide confirmatory evidence of the most lurid speculations about the evil consequences of clerical celibacy and the confessional. In his *Lectures* of 1851 Newman had attacked Giacinto Achilli, an Italian former priest who was now a

---

[69] French anti-clericals, however, similarly seized on the 'aliment impur et funeste' propagated by tracts on the subject. See J. Stengers, 'Les Pratiques anti-conceptionelles dans le mariage au XIXe et au XXe siècle: Problèmes humains et attitudes religieuses', *Revue belge de philologie et d'histoire*, 49 (1971), 403–81, esp. pp. 413, 451–2. I am indebted to Dr James McMillan for this reference.

[70] *Extracts from Peter Dens on the Nature of Confession and the Obligation of the Seal* (Dublin, 1836).

[71] W. L. Arnstein, *Protestant versus Catholic in Mid-Victorian England* (Columbia, Mo., 1982), 90.

[72] G. H. Smyth, *Maynooth College: Justification of the Term 'Beastly', as Applied to the Instruction Authorized at Maynooth College*, 2nd edn. (Colchester, 1845), 15–16, 22, 27–9.

[73] *R*, 10 May 1841.

professed Protestant touring Britain as a 'No Popery' lecturer. Newman alleged that Achilli had enjoyed a promiscuous career while in holy orders in Italy. When the case was heard in the Queen's Bench from 21 to 24 June 1852, a packed court-room was treated to a succession of women appearing on Newman's behalf to claim that they had been deflowered by Achilli. Some of their evidence appeared very convincing, but the Italian continued to protest his innocence, and the jury, which was clearly biased, found in his favour. Nevertheless, while there was not sufficient evidence to convince this particular court of law, the public as a whole was left in no doubt that Achilli was most profligate.[74] However, whatever the truth of the matter, the Roman Catholic Church was the loser: as one Protestant pamphleteer put it, she was 'either guilty of . . . wholesale subornation of perjury, or, on the other hand she is guilty of complicity in the foulest crimes and immoralities'.[75]

A further area of concern about the impact of Rome on sexuality focused on antagonism to the conventual system. This received a direct stimulus from the circulation in Britain of editions of *The Awful Disclosures of Maria Monk*, originally published in New York in 1836. This notorious book purported to be the memoirs of a renegade nun from the Hôtel Dieu in Montreal, and alleged that nuns regularly performed sexual services for priests. The resulting infants were routinely murdered and buried in a pit under the convent.[76] Despite devastatingly effective refutations of the charges, the book had a great impact in stirring anti-Catholicism in the United States.[77] In Britain, relatively speaking, its appeal was more limited: little direct allusion was made to Maria Monk in the 'respectable' Protestant literature surveyed in this chapter, and the allegations did not provoke any significant campaign against British toleration of Catholicism in Canada.

Maria Monk represented a cultural milieu which, in the area of sexuality, had some points of contact with evangelicalism but had a

[74] *Achilli v. Newman: A Full and Authentic Report of the Above Prosecution for Libel* (1852); W. F. Furlason, *Report on the Trial and Preliminary Proceedings in the case of the Queen on the Prosecution of G. Achilli v. Dr Newman* (1852); Lord Shaftesbury's diary, a source predisposed to the Protestant side, is the authority for the biased nature of the jury (Southampton University Library, Shaftesbury MSS, SHA/PD/6. Diary, 24, 26 June 1852.)

[75] P. D. Hardy, *Achilli v. Newman: An Action for Libel* (Dublin, 1852), 112.

[76] *The Awful Disclosures of Maria Monk* (1836, 1851); Catholic Institute of Great Britain, *Interim Report* (1843), 4.

[77] W. L. Stone, *Maria Monk and the Nunnery of the Hôtel Dieu* (New York, 1836).

fundamentally different focus, owing more to pornography and a popular fascination with mystery and violent crime than to religion.[78] The Protestant societies were relatively slow to develop a specific polemic against convents, and in this context the issue did not become prominent until the 1850s. Even then, although the possibility of systematic hypocrisy and illicit sexual activity was hinted at, the case was couched more in terms of the 'unnaturalness' of perpetual celibacy and the repressive nature of conventual vows, both in relation to physical liberty and emotional expression.[79] Conventionally, such attitudes are interpreted as representing the hostility of the Victorian paterfamilias to a rival patriarchalism.[80] It could conversely be argued that this viewpoint, which received active support from women themselves,[81] contained an embryonic feminism in the perceived resistance to sexual oppression in the form of priestly seduction and authoritarianism.

There was clearly a tension in anti-Catholicism between the view that 'Popery' was a spiritually corrupting influence pandering to the sinful desires of the 'natural' man, and the criticism of celibacy and Catholic 'virtuoso religion' as unnatural. In part, especially at a popular level, it undoubtedly reflected a preconceived mental framework which meant that the highest professions of purity by Catholics were regarded simply as confirmation of the depths of their hypocrisy. For evangelicals, however, there was a genuine clash in attitudes towards spirituality: the Protestant view of an ideal of marital fidelity against a Catholic exaltation of celibacy, or, to put it in broader terms, of holiness expressed as a distinctive way of life lived in the world rather than by withdrawal from it. Hence there was an ambivalence towards making explicit sexual allegations against Rome for fear that the circulation of such material might make the proper control of sexuality more difficult. There was anxiety that such material might fall into the 'wrong' hands, while in February 1856 a bachelor was upbraided for promoting a meeting on these lines in Edinburgh: 'You send home to

[78] Cf. S. Marcus, *The Other Victorians* (1966). I am also indebted to Ms Karen Haltunnen for this observation.

[79] *PM*, 14 (1852), 224–9; 15 (1853), 210, 330. There was an echo here of Puritan views on sexuality: cf. K. M. Davies, 'Continuity and Change in Literary Advice on Marriage', in R. B. Outhwaite (ed.), *Marriage and Society: Studies in the Social History of Marriage* (1981), 73–4.

[80] G. F. A. Best, 'Popular Protestantism in Victorian Britain', in R. Robson (ed.), *Ideas and Institutions of Victorian Britain* (1967), 135–6.

[81] *Bulwark*, 2 (1852–3), 269, 284–5.

their beds men filled with profanity fit for a Brothel and your position (unmarried) in the Chair . . . is a very doubtful one.'[82]

The third key strand in criticism of Roman Catholicism was the charge that it was antipathetic to 'liberty', conceptualized in broadly Whiggish terms, as mediated by Burke, as a balance between arbitrary government and anarchy.[83] This framework made it possible to identify the anarchic tendencies of Irish Catholicism with continental absolutism, as part of an integrated antithesis to true liberty. Between 1830 and 1848, however, with Catholic absolutism in Europe apparently in relative eclipse, especially in France, it was the Irish side of the equation which dominated Protestant consciousness in Britain.[84] Once again Dens's *Theologia*, which synthesized a good deal of militantly Tridentine material, was used as a central-proof text, providing apparent substantiation for the following propositions:

1. That Protestants of all denominations are accounted heretics by the Church of Rome, and worse than Jews and Pagans.
2. That all are by baptism placed under the power and domination of the Church of Rome.
3. It is the duty of the Roman Catholic Church to exterminate the rites of our religion.
4. That it is the duty of the Roman Catholic Church to compel heretics, by corporal punishment to submit to the faith.
5. That the punishments which the Church of Rome decrees against heretics are confiscation of property, exile, imprisonment and death.[85]

It was true that in 1826 the Irish Roman Catholic bishops had denied on oath that they held such doctrines, but Dens himself argued that the Church could give dispensations from the obligations arising from oaths.[86] Violence against Protestants in Ireland was recounted at great length and associated with the persecuting principles contained in Dens. Perjury and murder, it was claimed, were the natural outcome of

---

[82] Hope MSS 226/9, p. 408, Hope to Blakeney, 29 Mar. 1851; 39/2/168, W. B. Turnbull to Hope, 25 Feb. 1856. Cf. ibid. 33/5/16, Blakeney to Hope, 22 May 1852. Cf. M. Hill, *The Religious Order* (1973).

[83] Cf. R. Eccleshall, *British Liberalism* (New York, 1986), 13; E. Burke, *Reflections on the Revolution in France*, ed. C. C. O'Brien (1969), 118–20.

[84] This represents a revealing contrast with anti-Catholicism in the United States, which was shaped much more by antagonism to European absolutism. Cf. S. F. B. Morse, *Foreign Conspiracy against the Liberties of the United States* (New York, 1835).

[85] Quoted from O'Sullivan and M'Ghee, *Romanism*, i. 16–21.

[86] Ibid. 110; ii. 79–80.

Roman Catholic belief, and, if this gained a hold in Britain, the country would become a corrupt, violent, and backward society.[87]

Archbishop Murray admitted that Dens was used by the Irish clergy, but pointed out that this did not necessarily mean that they adhered to his opinions, maintaining that Dens's doctrines were the product of a bygone age in which religious persecution was general. Protestants represented this as a further instance of 'Romish' dissimulation, and argued that a Church claiming infallibility could not thus repudiate published statements. There was a genuine gulf in perceptions here, reflecting the unwillingness of most Protestants to see theological statements in their historical context.[88] Moreover, in the mid-1830s the charges against Dens appeared consistent with the prevalence of sectarian violence in Ireland. Catholic priests, although generally loyal to the British State, were becoming sufficiently politicized to provide evidence to substantiate claims that the Catholic Church was the real instigator of unrest in Ireland.[89]

The Protestant Association placed the attack on the perceived subversive political influence of Rome in the context of a revivified Protestant constitutionalism. The British State, it was contended, was unlike any other in human history, except Old Testament Israel, in that the objective of legislation was not simply utilitarian but also the statement of the divine law expressing the duty which individuals and the State owed to God. Those who asserted that the State was neutral in religion were promoting a spurious liberalism alien to the British tradition, giving dangerous openings to 'Popery' and, at worst, itself tending to 'Infidelity'. Protestants were deluded when they subscribed to such a doctrine. It was a religious and patriotic duty for the Christian to be involved in politics in order to give testimony to the true nature of the connection between God and the State, and also to protect the State from the danger of collapse that would come from the inherent contradiction of legislation based on fundamentally opposed principles.[90] Moreover, for those who believed in God's current activity in judging nations, there was the pressing concern that this compromise of essentials would lead to imminent and direct divine punishment.[91] Such arguments gained the support of clergy such as

---

[87] O'Sullivan and M'Ghee, *Romanism*, i. 55–73.
[88] Ibid. 84–5.
[89] S. J. Connolly, *Priests and People in Pre-Famine Ireland* (Dublin, 1982), 219 ff.
[90] PAss, *Statement of Views and Objects*, p. 4.
[91] G. Croly, *England the Fortress of Christianity* (1839).

Hugh Stowell and Hugh McNeile, who felt that they represented a compelling case for political involvement by Churchmen. In May 1841 McNeile declared his belief that 'no man can be a Protestant who is not a politician'.[92] Conversely, for an Ultra-Tory like Newcastle, such considerations gave a religious significance and intensity to political events. Commenting on the bill to legalize diplomatic relations with Rome in 1848, he observed that it rendered the nation culpable in the sight of God, and 'must bring a curse upon us'.[93]

The Protestant Association's position was less reactionary than the Ultra-Tory one, in that it did not rest the defence of the 'Protestant' character of the State on the circular argument that the status quo, which was *ipso facto* divinely sanctioned, was fundamentally anti-Catholic. In 1829 this approach had lost whatever intellectual coherence it might hitherto have possessed. Instead, the Protestant Association's reference was to a dynamic Protestant principle, rooted in evangelical theology rather than political theory. It was not compromised by individual pieces of legislation and did not imply resistance to all change. It made it possible to argue, with theoretical consistency, that Emancipation should be repealed as a temporary aberration and that the Maynooth grant, although long-established, should also be ended because it, too, was inconsistent with the true spirit of the constitution.

Confirmatory evidence that the anti-Catholic movement's ideology comprised elements of a Whiggish concern for controlled liberty and reform is provided by its capacity to attract the loyalty of Whigs such as Plumptre, Sinclair, and Johnston and even the Radical Colquhoun. A link with the liberal wing of Toryism was also evident in the later 1840s, when A. G. Stapleton, formerly private secretary to George Canning, became an active member of the National Club and argued publicly that the very convictions that had led Canning to advocate Emancipation in the 1820s now provided grounds to resist further concession. Stapleton saw no incompatibility in advocating parliamentary reform at the same time as anti-Catholicism.[94]

The view of Rome as authoritarian in its aspirations and anarchic in its methods was influential not only because it drew on traditional

[92] *PM*, 2 (1840), 186; 3 (1841), 188.

[93] Newcastle Diary, Ne2F8, 8 Feb. 1848.

[94] *A Report of the Speeches Delivered at the Dinner of the Members and Friends of the National Club, Held in the Club House, Old Palace Yard, May 12 1847* (1847); A. G. Stapleton, *Suggestions for a Conservative and Popular Reform in the Commons House of Parliament* (1850).

political motifs, but also because, to a hostile eye, it continued to be vindicated by events. This was the case especially in the later 1840s, when some priests were clearly implicated in Irish agrarian violence, and the Earl of Arundel incautiously declared in a Commons debate on a Catholic Relief measure that 'My hon Friend [Inglis] . . . says that the Church of Rome is antagonistic to Protestantism. I quite agree with him; it is antagonistic and will be while the world lasts, until Protestantism is extinguished.'[95] This statement by a leading English Catholic was linked by Arundel's critics to the activities of his co-religionists in Ireland, who were murdering Protestants. Arundel himself published a pamphlet aiming to demonstrate that spiritual allegiance to the pope was not incompatile with 'perfect loyalty' to the queen:[96] but this was followed by the National Club publication of the papal Bull 'In Coena Domini', which, it was claimed, authorized the anathematization of heretics and was a root cause of the troubles in Ireland.[97]

Aristocratic English Catholics like the Earls of Arundel and Shrewsbury, aware of the adverse reactions of Protestants in Britain, did their utmost to restrain Archbishop MacHale, the *Tablet*, and the more extreme and political wing of Catholicism. Arundel thought that the present conduct of the Irish priests was indefensible, and believed that 'The fierce declamations of Exeter Hall and all the vehemence of Parliamentary opponents and all the freedom of Protestant assertion have not done so much injury to the cause of the Catholic faith in this country as these unhappy circumstances.'[98] Shrewsbury regarded the *Tablet* as 'that vilest of vile papers', and feared that the English Catholics were in danger of appearing before the public 'only as a turbulent emanation from Conciliation Hall'.[99]

Shrewsbury entered into correspondence with George Biber, who had edited 'In Coena Domini' for the National Club, arguing that disorder in Ireland had far more to do with poor distribution of resources than with an obsolescent papal document.[100] Arundel, in an

[95] 3 *Hansard*, xci. 764, 14 Apr. 1847.

[96] Earl of Arundel and Surrey, *A Few Remarks on the Social and Political Condition of English Catholics* (1847), 9.

[97] *The Bull 'In Coena Domini'* (1848).

[98] Arundel Castle, Sussex, Norfolk MSS, correspondence of 14th duke, Arundel to unnamed archbishop (MacHale?), 26 Nov. 1847.

[99] Norfolk MSS, MD 2062, Shrewsbury to Arundel, 25 Jan. 1848.

[100] Ibid. Shrewsbury to the writer of the pamphlet on the Bull, 31 Jan. 1848; editor of Bull to Shrewsbury, 5 Feb. 1848; Shrewsbury to Arundel, n.d. (Feb. 1848). On Biber, see below, Chap. 6, p. 215.

open letter to Plumptre, pointed out that publication of the Bull had in fact ceased in 1773.[101] In response to such pressure, Biber was willing to pay a backhanded compliment to the Roman Catholic laity, while indicating that his view of the tendency of official Catholic publications was as entrenched as ever: 'there are . . . many men incapable of reducing to practice the principles of disloyalty and duplicity inherent . . . in the Papal system'.[102]

This conviction that antagonism to Rome, far from being intolerant, asserted true liberty against a persecuting and devious power, was central to the outcry against the establishment of the Catholic hierarchy in 1850 and 1851. The point was made in refreshingly light-hearted fashion by John MacGregor,[103] the honorary secretary of the newly formed Protestant Alliance, in 1852 in a pamphlet entitled 'Popery in 1900'. MacGregor visualized a nightmarish future in which a system of 1,134 district courts of inquisition had been set up, English had been superseded by Anglo-Latin, MPs had been replaced by mechanical talking-machines, and *Punch* had been suppressed at the instigation of the Speaker's private confessor.[104] Such fears need to be placed in the context of a general suspicion of absolutist Catholic powers in Europe, which acquired renewed force in the aftermath of the 1848 Revolutions. During the 1850s this became centred in support for the Italian struggle for liberty against Austrian and papal oppression. In 1853 Lord Roden wrote of the need to maintain 'the principles of true liberty threatened by the tyranny of the Roman Catholick Church in the several R. Catholick Countries in Europe'.[105]

Anti-Catholics felt that they were confronting a system with enormous potentiality for evil in spiritual, social, and political matters which was fundamentally inimical to British society and its embodiment in constitutional and political life. There is a significant parallel

[101] Earl of Arundel and Surrey, *A Letter to J. P. Plumptre, Esq., MP on the Bull 'In Coena Domini'* (1848).

[102] *A Letter to the Earl of Arundel and Surrey on the Bull 'In Coena Domini'* (1848), 3–4.

[103] John ('Rob Roy') MacGregor (1825–92) was an archetypal 'muscular Christian'. A barrister by profession, he travelled widely and was involved in a number of philanthropic activities. A small collection of his papers survive in the Greater London Record Office (*DNB*, xxxv. 97; E. Hodder, *John MacGregor ('Rob Roy')* (1894)).

[104] J. M., *Popery in 1900* (1852).

[105] Greater London Record Office, MacGregor MSS, F/MM/76, Roden to MacGregor, 24 Jan. 1853; J. R. Wolffe, 'Protestant Societies and Anti-Catholic Agitation in Great Britain, 1829–1860', D.Phil. thesis (Oxford, 1984), 340–1; C. T. McIntire, *England against the Papacy 1858–1861* (Cambridge, 1983), 1–12; B. Hall, 'Alessandro Gavazzi: A Barnebite Friar and the Risorgimento', *Studies in Church History*, 12 (1975), 342 ff.

to be drawn with anti-slavery ideology, which similarly bridged the spiritual, theological, and political. Both movements had their roots in a common evangelical consciousness: and it comes as no surprise to find personal links between them.[106] In the late 1830s Hugh McNeile became a passionate opponent of slavery as well as of 'Popery', explicitly linking the two together.[107] Such connections, though, were more often ones of general sympathy than of substantial dual involvement: the membership of the British and Foreign Anti-Slavery Society, founded in 1839, did not include any prominent anti-Catholics.[108] To a considerable extent this may simply reflect the pressures on the time of individuals who could not actively involve themselves in more than one cause: indeed, the very parallels between anti-slavery and anti-Catholicism probably made them appear substitutes for each other. In 1838, however, McNeile hinted that anti-slavery Dissenters were sympathetic to the cause of Irish Catholicism, while anti-papal Anglicans were associated with the West Indian interest. He maintained that the consistent Christian should oppose both slavery and Rome.[109] Nevertheless, it was only in the broader context later provided by the Evangelical Alliance that anti-slavery became institutionally associated with anti-Catholicism.

The failure to build a strong link with anti-slavery was a symptom of a wider incapacity to develop a coherent ideology which might have brought the diverse strands in the anti-Catholic movement together. In practice there was continual fragmentation as particular organizations and individuals stressed their own reasons for opposing 'Popery'. In the remainder of this chapter specific sources of division will be explored, particularly the distinction between 'political' and 'religious' Protestantism, closely related to the fundamental problem of the position of the Established Churches: were they a bulwark of the Reformation or a means by which Rome could gain insidiously in influence?

Throughout this period the Reformation Society continued to struggle to dissociate itself from political movements. In November 1835, at the height of the M'Ghee and O'Sullivan agitation, the Revd Robert Shanks, its missionary in Scotland, was firmly instructed 'on no

---

[106] Cf. E. F. Hurwitz, *Politics and the Public Conscience* (1973), 33–47.

[107] H. McNeile, *Anti-Slavery and Anti-Popery: A Letter Addressed to Edward Cropper, Esq. and Thomas Berry Horsfall, Esq.*, 2nd edn. (1838); *Slave Labor versus Free Labor Sugar* (1848). Cf. above, Chap. 3 n. 19.

[108] British and Foreign Anti-Slavery Society, *First Annual Report* (1840), 3.

[109] McNeile, *Anti-Slavery and Anti-Popery*, pp. 17–21.

account to mix up his labours with those of any associations having a political aspect or character'.[110] During the 'Papal Aggression' crisis of 1850–1 the Society was careful not to publish tracts of a 'political' tendency.[111] In April 1858 Bishop Bickersteth, while acknowledging that there were strong political and social grounds for denouncing Rome, felt that it would be 'unbecoming' to discuss them when preaching on behalf of the Reformation Society.[112]

Two main arguments were adduced in favour of this position. Firstly, politics was seen as an inferior calling, a distraction into issues of a transient nature away from the primary concern of saving souls from error. In 1840 Cumming, having recounted his opposition to Catholic Relief in 1829, went on to declare that 'now he would rather bring one soul to Christ than deprive St Stephen's of all its Papal partisans, or even repeal the Catholic Emancipation Act'.[113] Secondly, it was felt that there was wrong on both sides in political matters, and that any clear stance on a political issue, let alone consistent support for a political party, would alienate some of 'God's people'.[114]

The maintenance of the purity of 'religious' anti-Catholicism was difficult in practice. The Reformation Society itself could not resist the temptation to pronounce on political issues at times of crisis, notably in 1845, when its magazine the *British Protestant* devoted much space to criticizing Peel's policy over Maynooth.[115] The distinction was sometimes blurred at a local level, as in Bristol and Hertford, where the local societies supported both the Reformation Society and the Protestant Association. In the latter case, this was with the active support of Edward Bickersteth.[116] This confusion reflected the root problem stated by a speaker at the Reformation Society's annual meeting in 1835, who argued that 'Popery' was a politico-religious system and that it was impossible to touch one side without the other. Others were less candid about their presuppositions, but most involved in the anti-Catholic movement would tacitly have agreed, a view implicit in Blakeney's *Popery in its Social Aspect*.[117] Thus, rigid distinctions between the 'religious' and 'political' dimensions of the struggle were apt to seem strained and artificial.

[110] RS minutes, 4 Nov. 1835.
[111] Ibid. 6 Jan. 1851.
[112] *BP*, 14 (1858), 155.
[113] *Protestant Journal*, 6 (1836), 192–3; *R*, 25 May 1840.
[114] RS, *12th AR* (1839), 26; *R*, 6 May 1839, 7 May 1845.
[115] *BP*, 1 (1845), *passim*.
[116] RS minutes, 8 June 1840; Birks, *Memoir of E. Bickersteth*, ii. 136, 377–9.
[117] *R*, 14 May 1835; Blakeney, *Popery in its Social Aspect*, p. iii.

The major practical reason for making these distinctions lay in the effort to attract a degree of Nonconformist support, an endeavour that achieved only very limited success. The political stance adopted by the Protestant Association was inevitably thoroughly distasteful to the majority of Dissenters: within the organization, even relative moderates linked professions of limited toleration with pledges of unshakeable loyalty to the Church of England. The Marquis of Westmeath came to the conclusion that O'Sullivan's speeches had an adverse effect on English Dissenters, who would sympathize with Catholics when they heard them being abused. At Sheffield in 1840 the deacons of an Independent chapel forced the minister to resign after he had joined the Protestant Association.[118]

The *Eclectic Review*, a mouthpiece of radical Dissent, admitted that the growth of the Roman Catholic Church in England was a legitimate cause for concern, but felt that the Protestant Association's fears were exaggerated. The 'No Popery' cry was associated with 'disgusting hypocrisy' because it was in reality linked with the defence of the Established Church, the interest of the Tory party, and the suppression of 'the things that are equal'. The religious zeal of the promoters of the Association was genuine, but founded on dangerous self-deception. A defence against Rome that took its stand upon the Established Church was fatally flawed because the Church of England was itself 'Popish' in tendency, and, as long as its link with the State survived, Rome would seek to gain control of this for herself. Disestablishment would therefore be the heaviest blow that could be struck against 'Romanism'. The development of Tractarianism gave additional force to this argument, and by 1844 the *Eclectic* was predicting the gradual melting-away of Evangelicalism within the Church of England and the complete passing of the cause of the Gospel to the Dissenters. 'Popery' must be resisted not by societies but through the better education of ministers in controversy with Rome, the quest for unity among Protestants, and outreach to the unchurched masses.[119] A similar attitude was evident in the pages of the *Baptist Magazine*, which lacked interest in active anti-Catholicism, directing occasional Protestant darts more against Oxford than against Rome. It noted with satisfaction that exhibitions of 'Church of England Popery'

---

[118] *PPO*, 3 (1842), 25–6; Public Record Office of Northern Ireland, Belfast, Roden MSS, MIC 147/6, xiii. 467–8, Westmeath to Roden, 18 Jan. 1837; *PM*, 2 (1840), 128.

[119] *Eclectic Review*, 3rd series, 15 (1836), 29; 4th series, 6 (1839), 241–61; 9 (1841), 608–24; 10 (1841), 609–22; 15 (1844), 448–59.

showed the senselessness of Anglican attempts to link Dissenters with
Roman Catholics. Vigilance against Roman Catholicism was required,
but this should be achieved through a positive concern for Protestant
truth and spirituality. There should be union among those agreed on
fundamental truths, although, under present circumstances, separate
organizations were a regrettable necessity.[120]

From the early 1840s the development of the campaign for
disestablishment led to views even more hostile to the Anglican
position being expressed in the pages of the *Nonconformist*, which took
as its motto, 'The dissidence of dissent and the protestantism of the
protestant religion'. It was argued that the root cause of religious
corruption was not 'Popery' but the continuation of the link between
Church and State, and hence the Irish Catholic Church, however
distasteful some of its beliefs and activities might be, was more victim
than villain.[121] For its part, the *Protestant Magazine* was professing
friendliness towards Dissenters and complaining that, with only a few
exceptions 'we have met none who will even fairly consider our proofs
or candidly construe our motives'. This attitude, it was alleged, was
greatly contributing to the growth of 'Popery' and 'Infidelity', and,
Stowell maintained, Dissenters should mourn rather than triumph at
the divisions in the Church of England. In 1843 the *Protestant
Magazine* strongly denounced a meeting of Dissenters at which the
Established Church had been attacked, and maintained that such
attitudes, although linked with professions of attachment to the
Reformation, in reality showed a complete absence of Protestant
feeling.[122] Thus both Anglicans and Dissenters blended their own
characteristic views with the attack on 'Popery'. To Dissenters,
especially after the Romeward trend at Oxford became evident,
religious Establishments were an agency of Rome just as surely as to
Anglicans Voluntaryism was seen as a Jesuit plot. Hence the very depth
and pervasiveness of anti-Catholic feeling carried the seeds of its own
division and weakness.

However, there were some instances in which Dissenters allowed
their fear of Rome to overcome their hatred of the Establishment. The
Revd Joseph Irons, an Independent minister, was among the speakers
at the Protestant Association's meeting in May 1836, and fourteen
Dissenting ministers in the Hereford area were willing to be involved

[120] *Baptist Magazine*, 31 (1839), 432; 33 (1841), 226; 36 (1844), 449–54 and *passim*.
[121] *Nonconformist*, 7, 28 May 1845.
[122] *PM*, 1 (1839), 188–90; 3 (1841), 118; 4 (1842), 196–7; 5 (1843), 225.

in the early activities of the local association.[123] The Wesleyans in particular were more friendly towards the Protestant Association than were the older Dissenting denominations. Wesleyans disavowed having any sentiments unfriendly to the Established Church, seeing it, on the contrary, as an essential bulwark and ally against 'Popery'.[124] They were driven further into the arms of the Protestant Association by their opposition to Russell's education proposals in 1839 and by an attack on them from O'Connell, who alleged that the Methodists had little sympathy for religious liberty and that John Wesley had been a major instigator of the Gordon Riots. This allegation was refuted with more indignation than cogency, and interpreted as evidence of the 'diabolically malignant' character of 'Popery'.[125] However, even among the Wesleyans, support for the Protestant Association was not unqualified. Although they were united in their opposition to Rome, there was internal disagreement about how far this should be linked with support for the Establishment, especially as their concern over Tractarianism grew during the early 1840s. In 1843, against the background of the dispute over Graham's factory education proposals, the *Wesleyan Methodist Magazine* attacked Stowell for making remarks of a 'painfully exclusive' character, appearing to meet the claims of the Church of Rome by similarly extravagant assertions on behalf of the Church of England. The participation of Charles Prest, a leading member of the younger generation of ministers, in the Protestant Association's annual meeting in 1844 should thus be interpreted as an attempt to patch up a quarrel. He was at pains to assure the Association of official Wesleyan support in spite of attacks on it by a vociferous minority.[126]

A similar Anglican dominance was evident in the Reformation Society. Dissenters participated in meetings at Louth and Ramsgate in 1835, but such involvement was increasingly unusual.[127] The committee continued to be almost exclusively Anglican, and in 1838 a proposal that half its members should be Dissenters was rejected.[128]

[123] O'Sullivan and M'Ghee, *Romanism*, ii. 484; *R*, 16 May 1836.

[124] *PM*, 6 (1844), 189 ff.; D. N. Hempton, *Methodism and Politics in British Society 1750–1850* (1984), 183–6.

[125] D. O'Connell, *Letter to the Ministers and Office Bearers of the Wesleyan Methodist Societies in Manchester* (1839), 39–40, 45, 46 ff.; *Wesleyan Methodist Magazine*, 63 (1840), 151–4, 321; Hempton, *Methodism and Politics*, pp. 158–64.

[126] *Wesleyan Methodist Magazine*, 66 (1843), 602; *PM*, 6 (1844), 195; Hempton, *Methodism and Politics*, pp. 164–74.

[127] *Protestant Journal*, 5 (1835), 448–9, 642.

[128] *R*, 10 May 1838.

In 1841 there was even an attempt formally to limit participation in the government of the Society to Churchmen.[129] The involvement of John Cumming, technically a Dissenter when on English soil, was used by High-Churchmen to charge that there was in reality only a lukewarm adherence to Church principles, but Cumming himself denied that he was a Dissenter, stressed the Establishment principle, and argued that both the Church of England and the Church of Scotland were the finest developments of Reformation principles. This linking of the Scottish and English Churches in a common anti-Catholicism and defence of Establishment was to be a distinctive feature of the Reformation Society's stance in the 1850s.[130]

Given the impossibility of devising a coherent, comprehensive anti-Catholic political ideology, religion detached from explicit political programmes seemed to provide the most promising basis for Protestant co-operation. This perception lay behind the development of the Evangelical Alliance in the mid-1840s, generally seen as evidence that shared anti-Catholicism was able to lead to a significant suspension of conflict over the Establishment. During the 1830s direct efforts towards evangelical union, as opposed to somewhat uneasy co-operation, had appeared isolated and superficial.[131] The impetus for the initial Evangelical Alliance meeting of October 1845 can be traced back to an address by the prominent Birmingham Independent minister, John Angell James, to the Congregational Union in May 1842, in which he called for extensive union as a defence against 'Infidelity, Popery, Puseyism and Plymouth Brethrenism'.[132] A meeting for Christian Union was held in London on 2 January 1843, attracting Baptists, Independents, Moravians, Presbyterians, and Wesleyans. No Anglicans participated at this stage, and, although a few, notably Baptist Noel, became involved later in the year, the movement was dominated by Dissent.[133]

The Disruption of the Church of Scotland in May 1843 had a substantial but complex impact on both the anti-Catholic and pan-evangelical movements. The effective and dramatic settlement of the non-intrusion controversy which had dominated Scottish religious and

---

[129] RS minutes, 21 Dec. 1841.

[130] *R*, 11 May 1837, 23 Apr. 1849; see below, Chap. 7, pp. 255–8.

[131] J. R. Wolffe, 'The Evangelical Alliance in the 1840s', *Studies in Church History*, 23 (1986), 334–5. This article gives a more detailed account of the events summarized here.

[132] R. W. Dale, *The Life and Letters of John Angell James*, 2nd edn. (1861), 397–8.

[133] *Congregational Magazine*, New series, 7 (1843), 140–52, 376–8, 542–4.

political life for the previous decade meant that there was now
sufficient energy for other matters to be taken up north of the Border,
while inevitably these issues would, in the aftermath of the Disruption,
be coloured by recent events. The manner in which denominational
suspicions hampered anti-Catholic organization was evident in the
experience of John Hope, an Edinburgh solicitor who began a long
involvement with anti-Catholicism by attempting to set up a local
Protestant society in the autumn of 1845 to sustain the enthusiasm
stirred by resistance to the Maynooth Bill. Hope, a member of the
Established Church himself, was able to gain the support of some of
the Church of Scotland ministers in the city, but then found that most
Free Church clergy refused to be associated in a joint movement with
the Kirk.[134] This was in spite of the vigorously anti-Catholic tone of
the Free Church newspaper, the *Witness*.[135] Dissenters, too, were
lukewarm about Hope's plans. W. L. Alexander, a Congregationalist,
was uneasy about forging links with the Reformation Society which
might prove inconsistent with Nonconformist conviction.[136] The
Episcopalians held aloof, apart from D. T. K. Drummond of St
Thomas's, who was in schism with the Scottish Episcopal Church, and
he withdrew when he heard of Hope's contact with Alexander, who
possessed, Drummond thought, 'a zeal which tended *to* popery and not
from it'. Meanwhile, James Manson, a Free Church minister, was wary
about contact with the Episcopal Church, believing that it differed
little from 'Popery'.[137]

On the other hand, among Free Churchmen and Voluntaries on
both sides of the Border the Disruption aroused expectations of a
similar anti-Erastian movement in England serving as a catalyst for
wider Christian union. These hopes were articulated in a meeting at

---

[134] Hope MSS 226/4, pp. 455–62, Hope to Hill, 25 Nov. 1845; p. 494, Hope to
Blakeney, 2 Dec. 1845; 28/12–15, *passim*, replies of Edinburgh ministers to Hope,
1845–6. On Hope, whose copious surviving papers have been an important source for
this book, see D. Jamie, *John Hope* (Edinburgh, 1900).

[135] *Witness*, 5, 16 Apr. 1845, and *passim*.

[136] Hope MSS 28/11/12, Alexander to Hope, 25 Nov. 1845; *New Edinburgh Almanac*
(Edinburgh, 1845), 403.

[137] Hope MSS 28/12/60, Bishop Terrot to Hope, 16 Dec. 1845; 28/14/73,
Drummond to Hope, 4 Feb. 1846; 28/14/83–4, Manson to Hope, 3 Feb. 1846; *New
Edinburgh Almanac*, p. 407. It appears that Manson and others excepted Drummond
from their general condemnation of Episcopalians. On Drummond and his differences
with the Scottish Episcopal Church, see R. Foskett, 'The Drummond Controversy,
1842', *Records of the Scottish Church History Society*, 16 (1968), 99–109; A. L. Drummond
and J. Bulloch, *The Church in Victorian Scotland, 1843–1874* (Edinburgh, 1975), 58–9;
Birks, *Memoir of E. Bickersteth*, ii. 255–73.

Edinburgh in July to commemorate the bicentenary of the West-minster Confession and in a series of essays on Christian union that appeared in 1845.[138] This impulse was also evident in the secession of the militant Voluntaryists from the Anti-Maynooth Conference at the Crown and Anchor Tavern at the end of April 1845 in order to hold their own conference at Crosby Hall.

The Anti-Maynooth Committee had been called upon to set up a Protestant confederation, but felt that an initiative from them would have an unduly political character. Thus the invitation to the October conference was issued not by them but by a group of Scottish Free Churchmen and Dissenters, probably at the instigation of John Angell James. In the light of recent events and utterances, an initiative from such quarters was hardly likely to reassure wavering Anglicans, especially as the invitation alluded-to the 'encroachments of Puseyism' as well as those of 'Popery'.[139] Edward Bickersteth, however, was won over. He had himself been advocating Christian union in a series of letters to the *Record*, and in a letter to Sir Culling Eardley Smith, the chairman of the Anti-Maynooth Committee, he maintained that unity should be wholeheartedly pursued:

We are agreed on the great essential elements of Divine truth . . . We are agreed also on the soul destructive character of Popery—and in cordial love to all Papists and earnest desire for their salvation . . . Let us then *lay aside all political feelings* for this end . . . Let us for the same end *subordinate all ecclesiastical preferences* of particular forms of Church Government and State connection . . . [149]

Nevertheless, he agonized for a month before replying to the Scottish invitation, considered specifically requiring as a pre-condition that Dissenters should suspend the Church and State controversy, and only in 'fear and trembling' agreed to go to the meeting.[141]

Bickersteth's judgement appeared to be vindicated in October 1845, when a conference of 216 clergy and laymen from seventeen different

[138] W. Hanna, *Memoirs of the Life and Writings of Thomas Chalmers, DD*, 4 vols. (Edinburgh, 1849–52), iv. 378–9; *Congregational Magazine*, New series, 7 (1843), 617–19; *Essays on Christian Union* (1845).
[139] J. W. Massie, *The Evangelical Alliance: Its Origins and Development* (1847), 109; Dale, *John Angell James*, p. 412; A. S. Thelwall, *Proceedings of the Anti-Maynooth Conference* (1845), pp. clxxxvi–clxxxvii; *Conference on Christian Union—Narrative of the Proceedings of the Meeting held in Liverpool, October 1845* (1845), 59.
[140] Bod. Lib., Bickersteth MSS, Box 25, Bickersteth to Eardley, 23 June 1845.
[141] Birks, *Memoir of E. Bickersteth*, ii. 303–8; C. E. Eardley, *A Brief Notice of the Life of the Rev. Edward Bickersteth* (1850), 13.

denominations from all parts of the United Kingdom met in Liverpool. This was followed in the summer of 1846 by a conference in London that attracted evangelicals from Europe and North America and marked the formal inauguration of the Evangelical Alliance as an international organization, although it was immediately seriously divided by the slavery issue.[142] From the outset there were other signs of tension. Militant Voluntaryists had little time for the Evangelical Alliance. The *Eclectic*, whose editor Thomas Price had been among those convening the Crosby Hall meeting, considered that the admission of Churchmen degraded the whole initiative to the level of a farce.[143] Many Anglican Evangelicals, for the converse reason, remained equally suspicious, struck particularly by the almost complete absence of the Church of Scotland from the movement.[144] Participation by the other Established Churches was strikingly small, with the majority of participants coming from moderate Nonconformity. Table 2 provides a breakdown of the attendance.

TABLE 2. *Attenders at the Christian Union conference, 1845*

Church of England	15	Free Church of Scotland	14
Church of Ireland	4	United Secession	17
Church of Scotland	2	Reformed Presbyterian	11
		Original Secession	3
Congregationalist	54	Relief Synod	3
Wesleyan	40	Irish Presbyterian	6
Methodist New Connexion	5	Associate Synod of Ulster	1
Calvinistic Methodist	5		
English Presbyterian	18		
Baptist	18		
Quaker	1		

Source: Conference on Liverpool, pp. 6–13.

Anglican caution towards the Evangelical Alliance is particularly significant because it affected not only the moderate Evangelical

[142] Birks, *Memoir of E. Bickersteth*, ii. 303–8; *Conference on Christian Union held at Liverpool on Wednesday the 1st of October 1845 and Subsequent Days* (Liverpool, 1845); Evangelical Alliance, *Report of the Proceedings of the Conference at Freemasons' Hall, London from August 19th to September 2nd Inclusive* (1847). The American participants refused to accept the unequivocable exclusion of slave-holders required by some British members. On the American background, see P. D. Jordan, *The Evangelical Alliance for the United States of America 1847–1900* (New York, 1983).
[143] *Eclectic Review*, 4th series, 19 (1846), 500.
[144] Wolffe, 'Evangelical Alliance', pp. 339–40.

Christian Observer but also such staunch anti-Catholics as McNeile and Stowell. The *Observer* felt that Anglican supporters of the Alliance were giving ammunition to the Tractarians, who could suggest that Evangelicals were not sound Churchmen.[145] McNeile considered that many of the leaders of the Scottish Disruption were anticipating a similar movement in England, and were now looking to the Evangelical Alliance as a means of promoting it. His reservations also rested on a broader sense of the difficulties involved: 'The honest Churchman in opposing Popery is opposing false doctrine; but the honest Dissenter, the conscientious Voluntary, in opposing Popery, is opposing Church Establishments and endowments also. There can therefore be no real *bona fide* co-operation.'[146]

The Evangelical Alliance did not lack influential defenders. Bickersteth told Candlish, who in reality was struggling to persuade the Free Church, itself suspicious of co-operation, to maintain support for the Alliance, that he thought 'the designs charged against you are as alien from your minds as possible'. He continued strenuously to advocate the cause of the Alliance, but his efforts suffered a severe set-back when he was incapacitated for several months in 1846 as a result of a street accident.[147] The *Record* also was in favour of the Evangelical Alliance, suggesting, in a scarcely flattering analogy, that to be suspicious of it because of the prevalence of political Dissent was like refusing to join 'an Institution for the amelioration or suppression of immorality, because immorality dreadfully abounded, and was even exhibited by some of those who talked of joining the Society'.[148] The Evangelical controversy over the Alliance had a significant impact in souring relations between Anglican anti-Catholics.[149]

It is clear, therefore, that anti-Catholicism in itself was an insufficiently cohesive force in the Evangelical Alliance to overcome tensions over the Establishment and denominationalism. Indeed, it is important to recognize the extent to which the supporters of the Alliance were motivated by a positive spiritual desire for unity, fired by

[145] *Christian Observer*, 45 (1845), 739, 752–5; 46 (1846), 34–5; *BP*, 2 (1846), 113–16.
[146] *R*, 22 Dec. 1845.
[147] Birks, *Memoir of E. Bickersteth*, ii. 315–17, 323–7; W. Wilson, *Memorials of Robert Smith Candlish, DD* (Edinburgh, 1880), 375–7.
[148] *R*, 18 Dec. 1845.
[149] *R*, 22 Dec. 1845 and *passim*. Lewis (*Lighten their Darkness*, pp. 101–3) relates the suspicion of McNeile and others towards the Alliance to their futurist eschatology, which meant that they, unlike the historicists, could not see it as part of a divinely ordained plan.

the millennialism and revivalism of the 1840s rather than by negative anti-Popery. For example, James Hamilton, Free Church minister of the Scottish Church at Regent Square, thought it undesirable 'that this were, even chiefly or principally, an Anti-papal movement, or even an Anti-infidel movement, or that it took any mere anti form'.[150] His sentiments appeared to strike a chord with his hearers at Liverpool, and were reinforced by the warm spirit of fellowship evident in the early Evangelical Alliance meetings, developed particularly in shared acts of worship and prayer. In practice, the attitude towards Rome was noticeably more moderate than that of the Reformation Society and the Protestant Association.[151] The 1846 conference contented itself with resolving to collect information on 'the facts bearing on the growth of Popery', a measure seen as inadequate by a number of members, particularly Jabez Bunting and some Irish representatives, both Anglican and Presbyterian. On the other hand, Congregationalists, Baptists, and continental Protestants were all opposed to a headlong assault on Rome.[152] In November 1846 a British conference considered allocating subjects for enquiry to different regional divisions, but felt the Irish to be too fiery to be entrusted with 'Popery'. It was eventually assigned to the Scots, but some feared that they too would be over-enthusiastic.[153]

The Evangelical Alliance serves to indicate further the nature of the distinction between 'religious' and 'political' Protestantism and its ambiguities. It was recognized that any stand on matters concerning the relationship of Roman Catholicism to the State was inseparable from the whole Establishment controversy and hence would inevitably divide the membership. However, its apolitical claims were not merely a matter of negative necessity, but reflected a sense that political involvement was divisive and corrupting, and a positive spiritual yearning for a revival of Christian love. The Evangelical Alliance was at an opposite pole from the Protestant Association and the National Club, with their conviction that political involvement by Protestants was essential to the salvation of the nation.

[150] *Narrative of the Proceedings of the Meeting Held in Liverpool*, p. 16; W. Arnot, *Life of James Hamilton, DD* (1870), 188, 203, 231; Massie, *Evangelical Alliance*, p. 149.
[151] Those who wanted a militantly anti-Catholic interdenominational movement thus decided in the aftermath of the 'Papal Aggression' of 1850 that it was necessary to form a new organization, the Protestant Alliance. See below, Chap. 7.
[152] *Conference at Freemasons' Hall*, pp. 194–280.
[153] Evangelical Alliance, British Organization, *Report of the Proceedings of the Conference of British Members held at Manchester, from Nov. 4th to the 9th Inclusive 1846* (1847), 152–65.

The Alliance can be seen as part of a wider cultural trend, dividing the anti-Catholic movement itself, away from the identification of Church and State. This was reflected not only in the militancy of Dissent, but also in the attitude of Anglicans, both Evangelical and Tractarian, that the State and political involvement were a corrupting influence on the Church, a consciousness that led to Gladstone's change of heart over Maynooth in 1845. The involvement of American evangelicals in the founding conference of the Evangelical Alliance in August and September 1846 reinforced this trend. The anti-Catholic movement that had developed in the United States since the early 1830s naturally treated as axiomatic the separation of Church and State, and hence had made the assault on the Roman Church even more of a direct attack upon 'political' Christianity than English Nonconformists had done. On the other hand, it proved very difficult for the Alliance to carry this subjective aspiration to religious purity into practical action: James himself accused it of being an unduly refined 'do nothing society'.[154] This is an indication that, although political intent was disavowed, participants found it impossible to move beyond the formulation of modes of action that were essentially 'political' in character. For the present, the only course a broad 'religious' anti-Catholic movement could pursue was pious inertia.

By the late 1840s sympathy for anti-Catholicism had been diffused substantially beyond the 'Recordite' core of the early 1830s, but the price of this impact was a growing loss of coherence. Examination of the Evangelical Alliance underlines the inexorable tendency of the anti-Catholic movement to fragmentation, and its inability when it did try to form broader alignments to agree on anything beyond an abstract hostility to Rome that could not be carried into a practical programme of action. This stemmed from the fact that anti-Catholicism was neither a superficial prejudice nor a coherent ideology, but rather a frame of mind, an integral part of religious, political, and social belief and experience, ingrained into the consciousness of individuals in diverse ways that led inevitably to conflicting assumptions and aspirations. It was inextricably linked with the urge to promote spiritual revival, social and political advance, and controlled civil liberty. It was a crucial strand in an evangelical world-view that made far-reaching connections which seem strange to a later age with different presuppositions but which had an inherent logic of their own. One

---

[154] Dale, *John Angell James*, p. 418.

cannot divorce negative anti-Catholicism from the positive development and influence of Protestant forms of Christianity, with their roots
deep in nineteenth-century British life and forming an essential part of
national consciousness.

5
THE MOBILIZATION OF POPULAR
ANTI-CATHOLICISM

THE examination of the Protestant outlook carried out in the preceding chapter naturally raises the question of how widespread these ideas were in mid-nineteenth-century Britain, and how 'No Popery' feeling was stimulated and maintained. These problems are also fundamental to the evaluation of the political impact of anti-Catholicism in the 1840s and 1850s, which will form the subject-matter of Chapters 6 and 7. In this chapter organized popular anti-Catholicism will be examined at both a middle-class and working-class level. The activities of the Protestant societies will be considered first, including their efforts to mobilize public opinion, the response to them, and Catholic counter-agitation. The analysis will then turn to Protestant initiatives aimed more specifically at the lower levels in society, especially Operative Associations, Protestant Institutes, and missionary and educational activities.

How strong was popular anti-Catholicism when left untouched by the societies? It was argued in Chapter 1, that, at the beginning of the period under consideration, 'traditional' forms of anti-Catholicism had been in decline for some decades. This conclusion is confirmed by studying Guy Fawkes celebrations, which appear to have become rather less conspicuous during the early nineteenth century than they had been in the seventeenth and eighteenth centuries. Local élites, particularly concerned about the problem of public order following the French Revolution, tended to withdraw their patronage. Although 5 November was still widely marked by popular demonstrations, these seem to have become distinguished more by rowdyism than by specific religious statements.[1] This is evident from accounts of events at

---

[1] R. D. Storch, 'Please to Remember the Fifth of November', in R. D. Storch (ed.), *Popular Culture and Custom in Nineteenth-Century Britain* (1982), 71–99; G. Morgan, 'The Guildford Guy Riots (1842–1865)', *Surrey Archaeological Collections*, 76 (1985), 61–8. See also, D. G. Paz, 'Bonfire Night in Mid-Victorian Northants.: The Politics of a Popular Revel', *Historical Research*, forthcoming. I am indebted to Professor Paz for sending a copy of the typescript of this article.

Gravesend and Guildford, and is stated explicitly in a newspaper report on 5 November 1834 in Exeter:

Even those ragged urchins, who will be in at the death of the gunpowder plot commemoration; who will live to see the last of the first festival in our national calender . . . are themselves in such a state of oblivious confusion, that in the figure they fabricate, the attributes are blended of the Pope and the conspirator . . . The gunpowder thanksgiving is damped beyond all possibility of future igniting. It has missed fire for so many years that it will never blaze again; and the paupers in the streets, like the priests in the churches, poorly preserve, for the sake of the peace, the ragged remnants of the ceremony. As a public anniversary, as a national commemoration, the 5th of November has now, for a long time, been dead and gone, rotten and forgotten. Even the Perceval 'No Popery' cry could not blow-up the blown-out embers of the great blow-up that was to have been; and in later attempts, how many anti-catholic crackers have proved to be very harmless serpents. The feeling has passed away, and the fireworks follow.[2]

Reports from the agents of the Protestant societies frequently complained of apathy and complacency among the 'respectable' middle class to whom they initially directed their efforts. This was especially evident in more remote areas and in places where there were neither many Catholics nor hardline Evangelical clergy. A correspondent of the Protestant Association in Ulverston in April 1838 described the local mood as 'quiet persuasion that the efforts of Papists are too insignificant to excite alarm'.[3] At St Keverne in Cornwall, however, inertia appeared simply to reflect ignorance; when the parishioners became aware in January 1840 that public money was given to Maynooth, they gave their 'unanimous' support to a petition against it.[4] In the spring of 1841 the Revd Richard Parkinson toured the less urbanized parts of the Midlands on behalf of the Reformation Society, usually finding that little local activity was taking place.[5] Such attitudes were also evident in Scotland: at Musselburgh in the early 1850s there appeared to be little local support for the Protestant Association, 'since as Popery is not hurting them we have got nothing to do with popery, thus they reason'.[6]

The activity of the Protestant societies needs to be seen against the

---

[2] *Western Times*, 8 Nov. 1834; cf. R. Swift, 'Guy Fawkes Celebrations in Victorian Exeter', *History Today*, 31 (1981), 5–9.

[3] PAss, *2ndAR* (1838), 15.

[4] *PM*, 2 (1840), 87.

[5] RS minutes, 26 Apr. 1841.

[6] SRO, Edinburgh, John Hope MSS (GD 253) 36/4/26, James Simpson to Hope,

background of the spectacular Catholic advances of the 1830s and 1840s. The internal history of Catholicism in the period, the implications of mass Irish immigration, the spread of Ultramontanism under the leadership of Nicholas Wiseman, the triumphalist aspirations for the conversion of England, and the boost to morale provided by the Oxford converts have all been well described elsewhere, and it is unnecessary to repeat the details here.[7] Some specific points do, however, need to be made. Traditional Catholic historiography has presented these developments in the terms set by J. H. Newman's famous sermon of 1852 as a 'Second Spring'. John Bossy rightly criticizes this perspective because it ignores the substantial continuities and internal growth of pre-Emancipation English Catholicism.[8] However, a corollary of Bossy's evidence that growth was occurring in the English Catholic community as well as through Irish immigration is that there was a basis for friction in places with a long-standing recusant presence as well as in districts affected by the Irish influx. Indeed, recognition that the 'Second Spring' was in some respects a myth must be accompanied with the realization that it was an extremely potent contemporary perception both in boosting Catholic morale and in stirring Protestant fears. For people who, like the young J. H. Newman, had believed that Catholicism was indeed almost extinct, its apparent dramatic rebirth came as a significant surprise.[9] For others, the conversions to Rome, however small in absolute numbers, were a profound psychological and emotional shock, because they affected relatives and friends.[10] The language of Wiseman and Newman was echoed at a local level in material such as the verse written to celebrate the first tolling of a bell at a chapel in Preston:

> Sweet bell! As I list to thy sounds on the wind,

26 Oct. 1854. There were, of course, occasions on which local 'apathy' stemmed from unease about the reputation and methods of a particular Protestant society, a point that will be explored below.

[7] See J. D. Holmes, *More Roman than Rome: English Catholicism in the Nineteenth Century* (1978); J. Bossy, *The English Catholic Community 1570–1850* (1975), 296–401; E. R. Norman, *The English Catholic Church in the Nineteenth Century* (Oxford, 1984); P. A. Adams, 'Converts to the Roman Catholic Church in England, c.1830–1870', B.Litt. thesis (Oxford, 1977); G. Connolly, 'The Transubstantiation of Myth', *Journal of Ecclesiastical History*, 30 (1984), *passim*. The more specific implications of Irish immigration are considered below, pp. 180–96.

[8] Bossy, *English Catholic Community*, p. 297.

[9] J. H. Newman, 'The Second Spring', in *Sermons Preached on Various Occasions* (1857), 171–2.

[10] Adams, 'Converts to the Roman Church', p. 7.

> Cherished visions and hopes crowd uncalled on my mind;
> Do I *dream* that a long night of darkness is past?
> That streaks of the morning are dawning at last?
> That ere long the one Faith, in the brightness of day,
> Shall shine o'er proud 'Priest-town' in unclouded ray?
> Yea—broad England, my country, as fair as of old,
> Shall be blest in the peace of the one Faith and fold![11]

We have already seen how, in the late 1820s and early 1830s, local Catholic militancy could produce a Protestant backlash which interacted with outside influences. A later illustration of this is provided by events in Worksop and Gainsborough in 1850. The Catholic priest at Brigg and Gainsborough began a series of controversial lectures and also engaged in a discussion with Richard Blakeney at Worksop. The priest then decided that he wanted to pull out of the Worksop discussion, but local Catholics insisted that he continue. The discussion brought to a head local Protestant feeling which appears to have been growing for some time in the face of Catholic activity.[12] Meanwhile, in rural Dorset it was the activities of a Catholic landlord, Mr Weld of Lulworth, that produced a hostile reaction. According to William Palmer, an early member of the Oxford Movement now incumbent of Whitchurch Canonicorum, Weld had employed an Ultramontane priest who had been distributing tracts and threatening lapsed Catholics with eternal damnation. Palmer had retaliated by circulating a tract himself and preaching controversial sermons, but the priest ordered the Protestant tract to be burnt, and the Catholics started up their own lectures. Palmer alleged that Weld was making improper use of his influence as a landlord to support Catholicism. He continued his own campaign with assistance from Protestant societies, with the result that 'our own people are zealous Protestants and are now well able to argue with and overcome the Romanists in controversy'.[13] A third instance suggests that the appearance of Catholic intrigue could also fuel hostility: in distant Wick there were believed to be only two Catholics in the town outside the fishing-season, but 'One has no visible means of support and more Postal correspondence than any other in Wick. Thought to be a Jesuit.'[14] Elsewhere, from the mid-1840s onwards, hostility to

[11] Archives of the English Province of the Society of Jesus, Preston Scrap-book, f. 74.

[12] *BP*, 6 (1850), 17–24, 33–46.

[13] Hope MSS 35/3/53, W. Palmer to Hope, 18 Mar. 1854.

[14] SRS Archives, Branch Associations Book.

Tractarianism could stir a broader anti-Catholicism, particularly noticeable in the diocese of Exeter in the face of Phillpotts's supposed countenancing of Romanizing practices.[15]

The Protestant societies faced the task of giving national cohesion to a movement stirred by a variety of local impulses, and of promoting anti-Catholicism where local conditions were not so immediately favourable, assisted by national events, as in 1828–9, 1834–5, 1845, and 1850–1. Before analysing the methods used, the institutional development of anti-Catholic organizations must be surveyed. Gordon was largely responsible for the formation of the Protestant Association, but by 1837 his failing health obliged him to retire from active involvement.[16] The most prominent figures were initially M'Ghee and O'Sullivan, themselves increasingly overshadowed by McNeile and Stowell. None of these four, however, held any formal office, and the secretary by 1839 was Edward Dalton, who was succeeded in 1844 by James Lord, a barrister and writer of a history of debates and legislation relating to Maynooth College. The committee consisted predominantly of laymen, notably the Evangelical publishers James Nisbet and Robert Benton Seeley, but there were five clergymen on the initial committee of twenty-four.[17]

Clergy were dominant in the Reformation Society. Although Finch and Harcourt continued to be active throughout the period, Cumming and Blakeney became the central figures. Leading supporters included C. J. Goodhart, minister of St Mary's Chapel, Reading from 1836 to 1852 and then of Park Chapel, Chelsea, and John Hatchard, vicar of St Andrew's, Plymouth, who saw the Society as a useful ally in his local struggles against Tractarianism.[18] Both Edward and Robert Bickersteth were also energetic sympathizers.[19] As in the Protestant Association, laymen carried out the routine administration. The minute-books record the regular attendance at committee meetings over many years of a hard core of half a dozen individuals, particularly

---

[15] *BP*, 4 (1848), 174–5; 5 (1849), 49–61; 6 (1850), 197–212.

[16] *R*, 5 June 1837, 9, 13 May 1839, 23 June 1853; 'C. B.' [Charlotte Bickersteth], *Dawn and Sunrise: Brief Notes of the Life and Early Death of Barbara Sophia Gordon* (1860), 7–10.

[17] PAss, *3rd AR* (1839), p. iii; *PM*, 3 (1841), 92; 6 (1844), 171; PAss *Publications*, *passim*.

[18] J. Venn, *Alumni Cantabrigienses*, ii. *1752–1900* (6 vols.), iii. 83, 285; J. R. Wolffe, 'Bishop Henry Phillpotts and the Administration of the Diocese of Exeter, 1830–1869', *Transactions of the Devonshire Association*, 114 (1982), 109.

[19] *R*, 29 Apr. 1847, 8 May 1854.

Mr James Miller, who was the principal salaried official from 1840 onwards.[20]

Both societies followed broadly similar patterns of deputation activity with a view to fund-raising and the establishment of local branches. The Protestant Association, with the advantages of novelty and political interest, received greater publicity in the later 1830s, but the Reformation Society's operations proved more enduring. The Protestant meetings of 1835 and 1836 led to the formation of local Protestant Associations at Liverpool, Edinburgh, Glasgow, and Hereford.[21] In 1837 the London committee decided that such local initiatives must be assisted by organization from the centre, and, beginning in the metropolitan area, they began to promote further branch associations.[22] They appointed a travelling agent in April 1839, a second in January 1840, and a third, with specific responsibility for Scotland, was hard at work by July 1840, addressing crowded meetings in the Dundee and Aberdeen areas.[23] In November 1839 the *Protestant Magazine* published advice on the formation of local Protestant Associations, recommending an initial private meeting to establish basic principles and circulate tracts in preparation for a public meeting. Potential subscribers should be quickly enlisted before their enthusiasm waned. Dissenters were only admissible if they supported religious Establishments, but the 'poor' were welcome at a reduced subscription. The duties of local associations were to be the diffusion of information by means of public meetings, sermons, and publications, petitioning, and the collection of funds.[24]

Figure 2 indicates the geographical extent of the Protestant Association's activities.[25] Nearly fifty branches were formed between 1836 and 1844, although they were not all in existence at any one time, and many survived only for short periods. Their distribution suggests that they were heavily dependent on the enthusiasm generated by visiting speakers. Some of the Protestant Association's orators, above all O'Sullivan and McNeile, had quite exceptional power and appeal as speakers, and could be relied upon to stir a powerful, if short-lived,

[20] RS minutes, 6 Jan. 1840, 16 May 1853, and *passim*.
[21] M. O'Sullivan and R. J. M'Ghee, *Romanism as it Rules in Ireland* (1840), ii. 1, 62, 385, 434.
[22] PAss, *1st AR* (1837), 12–13.
[23] *PM*. 1 (1839), 13, 236; 2 (1840), 96, 330–3; PAss, *3rd AR* (1839), 16.
[24] *PM*, 1 (1839), 199–203.
[25] *Annual Reports, Protestant Magazine*.

Figure 2. Protestant Association activity: Meetings and branches, 1836–1845

response from an audience.[26] Obviously they were unlikely to visit regularly areas which were remote from their bases in Lancashire and London. Occasionally, however, there were local initiatives, like the one at Whitchurch (Shropshire), where the town was systematically divided up with a view to the efficient distribution of tracts and collection of signatures for petitions.[27] In Derbyshire the local Evangelical clergy, not content with a branch in the county town, held meetings and formed auxiliaries in a number of smaller towns and villages. The *Protestant Magazine* held up the case of Derbyshire as an example to the rest of England, where such intensive local activity was clearly unusual.[28] In Hertfordshire the local society found it difficult to get a good attendance at public meetings, and even in Liverpool the local branch did little more than hold an annual meeting and engage in occasional petitioning and tract distribution.[29]

A similar pattern of energetic deputation activity and limited local response is evident in the case of the Reformation Society. By 1839 the committee had divided England into four regions and appointed a secretary for each as well as one for Scotland.[30] In addition, 'missionaries' and other agents were employed at various times. When this structure operated efficiently, as it did for much of the period, it enabled the Society to visit most major centres every year or so. Reports of the meetings claimed that there were often large and enthusiastic audiences.[31] However, the income raised by deputation tours was usually fairly small, suggesting that much of the audience at the public meetings was there more out of curiosity or in search of the entertainment that could be provided by an eloquent Protestant speaker than from commitment to the cause. Evidence of meetings held as a result of local initiatives rather than in association with a visit from a travelling agent is comparatively rare.[32]

Figure 3 provides an indication of the geographical distribution of

[26] C. E. Trevelyan, *The No Popery Agitation*, 4th edn. (1840), 8; J. C. Colquhoun, *Memorials of H. M. C.* (1870), 72–4; J. A. Wardle, 'The Life and Times of the Rev. Dr Hugh M'Neile, DD, 1795–1875', MA thesis (Manchester, 1981), 429–37.

[27] *PM*, 2 (1840), 360.

[28] *PM*, 1 (1839), 143.

[29] Ibid. 111–12; 2 (1840), 283–6.

[30] RS, *11th AR* (1838).

[31] See e.g. RS, *12th AR* (1839), 8–20; *BP*, 3 (1847), 50–1.

[32] One recorded instance of local activity was at Nottingham, although this was associated with Blakeney's ministry there (*BP*, 1 (1845), 112–14). It should be noted, however, that only the publications of central Protestant societies have been systematically searched, and examination of provincial newspapers might well provide evidence of further local activity.

Figure 3. Reformation Society branches, 1827–1860

the Reformation Society's support, based on the figures for income given in the *Annual Reports*.[33] The most striking conclusion to be drawn is that, while this support was likely to be somewhat stronger in areas with a substantial Catholic presence, it was in fact widely distributed over the country, with the exception of Wales. This suggests that the key factor in determining the extent of the Reformation Society's appeal was as much the energy of local Evangelical clergy as the number of Roman Catholics in an area. For example, it appears that Yorkshire, with its strong Evangelicalism, gave almost as much support to the Reformation Society as Lancashire, with its much larger Catholic population. Conversely, in South Wales, which had a significant Catholic presence, organized anti-Catholic activity was minimal. An agent of the Reformation Society made a tour in 1847 and reported that 'there is a spirit of Protestantism alive in the Principality which needs only to be awakened and brought into action', but no one appears to have taken an initiative.[34] However, some credible Catholic presence was necessary to give grist to the mill of anti-Catholic activity: this was especially apparent in Scotland, where a number of ministers, particularly in rural areas, gave the total absence or insignificance of local Catholicism as a reason for being unable to get a Protestant movement under way.[35] Above all, it is clear that organized anti-Catholicism, like Catholicism itself, was primarily an urban phenomenon. It was unusual for a district to sustain more than one active Protestant society: for example, the Protestant Association was strong in Hereford, Derby, and Glasgow; the Reformation Society in Cheltenham, Preston, and Edinburgh.[36] It would be hard to discern any pattern either of a socio-economic or politico-religious kind in the affiliations of towns to particular societies, as this was attributable largely to the chances of personal contacts and the visits of deputations. Indeed, there were instances, such as that of Liverpool, of a town supporting both societies, but at different periods.[37]

---

[33] *British Protestant*; RS, *Annual Reports*.

[34] *BP*, 3 (1847), 168–71.

[35] Hope MSS 43/1/166, Revd James Cochrane, 6 Jan. 1858, on Cupar, where there were only 4 or 5 Roman Catholics; SRS Archives, Branch Associations Book, reports on Thurso, Selkirk, Ecclefechan, etc. Cf. B. Stanley, 'Home Support for Overseas Missions in Early Victorian England, *c*.1838–1873', Ph.D. thesis (Cambridge, 1979), 156–200; E. Jay, *The Religion of the Heart: Anglican Evangelicalism and the Nineteenth-Century Novel* (Oxford, 1979), 31–7.

[36] This judgement rests on a large number of sources, particularly *Annual Reports*, *Protestant Magazine*, and *British Protestant*.

[37] Liverpool supported the Protestant Association in the 1830s, but by the 1850s had switched its allegiance to the Reformation Society.

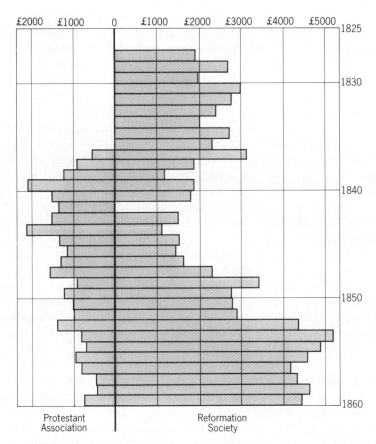

Figure 4. Reformation Society and Protestant Association income, 1827–1860

The insubstantial nature of support is also evident in the almost continual financial difficulties of both societies, although these can be partially explained by a tendency to extend operations faster than resources permitted. Figure 4 shows how gains by one society were frequently at the expense of the other.[38] The Protestant Association's income rose from £561 in 1836–7 to £2,073 in 1839–40 as systematic methods of collecting subscriptions were employed, but during the same years the income of the Reformation Society fell. By 1840 the older body had a debt of £955 and was only saved from bankruptcy

[38] *Annual Reports, British Protestant, Protestant Magazine.*

during the early 1840s by large donations from Finch.[39] Throughout
the early 1840s, years of relatively limited anti-Catholic activity, the
income of the Protestant Association fell off, while that of the
Reformation Society showed little sign of recovering to the levels of
the early to mid-1830s. At the end of the decade, however, there was
an upturn in the Reformation Society's income, while that of the
Protestant Association slipped back further. In the 1850s the Reformation Society enjoyed substantially increased financial support, but this
did not save it from a further acute crisis in 1856–8, when there was a
minor downturn which forced a curtailment in the scale of operations.
In 1857 it was belatedly decided to attempt to build up a reserve
fund.[40]

Financial worries took their toll on the attitudes of committees and
of employees, who were sometimes specifically expected to pay their
own way. For example, in 1846 the Revd Peter Hall was appointed by
the Reformation Society as district secretary for the West of England,
with a salary of £100, but he was told that he would be expected to
raise the Society's income from that region by at least that amount.
Evidently Hall found the struggle an uphill one and he resigned in
March 1848.[41] A sympathetic critic of the Society's efforts in London
observed in December 1852 that 'the whole work seems to be *money,
money*'.[42]

A further difficulty, which the Protestant societies shared with
contemporary missionary societies, was the limited supply of suitable
agents for deputation tours. They employed both young men, marking
time between graduation and ordination, and older clergymen, like
Hall, hoping to supplement their income by part-time work.[43] The
former category were likely to be inexperienced and to leave as soon as
they had acquired sufficient knowledge to be useful, while the latter
were prone to be overworked.[44] The problem was particularly acute
for the Reformation Society, whose agents continued to engage in
theological controversy with Roman Catholics. They increasingly
recognized that the advocacy of men whose ardour was untempered by

[39] RS minutes, 13 Jan. 1840; RS, *14th AR* (1841), 39; *15th AR* (1842), 33.

[40] RS minutes, 3 Nov. 1856, 25 Jan., 1 Mar. 1858; *R*, 6 May 1857, 5 May 1858.

[41] RS minutes, 16 Mar. 1846, 20 Mar. 1848. Hall was minister of St Thomas's
Chapel, Bath from 1843 to 1849 (J. Foster, *Alumni Oxonienses*, 4 vols. (1887–8), i. 588).

[42] Hope MSS 33/12/66, Turnbull to Hope, 20 Dec. 1848.

[43] The men employed as Scripture readers were generally from a very different kind
of social background.

[44] *R*, 22 May 1844; RS minutes, 2 Nov. 1846, 19 June 1854; Stanley, 'Home
Support for Overseas Missions', pp. 222–50.

discretion or basic theological knowledge was likely to be counter-productive. In 1845 a prospective secretary was warned that the 'Romish controversy' required long study, and in 1852 Blakeney emphasized how essential it was for the agent who was to be trained for work in Edinburgh to be 'thoroughly made up'. 'One blunder', he thought, 'might do such harm as twenty lectures would not repair.'[45] The recognition that trained manpower was limited led to disagreements over the best means of deploying available resources. John Hope argued that it was most effective to mount a sustained campaign in a particular locality, but the London committee usually preferred to seek to maintain footholds over the country as a whole.[46]

The Reformation Society remained a centralized body with a nation-wide coverage but limited local impact, while the Protestant Association during the 1840s became increasingly concentrated in particular areas. The central organization continued in existence, holding show-piece annual meetings in Exeter Hall and co-ordinating publishing activity, but there was little deputation work on behalf of the London committee.[47] The low level of its income reflected the local expenditure of significant energy and resources, as the committee explained in 1847: 'Parties do not like to move in opposition to Popery till some local cause arises, and then employ the whole of their funds, or nearly so, in local operations. So that, from those places where Protestant zeal, energy and judgement are most displayed, as Liverpool, Manchester, York, Norwich etc., your Association has rarely received any assistance.'[48] The example of Birmingham serves to illustrate the kind of activity promoted at a local level. A Protestant Association was formed in Birmingham in the summer of 1847 with an initial membership of fourteen. During the course of the next year it held seven lectures, collected a library of fifty volumes, and saw its membership grow to between sixty and seventy.[49] It gained further support from the local reaction to the burning of a Bible by a priest in late 1848 and the publicity given to an alleged fugitive monk from Mount St Bernard's in Leicestershire.[50] Local clergy had initially been

[45] RS minutes, 17 Apr. 1845; Hope MSS 33/11/17, 5 Nov. 1852.
[46] Hope MSS 32/11/51, Miller to Hope, 10 Oct. 1851; 226/10, p. 69, Hope to Miller, 21 Oct. 1851.
[47] *PM*, 9 (1847), 161–5 and *passim*.
[48] Ibid. 167–8.
[49] *PM*, 10 (1848), 243–5; *Protestant Watchman* (Birmingham 1849–50), 60–2, 68–70.
[50] The 'monk' was eventually found to be an imposter. *PM*, 11 (1849), 10; *Protestant Watchman*, July 1849, pp. 60–2.

cautious about supporting the society, fearful lest they should be associating themselves with an unstable and short-lived body, but by March 1849 seventeen of them were listed as vice-presidents. There was a committee of twenty-two laymen which met monthly, with Thomas Ragg, a publisher and bookseller, serving as secretary.[51] The second annual meeting in July 1849, attended by 300 people, received a report of further steady progress. The membership had doubled during the previous year, the number of books in the library had trebled, 'thousands' of tracts had been distributed, and the branch association had begun to publish its own monthly magazine, the *Protestant Watchman*, which had achieved a circulation of 3,000.[52] The 1850 annual report showed a somewhat less encouraging state of affairs: six of the committee had either died or left the district, and the increase in membership had levelled off. Nevertheless, lectures were continuing, with an attendance which was always satisfactory and sometimes 'very numerous'.[53]

The printing-press was extensively used as an instrument of agitation at both national and local level. Between 1836 and 1839 the Protestant Association published over twenty tracts, which could be purchased in bulk at a discount for distribution in the street or from door-to-door.[54] By 1842 the Protestant Association alone had distributed or sold over three-quarters of a million tracts, and these, together with extensive coverage of its activities in sympathetic newspapers, including *The Times* up to 1841, enabled it to convey its views to an extensive readership.[55] A few local branches, such as those at Hereford and Glasgow in the mid-1830s, assisted these efforts by issuing their own publications.[56]

From the later 1830s there was a tendency to move away from tracts and pamphlets in favour of periodicals. In 1839 the Protestant Association began to publish the *Protestant Magazine*, which reported on Roman Catholic activities, political developments, and Protestant meetings.[57] The Reformation Society followed in 1845 with the *British*

---

[51] *PM*, 10 (1848), 243; *Protestant Watchman*, cover and p. 15.

[52] *PM*, 11 (1849), 134.

[53] *PM*, 12 (1850), 142, 149.

[54] PAss, *Publications of the PAss* (1839).

[55] *PM*, 3 (1841), 176; 4 (1842), 184; J. Murphy, *The Religious Problem in English Education* (Liverpool, 1959), 229.

[56] O'Sullivan and M'Ghee, *Romanism*, ii. 389; *Glasgow Protestant Association Tracts* (Glasgow, 1835–6). It is probable that more literature of this kind was published but has since disappeared without trace.

[57] *PM*, 5 (1843), 128 and *passim*; Charlotte Elizabeth, *Personal Reminiscences*, 4th edn. (1854), 392–3.

Protestant, edited during the 1850s by William Clementson, the superintendent of the Society's Special Mission to Roman Catholics. It contained news of the Society's operations, extracts from the journals of Scripture readers, and articles on theological and historical themes.[58] In addition, there were several local short-lived periodicals, such as the *Bath Protestant* (1838–45), the *Norwich Protestant Herald* (1841–2), and the *Protestant Witness*, which appeared fortnightly in Manchester from 1848 to 1852.

During the 1850s the Reformation Society acquired renewed support following the promotion of missions to Roman Catholics, but the Protestant Association, burdened by growing indebtedness, declined further. It increasingly seemed to be little more than a 'one-man show' for James Lord, who edited the *Protestant Magazine*, published addresses and circulars when circumstances warranted, and engaged in an extensive correspondence with contacts at home and overseas.[59] He made occasional lecture tours, but no consistent attempt to maintain a network of branches. Where these survived, as at Birmingham, Derby, and Clare in Suffolk, they did so by drawing on their own resources.[60] The clerical Protestant orators of the 1830s and 1840s were much less active than hitherto. O'Sullivan returned to Ireland, and McNeile did little outside Liverpool.[61] M'Ghee, now rector of Holywell in Huntingdonshire, took an intermittent interest in Protestant affairs, but lacked his old energy.[62] Stowell was still engaging in speaking-tours in 1853, but, like McNeile, he localized his efforts, ensuring the survival of vigorous Protestant Associations in the Manchester area, but not arresting decline elsewhere.[63]

The weakness of the Protestant Association in the 1850s was counteracted by the formation of new societies, particularly the Protestant Alliance and the Scottish Reformation Society.[64] John MacGregor threw himself into promoting the formation of local societies during the winter of 1851–2. He was rewarded with news of the existence of thirty provincial societies in January 1852, and a further fourteen had emerged by the beginning of April. They were

[58] *BP, passim*; Hope MSS 34/3/67, Blakeney to Hope, 14 Mar. 1853.
[59] *PM*, 15 (1853), 168–73; 18 (1856), 116–27 and *passim*; *R*, 6 Feb. 1856.
[60] *PM*, 14 (1852), 159–60, 360, 383–6; 17 (1855), 259; 19 (1857), 60–4.
[61] *DNB*, xlii. 319; Hope MSS 35/2/70, McNeile to Hope, 17 Feb. 1854.
[62] Derby MSS 142/4, M'Ghee to Derby, 30 Mar. 1852; *PM*, 21 (1859), 85.
[63] *PM*, 15 (1853), 99, 163, 373–8.
[64] The implications for the character of the Protestant movement as a whole of this shift from an exclusively Anglican society to interdenominational bodies will be considered in Chap. 7.

fairly evenly dispersed over the whole of England from Plymouth to Newcastle, but the Protestant Alliance did not fare any better in Wales than the other societies had done.[65] Although the speed with which the organization was built up was impressive, there was a loss of momentum after 1852. The Alliance employed only one travelling secretary, who could hardly be expected to cover the whole of England efficiently. It did not engage in publishing activity, although Mac-Gregor did issue several pamphlets under his own name.[66]

The Scottish Reformation Society, founded in 1850, proved to be particularly efficient in its sphere of operation. It was dominated by two leading Free Church clergymen. James Begg, born in 1808,[67] was an eager follower of Thomas Chalmers on social issues, but took a much more extreme stance on Roman Catholicism. He was a forceful and eloquent leader, albeit a somewhat inflexible one.[68] James Aitken Wylie, also born in 1808, was an Original Secession minister who joined the Free Church in 1852. His interests were of a literary and academic character, thus complementing Begg's organizational abilities.[69] The Scottish Reformation Society was also well served by its officers, George Lyon, WS, the honorary secretary, and Edward Marcus Dill, the acting secretary, an Irish Presbyterian minister. Dill was succeeded in 1858 by G. R. Badenoch, who was still active in Protestant movements in 1901.[70]

The Society operated over the whole of Scotland, with the exception of the city of Glasgow, where there was a separate body, the Glasgow Protestant Laymen's Society. In February 1855 the *Bulwark* claimed that there were sixty-four branches in existence, of which thirty-seven supplied details of their activities. The information given is summarized in Table 3, which covers the year from November 1853 to November 1854. This shows clearly the nature of the Scottish Reformation Society: it was not a mass movement, but it did maintain

[65] Southampton City Record Office, Croft Moody MSS, D/PM/10/5/6, PAll circular, Jan. 1852; D/PM/10/8/18, List of local societies connected with the PAll, 1 May 1852.

[66] Croft Moody MSS, D/PM/10/8/23, summary of Protestant Alliance activities; SRS minutes, 6 June 1854; E. Hodder, *John MacGregor* (1894), 103.

[67] He should not be confused with his father, also James, a prominent member of the Evangelical party in the Kirk in the first half of the nineteenth century.

[68] T. Smith, *Memoirs of James Begg, DD* (Edinburgh, 1885), i. 1–77 (autobiographical memoir by Begg); *DNB*, iv. 127–8.

[69] *DNB*, lxiii. 237.

[70] SRS, *AR* (1859), 1; SRS minutes, 23 Dec. 1869; Bod. Lib., NC Papers, MS letter from Badenoch to Col. Robinson, 25 Mar. 1901.

TABLE 3. *Scottish Reformation Society activity, 1853–1854*

Activity	Branches making return	Overall total	Average per branch
Circulation of *Bulwark*	30	2339	77.6
Committee meetings	35	249	7.1
Public meetings	33	50	1.5
Lectures	34	211	6.2
Memorials and petitions	33	73	2.1

an active presence in a substantial number of Scottish towns.[71] Nine branches appear to have been holding committee meetings at least once a month, and those at Edinburgh and Hamilton were gathering even more frequently. At Leith no less than twenty-six lectures had been given during the last year, and Edinburgh, Elgin, Falkirk, Haddington, and Stranraer also reported that they had held ten or more. The Alloa branch was publishing quarterly tracts; at Falkirk a library of nearly 300 volumes had been set up; and the Dunbar and Paisley branches had plans to do likewise. However, several branches did not appear to be in such a flourishing state, and one or two were teetering on the edge of viability. This machinery was maintained by vigorous deputation work. For example, during six months in 1855 Dill and his assistant covered 4,835 miles between them, visiting about seventy towns in Scotland and the north of Ireland and holding approximately 150 meetings. At one stage in 1860 the Society was employing six agents on work of this sort.[72]

The *Bulwark*, a journal closely associated with the Scottish Reformation Society, was of considerable importance as a stimulus to anti-Catholic feeling in England as well as Scotland. It aimed 'to convert, by means of full intelligence, the instinctive and traditional hatred of [Roman Catholicism] which prevails amongst our population, into an enlightened determination to resist its progress and seek . . . to convert its adherents'.[73] Editorial policy was controlled by Begg, who pursued his task with a virulence extreme even by the standards of

[71] *Bulwark*, 4 (1854–5), 200–1. The large discrepancy between the circulation figures for the *Bulwark* here and those claimed for 1852 is accounted for by the partial nature of the return, by distribution independent of the SRS, and by circulation outside Scotland.
[72] SRS minutes, 15 Nov. 1855; *Bulwark*, 9 (1859–60), 233.
[73] *Bulwark*, 1 (1851–2), 1–2.

the Protestant literature of the period, although he was at pains to point out that he never rendered himself open to a libel action. Illustrated with lurid woodcuts, it was the most successful of the nineteenth-century Protestant journals, claiming a circulation of 30,000 by May 1852.[74]

There were also tentative attempts in Scotland to fortify the intellectual basis of Protestant polemic. Hope sponsored a competition for theological students, and Blakeney wanted to see a university chair established for the study of the controversy with Rome. Nothing came of this scheme, but an anti-Roman society was formed among Edinburgh University students.[75] In 1862 the Free Presbytery of Edinburgh and the Scottish Reformation Society jointly established the Protestant Institute of Scotland 'for the training of Missionaries, Students, Teachers and others'. A building was constructed on George IV Bridge, and contains a lecture-hall to seat about a hundred people and various other classrooms and offices.[76]

Direct Irish influence also continued to have an impact. In 1834 the Revd Edward Nangle began a Protestant mission on Achill Island in the remote west of Connaught. He had the significant advantage of speaking Gaelic, and was operating in an area where Roman Catholic religious provision was weak. Consequently he enjoyed substantial, if localized, success. From 1837 Nangle began to publish the *Achill Missionary Herald*, which was circulated among Evangelicals in Britain and contained reports of the mission on Achill Island with more general comment on matters of Protestant concern.[77] A more far-reaching revival of the kind of involvement in Ireland that had been crucial in the early years of the Reformation Society's history came in 1849 with the establishment of the Irish Church Missions to Roman Catholics, led by Alexander Dallas. Dallas's vigorous anti-Catholic oratory was linked to his efforts to raise funds for his Irish operations and was given heightened intensity by his fervent pre-millennialism. Particularly in the early 1850s he was very active as a speaker in England.[78]

---

[74] *Bulwark*, 1 (1851–2), 289; Smith, *Begg*, ii. 175.

[75] D. Jamie, *John Hope: Philanthropist and Reformer* (Edinburgh, 1900), 267; Hope MSS 32/2/63, Blakeney to Hope, 21 Feb. 1851; 41/3/52, 68, G. R. Badenoch to Hope, 9, 11 Feb. 1851.

[76] The building still stands, almost opposite the National Library.

[77] D. Bowen, *The Protestant Crusade in Ireland* (Dublin, 1978), 204; *Achill Missionary Herald, passim.*

[78] Bowen, *Protestant Crusade*, pp. 208–56, gives a detailed account of Dallas's

Several smaller Protestant societies also emerged in the 1850s. The Church Protestant Defence Society, commenced in March 1853, was a response to the growth of ritualism and the movement to revive Convocation, and was aimed specifically at maintaining 'the pure and practical doctrines of the Gospel within the bosom of the Church of England'. The committee was chaired by the Earl of Shaftesbury, and the secretary was Wilbraham Taylor, also a member of the committee of the Protestant Alliance. There was an active branch in Brighton, a Tractarian stronghold.[79] The British Protestant League and Bible and Anti-Popery Mission was active during 1852. It was supported almost exclusively by clergy and led by the Revd T. Tenison Cuffe, who had left the Church of England in November 1850 and joined the Countess of Huntingdon's Connexion because he considered that the Gorham Judgement did not go sufficiently far in condemnation of Phillpotts.[80] In March 1856 the 'Young Men's Tract Association for the Publication . . . of Popular Tracts on the Roman Catholic Controversy' issued a circular announcing its intention of issuing a continuous series of tracts, but no more was heard of it.[81] There were also regional initiatives, notably the North of England Protestant Organization centred on Manchester, which commenced operations in November 1855. It was inspired by the Scottish Reformation Society and aimed to follow the pattern of intensive regional activity in the seven northern counties of England, an approach which its promoters believed to be more effective than attempts to embrace the whole country. It was very effective for a short period, but appears to have collapsed in 1857.[82]

This survey indicates that, while Protestant societies attracted extensive interest, their committed support was relatively limited. This is confirmed by Tables 4 and 5, which break down the social profile of the membership of two societies in sample years. Table 5, the

---

activities. The implication that the ICM were not merely significant but central to anti-Catholicism in the 1850s cannot be sustained, however. See also D. Bowen, 'Alexander R. C. Dallas: The Warrior Saint', in P. T. Phillips (ed.), *The View from the Pulpit* (Toronto, 1978), 17–44.

[79] Church Protestant Defence Society, *Address No. 1* (1853), 2, 6; *Address No. 3* (1853), 8; Croft Moody MSS, D/PM/10/8/23, Summary of Protestant Alliance activities; Southampton University Library, Shaftesbury MSS, SHA/PD/6, Diary, 7 Jan. 1854.

[80] Croft Moody MSS, D/PM/10/5/45, Cuffe to Croft Moody, 3 Mar. 1852; D/PM/10/8/35, Circular of British Protestant League; *Baptist Magazine*, 43 (1851), 705.

[81] Hope MSS 39/3/75, Prospectus of Young Men's Tract Association.

[82] SRS minutes, 30 Apr. 1855; *R*, 11 Feb. 1857.

TABLE 4. *Protestant Association subscribers, 1839*

	No.	%
Peers	10	1.9
Other titled laymen	9	1.7
MPs	9	1.7
Clergy	110	20.6
Laymen styled 'Esq.'	213	39.8
Laymen styled 'Mr'	61	11.4
Women	123	23.0
TOTAL	535	

TABLE 5. *Reformation Society subscribers, 1850*

	No.	%
Peers	1	0.1
Other titled laymen	7	0.9
MPs	3	0.4
Clergy	171	20.9
Laymen styled 'Esq.'	277	33.9
Laymen styled 'Mr'	91	11.1
Women	267	32.7
TOTAL	817	

Note: Doctors and officers are subsumed under the heading of 'laymen styled "Esq." '. It should be noted that the information on which these tables are based is incomplete: provincial branches are not included, nor are donors of less than 5s. The evidence advanced here is therefore useful only to indicate the nature of support within the middle and upper classes.

Source: BP, 6 (1850), 111–27; PAss, 3rd AR (1839), 23 ff.

Reformation Society in 1850, can also constructively be compared with Table 1 (p. 52), which provides figures for the same organization in 1828–9. There are obvious similarities: the proportion of clerics, almost exclusively parochial clergy, is identical in the sample years, and in each case the backbone of membership clearly came from the minor gentry and professions. However, the Protestant Association's political interests gave it somewhat higher support from MPs and the aristocracy, while, conversely, the proportion of women in the Reformation Society was substantially higher. The changing composi-

tion of the Reformation Society's membership is also instructive. It is
clear that politically involved individuals tended to lose enthusiasm,
while women and, to some extent, men, of somewhat lower social
status were recruited in their place. Overall, the two decades saw a
modest increase in membership, but one hardly proportionate to the
efforts put in by deputations.

The limited extent of committed public support for the Protestant
societies reflected a distaste for the methods and character of
particular organizations rather than a lack of sympathy with the broad
goal of attacking Roman Catholicism. On occasions, unenthusiastic
local receptions for Protestant societies stemmed directly from
unhappy experiences of their activities in the past. At Newcastle in
1835 Cumming met with a very cool reception, but conceded that 'if
ever there was ground for holding back from a society . . . that ground
was at Newcastle'.[83] At Cheltenham Francis Close, despite his own
staunch Evangelicalism, opposed the Reformation Society for years,
but became more sympathetic in the early 1840s in the belief that it
had moderated.[84] At Winchester and at Bridport in 1850 the
Reformation Society found that disturbances at meetings held by the
Protestant Association had given rise to a general prejudice against all
anti-Catholic activities.[85]

Criticism of the Protestant societies was especially significant when
it came from potential supporters. A Bath Dissenting minister
considered that offensive attacks on Catholics were leading to a
reaction in their favour.[86] The *Protestant Magazine* did not deny this,
but saw it as the divinely ordained separation of the chaff from the
wheat, a view hardly likely to appeal to the uncommitted.[87] Lord
Ashley was particularly concerned at the language used against Roman
Catholicism by the *Record*: while concurring in the newspaper's basic
position, he thought the motives and style adopted to be thoroughly
undesirable and suspected that it resorted to hearsay when facts were
not available.[88] An Edinburgh clergyman approved of moderate
Protestant activity, but refused to associate himself with Hope's
movement 'because I was apprehensive that the pernicious weapons of
invective and ridicule might be employed against the Romanists which

[83] *Protestant Journal*, 5 (1835), 55.
[84] RS minutes, 26 Apr. 1841.
[85] *BP*, 6 (1850), 149–55.
[86] J. Murch, *The Trial of Maynooth* (Bath, 1838), 25.
[87] *PM*, 4 (1842), 218.
[88] Shaftesbury Diary, SHA/PD/2, 22 Nov. 1841, 25 Jan. 1842.

... have only the effect of deepening prejudice and exciting hostility'.[89] Such opinions were quite commonly held in Scotland in the 1850s: there was concern that vigorous Protestant activity would produce a Catholic backlash in areas where relations had hitherto been reasonably harmonious.[90] Some Edinburgh clergy thought that the normal operations of the Churches were more likely to secure conversions than para-ecclesiastical societies were, a factor probably influential in England as well.[91] A similar distaste for the methods of Protestant societies was evident in the Scottish universities: an Edinburgh student thought that crude controversial methods could not hope to combat an intellectual system with the subtlety of Roman Catholicism, while the principal of St Andrews pointedly informed Hope that he considered his students sufficiently instructed in Protestantism. He, too, questioned 'whether the promotion of a spirit of controversy on the subject is likely to prove beneficial'.[92]

More unqualified opposition was also apparent. In particular, the meetings held by the Reformation Society in the early 1830s and by the Protestant Association in the latter part of the decade produced strong adverse reactions. The *Caledonian Mercury* attacked M'Ghee's 'coarse, vulgar and ridiculous' exhibitions, which, it thought, displayed the same persecuting spirit denounced in the Catholics themselves, while the *Liverpool Mail* dismissed the efforts of anti-Catholic orators as 'disjointed trash'.[93] Protestant allegations of Catholic conspiracy were also turned back on their authors: when, in 1839, Hugh McNeile exclaimed with reference to the Papacy: 'What peace so long as that woman Jezebel lives?', he was accused of inciting his audience to assassinate the queen.[94] In 1851 Newman put a brilliant parody of

[89] Hope MSS 28/15/56, Dr Birkmyre to Dr Muir, 13 Mar. 1846.

[90] Ibid. 39/5/31, John Kinross to Hope, 24 May 1856 (on Largs); 41/1/150, Revd Robert Angust to Mr Stewart, 26 Feb. 1857 (copy, on Peebles); 41/4/88, Revd Robert Tait to Hope, 17 Apr. 1857 (on Kirkliston), and *passim*.

[91] Ibid. 28/15/9, Revd William Glover to Hope, 21 Mar. 1846; 28/15/27–8, Revd T. Addis to Hope, 27 Mar. 1846.

[92] Ibid. 42/5/24, P. Cameron Black to Hope, 24 Nov. 1857; 43/1/142, Principal Tulloch to Hope, 11 Jan. 1858. On John Tulloch, principal of St Andrews from 1854, see *DNB*, lvii. 303.

[93] O'Sullivan and M'Ghee, *Romanism*, ii. 108–9 (Citing *Caledonian Mercury*); T. Butler, *Letter . . . Containing Strictures on the Rev. J. Baylee's Challenge to Dr Butler* (Liverpool, 1841), 3 (citing *Liverpool Mail*).

[94] *Jezebel: Speech of the Rev. Hugh McNeile at Market Drayton, Salop* (1839); *Eclectic Review*, 4th series, 9 (1841), 621 n.

Protestant rhetoric into the mouth of a fictional Russian count engaged in passionate denunciation of 'John Bullism'.[95]

From the late 1830s there were serious efforts to mount a Catholic counter-agitation. In February 1838, at the instigation of O'Connell, it was decided to form an organization 'for the protection and encouragement of the Catholic religion and Catholic people'. The objects of the Catholic Institute of Great Britain, formally inaugurated later in 1838, were the publication and circulation of tracts in order to meet the charges against the Roman Catholic religion, the supply of devotional books to poor Catholics, the removing of obstacles to freedom of worship in the armed services and in workhouses, hospitals, and prisons, and the vindication of the legal rights of all Catholics, especially the poor. This plan of action received the unanimous approval of the vicars apostolic, on condition that all tracts issued should be subject to inspection by an ecclesiastic as a guarantee of their moderation and orthodoxy.[96] The Institute republished a declaration by the vicars apostolic, originally issued in 1826, in which the misrepresentation of Catholic doctrines was lamented and beliefs on contentious points summarized. Subsequent tracts provided a more elaborate treatment of Catholic beliefs, consisting primarily of reprints of the works of medieval and recusant writers from Alcuin to Milner.[97]

The methods of agitation adopted by the Catholic Institute were strikingly similar to those of the Protestant societies, suggesting that the Catholics observed their adversaries closely and thought their approach sufficiently successful to be worthy of imitation. Lectures were delivered in which there was an explicit attempt to respond to Protestant attacks; about half a million tracts had been distributed by 1843, some of them handed out at anti-Catholic meetings, and 124 branch societies formed. It was claimed that in some cases these efforts were effective in counteracting the Protestant campaign, and even in leading to conversions to Catholicism, but elsewhere, 'from the gross misrepresentations of the emissaries of religious discord, our holy religion has been depicted in colours calculated to deter our

---

[95] J. H. Newman, *Lectures on the Present Position of Catholics in England* (1892 edn.), 27–41, Lecture I.

[96] Catholic Institute of Great Britain, *A Short Account of the Catholic Institute of Great Britain* (1839).

[97] Catholic Institute of Great Britain, *Declaration of the Catholic Bishops, the Vicars Apostolic and their Coadjutors in Great Britain* (1826, 1838), *Tracts* (1838–41).

countrymen from the examination of its truth'.[98] From 1839 onwards
the Catholic Institute held large meetings in London, patronized by
leading laymen, particularly Charles Langdale and Lord Camoys, at
which O'Connell himself was the star performer. His rhetoric,
although primarily intended to boost Catholic morale, was hardly
calculated to calm Protestant apprehensions. In June 1842, for
example, he professed himself a 'moderate' and 'easily contented' man
who merely wanted to hear High Mass sung again in Westminister
Abbey.[99] Meanwhile, in June 1840 Frederick Lucas commenced
publication of the *Tablet*, the zealous Ultramontane tone of which was
to prove too vigorous for some of his fellow-Catholics.[100]

The response of the Protestant Association was predictable. The
Protestant Magazine compared the Catholic Institute to the Catholic
Association in the Ireland of the 1820s and attributed sinister political
objectives to it, while believing its contacts with Rome to be felonious.
The force of the Catholic response was held to be gratifying, as it
showed that the Protestant campaign was striking home.[101] Sub-
sequently the Catholic Institute experienced the same decline as the
Protestant Association. No annual meeting was held in 1844.
However, in 1845, at the time of the anti-Maynooth agitation, an
attempt at revival was made, with a particular emphasis now being
given to the promotion of Catholic education.[102] The Catholic
Institute, however, fell victim to the differences between moderates,
represented in this case by Langdale, who was anxious not to provoke
Protestant feeling by political activity, and the militant sympathizers
with Irish Catholicism, headed by Lucas and the *Tablet*. Thus it was
eventually dissolved and its funds divided between the Catholic Poor
School Committee and the Association for the Vindication of Catholic
Rights.[103]

The tension between English aristocratic and Irish Catholic
responses to Protestant attacks was still evident in the early 1850s.
The first was represented by Newman's *Lectures on the Present Position of
Catholics in England*, which themselves provoked a number of

---

[98] Catholic Institute of Great Britain, *1st AR* (1839), 12–13; *2nd AR* (1840), 11; *5th
AR* (1843), 11 (Newberry Library, Chicago).

[99] D. O'Connell (ed.), *A Full Account of the . . . Great Meeting of the Catholics of London*
(1839); *Tablet*, 30 May 1840, 15 May 1841, 11 June 1842; *PM*, 5 (1843), 239.

[100] See above, Chap. 4, p. 130.

[101] *PM*, 2 (1840), 289–91; 4 (1842), 130–3.

[102] *Tablet*, 12 Apr., 17, 24 May 1845, 2 May 1846.

[103] *Month*, 51 (1884), 509–26.

Protestant rejoinders and Achilli's famous libel suit. However, they were mild in comparison with the defence of Roman Catholicism undertaken by an Irishman, Daniel Cahill. Born in Queen's County in 1796, Cahill cut his controversial teeth by attacking the 'Second Reformation' movement in the 1820s, and during the famine he became a passionate critic of British rule in Ireland.[104] The Durham Letter of 1850 provoked him into issuing a series of open letters to Russell, and he followed these with similarly combative thrusts at other leading Protestant figures. His language was quite as extreme as that of his anti-Catholic opponents. For example, he maintained that there was a 'deep, wide and almost universal conspiracy of the English Cabinet to annihilate Catholic liberty, and to crush the Catholic faith throughout the entire continent of Europe, and in America and the English colonies'. Protestants made repeated attempts to hold public debates with Cahill, but he always refused to rise to the bait, fearful perhaps that such an occasion would implicate him directly in sectarian violence.[105]

Catholic political action entered a new phase in the early 1850s. Opposition to the Ecclesiastical Titles Bill in 1851 was a major stage in the formation of the Independent Irish party, an important force in the Parliaments of the early 1850s.[106] English Catholics were associated with this in the Catholic Defence Association of Great Britain and Ireland, set up at a meeting in Dublin on 19 August 1851. A branch in Preston was formed in October with the aim of repealing the Ecclesiastical Titles Act, described as a 'tyrannical and offensive enactment'. However, Catholic support for the organization was limited, and such efforts, obviously only viable in areas where there was a substantial Catholic presence, were short-lived; the Catholic Defence Association disappeared after the 1852 general election.[107]

The anti-Catholic activity analysed so far in this chapter was in theory directed at all social groups, but in practice its impact was limited largely to the middle class. Indeed, working-class anti-

---

[104] *Life, Letters and Lectures of the late Dr Cahill, Biographical Sketch* (Dublin, 1880); W. Kinsella and D. W. Cahill, *Letter on the Subject of the New Reformation* (Carlow, 1827); *DNB*, viii. 210.

[105] D. W. Cahill, *Letters Addressed to Several Members of the British Cabinet; and Speeches on Various Subjects Delivered in Several Towns and Cities in England, Ireland and Scotland* (Dublin, 1856), pp. v–vi.

[106] J. H. Whyte, *The Independent Irish Party, 1850–9* (Oxford, 1958), 19–24.

[107] Archives of the English Province of the Society of Jesus, Preston Scrap-book, ff. 215–17; Whyte, *Independent Irish Party*, pp. 28–9.

Catholicism was viewed intially with coolness by organizations anxious to assert their own 'respectability' and to avoid contact with possible disorder. Furthermore, the poorer classes could be of little direct service in the primary purposes of political lobbying and fund-raising for missionary operations among Roman Catholics. Thus, for most of the 1830s, although a few tracts and handbills were issued with relatively poorly educated people in mind,[108] no systematic efforts were made to involve them in the societies. From the late 1830s, however, there were serious efforts to widen the social base of the Protestant societies. These efforts were intially motivated by two factors. Firstly, the growth in the Irish Catholic presence in British towns highlighted the need for activity in the slums, not only to 'convert' the Catholics but also to protect the nominally Protestant population from 'perversion' by fortifying them with anti-Catholic arguments. Secondly, the resurgence of lower-class radicalism in the later 1830s influenced the Protestant societies, predisposed to believe that political and social unrest stemmed from spiritual destitution, to turn their attention to the urban poor. Given their dualistic outlook, the anti-Catholic leaders were especially prone to view Chartism, 'socialism', and 'Popery' as phenomena with common roots.[109]

The reports of urban missionaries provide support, from a different quarter, for the evidence derived from the study of Guy Fawkes celebrations that British lower-class anti-Catholicism was declining when untouched by Protestant agitation. An agent in Bermondsey in 1845 found that one family he visited did not know whether they were Protestants or Catholics. In Aberdeen in 1860 it was reported that 'very many' Protestants believed Roman Catholicism to be 'a very good thing'.[110] Probably more representative was the response of a 'poor labouring man' attending a Protestant meeting at Westminster who had 'always thought Romanism was something bad, but this was the first time he had heard its principles explained and exposed'.[111] There were also instances of such vague eclecticism as was displayed by a

---

[108] See e.g. the handbills published by the Protestant Association, *Popery the Enemy of God and Man*; *Popery Unchanged*; *Startling Facts* (*c*.1839).

[109] This paragraph draws on a wide range of sources. For the connection between religious and political concerns, see *PPO*, 1 (1840), 1. A good illustration of wider Evangelical concern for Church extension linked with the maintenance of good order is provided by R. H. Inglis, *Church Extension: Substance of a Speech Delivered in the House of Commons, 30 June 1840* (1840).

[110] *BP*, 1 (1845), 117; Hope MSS 46/11/60, J. H. Gildard to Hope, 17 Mar. 1860.

[111] *BP*, 1 (1845), 48.

woman in Manchester who engaged in lengthy argument with a missionary and 'professed formerly to be a Methodist and afterwards a Catholic and has recently imbibed the sentiments of Infidelity',[112] Mixed marriages were quite common: in Scotland it was reported in 1859 that these were the most common cause of 'conversion' and 'perversion'. In Manchester a nominally Protestant husband explained that 'in order to have peace at home he must either attend the Catholic Chapel or none at all'.[113] Confident generalization is impossible, but it would seem that those indifferent to religion commonly lacked sectarian commitment also. Areas with an extensive Irish Protestant immigrant presence were likely to be an exception to this, of course, as a residual Orange influence was generally in evidence there, but this was unusual in those localities, particularly Edinburgh and the London area, in which the Protestant societies were most actively engaged in the development of working-class Protestantism. Catholics, for their part, were more likely to have a sense of communal loyalty, ingrained in the case of recent immigrants by the sectarian struggles in Ireland from the later 1820s to the early 1840s. However, the extent of actively spiritual commitment was often limited, and non-observance was very common, especially among recent immigrants.[114] Faced with widespread Protestant indifference and Catholic responses that ranged from cautious welcome to violent hostility, the Protestant societies had the integrated aims of fortifying nominal loyalty to their own faith and of winning over Catholics disillusioned with theirs. The first objective was advanced initially by Protestant operative societies and later by a wide range of educational and propagandist techniques; the latter one by active missions to the Irish Catholic poor.

It was in 1839 that McNeile had the idea of forming Protestant Operative Associations on the lines of the Conservative Operative Associations, which had already existed for some years. The first such organization was established in Liverpool, and by mid-1839 it was

---

[112] Manchester Central Library, Archives Dept., BR.MS.259.31, Bembridge Journal, v. 7 June 1844.

[113] Ibid. i. 15 Aug. 1842; Church of Scotland, *Annual Report to the General Assembly by the Committee on Popery* (Edinburgh?, 1859), 18.

[114] This statement represents a summary of a consensus that seems to emerge from recent studies of Irish Catholicism in Britain. See e.g. Connolly, 'Transubstantiation of Myth', p. 88; L. H. Lees, *Exiles of Erin* (Manchester, 1979), 175. It is important, as Raphael Samuel points out ('The Catholic Church and the Irish Poor', in R. Swift and S. Gilley (eds.), *The Irish in the Victorian City* (1985), 290) not to read back the greater cohesion of commitment achieved by the Catholic Church in the later nineteenth century into the conditions of the 1840s and 1850s.

holding regular monthly meetings with an average attendance of over
500. There were branches in suburbs and villages, and a committee
visited working men in order to circulate tracts, to invite them to join
the association, and to urge them to attend church more regularly.[115]
Stowell quickly followed McNeile's example and started an Operative
Association in Salford, which held quarterly meetings and distributed
tracts. Stowell divided the town into districts, assigning a 'Protestant
watchman' to each, with responsibility for diffusing information orally
and by means of tracts, and to look out 'against any intrusions of the
enemy into their beats'. These stalwarts met regularly to report on
their activities and receive instruction.[116]

The lead taken in Liverpool and Salford was quickly followed in
York in August 1839, Norwich in November 1839, and Sheffield in
January 1840. London was relatively slow to move, but a Protestant
Operative Association was formed in Finsbury in March 1840, and
during the next two years similar bodies were established in a number
of other suburbs and districts.[117] Edward Dalton, the Protestant
Association secretary, took a particular interest in the promotion of
operative organization in the London area. In 1840 he began to edit
the *Penny Protestant Operative*, intended as a working man's version of
the *Protestant Magazine* and distributed to members of Operative
Associations.[118] The London Operative Associations met regularly for
lectures, and formed classes for 'mutual instruction'.[119] Libraries of
suitable literature were also set up, and a wider educational and social
function was served. The young men's society of the Marylebone
Operative Association sought to instruct its members not just on points
relating to 'Popery' but also on history and other subjects. At York the
membership included a substantial proportion of women, and the
presence of both sexes in the London societies is suggested by the
commencement of a series of singing-classes in February 1843 and the
arrangement of a steam-packet excursion to Richmond that summer.[120]

The earliest Protestant operative societies were linked with the

[115] *PM*, 1 (1839), 111–12; Murphy, *Religious Problem*, pp. 220–1.
[116] *PM*, 2 (1840), 334; 4 (1842), 83; Murphy, *Religious Problem*, p. 221.
[117] *PM*, 1 (1839), 143, 236; 2 (1840), 85, 123, and *passim*. There are references in
the *Penny Protestant Operative* to branches at Lambeth, Marylebone, Peckham,
Southwark, and Tower Hamlets.
[118] *PM*, 4 (1842), 157. The authority for the statement that Dalton was editor of the
Penny Protestant Operative is an advertisement on the back cover of his pamphlet *No Peace
with Rome* (1841).
[119] *PPO*, 3 (1842), 15, 37, 93, and *passim*.
[120] Ibid. 15; 4 (1843), 16, 48; *Yorkshire Gazette*, 17 Oct. 1840.

Protestant Association, but from 1841 the Reformation Society took up the idea, concentrating its efforts in the London area and forming operative auxiliaries in those districts such as Westminster, Bermondsey, and Chelsea where the Protestant Association had not established itself. In July 1843 they appointed a general operative secretary to oversee these societies.[121] In most respects they resembled the organizations set up by the Protestant Association, although, in accordance with the interests of the parent body, they generally avoided activity of an explicitly political kind and gave more attention to missionary work among Roman Catholics, who were systematically visited and encouraged to attend meetings and discussions.[122]

Tight social control of the operative societies was exercised. Local clergy and lay members of the parent committee of the Protestant Association or the Reformation Society served as chairmen and speakers. A condescending attitude was widely in evidence: the Reformation Society's *Annual Report* in 1842 spoke of the 'intellectual limitations' of its operative supporters, and when the Manchester Association discovered in 1849 that the winner of their essay competition really was 'a *bona fide* shoemaker', 'they could hardly suppose that the essay was his own composition. But they learned a good lesson—not to judge of the value of the diamond by the roughness of the coating.'[123] The *Penny Protestant Operative* adopted a patronizing attitude to working-class participation in meetings, while Edward Dalton attempted, rather quaintly, to communicate arguments against Rome in a lecture consisting entirely of words of one syllable.[124]

The first issue of the *Penny Protestant Operative* made explicit the motives for setting up the associations, condemning 'Socialism' and 'Chartism' in the same breath as 'Socinianism' and 'Popery'. It continued: 'If the higher classes do not furnish their less privileged brethren with sound and nutritious food for the mind, how can they wonder that the corrupt seed sown among them by the enemy should

[121] RS, *14th AR* (1841), 12–13; *15th AR* (1842), 10; RS minutes, 3 July 1843. Other recorded Reformation Society operative branches were at Greenwich, Hammersmith, Islington, Lambeth, Poplar, St John's Wood, Somers Town, Southwark, and Woolwich. The general operative secretary was a Mr John Ballard who, in a letter of 30 Nov. 1852 (Hope MSS 33/11/92), later gave an interesting account of the work.

[122] BP, 1 (1845), 46–9, 114–23; 2 (1846), 142–4 and *passim*; cf. S. Gilley, 'Protestant London, No-Popery and the Irish Poor, 1830–1860', *Recusant History*, 10 (1970), 218.

[123] RS, *15th AR* (1842), 11; *Protestant Witness*, 17 Nov. 1849, pp. 252–3.

[124] PPO, 1 (1840), 47, 63–4; E. Dalton, *No Peace with Rome* (1841).

spring up, and bring forth bad fruit.'[125] In February 1842 the London Protestant Operative Associations were circulating Brindley's *Anti-Socialist Gazette* as well as anti-Catholic publications.[126] In 1844 the Revd M. H. Seymour, replying to an address from the Southwark Protestant Operative Association, acknowledged that the lower classes had an importance 'far greater than our statesmen are disposed to ascribe to them', and that there could be no security for national institutions if the poor were alienated from them.[127]

Clumsy though these efforts were, they do seem to have struck a vein in lower-class consciousness and to have enjoyed a success that was significant, albeit short-lived and geographically limited. There were clear links with the radical Tory tradition, indicated, for example, by a letter in the *Penny Protestant Operative* in March 1842 which alleged that the New Poor Law served the purposes of the pope.[128] The rhetoric of liberty and resistance to oppression, linked with a strong patriotism, was likely to strike a chord in popular consciousness, and to deflect antagonism that in other circles was directed against the established constitutional order on to the attack on Rome. This is well illustrated by a poem published in the *Penny Protestant Operative* in October 1840:

> Ye Protestant Christians arise!
> England summons you now to her aid
> Protect and defend me, she cries
> Ere freedom and liberty fade . . .
>
> Firm as a rock be the trust
> Of our loyal and Protestant bands
> Rome never shall crush to the dust
> Our Protestant free artisans.[129]

In similar vein, Stowell, speaking in York in 1844, charged that 'Popery' oppressed the poor man by its élitist use of Latin and its financial exactions for Masses for the dead.[130]

[125] *PPO*, 1 (1840), 1.

[126] *PPO*, 3 (1842), 16.

[127] *PPO*, 5 (1844), 59–60.

[128] *PPO*, 3 (1842), 18–19.

[129] *PPO*, 1 (1840), 55. On popular patriotism, see H. Cunningham, 'The Language of Patriotism, 1750–1914', *History Workshop Journal*, 12 (1981), 8–33. Cf. J. Wolffe, 'Evangelicalism in Mid-Nineteenth-Century England', in R. Samuel (ed.), *Patriotism: The Making and Unmaking of British National Identity*, i. *History and Politics* (1989), 188–200.

[130] H. Stowell, *A Speech Delivered at the Fifth Anniversary of the York Operative Protestant Association* (York, 1844), 13–14 (York City Library).

The Protestant operative movement was at its height in 1842 and was viewed by both the Protestant Association and the Reformation Society as an important aspect of their operations.[131] The numbers of people involved were quite substantial, with memberships of 412 at Norwich in February 1841, 228 at Tower Hamlets in 1842, and 631 at Southwark in September 1842.[132] Numerous meetings were held, and there was a considerable amount of tract distribution and door-to-door visiting. There is no evidence regarding the 'trade' composition of the operative societies' membership, but the disproportionate extent of their impact in the London area suggests that the backbone of their support came from the small tradesmen and independent artisans who dominated the occupational struture of the capital.[133]

The close correlation of the movement's rise and decline with that of Chartism can hardly have been coincidental. In part, as we have seen, it was consciously promoted as a counterweight to radical agitation, but it would seem that the Protestant operative societies thrived on the same adverse economic conditions as the Chartist organizations did. In those areas supporting Protestant Operative Associations, Chartism had a significant pressure but not a dominant one; and in districts such as Halifax, Oldham, or the North-East, where Chartists challenged traditional authority most forcefully, operative societies usually do not appear to have got off the ground. In centres like Liverpool, York, and, above all, London, the working class was more divided occupationally and more exposed to Anglican Evangelical influence. A substantial Catholic presence also provided the *raison d'être* for operative associations and made it possible for them to co-exist with Chartism. The relatively late development of organized working-class Protestantism in London coincides interestingly with the similarly slow emergence of an effective metropolitan Chartist movement. Furthermore, the eventual strength of the anti-Catholic movement in London may well stem from the secularist flavour of London Chartism, which presumably repelled those with at least a minimal religious allegiance. In the North of England, on the

---

[131] *PM*, 6 (1844), p. iv; RS, *15th AR* (1842), 10.

[132] *Yorkshire Gazette*, 17 Oct. 1840; *PPO*, 2 (1841), 15, 57; 3 (1842), 37, 75. It was stated in relation to Southwark that only a small proportion of the membership was really active (*PPO*, 2 (1841), 58).

[133] D. Goodway, *London Chartism 1838–1848* (Cambridge, 1982), 5–11.

[134] D. Thompson, *The Chartists* (1984), 61–2. There was an isolated Protestant meeting, clearly dominated by Wesleyans, at Bradford, where Chartism was very strong (*PPO*, 2 (1841), 32).

other hand, the more extensive use of Christian motifs by the Chartists would enable them to gain and retain the loyalty of such people.[135]

It might also be argued that the Operative Associations were exploiting an antipathy to Chartism among some of the labour aristocracy stirred by sectarian suspicions of links between radicalism and the Irish. This, however, would be to build too much on the evidence. The anti-Chartist rhetoric in the *Penny Protestant Operative* appears to be derived more from the perceptions of the upper-class patrons of the movement than the real grievances of its working-class members. Furthermore, until 1848 the links between Chartism and the Irish were weak.[136]

The operative societies declined in the mid-1840s, although the missionary focus of the branches linked with the Reformation Society meant that they proved somewhat more enduring than those of the Protestant Association. The *Penny Protestant Operative*, which in its early years had contained much original matter aimed at a working-class readership, degenerated into a potted version of the *Protestant Magazine*, and at the end of 1848 it ceased publication altogether. Where Operative Associations did survive, as in Manchester, they tended to become more middle-class in character, with little to distinguish them from ordinary branches of the Protestant societies.[137]

The gap left by the decline of the operative societies was filled to some extent in the later 1840s and early 1850s by the development of Protestant classes. When John Hope began to promote a Protestant movement in Edinburgh in 1845, he felt that machinery going beyond occasional public meetings was required. He had already had extensive experience organizing teetotalism, and now sought to teach children 'to avoid the Mass House as the public House and Popery as alcohol'.[138] As this aphorism implied, he saw the anti-Catholic campaign primarily in the context of education directed towards the younger generation. Initially he worked through his existing structure of apprentice schools in the city, which had an attendance of about 800

---

[135] Goodway, *London Chartism*, pp. 12, 59; E. Yeo, 'Christianity in Chartist Struggle, 1838–1842', *Past and Present*, 91 (1981), 109–39.

[136] Goodway, *London Chartism*, pp. 61–8; J. Belchem, 'English Working Class Radicalism and the Irish, 1815–50', in Swift and Gilley, *Irish in the Victorian City*, pp. 85–94.

[137] *PPO, passim*. The social profile of the supporters of the Manchester Operative Protestant Association can be inferred from the charges made for tickets to its annual meeting (*Protestant Witness*, 2 Dec. 1848, p. 56).

[138] Hope MSS 226/6, pp. 669–70, 226/7, pp. 319–21, 226/8, pp. 31–2, Hope to Cumming, 7 Mar., 3 Nov. 1848, 20 Aug. 1849.

in 1849.[139] Weekly classes were subsequently formed specifically to study the controversy with Rome.[140] Hope's activities in Edinburgh appear to have had a formative influence on the development of classes elsewhere, both of children and young men. One of the earliest to come into existence was associated with Blakeney's ministry at Nottingham, and by the end of 1848 a class of nearly thirty had been formed by the Islington Protestant Institute.[141] During the 1850s Protestant classes were set up in a number of places in Scotland outside Edinburgh, but the idea does not appear to have been taken up to the same extent in England.[142]

Hope's copious correspondence provides insights into the nature of the instruction given at Protestant classes. His first step was to pester the leaders of the Reformation Society to write tracts for them, suggesting that they should consist of only four pages, this being the maximum that classes could absorb at one sitting, with questions and answers at the end.[143] Blakeney was ultimately persuaded to write the tracts, and the collected results were later published as the *Manual of the Romish Controversy* and *Popery in its Social Aspect*.[144] These works, like the Protestant catechisms produced by Blakeney, Vernon Harcourt, and others, were structured in a manner designed to encourage rote-learning of standard replies to Catholic arguments which could then be employed in polemical debates. Hope offered prizes for proficiency in the acquisition of such knowledge.[145]

It was common for a member of a class to assume the persona of a Catholic in order to stimulate supposedly realistic debate. William Turnbull, an agent employed by Hope but seconded to the Reformation Society for training, explained how this was done in a young men's class he was conducting in London in March 1853. After three nights studying Blakeney's *Manual*, on the fourth night he would 'give out a subject, make one of the Class read . . . all the Romish arguments for that subject he can in fifteen minutes, then any member may get up

---

[139] Ibid. 226/8, pp. 206–7, Hope to Miller, 24 Oct. 1849.
[140] Ibid. 43/5/161–2, enc. handbill on 'Popery' classes.
[141] Islington Protestant Institute, *2nd AR* (1848), 29.
[142] Hope MSS 44/4/79, James Sommerville to Hope, 8 Oct. 1858 (Irvine); 44/4/115, Robert Ovens to Hope, 29 Oct. 1858 (Belford); 45/7/75, J. H. Gildard to Hope, 19 July 1859 (Aberdeen).
[143] Ibid. 226/8, p. 32, Hope to Cumming, 20 Aug. 1849.
[144] R. P. Blakeney, *A Manual of Romish Controversy* (Edinburgh, 1851); *Popery in its Social Aspect* (Edinburgh, 1852); Hope MSS 32/9/51, Blakeney to Hope, 26 Sept. 1851.
[145] R. P. Blakeney, *Protestant Catechism* (1853); F. E. Vernon Harcourt, *The Protestant Missionary's Catechism* (1853); Jamie, *John Hope*, pp. 262–3.

and reply to those arguments *extempore* for ten minutes while I look for errors in views or methods of controverting any point . . . '.[146] Turnbull's methods reflected his belief in the desirability of encouraging independent thought rather than parrot-like repetition. Such convictions were rare among the teachers of Protestant classes: one discontented pupil explained to Hope that he had left a class because he felt that the instruction was more suited to children than to grown men.[147] This became a more pressing problem within a few years, when Catholics had sufficiently familiarized themselves with Protestant controversial works to ensure that debate would be conducted on lines with which their adversaries were unfamiliar. Other critics expressed unease about the moral and spiritual dangers of poorly controlled debate and the role-playing of Catholics.[148]

The surviving minutes of an adult male Antipopery Class in Leith in 1859 and 1860 provide evidence of the occupational make-up of one of these bodies. This gathering was a major formative influence on Jacob Primmer, later a leader of anti-Catholicism in Scotland at the turn of the century. Of the forty-two men on the roll, the largest single group comprised six joiners. There were also five engineers, four confectioners, three masons, two sugar-refiners, two printers, two warehousemen, two gardeners, two blacksmiths, a rope-spinner, a brass-founder, a sawyer, a porter, a tinsmith, a draper, and a bookbinder. Only seven members of the class, four pupil-teachers and three clerks, came from occupations not of a trading or artisan character. Thus the gathering was predominantly one of the 'respectable' working class and lower middle class: there were no labourers, and, in a port, dockers were also conspicuously absent.[149] Parallel evidence is not available for other classes, but it is clear that their members were generally men of limited education, with social and cultural ambitions blending with religious motives for involvement. Tension arose in 1857 between Hope and one of his classes in Rose Street, Edinburgh, when a number of members expressed an intention to leave if the programme continued to be limited to anti-Catholicism. They called their class 'The Young Men's Saturday Evening Popery

[146] Hope MSS 34/3/18, Turnbull to Hope, 3 Mar. 1853.

[147] Ibid. 43/2/74, John Stevenson to Hope, 10 Feb. 1858.

[148] Ibid. 43/1/207, James Mathison to Hope, n.d.; 45/1/133, Muir to Turnbull, 20 Jan. 1859; 45/4/139, Revd Alex Maclaren to Hope, 1 Apr. 1859.

[149] Ibid. 18/5, Minute-Book of Leith Antipopery Class, Sept. 1859–July 1861; J. B. Primmer (ed.), *Life of Jacob Primmer, Minister of the Church of Scotland* (Edinburgh, 1916), 7–8; S. Bruce, *No Pope of Rome*, (Edinburgh, 1985), 40.

Class for Mutual Improvement'. Debates on 'Popery' continued to be an important part of their activities, however, not only in deference to Hope but because the members enjoyed the sharpness of polemical discussion and realized that they were acquiring valuable verbal skills. Their anxiety to score points off each other became a source of concern to a leadership more preoccupied with united and effective mission to Roman Catholics.[150]

Most Protestant instruction was directed at men and boys, but women and girls were not wholly neglected. A speaker at a Protestant operative meeting in York in October 1840 emphasized how important women were in influencing young minds.[151] There was a girls class in Edinburgh in the 1850s, and at Bathgate in March 1859 it was noted that the majority of attenders at a class for young people open to both sexes were girls. However, exclusively male classes were far more common than female ones, and when classes for women did exist, they did not receive the same degree of attention.[152]

On a few occasions Protestant missions set up elementary schools for children, giving a general education to both Protestants and Catholics, although the majority of the children attending were Protestants.[153] The Free Church mission in Edinburgh in 1855 had two day-schools, one for ordinary education, the other offering industrial education for girls. Although 164 children were enrolled, the actual attendance was only around 55.[154] In 1856 Hope's mission had six classes meeting in the densely populated slum districts immediately to the south of the Old Town. They operated on five evenings each week and attracted a total average attendance of over 400, but the wide variations in numbers at some of them suggest that there, too, children had only a limited commitment.[155] A teacher commented in 1859 that they were 'of that Class that take it into their heads to attend for a while and then disappear'. Various direct material incentives, such as gifts of clothes to regular attenders, were developed

---

[150] Hope MSS 42/3/58, J. W. Cox to Hope, 14 Sept. 1857; 43/1/207, James Mathison to Hope, n.d.; 44/6/23, Turnbull to Hope, 27 Dec. 1858. The location of a class in Rose St., in the heart of the New Town, suggests that the membership consisted of domestic servants and of men employed in service industries.

[151] *Yorkshire Gazette*, 17 Oct. 1840.

[152] Hope MSS 45/3/115, John Byres to Hope, 5 Mar. 1859; 46/5/43, Miss Pritty to Hope, 21 Dec. 1859.

[153] Catholic participation in these schools is discussed below.

[154] SRO, CH 3/111/26, p.614, Minutes of the Free Presbytery of Edinburgh, 20 June 1855.

[155] Hope MSS 40/3/9, Turnbull to Hope, 29 Sept. 1856.

in an attempt to rectify this position.[156] The Islington Protestant Institute ran a number of mission schools which, in 1859, had 420 children on their books and an average daily attendance of 342.[157] Both in Edinburgh and in Islington staunchly Protestant religious teaching was a prominent feature of the curriculum. However, such educational provision by Protestant societies was quite unusual: in most places they preferred to concentrate their limited manpower on exclusively religious education.

From the early 1850s the Reformation Society and other bodies sought to develop more extensive missionary operations. These had the primary aim of proselytism among the Roman Catholic poor, but they were also intended to reinforce Protestant conviction among the non-Catholic working class. At the end of 1851 the committee, at Blakeney's instigation, founded a 'Special Mission to Roman Catholics in London', an operation which was quickly extended to the provinces. In collaboration with John Hope and the Anti-Popery Committee of the Church of Scotland, they also pursued missionary work north of the Border.[158] The localities in which missions were set up during the 1850s are indicated in Figure 3 (p. 153). This aspect of the Reformation Society's work should be understood in the context not only of the anti-Catholic movement but also of the urban mission societies. In 1855 the London City Mission and the Scripture Readers' Association had between them 449 workers in the metropolis, and there were over 250 missionaries and Scripture readers working elsewhere in England.[159] In Scotland the Glasgow City Mission was founded in January 1826 and was employing 22 agents in 1831 and 52 in 1864. A comparable Edinburgh organization opened in 1832.[160] Although these major societies were concerned with the general problem of 'spiritual destitution', the London City Mission gave particular attention to the needs of the Catholic poor, and recruited a number of missionaries specifically to work among them. Conversely, there were some respects, such as the educational work at

---

[156] Hope MSS 46/2/14, Patrick Corbett to Hope, 28 Sept. 1859; 47/2/36, Sullivan to Hope, 18 June 1860.

[157] Islington Protestant Institute, *12th AR* (1859), 14–15.

[158] *BP*, 9 (1853), 94–5; 10 (1854), 177 ff.; Hope MSS 32/12/45, Blakeney to Hope, Dec. 1851.

[159] D. M. Lewis, *Lighten their Darkness* (Westport, Conn., 1986) Appendix B; id., 'The Evangelical Mission to the British Working Class', D.Phil. thesis (Oxford, 1981), 191.

[160] O. Checkland, *Philanthropy in Victorian Scotland* (Edinburgh, 1980), 66–71.

Edinburgh and Islington, in which the Protestant missions performed a function substantially wider than that of proselytism.

In addition to the Reformation Society, there were three smaller urban missionary bodies working predominantly among Catholics. The English Church Missions to Roman Catholics was set up in 1853 and lasted until 1858. It was most actively supported by the Revd J. E. Armstrong of St Paul's, Bermondsey, but it also maintained missions in other parts of London and in the provinces.[161] In north London in 1852 the Islington Protestant Institute was employing a clerical secretary and superintendent, the Revd Robert Maguire, two lay agents, and two schoolmasters.[162] In Edinburgh the Free Church set up its own missions amidst the poor Irish in the Grassmarket area of the city.[163] Thus the total number of men involved specifically in proselytism among professing Catholics rose quickly to a peak of about sixty in 1855 before declining somewhat at the end of the decade. About a third were at work in London, a third elsewhere in England, and a third in Scotland, mainly in the Edinburgh area. Wales was entirely neglected apart from a brief attempt to establish an agent in Swansea. The Reformation Society provided much the largest group of missionaries, about half the total.[164]

The agents employed were frequently themselves converts from Roman Catholicism who had migrated from Ireland. They had a certain cultural affinity with the targets of proselytism, particularly when they were able to converse in Gaelic. For example, one Michael Quin was converted to Protestantism in Ireland, worked there as a Scripture reader for twelve years, but then claimed that he was driven from the country by the antagonism of the priests, rendered more intense by knowledge of his apostasy. He continued in a similar occupation in England for eleven years, and in July 1856 he wrote to Hope from Liverpool to ask for work in Edinburgh: 'I am quite adiquate [*sic*] to hold and address a meeting in a Room to the Irish people and also you will find me active and energetick [*sic*] to go read

[161] *R*, 16 June 1853, 24 May 1854, 8 May 1857, 5 May 1858. Armstrong was born and educated in Ireland, appointed to St Paul's in 1848, and learnt Gaelic in order more effectively to evangelize the Irish poor (newspaper cuttings and handbills in Southwark Local Studies Library).
[162] Islington Public Library, Islington Protestant Institute materials, YK701(1). On Maguire, see *DNB*, xxxv. 332.
[163] J. E. Handley, *The Irish in Modern Scotland* (Cork, 1947), 102.
[164] *BP*, 12 (1856), 59 and *passim*. These estimates do not include men employed by the London City Mission and other similar general mission societies.

[*sic*] the Scriptures among them from house to house in English as well as Irish. I know all the leading doctrines of the papal religion both in Latin as well as Irish and English.''[165] In October 1857 Hope received a further letter from Quin, now living in an Edinburgh tenement, pathetically entreating him to find him a job of any kind, secular or missionary, as his wife and four children would otherwise starve.[166] Such indications suggest that the position of convert missionaries was vulnerable and insecure. They could labour with heroic commitment,[167] but their background and circumstances were such that several of them were unstable men with an eye to the main chance. For example, in 1857 the Reformation Society dismissed a man when they discovered that he had been obtaining money from a Catholic priest by making false professions that he was about to return to Rome.[168]

Missionary agents brought up as Protestants usually appear to have come from a similar kind of social background to that of the members of the Leith AntiPopery Class: indeed, it is clear that such classes were a major source of recruitment for the missions. While zeal against 'Popery' was usually sincere, there was also a consciousness that employment as a Protestant missionary offered prospects and status somewhat in advance of alternative occupations, and a decisive step to 'respectability'. In 1858 missionaries in training in Edinburgh were paid £52 a year if single, £60 if married; when qualified, single men received £70 and married men £80.[169] However, an experienced man might expect to receive as much as £150. At approximately the same period, the majority of the Edinburgh labour aristocracy were receiving between 15s. and 22s. a week.[170] In some cases, working for the Protestant missions clearly did not come up to expectations. For example, Thomas Robertson wrote in February 1858 to ask for a pay increase, claiming that his accommodation was inadequate and that he needed better clothes than when he had been working in a bakery.[172] William Smith complained in August 1858 that he did not really like

[165] Hope MSS 40/1/176, Quin to Hope, 29 July 1856.
[166] Ibid. 42/4/118, Quin to Hope, 1 Oct. 1857.
[167] *BP*, 3 (1847), 54–62, 120–32, and *passim*.
[168] RS minutes, 23 Mar. 1857.
[169] Hope MSS 44/5/92, notes by Turnbull. It is not entirely clear from the document whether this salary scale was actually implemented or merely recommended.
[170] Hope MSS 44/2/18–19, Dunlop to Hope, 24 Aug. 1858; Robert Q. Gray, *The Labour Aristocracy in Victorian Edinburgh* (Oxford, 1976), 45, 136–43.
[171] Hope MSS 43/2/86, Robertson to Hope, 8 Feb. 1858.
[172] Ibid. 44/2/33, bundle relating to Smith, especially Smith to Hope, 18 Aug. 1858, 19 Feb. 1859, Hope to Smith, 24 Feb. 1859.

visiting Roman Catholics and would like to be given the opportunity to learn Latin. Hope did not think that this would be of any use to him. By February 1859 Smith had shifted to financial ground, asking for a pay increase of fifteen pounds per annum. Hope's reply alleged that Smith was living beyond his means, thus reflecting his own anxiety that his agents should continue to be closely identified with the working class. However, he did agree that Smith required somewhat superior clothing and accommodation, and gave him £9 for the purpose. Smith was still dissatisfied, feeling that he could not dress his family in a manner befitting his status, bemoaning the penance of living on porridge, and revealing that his ultimate aspiration was to enter the ministry.[172] This was probably the ambition of many of his colleagues: Turnbull, after some years as superintendent of Hope's operations in Edinburgh, was eventually ordained.[173] Other agents displayed a similar, if less fruitful, autodidacticism: one Scripture reader settled down to learn Syriac in the belief that it would equip him better to rebut Catholic arguments, while another wrote a lengthy tract on infidelity.[174] Meanwhile, other, frailer brethren found the moral demands made upon them too exacting: the Reformation Society, increasingly influenced by Hope's rigid teetotalism, dismissed two employees for drunkenness in 1854, and in 1855 a former superintendent of the Free Church Grassmarket mission was arrested in a disturbance in a Liverpool brothel.[175]

Given this variable human material, the Reformation Society took an interesting initiative by establishing a training institute for its agents. The course included a mixture of reading and practical experience and lasted six months, divided into three terms.[176] The first was spent on the Bible, the second on Blakeney's *Manual of Romish Controversy* and Chillingworth's *Religion of Protestants*, and the third on ecclesiastical history. Clementson, the superintendent, was to catechize the students every week and they were to write essays every month. Throughout their training they were expected to spend six hours a week visiting and to keep a journal which would be regularly inspected. At the end of the

[173] Jamie, *John Hope*, p. 371.
[174] Hope MSS 42/6/119, 43/3/120, Coghlan to Hope, 9 Dec. 1857, 8 Mar. 1858; 43/6/30, Dunlop to Hope, 25 June 1858.
[175] RS minutes, 27 Feb., 21 Apr. 1854; Handley, *Irish in Modern Scotland*, p. 104. Given the natural tendency of Catholic sources to make the maximum propaganda capital out of such incidents, and the equally understandable Protestant anxiety to ensure that they did not receive any publicity, it is hard to judge how common they were.
[176] *BP*, 11 (1855), 85.

course the students would undergo a general examination.[177] An extract from Turnbull's journal for 13 January 1853 gives an idea of how a typical day was spent: 'Got up this morning at 7—wrote out some extracts I took from Dr Cahill last night—which I hope to use soon in Edinb. Went to Southwark, visited one hour, came home, studied the Manual for tomorrow's lesson—at eight o'clock went to Parker St. St Giles to hear a discussion.'[178] Turnbull's letters to Hope suggest, however, that in many respects the reality of the institute fell short of the ideal: matters were much more casually arranged than the printed sources suggest, and the standard of the teaching was poor.[179]

In communicating with a semi-literate population, among whom Protestant feelings might have to be awakened rather than assumed, the societies and missions developed increasingly sophisticated propaganda techniques. Blakeney thought that Roman Catholics should be encouraged to attend in order to increase the excitement. He preferred to hold meetings in halls rather than churches so that there would be no sense of decorum to restrain any 'ebullition of feeling'.[180] Visual aids were also employed: the Protestant Alliance was using a portrait of Hus, although MacGregor considered that illustrations associated with the English Reformation were likely to have a greater appeal.[181] Blakeney's pictorial sense was cruder, however: in April 1851 he was using a 'number of the beast' 2 yards long by $1\frac{1}{2}$ wide. In 1852 Hope was eagerly investigating the possible use of magic-lantern slides to discredit the Mass, images, the confessional, nunneries, and other Catholic practices. He was informed of a mechanism whereby a picture of the pope could be transformed gradually into that of a gentleman in black with a tail and cloven hooves.[182]

Debates with Roman Catholics continued to be a regular feature of the operations of Protestant societies and attracted considerable audiences. These could occur casually in the open air and were prone to become disorderly. For example, an open-air meeting on Prince's Pier, Liverpool on a Sunday afternoon in June 1852 drew a crowd of

---

[177] Hope MSS 32/12/45, Blakeney to Hope, Dec. 1851; *BP*, 9 (1853), 104.
[178] Hope MSS 34/1/72–3, Turnbull to Hope, 14 Jan. 1853.
[179] Ibid. 33/9/30, 27 Sept. 1852; 33/10/9, 9 Oct. 1852; 33/11/67, 20 Nov. 1852; 33/12/7, 2 Dec. 1852; J. R. Wolffe, 'Protestant Societies and Anti-Catholic Agitation in Great Britain, 1829–1860', D. Phil. thesis (Oxford, 1984), 265.
[180] Hope MSS 32/1/68, Blakeney to Hope, 20 Jan. 1851.
[181] Ibid. 36/1/40, 36/5/121, MacGregor to Hope, 18 July, 18 Nov. 1854.
[182] Ibid. 32/4/45, Blakeney to Hope, 16 Apr. 1851; 226/11, p. 716, Hope to Turnbull, 27 Jan. 1853; 34/3/21, Dundas to Hope, 4 Mar. 1853.

500, including two Roman Catholic hecklers.[183] Similarly, in September 1852 Turnbull engaged upon a discussion on Kennington Common in front of a crowd of several hundred. At Birkenhead in late 1853 or early 1854 a missionary who conversed with a few Roman Catholic workmen drew a crowd that was initially peaceful but ultimately assaulted him.[184]

Indoor meetings were more readily controllable, and there were still frequently Catholic spokesmen, usually laymen, who were willing to engage in formal debate. One Catholic debater was reduced to a state of fury by Turnbull in three hours at Chelsea in October 1852, but at Southwark another was prepared to carry on weekly discussions with the Reformation Society's missionary for a period of ten months.[185] Despite the general caution of the Catholic clergy towards such events, the missionary at Preston claimed that no less than seven priests had participated in debate.[186] In Glasgow in 1859 debates were attracting large audiences of both Protestants and Catholics. These occasions were generally good-humoured, although in one instance a group of thugs intending to cause trouble was observed.[187] Both religious groups had their preferred champions, and at times debaters seemed to be as much in competition with their co-religionists for the loyalty of their own community as they were with the other side.[188]

Nevertheless, it was clear that Catholic opponents were not always forthcoming, and missionaries then resorted to lecturing. The Preston missionary claimed an attendance of between 400 and 500 at his weekly meetings, including a high proportion of Catholics. In Liverpool the agent delivered twenty-one indoor lectures and thirty-six outdoor ones between May 1859 and May 1860. The attendance at the former averaged 300 and at the latter 600, again including numerous Catholics. During the same period up to a dozen controversial lectures were being delivered each week in Glasgow.[189]

An intriguing insight into the more disreputable side of Protestant missionary activity is provided by the correspondence between John

[183] *BP*, 8 (1852), 128.
[184] Hope MSS 33/9/4, Turnbull to Hope, 6 Sept. 1852; *BP*, 10 (1854), 29–30.
[185] Hope MSS 33/10/23, Turnbull to Hope, 28 Oct. 1852; *BP*, 10 (1854), 246 ff.
[186] *BP*, 11 (1855), 9.
[187] Hope MSS 45/7/56, 46/2/22, Dunlop to Hope, 16 July, 24 Sept. 1859; 45/5/43, newspaper cutting.
[188] Ibid. 45/5/26, 45/6/103, Dunlop to Hope, 25 May, 4 June 1859.
[189] *BP*, 11 (1855), 9; 16 (1860), 21; Hope MSS 46/8/41, Dunlop to Hope, 4 Feb. 1860.

Hope and James Mathison, a Catholic living by his wits in the slums of Edinburgh and Glasgow. Mathison's barely literate letters indicate a shrewd ability to exploit Protestant leaders to his own advantage.[190] Mathison had some contact with Hope's mission during the mid-1850s and claimed that he had become convinced of the errors of Rome.[191] However, he remained a professing Catholic while Hope gave him money to provide tame Catholic opposition for Protestant debaters.[192] By March 1859 Mathison decided that it was time for him to make a public recantation of Catholicism, and, never a man to engage in false modesty, he urged Hope to hire Glasgow City Hall for the purpose, claiming that no other building in the city would be large enough. Admission should be charged to the meeting, and the proceeds were to go to Mathison himself. In order to ensure a large turn-out, Mathison suggested that the town should be placarded and interest excited by his participation in one final discussion as a Catholic, thereby enhancing the drama of his 'conversion'.[193] However, this ingenious scheme was frustrated when news of Mathison's surreptitious contacts with Hope leaked out, apparently disseminated by rival Protestant missionaries who sought to discredit Hope's organization.[194] In the end Mathison found Scotland too hot to hold him; he enlisted in the army, but he quickly deserted and, with Hope's assistance, emigrated to America, where he renewed his career as a religious orator in New York.[195]

Through James Mathison's career one glimpses something of the complex variety of perceptions focused on Protestant activity in the Irish slums. For the middle-class and aristocratic leaders like Hope it was a struggle against an elemental power of spiritual and social evil in which the end seemed to justify occasionally dubious means. For the poor themselves it was a source of enjoyment and excitement in which

---

[190] Unfortunately, many of these are inadequately dated and, as their order in the Scottish Record Office has become muddled, it is difficult to be sure about the detailed sequence of events. However, the general development of Mathison's activities seems clear.

[191] Hope MSS 44/1/132, 46/1/58, Mathison to Hope 2 [July 1858?], 24 [Aug. 1859?].

[192] Ibid. 43/1/210, Mathison to Hope, n.d. [Jan. 1858?]. It was claimed that something similar was happening at debates in Edinburgh (Hope MSS 43/1/203, anonymous note, n.d.).

[193] Ibid. 45/3/46, 45/4/49, Mathison to Hope, 16 [Mar. 1859?], 26 [Apr. 1859?].

[194] Ibid 45/5/96, Mathison to Hope, 16 [May 1859?].

[195] Ibid. 46/1/58, 149, Mathison to Hope, 19, 24 [Aug. 1859?]; 47/1/79, James McClelland to Hope, May 1860.

communal consciousness was developed and reinforced in a manner which in a later generation, in Glasgow at least, was to be translated from the religious platform to the football field. The lower-class speakers and missionary agents might share something of the ideology of the élites and be influenced by the sectarian loyalties of the poor, but for them the controversy was also a source of employment and income, and a way of life which both Protestants and Catholics had a vested interest in maintaining, while scoring points off each other.

A similar complexity of motive and response is evident when one turns to consider the impact of door-to-door visitation of Catholics. This was a staple occupation of Protestant missionaries, and a task which the Reformation Society's agents in London were instructed to undertake for three hours each day.[196] In 1854 the missionary at Birkenhead reported that, throughout the previous year, he had visited an average of five families for 2½ hours a day, not counting Protestant households. At Liverpool 2,250 visits were claimed in 1860, while at Bradford there had been 2,143.[197] The Church of Scotland Anti-Popery Mission carried out 7,961 visits to Roman Catholics and 2,598 to Protestants in the year from May 1857 to April 1858, the majority of which would have been in Edinburgh.[198] Such precise indications of the number of visits were not recorded sufficiently widely to permit any systematic calculations, especially as there is usually no means of ascertaining the proportion of return visits, but it is clear that Protestant missionaries were a common sight in the Irish slums, particularly in Edinburgh and London. Visits normally took the form of an offer to read the Bible, sometimes in the Catholic Douai version and in Irish if the missionary was fluent in the language. An exposition and discussion would then follow.

The varying beliefs and levels of commitment among Irish Catholics are reflected in the wide range of responses received. The most common reactions were hostile, but expressed in a variety of different ways. Doors were slammed in the missionaries' faces, tracts were refused, or taken and then ostentatiously torn up.[199] One woman visited in St Giles in March 1847 declared that she wanted 'no religion but her own', forcing the missionary to retreat, while another, he reported, 'took a shovel and swore that if I did not take myself and the

---

[196] Ibid. 33/11/40, Blakeney to Hope, 11 Nov. 1852.
[197] *BP*, 10 (1854), 231; 16 (July 1860), 14.
[198] Hope MSS 43/5/176, notes by Turnbull, May 1858.
[199] *BP*, 1 (1845), 23; 2 (1846), 142 and *passim*.

Devil's book away, she would split my head'.[200] Physical violence was more often threatened than carried out, because missionaries generally retreated from confrontation and were attacked only if they behaved particularly provocatively, like the man who put a tract in a carriage belonging to visiting ecclesiastical dignitaries at the consecration of a chapel.[201] However, they might also be waylaid in premeditated assaults, to which missionaries who were themselves converts from Catholicism appear to have been particularly subject. One agent, reporting on such an attack in Bermondsey early in 1852, remarked that it was the fifth time he had been treated in this manner. Clearly, however, the motive was to intimidate not to murder, and the injuries received, although unpleasant, seldom appear to have been serious.[202]

On occasions there were hints that hostile reactions reflected pressure from relations, community, or the priests as much as individual conviction. A woman in Bermondsey explained that her husband had abused her for taking a tract, and on another occasion a man who engaged in a discussion was brusquely called away by his wife.[203] A group accosted in the street declared that they 'were Roman Catholics and not turn-coats'.[204] Similar instances of community solidarity were noted among children: in June 1857 boys in Edinburgh were noticed snatching a Protestant tract from a girl, and a few months later a Protestant Sunday School teacher expressed an anxiety to equip his charges verbally 'to shew fight to the young defenders of the Pope'.[205] The Catholic clergy took firm steps to discourage contact with missionaries: in London in the summer of 1847 a congregation was warned about 'false teachers that are going about in sheep's clothing' and told not to admit them to their houses.[206] A priest's influence is evident in the reaction of a woman who said that 'we don't belong to Bible religion, we belong to the Holy Roman Catholic religion . . . we must not talk to any of your church people'.[207] An agent at work in Stirling in 1856 gave the following account of his efforts:

I have . . . a pretty free access to them [the Roman Catholics], as I speak the Irish

---

[200] *BP*, 3 (1847), 57–8.
[201] *BP*, 4 (1848), 127–8.
[202] *BP*, 5 (1849), 175; 8 (1852), 48.
[203] *BP*, 1 (1845), 49; 2 (1846), 188.
[204] *BP*, 3 (1847), 129.
[205] Hope MSS 41/6/44, Charles Hardie to Hope, 10 June 1857; 43/3/118, John Maconochie to Hope, 8 Mar. 1858.
[206] *BP*, 3 (1847), 172.
[207] Ibid. 137. See also *BP*, 1 (1845), 49.

language freely to them, and read that tongue for all such as don't comprehend English . . . I have held meetings in the Raploch for over twelve months, at the three first of which they crowded to overflowing, hearing me lecture in their native tongue and read God's blessed word. But when the priest interfered and threatened to curse them if they would continue to attend, they gradually withdrew from our meetings.[208]

Only in a minority of cases did missionaries find Catholics ready to listen to them. A rare indication of the frequency of such a response was given by a Scripture reader in Bermondsey in December 1850 who said that he was allowed to read to eight out of the sixty-two families he visited.[209] Such contacts, however, naturally took up the majority of their time and were sufficiently numerous to give them some basis for encouragement. Well-informed Catholics were willing to engage in friendly discussions, presumably in the hope of convincing the missionary himself of his error or of reducing his antagonism to Roman beliefs. In Westminster in 1845 a Roman Catholic told a tract distributor that 'he only spoke from a desire to shew him his error'. In Northampton in 1854 the missionary had 'much conversation' with a Roman Catholic woman who ultimately exclaimed: 'I wish your honour would betake yourself to the patronage of the blessed Mother of God.'[210]

Clearly, some Irish speakers were pleased to have the Bible read to them in their own language and were even prepared to listen to Protestant expositions of it without taking offence.[211] Such people often had only minimal contact with the overworked priests, for whom effective pastoral oversight was a physical impossibility, and welcomed religious ministrations from whatever source they came. A woman in Birkenhead explained: 'No sir, it is not poor people like us he [the priest] goes to see, he never darkens our door, except, one of us were sick and he was sent for.' When the missionary said that his visits would be likely to stimulate the priests to pay them more attention, the woman replied: 'Well sir, if you wont do us any other good, you will bring the priest to us, and we ought to be obliged to you for that.'[212] On several occasions the Catholics visited expressed a wish that the priests themselves would send round Scripture readers.[213] Where

[208] Hope MSS 40/5/167, James O'Sullivan to Hope, 3 Nov. 1856.
[209] *BP*, 6 (1851), 32.
[210] *BP*, 1 (1845), 48; 10 (1854), 198.
[211] *BP*, 3 (1847), 58–9.
[212] *BP*, 9 (1853), 155.
[213] *BP*, 3 (1847), 59, 176.

contact with the Catholic Church had been completely lost, missionaries saw definite hopes of securing conversions. In Aberdeen the agent wrote: 'I have come across several "bad catholics" who having lived years out of the communion of the Ch. might easily be persuaded to join any Protestant congregation.'[214] In other instances, however, especially in London, infidel influence meant that nominal Catholics, while lacking contact with their own Church, were equally unreceptive to the Protestant missionaries.[215]

Catholic anticlericalism provided an opening for Protestant missionaries. Resentment against the priests was especially evident among recent immigrants, who had hostile memories of the Irish clergy. Some felt that the priests had done little for them and, it was alleged on one occasion, had even misappropriated British and American famine relief.[216] There was also tension over confession: one man declared that he was 'not going to tell my sins nor my faults to priests nor to any other man'. A woman in Drury Lane felt that she was defiled by the inquisitions on sexual matters to which the priest subjected her.[217] On occasions, too, the efforts of the priests to assert their authority were counter-productive: missionaries were able to play on the curiosity thus raised about their activity, while exploiting the resentment stirred when the moral yoke of the Church was felt to be too heavy.[218]

The educational facilities of Protestantism were also deployed against the priests. A woman in Northampton said that the priest was very angry that she had sent her son to the Protestant school, but emphasized: 'he may be angry as long as he pleases, I shall do as I think best with my own child'.[219] At Islington in 1854 Catholic children were attending the Protestant Institute schools, and Frederick Oakeley, serving as the local priest, threatened to excommunicate their parents, but even this did not stop the practice.[220] Clearly, faced with a desperate shortage of educational facilities, some of the Catholic poor were prepared to give a higher priority to ensuring that their children acquired at least a minimal literacy than to maintaining a rigorous allegiance to the Church.

[214] Hope MSS 46/11/60, Gildard to Hope, 17 Mar. 1860.
[215] *BP*, 4 (1848), 142; 7 (1851), 162.
[216] *BP*, 3 (1847), 142–3; 8 (1852), 156.
[217] *BP*, 7 (1851), 161; 8 (1852), 146–7.
[218] *BP*, 4 (1848), 32; 5 (1850), 193–5; 9 (1853), 154.
[219] *BP*, 10 (1854), 197.
[220] Islington Protestant Institute, *12th AR* (1859), 14–15; *Catholic Standard*, 4 Mar. 1854.

Given the tensions between priests and people, the temporal advantages to be gained, and the sheer persistence of the missionaries, it is not surprising that conversions to Protestantism were by no means unknown, although the strength of Catholic communal loyalty and the danger of ostracism and violence facing the convert ensured that they were relatively uncommon. A woman in Glasgow who renounced Catholicism in 1858 was attacked several times and deserted by her teenage daughters.[221] In another case a woman claimed that, after she had been converted, the priest had attempted to persuade her father to turn her out of his house.[222] One Catholic whole-heartedly agreed with a Scripture reader but would not change his religion because he was afraid he would be killed or persecuted by his workmates.[223] In 1860 the Liverpool mission claimed twenty-four converts, but of these only fourteen were prepared to renounce Roman Catholicism openly.[224] Those who did openly profess conversion appear usually to have been people already on the fringes of the Catholic community and very seldom active attenders at Catholic worship.[225] The impact of missionary activity was thus small everywhere, but there were interesting regional constrasts. By 1860 there had been about 2,000 conversions in London and about 250 in Liverpool, although there were more than three-quarters as many Irish-born in Liverpool as in London. This was probably attributable in part to the greater geographical dispersion of London's Catholic community, but it was also exposed to a more intensive Protestant missionary effort.[226]

More specific consideration must now be given to the nature and extent of the connections between Protestant activity and sectarian riots. In analysing this problem, it is worthwhile to distinguish those incidents in which Catholics struck the first blows, albeit generally in response to considerable Protestant provocation, from those in which the violence was initiated directly by Protestants. As has been shown above, violence against Protestant missionaries and debaters was

[221] Hope MSS 44/4/12, Martin McDona to Hope, 9, 12, 22 Nov., 1 Dec. 1858. The younger girl subsequently returned to her mother.
[222] Ibid. 47/7/54, Mary Warnock to Hope, 15 Nov. 1860.
[223] *BP*, 3 (1847), 138.
[224] *BP*, 16 (July 1860), 14.
[225] *Catholic Standard*, 28 Jan. 1854; cf. Gilley, 'Protestant London', p. 32; Lees, *Exiles of Erin*, pp. 195–6.
[226] *BP*, 16 (1860), 14; Gilley, 'Protestant London', p. 31. In 1851 there were about 109,000 (4.6%) Irish-born in London; 83,000 (22.3%) in Liverpool. It may well be that Sheridan Gilley's estimate for London is too high, and he does himself present it as an upper limit, but even so the difference appears significant.

generally of a limited and personal kind and did not lead to large-scale riots. For example, a meeting at Finsbury in 1841 was, according to the *Penny Protestant Operative*, 'violently interrupted by a body of Chartists, Papists and Socialists, whose unruly and boisterous behaviour entirely prevented anything being heard', but there is no evidence that blows were exchanged.[227] In London during the early 1840s Roman Catholics regularly hooted down Protestant speakers and threw brickbats at the windows of buildings where meetings were taking place. The sources keep a discreet silence regarding the precise nature of the steps taken to combat these interruptions, but claim that they were effective.[228] The occasions on which Catholics were goaded beyond endurance were generally at times when feelings were already running high and at meetings of a more extreme political kind. An ugly incident occurred at Birkenhead on 27 November 1850, when a mob, consisting mainly of Irish navvies, attacked the town hall during a meeting protesting about the 'Papal Aggression'. Every window in the building was broken, and a number of policemen were seriously hurt in the affray.[229]

Of course, Liverpool and Western Scotland were the areas in which Catholics were most prone to attack Protestants, especially as the Orange Order revived from the early 1850s onwards. There had been serious disorders in Liverpool at the general election of 1841, and in 1842 the police prohibited the Orangemen from meeting, thereby successfully keeping the peace.[230] The remainder of the 1840s do not appear to have seen significant incidents in the town, but in 1851 the police had difficulty maintaining order in the face of large Orange gatherings and ominous signs of consequent unrest among the Catholic population. On several occasions in the 1850s sectarian tensions ran high in Liverpool, but there was little physical violence.[231] Meanwhile, Orange demonstrations in the Lanarkshire coalfields in the 1850s regularly provoked Catholic attacks; on 13 July 1857 a few hundred Protestants returning from a parade were attacked by a larger

[227] *PPO*, 2 (1841), 24.

[228] Hope MSS 33/11/92, John Ballard to Hope, 30 Nov. 1852.

[229] PRO, HO45/3472J/25–30, 43, 68–74, 83–5, Reports by the authorities at Birkenhead; *Catholic Standard*, 12, 19 Apr. 1851.

[230] Murphy, *Religious Problem*, p. 223; PRO, HO45/249/42, HO45/249D/2, 16, J. S. Leigh (Mayor of Liverpool) to Home Office, 24, 28 June, 13 July 1842. The disorder in 1841 does not appear to have been directly associated with the Orangemen.

[231] PRO, HO45/3472M/18, Report from commissioner of Liverpool police, 14 July 1851; HO45/4085F/86–96, Reports and letters relating to July 1852; W. J. Lowe, 'The Irish in Lancashire, 1846–71', Ph.D. thesis (Trinity College, Dublin, 1974), 410–25.

mob of Catholics, and the rioters took over the centre of Coatbridge for several hours until quelled by the military.[232]

There was no occasion on which a Protestant society other than the Orange Order can be directly linked to disturbances of this kind. There were instances, however, when the authorities feared that anti-Catholic meetings would lead to riots and so tried to prevent them from taking place. At Walsall in October 1853 the magistrates required the Revd J. E. Armstrong to abandon a lecture to be held in the schoolroom on the grounds that a 'breach of the peace is likely to ensue', although they apparently did not object to him speaking in the church, where respect for the building would have been likely to restrain protest.[233] Similarly, at Windsor in 1854 the mayor banned a meeting for fear that it would cause a disturbance among Roman Catholic soldiers in the garrison. On both occasions, however, protests were made to the Home Office, and Palmerston clearly felt that the local authorities were over-reacting.[234]

Turning to consider violence initiated by Protestants, this can be further subdivided according to whether or not it was associated with Fifth of November celebrations. Guy Fawkes Day certainly revived during the period, especially after the 'Papal Aggression', but the distinctively religious element remained limited, and when violence resulted it was by no means purely sectarian in character. In 1853 the authorities at Guildford sought Home Office advice on how to deal with Fifth of November riots in the town, which, although a regular occurrence for many years, had recently become more dangerous. There was no suggestion that Catholics were the sole or even the chief victims of the drunken mobs, which simply seemed to attack everything in their paths.[235] At Gravesend the religious motive was more in evidence, but the town clerk, reporting on disturbances in the early 1850s, clearly saw it as subordinate:

For many years past a custom has prevailed in this Town on the nights of the 5th and 9th November, for noisy and disorderly mobs, with blackened faces and other disguises, to assemble; and in procession, with bludgeons and lighted torches, squibs and effigies to perambulate the Town and levy contributions (which few inhabitants have courage to refuse) from door to door.

[232] A. B. Campbell, *The Lanarkshire Miners* (Edinburgh, 1979), 183–4.
[233] PRO, HO45/5128W/580–615, Correspondence relating to the action of the Walsall magistrates Oct.–Nov. 1853.
[234] *BP*, 10 (1854), 49–58.
[235] PRO, HO45/5128N; cf. Morgan, 'Guildford Guy Riots'.

These processions cause great crowds to congregate, and as the scheme is a profitable one to the ringleaders, rival parties have latterly been formed and occasionally come into collision, when . . . violent affrays and scenes of extreme riot ensue.

Within the last two or three years the disturbances in the Town on the nights referred to, have been greatly increased, by a pseudo-religious hostility to the conversion of a Protestant Chapel of ease into a Roman Catholic place of worship; and last November [1852] especially, an excited and violent Mob of many hundreds of persons . . . assembled around the building, yelling and hooting, breaking the windows, and doing other damage to the property, burning tar barrels in dangerous proximity to the Chapel and adjoining houses, and exciting the gravest alarm in the minds of the Inhabitants.[236]

At other times of the year directly religious factors were more apparent, although the proximity of 12 July to most disturbances should be noted. At Greenock on 14 July 1851 a mob, stimulated by the presence of John Orr, an itinerant Protestant preacher calling himself the 'Angel Gabriel', caused £30 worth of damage to the Catholic chapel. Similar outrages followed, and on 5 August the Catholic inhabitants complained of being 'kept in a state of insecurity and continual terror'. The provost asked for military assistance to restore order.[237] On 15 June 1852 the Conservative government issued a proclamation against the use of Catholic vestments and ornaments in public, thus suggesting considerable nervousness about the consequences for public order were Protestants to consider themselves provoked at this period of the year. This did not prevent, and may indeed have stimulated, the outbreak of rioting at Stockport from 27 to 29 June, when 2 Catholic chapels and 24 houses were wrecked, 1 man was killed, 50 wounded, and 114 arrested. The Stockport riots were stimulated by a complex mixture of economic, social, and political factors, but here, as at Greenock, anti-Catholic preaching evidently played a part. A broadsheet published at the end of April 1852, two months before the riots, had observed that 'polemical excitement has lost none of its virulence during the past year' and pointed out that 'the feeling that prompts the educated man to the use of injurious words, will urge the ignorant man to resort to blows'.[238]

[236] PRO, HO45/5128M/422–3, 22 Oct. 1853.
[237] PRO, HO45/3472P/3–18; on Orr, see Handley, *Irish in Modern Scotland*, pp. 95–6.
[238] *Stockport Letter Bag*, 30 Apr. 1852 (Stockport Public Library, SF. 32); P. Millward, 'The Stockport Riots of 1852', in Swift and Gilley, *The Irish in the Victorian City*, pp. 207–24; V. Holland, 'Anti-Catholic Riot in Stockport 1852', unpublished paper

It is significant that, even in the disturbed early 1850s, London was almost free from outbreaks of violence against Roman Catholics. During the twelve months up to December 1851 there were only three cases recorded by the police. One of these appears to have been a common criminal assault, and in another the offender was found to be mentally deranged. In the third incident a priest merely complained of being 'insulted', not injured, in the street, and appears himself to have acted in an unnecessarily provocative fashion.[239] The relative calm of the capital can be attributed in part to the extensive involvement of the élite in organizing and directing Protestant feeling there into moderate channels, not only within operative societies but on such occasions as a demonstration at Greenwich, which was attended by a number of carriages and organized by 'between twenty and thirty persons all of whom were respectable tradesmen living in the neighbourhood'.[240]

Sectarian conflict in mid-nineteenth-century Britain thus appears to have operated on a number of different levels. There was the religious tension associated with Protestant missions but controlled by the organizers' vested interest in maintaining order and the aspiration of the participants to a modicum of 'respectability'. Secondly, there was the political rivalry stirred by the Protestant Operative Associations, and, finally, the outright physical conflict originating in long-standing tensions imported from Ireland, economic rivalries, and spatial segregation.[241] The evidence suggests that Catholics perceived the varying nature of these challenges and responded to them in different ways. This analysis can to some extent be used to highlight regional variations: in London religious and political factors predominated; on Merseyside social antagonisms stirred particularly by the massive influx of Irish following the Great Famine of 1847–8 were of greater importance. Scotland represented something of a middle ground, with considerable internal variations. Intensive, religiously directed missionary activity in the cities appears to have kept the cruder forms of

(Stockport Public Library). However, there is no evidence of which I am aware to support Millward's claim (p. 219) that the riots were 'deliberately fostered by the Protestant Association'. In any case this is implausible on prima-facie grounds.

[239] PRO, HO45/3783, Abstract of superintendent's report, 6 Dec. 1851.
[240] Ibid. Report from Greenwich division, 12 Dec. 1852.
[241] F. Neal, *Sectarian Violence: The Liverpool Experience 1819–1914* (Manchester, 1988), 80–130. See also M. A. G. O'Tuathaigh, 'The Irish in Nineteenth Century Britain: Problems of Integration', in Swift and Gilley, *Irish in the Victorian City*, pp. 13–36; Campbell, *Lanarkshire Miners*, pp. 178–204; J. A. Jackson, *The Irish in Britain* (1963); Lowe, 'Irish in Lancashire', pp. 386–472, *passim*; T. Gallagher, *Glasgow, The Uneasy Peace: Religious Tension in Modern Scotland* (Manchester, 1987).

conflict under control. This was evident above all in Edinburgh, but was also apparent in Glasgow, where sectarian violence was less endemic than in Liverpool. However, missionary efforts were not so extensive in smaller industrial centres such as Airdrie and Coatbridge, where the pattern of violence was more reminiscent of Merseyside.[242]

Religious, political, and social factors intermingled in practice, of course, but religion was often an important catalyst even when it was not the real substance of conflict. For example, while it would be hard to point to institutional links between McNeile and sectarian violence on Merseyside, it seems undeniable that the manner in which his activities inflamed local passions contributed considerably to the polarization of religious groups in the Liverpool of the 1830s and 1840s. Indeed, McNeile's influence was particularly explosive precisely because, after the early 1840s, he does not appear to have promoted the kind of Evangelical anti-Catholic classes and societies which were responsible for channelling anti-Catholic feeling in the Scottish cities in relatively non-violent directions.

Finally, how did anti-Catholicism relate to anti-Irish feeling? At a popular level, the terms 'Papist' and 'Irishman' were frequently seen as synonymous, and ethnic antagonisms accordingly fuelled religious ones. On the other hand, the Protestant societies themselves continued to stress the religious basis of their activity: Hugh Stowell proclaimed in 1849 that 'it is not Ireland, it is Popery—it is not the Celt, it is the Romanist, that makes the dark return'.[243] Protestant missionaries, themselves often Irish, also tried to maintain the distinction. They were successful in so far as institutionalized antagonism to the Irish Catholics, as it was expressed in the Orange Order, for example, was legitimized primarily in religious rather than ethnic terms. There is an illuminating contrast to be drawn here with the United States, where popular anti-Irish antagonisms were frequently expressed in 'nativist' movements in which explicit anti-Catholicism was played down and American nationality affirmed.[244]

[242] T. Gallagher, 'A Tale of Two Cities: Communal Strife in Glasgow and Liverpool before 1914', in Swift and Gilley, *Irish in the Victorian City*, pp. 106–29.

[243] *PM*, 11 (1849), 94; *BP*, 5 (1850), 64; S. Gilley, 'English Attitudes to the Irish in England, 1780–1900', in C. Holmes and K. Lunn (eds.), *Hosts, Immigrants and Minorities* (1980), 98; Lowe, 'Irish in Lancashire', pp. 393–4. L. P. Curtis, *Anglo-Saxons and Celts* (Bridgeport, 1968), presents a racial interpretation, but does not so much reject the religious dimension as ignore it. In any case, his work is concerned with middle-class attitudes at a rather later period.

[244] J. H. Lee, *The Origin and Progress of the American Party in Politics* (Philadelphia, 1855); *Proceedings of the Native American State Convention* (Newbury, Vermont, 1847); M. Feldberg, *The Philadelphia Riots of 1844* (Westport, Conn., 1975).

The Protestant societies were rooted in middle-class evangelicalism. Their importance lay not so much in the extent of their committed support as in their contribution to the continual stirring of the cooling embers of a wider anti-Catholic enthusiasm, which could thus be brought suddenly into flame in 1845 and 1850. An observer in Manchester commented in 1842: 'I could make affidavit that there is seven times the amount of Protestant information, and more than seven times the amount of Protestant feeling, amongst the middle and lower classes . . . than there was some years ago.'[245] In the remaining chapters of this book we must first consider the political implications of anti-Catholic opinion (Chapter 6), and then examine the reasons for Protestant decline in the 1850s (Chapter 7). The latter discussion can be anticipated by two further conclusions that can be drawn from the current chapter. Firstly, in the later 1840s and 1850s the anti-Catholic movement was increasingly extended to Scotland as well as England, and, indeed, much of the most vigorous activity was now taking place north of the Tweed.[246] Secondly, the critics of the Protestant movement were frequently people who shared their aspirations but feared their methods would be counter-productive. Against such a background, successes were very likely to constitute a source of future weakness.

[245] *PM*, 4 (1842), 84.
[246] Sheridan Gilley ('Protestant London', p. 212) wisely warns of the dangers of swelling an English narrative with Scottish material. These are minimized, however, if both writer and reader are aware that it is happening.

6

PROTESTANTISM AND POLITICS
1841–1850

THE decade to be surveyed in this chapter saw the high-water mark of Protestant activity in the nineteenth century as gauged by the anti-Maynooth agitation of 1845, the frustration in 1848 of the Russell government's plans for diplomatic relations with Rome and the concurrent endowment of the Irish Roman Catholic Church, and the reaction to the 'Papal Aggression' of 1851. If the nature and significance of the 'No Popery' outcries of 1845 and 1851 are to be fully appreciated, they must be placed in the context of the development of the anti-Catholic movement and its relationship to political life during the surrounding years. This is the task that will be undertaken here. The chapter will begin with an evaluation of the anti-Maynooth agitation from this perspective, and the organized Protestant movement of the late 1840s will then be considered. Particular attention will be given to the National Club, to efforts to influence elections, governmental and parliamentary decisions, and to the development of the Protectionist party.

The Maynooth crisis of 1845 can be briefly summarized.[1] On 4 February, when Gladstone announced in the Commons that he intended to resign from the government, Peel was forced to admit that he intended to propose 'a liberal increase of the Vote for the College of Maynooth' without making 'any regulations in respect of the doctrines and discipline of the Church of Rome'. The Protestant Association quickly called a meeting to discuss means of resisting the measure. This led to the formation of the Central Anti-Maynooth Committee, an *ad hoc* body on which most orthodox Protestant denominations were represented, and vigorous agitation was already under way by the time Peel

[1] There are more detailed accounts in G. A. Cahill, 'The Protestant Association and the Anti-Maynooth Agitation of 1845', *Catholic Historical Review*, 43 (1957), 273–308; I. S. Rennie, 'Evangelicalism and English Public Life', Ph.D. thesis (Toronto, 1962), 271–6; E. R. Norman, *Anti-Catholicism in Victorian England* (1962), 23–51; G. I. T. Machin, *Politics and the Churches in Great Britain, 1832–1868* (Oxford, 1977), 169–77; D. A. Kerr, *Peel, Priests and Politics* (Oxford, 1982), 224–89.

formally introduced his Bill on 3 April. He proposed to raise the annual grant from £9,000 to £26,360, to make it a permanent charge on the consolidated fund, and to make an additional non-recurrent grant of £30,000 to finance repairs to the College buildings. There were numerous public meetings, both in London and in the provinces, and during the session 10,204 petitions against the Bill, with a total of 1,284,296 signatures, were presented. The supporters of Maynooth were able to muster only 90 petitions with 17,482 signatures, which came almost exclusively from Catholics and Unitarians. The anti-Maynooth agitation reached its climax between 30 April and 3 May, when a conference at the Crown and Anchor Tavern was attended by 1,039 delegates from all parts of the United Kingdom. Meanwhile, in Parliament resistance to the measure was led by Sir Robert Inglis.[2] Half the Conservative party revolted against Peel, and in June the National Club was formed as a lasting focus for Protestant interests in Parliament. However, this did not halt the progress of the Bill, given the readiness of the opposition to support the measure. Although vigorously contested at all stages, it received the royal assent on 30 June.

As in the preceding decade, the Maynooth issue was contested both on the levels of expediency and of principle. Under the first heading were arguments relating to the government of Ireland and the effect of the teaching given at the College, which dominated Peel's speeches in support of his measure and provided the grounds on which Colquhoun opened the opposition to the second reading.[3] For others in Parliament, notably Inglis and Plumptre, the matter hung on the fundamental constitutional and religious principles seen to be threatened by the proposed strengthening of a link between the State and the Roman Catholic Church. This was the view most evident in the extra-parliamentary opposition to the measure.[4] While Peel and Russell both felt that the Bill should be judged primarily in relation to the needs and wishes of the people of Ireland itself, an underlying assumption made by their opponents was that Britain and Ireland were indissolubly linked.[5] The issue was seen as crucial to the whole religious character of the nation and its political stability. In an ironical

[2] Canterbury Cathedral Library, Inglis MSS, Diary, 3, 9 Apr. 1845.
[3] 3 *Hansard*, lxxix. 18–38, 501–20, 3, 11 Apr. 1845.
[4] Ibid. 88–90, 1023–4, 3, 18 Apr. 1845; Inglis Diary, 11 Apr. 1845; Kerr, *Peel, Priests and Politics*, p. 281.
[5] 3 *Hansard*, lxxix. 1004, 1011–14, 1025–9, 18 Apr. 1845; Kerr, *Peel, Priests and Politics*, p. 272.

leader, *The Times* 'praised' the manner in which Peel had exercised great economy in giving such a large amount of offence to so many people with the minimum of effort.[6] McNeile saw the measure as saddling 'upon this Nation the support of doctrines which are opposed to the word of . . . God', while Stowell argued that to pass the Bill would 'virtually destroy the right of the House of Brunswick to the Throne of England'.[7] The argument from principle, however, was one that many found difficult to maintain. Gladstone's eventual grudging support for the Bill stemmed from the recognition that such a position was ultimately unrealistic, while Russell saw its logical consequence as being opposition to endowment of Catholicism in the colonies as well, which, if carried into government policy, would 'shake the empire to its foundations'.[8] Furthermore, the very arguments used against the Bill by anti-Catholics were liable to be arguments in its favour among religious liberals and Catholics.

There was a widespread belief that Peel was using this intrinsically minor issue as a means of setting a precedent and testing the waters of public opinion, with a view subsequently to proposing the concurrent endowment of the Irish Catholic Church. *The Times* believed that 'no thoughtful person . . . can conceal from himself that a further grant to Maynooth does really involve the ultimate endowment of the Catholic Church in Ireland'.[9] From different standpoints, Russell and Ashley both publicly placed this interpretation on events.[10] Peel denied that he had any such intention, such a policy being unacceptable to the Irish Catholics themselves, although he refused to give an assurance that he would never consider the move.[11] The *Tablet* was unconvinced, and summarized its interpretation of government policy in picturesque terms:

Exeter Hall is to be bullied; the Conciliation Hall is to be cajoled. If the people of the Strand are found weak enough, and the people of Burgh Quay grateful enough, then will come the question of the pension.

As matters now seem, we fear we shall owe some part of our safety to the

[6] *The Times*, 17 Apr. 1845.
[7] A. S. Thelwall (ed.), *Proceedings of the Anti-Maynooth Conference* (1845), 16, 19.
[8] 3 *Hansard*, lxxix. 536–9, 1010, 11, 18 Apr. 1845.
[9] *The Times*, 1 Apr. 1845.
[10] 3 *Hansard*, lxxix. 93–4, 777, 3 16 Apr. 1845. Privately, however, Russell did not think that Peel had ulterior motives (National Library of Scotland, Minto MSS 11774, ff. 80–1, Russell to Minto, 14 May 1845).
[11] 3 *Hansard*, lxxix. 1035–6, 18 Apr. 1845. Inglis feared that taunting Peel with the possibility might in fact serve to fix him in 'his bad legislation' (Diary, 24 Apr. 1845).

English Saints . . . Doubtless Rome will be a second time saved by the cackling of geese.[12]

Another interesting feature of the crisis was the speed with which the Anti-Maynooth Committee, despite a somewhat sluggish start, was able to mount a large-scale campaign of extra-parliamentary agitation.[13] The government tried to push the Bill through as quickly as parliamentary procedure would permit in order to prevent the outcry gathering momentum: in early April Peel, to the fury of the *Record*, refused to delay the second reading at all, while Graham wrote to Heytesbury that 'we must press the measure forward with as little delay as possible'.[14] However, the opponents of the measure, assisted by Gladstone's revelation of Peel's plans in early February and by the improvement in communications brought about by the railways, were still able to mobilize a large degree of support in a short space of time. This partially reflected the experience gained by the Dissenting members of the Committee in the agitation against the educational clauses of Graham's Factory Bill in 1843 and probably in some cases in the Anti-Corn Law League, but it is noteworthy that the Anti-Maynooth Committee also included a number of active members of the Protestant Association, while James Lord served as secretary of both organizations.[15] The anti-Maynooth movement was thus able to draw directly on the experience and contacts of the preceding decade, as was evident in a circular issued on 28 March which showed a clear grasp of the practicalities of bringing public opinion to bear on Parliament. Detailed instructions were given on the form and procedure to be used in drawing up petititons and transmitting them to MPs for presentation. Local opponents of the Bill were urged to arrange public meetings, for which the Central Committee would endeavour to provide speakers, and to make personal and direct expressions of their views to their MP, who would be encouraged to ponder the possible effects of his conduct on his prospects at the next election. Agents of the London Committee were appointed to tour the provinces and stimulate local activity. It would seem that, at a time of perceived crisis, previously apathetic supporters could readily be stirred into action.[16]

[12] *Tablet*, 19 Apr. 1845, p. 242.

[13] Thelwall, *Anti-Maynooth Conference*, pp. vii–xi and *passim*.

[14] *R*., 7, 10 Apr. 1845; Bod. Lib., Graham MSS (microfilm, MS Films 120), Graham to Heytesbury, 4 Apr. 1845.

[15] Thelwall, *Anti-Maynooth Conference*, p. xvi

[16] Ibid. pp. xvii, lxxxvii–lxxxviii.

The critics of the Anti-Maynooth Committee were not slow to claim that the agitation was not truly representative of public opinion. Peel maintained that it was being artificially manufactured from London, and the *Tablet*, paying a backhanded compliment to 'the promptness, dexterity and universality' of 'the Protestants of Exeter Hall', made a similar point.[17] A. S. Thelwall,[18] in his account of the Committee's activities, was at pains to rebut such charges: 'It would be doing injustice to the friends of Protestantism in the Country, to say, that the Deputations from London were *necessary to awaken their opposition* to the Endowment of Maynooth. They *found* the feeling; and they *counselled* and *encouraged* it.'[19] This assessment is consistent with the evidence adduced in Chapter 5 that agents of Protestant societies found superficial enthusiasm but little sustained organization. Some provincial meetings were held in March and early April before the Exeter Hall agitation had gathered full momentum, and delegates to the Anti-Maynooth Conference indicated the force of the local feeling at their backs.[20] It was true that the petitioners against Maynooth, numerous though they were, represented only a small minority of the population and a substantially lower number than had opposed factory education two years before, but, while the almost total silence on the other side might be construed as apathy, it cannot readily be interpreted as support for the government. Indeed, MPs favourable to Maynooth were willing almost to make a virtue of their defiance of public opinion. Macaulay, for example, prided himself on having 'opposed myself manfully to a great popular delusion'.[21] It can thus be concluded that, while, like any major extra-parliamentary campaign, the anti-Maynooth agitation was far from 'spontaneous', it did represent widely held, albeit inarticulate, convictions.

The anti-Maynooth campaign opened up questions of the accountability of government and MPs to their constituents in a manner reminiscent of agitations on more apparently 'progressive' matters. Indeed, inasmuch as it was based on the forces of middle-class

[17] Thelwall, *Anti-Maynooth Conference*, p. xxxii; *Tablet*, 10 May 1845, p. 290.
[18] Algernon Sydney Thelwall (1795–1863), a son of the reformer John Thelwall, was an unbeneficed clergyman (Boase, iii. 919; A. S. Thelwall, *Memorial and Testimonials of A. S. Thelwall* (1858)).
[19] Thelwall, *Anti-Maynooth Conference*, p. lxxxviii.
[20] Ibid. *passim*; *The Times*, 12, 28, 29 Mar., 2 Apr. 1845.
[21] Cited by J. C. Williams, 'Edinburgh Politics, 1832–1852', Ph.D. thesis (Edinburgh, 1972), 233; cf. Gladstone's comments on public opinion, 3 *Hansard*, lxxix. 521–2, 11 Apr. 1845.

Dissent and Anglican Evangelicalism, it was promoted by similar social groups. *The Times* considered that the measure had no legitimate parentage in the national will, and attacked Peel for his disdain for public opinion.[22] Peel received a deputation from the Anti-Maynooth Committee on 9 April urging him to delay the second reading in order to permit a wider expression of public opinion, but he refused to do so.[23] At the end of the month, when the Crown and Anchor conference was in session, he declined to meet its representatives, commenting to his Cabinet colleagues that to do so 'would be giving a sanction and importance to their proceedings'.[24] Russell, too, was unsympathetic when he met a deputation: according to Thelwall, 'the advocate for the Rights of the People was resolutely bent on resisting those Rights'.[25] The *Record* also commented sarcastically on the behaviour of Whig and Radical advocates of parliamentary reform, who were now, it claimed, riding roughshod over the feelings of the majority of the public.[26]

These circumstances led certain anti-Catholic Tories to link their opposition to Maynooth with fears for the future of a political system under which the government was defying public opinion in a manner hardly conducive to class harmony. Newcastle believed that the people should 'resolutely require their representatives to support their opinions and wishes [and], if they will not, then require them to resign'.[27] Ashley was full of forebodings:

It is an alarming feature in this present day that the middling classes of all denominations are so zealous and sincere in the assertion of Protestant principle, while the Members of both Houses and the gentry at large, prompted either by policy or indifference stand aloof from the mass of the people. This separation on solemn subjects which involve alike the safety of civil and religious freedom, will soon be felt, recognised, and acted on, and will do more to alter the fundamentals and practice of the Constitution in Church and state, than every thing that broke out at the French Revolution, or followed in its train. The direct opposition in which these parties will be placed by the Maynooth-bill will open a gulf between them never to be passed.[28]

[22] *The Times*, 12 Apr., 3 May 1845.
[23] Thelwall, *Anti-Maynooth Conference*, p. xxxii.
[24] Ibid. 5; Peel Papers, BL Add. MS 40565, ff. 274–5, Peel to Smith, 29 Apr. 1845.
[25] Thelwall, *Anti-Maynooth Conference*, pp. xxxii–xxxiii.
[26] *R*, 28 Apr. 1845.
[27] Nottingham University Library, Newcastle MSS, Diary, Ne2F7, 19 Apr. 1845.
[28] Southampton University Library, Shaftesbury MSS, Diary, SHA/PD/3, 23 May 1845.

Irish Protestant agitation on Maynooth was muted in contrast to that in Britain. The Presbyterian leader, Henry Cooke, whose support for the anti-Catholic campaign of 1834–6 had been of great importance, now gave a grudging support to the government.[29] In general, active Irish opposition was confined to a limited number of Anglicans and Wesleyans. However, according to Mortimer O'Sullivan, caution on the part of the Protestant leadership stemmed from fear that strong popular feelings could easily be fanned and result in violence.[30] Anti-Maynooth meetings in Dublin and Belfast eventually attracted considerable support, but they were not held until early June and much of the organization was undertaken by the London Committee.[31] Thus, in 1845 Irish Protestantism was stimulated from England, the reverse of the position in 1834–5.

The vigour of the anti-Maynooth campaign barely concealed the underlying divisions of anti-Catholicism. The co-operation of Dissenters and Anglicans in opposing the Bill was always liable to be uneasy. Indeed, when viewed against the background of the 1830s and early 1840s, it is remarkable that this collaboration occurred at all. The Anti-Maynooth Committee consisted of thirty-nine Anglicans, nineteen Congregationalists, including the chairman Sir Culling Eardley Smith, nine Wesleyans, and four Presbyterians.[32] The *Congregational Magazine* explained: 'We are not such zealous *dissenters* as to forget we are *Protestants*; nor can we overlook the fact that the voluntary and established systems are but means to an end; the question at issue being, "Which method is more likely to preserve and extend the Protestant faith?" '[33] However, as this quotation suggests, unspoken assumptions about the nature of Protestantism itself were in underlying tension. Most Nonconformist opponents of the Maynooth Bill viewed their alliance with Anglicans as an essentially tactical device, made only because the measure raised the issue of state endowment of religion conjointly with that of support for Roman Catholicism. James

---

[29] Kerr, *Peel, Priests and Politics*, p. 284.

[30] Lambeth Palace Library, Wordsworth MSS 2143, ff. 157–8, Palmer to Wordsworth, 16 May 1845.

[31] Thelwall, *Anti-Maynooth Conference*, pp. cxxv ff.

[32] Machin, *Politics and the Churches*, p. 174. Sir Culling Eardley Smith (1805–63), 3rd baronet, son of Sir Culling Smith and Charlotte Elizabeth Eardley. He was MP for Pontefract, 1830–1 and an unsuccessful parliamentary candidate on a number of occasions. He was also interested in missions and the Jewish cause (*DNB*, xvi. 316; *Evangelical Christendom*, 1 June 1863: I am indebted to Mr Bruce Kupelnick for the latter reference).

[33] *Congregational Magazine*, 3rd series, 9 (1845), 397.

Massie, a Manchester Independent minister who was also an active member of the Anti-Corn Law League, explicitly linked the cause of free trade in corn with that of free trade in religion.[34] The very manner in which the *Congregational Magazine* defended those involved in the Anti-Maynooth Committee shows that other Congregationalists were opposed to such a combination. For stronger Voluntaryists, opposition to Establishments was ultimately a more powerful motivating force than was antagonism to Rome. When Eardley Smith made it clear on behalf of the Committee that the Crown and Anchor conference would not address the Establishment issue, they seceded and subsequently held their own conference at Crosby Hall. In Thelwall's view, this division in the anti-Maynooth movement at such a crucial juncture was disastrous, shattering the impression hitherto generated of united Protestant action against the measure.[35]

Conversely, the conspicuous role played by Dissent in the organized anti-Maynooth movement caused Anglicans other than 'Recordite' Evangelicals to view it with distaste. After the second reading of the Bill had been passed, the Anti-Maynooth Committee dispatched a circular to every clergyman and Dissenting minister in the country, a total of 30,000 in all.[36] Several of the recipients wrote to Peel to assure him of their support for the government. The agitation was attributed to Dissenters and to 'the Calvanistic [*sic*] portion of the Church of England', and a Dorset clergyman told the premier that 'in rural districts the measure neither excites the intense interest nor produces the great alarm indicated by this Circular'.[37] Meanwhile, William Rowe Lyall, the Archdeacon of Maidstone, although willing to petition against Maynooth, was only lukewarm in his opposition for fear of appearing to be associated with Voluntaries.[38] The aristocracy were conspicuous by their absence from the Crown and Anchor conference, and, although it was claimed that a number of bishops were sympathetic to it, none was willing to appear publicly in such dubious ecclesiastical company.[39]

[34] Thelwall, *Anti-Maynooth Conference*, p. 24; N. McCord, *The Anti-Corn-Law League 1838–1846* (1958), 192.

[35] Thelwall, *Anti-Maynooth Conference*, pp. cii–civ.

[36] Ibid. p. lxxiii.

[37] Peel Papers, BL Add. MS 40565, ff. 270–1, Edmund Peel to Peel, 28 Apr. 1845; f. 147, Revd Henry Hope to Peel, 25 Apr. 1845.

[38] Wordsworth MSS 2147, ff. 233–4, Elizabeth Frere to Mrs Wordsworth, 24 Apr. 1845.

[39] Thelwall, *Anti-Maynooth Conference*, pp. 64, 67.

There was an attempt to initiate a parallel conservative High-Church anti-Maynooth movement, centred on Christopher Wordsworth (1807–85), the future Bishop of Lincoln, then a canon of Westminster and the anonymous author of a pamphlet, *Maynooth, the Crown and the Country*, published in early April 1845. He made explicit the connection between the maintenance of the existing religious order and the stability of the political system: 'Unity in true religion being the great conservative principle of a Commonwealth, and civil discord and disquiet being the natural consequences of religious dissension, it is certain that when a nation is passing from the *Toleration* of various forms of religious belief to the *Encouragement* of them, its civil rulers have great cause for alarm . . .'.[40] Wordsworth argued that the establishment of the Maynooth grant under exceptional circumstances in 1795 was insufficient argument for its perpetuation in changed conditions; that in continental countries, unlike Ireland, the Roman Catholic Church was clearly controlled by the State, and that the teaching at the College was essentially subversive.[41] During April and May Wordsworth was in extensive communication with William Palmer of Worcester College (1803–85), who cherished the idea of forming some kind of association to defend the Church. Palmer was greatly alarmed by the prospects for relations between Church and State, but found Churchmen generally reluctant to take active steps. They disliked the prominence of Dissenters in the agitation and feared that to turn out Peel would play into the hands of the enemies of the Church. They were also constrained by the infighting among Anglicans themselves.[42]

The tensions apparent in the 'out-of-doors' opposition to the Bill were also strongly evident in Parliament itself, both on the grounds of ideology and of tactics. The protracted debate on the Bill, extending over six nights on the second reading in the Commons, showed the importance of the issues at stake, but also indicated that the opposition to Maynooth had been unable to find a basis for united action, despite several meetings to discuss the means of procedure.[43] The fundamental problem was that to argue against the measure on the grounds

[40] [C. Wordsworth], *Maynooth, the Crown and the Country* (1845), 3; J. H. Overton and E. Wordsworth, *Christopher Wordsworth, Bishop of Lincoln, 1867–1883* (1888), 113.

[41] *Maynooth, the Crown and Country*, pp. 7–10, 21–32, 55 ff.

[42] Wordsworth MSS 2143, ff. 133–4, 139–42, 155–6, Palmer to Wordsworth, 10, 22 Apr., 14 May 1845. Palmer, a participant in the Oxford Movement in its early stages, wrote in 1843 *A Narrative of Events Connected with the Publication of the Tracts for the Times*, which attacked the Romanizing party in Oxford (*DNB*, xliii. 168).

[43] Inglis Diary, 7, 9 Apr. 1845.

that it compromised the established relationship between the State and the Church of England was anathema to Dissenters. Ashley feared that he would be forced back on the 'trite, despised and unpalatable' theological objections to Roman Catholicism, which he recognized had only limited appeal in the House and were likely to be counter-productive because they would stir sympathy for the Catholics.[44] His honest statement of his dilemma during the second-reading debate won him Catholic respect, but showed how far he was separated from the Exeter Hall agitation.[45] Meanwhile, Inglis was privately critical of Colquhoun's tendency to rest his case on theological and prudential rather than constitutional grounds.[46] Such ideological and tempera-mental differences were compounded by disagreements on strategy. Inglis believed that the circumstances warranted ruthless exploitation of parliamentary procedures in order to frustrate the government. He was ready to advocate tactical support for Ward's amendment to provide the funds for Maynooth from the revenues of the Church of Ireland prior to joining with the government to defeat the revised substantive motion, but not all his supporters were prepared to resort to such factious measures.[47] Thelwall observed that in general the opposition to the Bill in the Commons did not have the determined spirit of the anti-Maynooth activity outside the House.[48]

The Conservative revolt was only loosely connected with the extra-parliamentary agitation. This applied not only to Disraeli, whose classic denunciation of Peel was based far more on questions of political style and leadership than on religious arguments, but also to those who shared the Protestant concerns of the Anti-Maynooth Committee.[49] This separation was consistent with developments in the political Protestant movement since 1841. After the general election victory, Conservatives who equated their own cause with that of Protestantism considered that agitation in the country had served its purpose. Plumptre was the only MP to attend the 1842 annual meeting of the Protestant Association.[50] Meanwhile, *The Times*, which had

[44] Shaftesbury Diary, SH/PD/3, 12 Apr. 1845.
[45] 3 *Hansard*, lxxix. 774–81, 16 Apr. 1845; Shaftesbury Diary, SH/PD/3, 19 Apr., 3 May 1845.
[46] Inglis Diary, 11, 24 Apr. 1845.
[47] Ibid. 3, 9 Apr. 1845.
[48] Thelwall, *Anti-Maynooth Conference*, p. cxii.
[49] 3 *Hansard*, lxxix. 555–69, 11 Apr. 1845.
[50] *PM*, 3 (1841), 376; 6 (1844), 133, 377; *R*, 16 May 1842; J. A. Wardle, 'The Life and Times of the Rev. Dr Hugh M'Neile, DD, 1795–1875', MA thesis (Manchester, 1981), 154–5.

given the Protestant Association considerable support during the late
1830s, stated in 1841 that 'we very decidedly disapprove of the
proceedings of that body', argued that its violent fanaticism was
ineffective, denied that Peel's 1835 administration gave any countenance to its principles, and urged a balanced policy towards Ireland.[51]
The effect of this was to leave the Protestant Association increasingly
under the control of clergy like Stowell who were innocent of political
realities.[52]

Meanwhile, anti-Catholic MPs had been at pains to give Peel the
benefit of the doubt: in opposing the annual grant to Maynooth in
September 1841, Plumptre hoped 'that the right hon. baronet below
him would not think that . . . he meant to offer the slightest opposition
to his general policy'. Inglis urged him not to divide the House.[53]
However, although parliamentarians did not generally engage in the
explicit criticism of Peel made by Protestants outside Westminster, a
growing unease was evident, certainly from 1843 onwards. In October
1843 Ashley gave credibility to a rumour that the government was
planning to endow the Irish priesthood, and in 1842, 1843, and 1844
the opponents of Maynooth divided the House with rather less scruple
and with a higher number of supporters than in 1841.[54] Particularly
for Evangelicals, the Dissenters' Chapels Act of 1844, seeming to
implicate the State in the propagation of religious error, gave rise to
concern and vigilance on religious issues.[55] Frustrated ambition was
also evident, however, especially in the case of Colquhoun.[56]

Nevertheless, unease on religion was not translated into sustained
rebellion against Peel, but fits into the pattern of isolated back-bench
revolts in which MPs were asserting their residual independence and
their convictions on particular issues. To a considerable extent, the
Maynooth rebellion itself can be seen in similar terms. Continuity with
the revolt on the sugar duties in the previous year was weak: out of 60
Conservative rebels on that occasion, 27 now supported the government.[57] Large though the Maynooth rebellion was, the continuing

[51] *The Times*, 8 Aug. 1841.

[52] *PM*, 6 (1844), 377–80.

[53] 3 *Hansard*, lix. 668–73, 20 Sept. 1841.

[54] Shaftesbury Diary, SHA/PD/3, 24 Oct. 1843; 3 *Hansard*, lxv. 379–95, 20 July
1842; lxviii. 727–30, 7 Apr. 1843; lxxvi. 1143, 19 July 1844.

[55] Machin, *Politics and the Churches*, pp. 165–6; Peel Papers, BL Add. MS 40546,
f. 127, Gordon to Peel, 5 June 1844.

[56] Bod. Lib., Disraeli MSS, A/X/A/13, memorandum on Colquhoun.

[57] D. R. Fisher, 'Peel and the Conservative Party: the Sugar Crisis of 1844 Re-

strength of loyalty to Peel was evident in the 66 Conservative abstentions on the second reading. Nearly half the Conservative rebels, 71 out of 147 on the second reading, had already opposed the annual grant on at least one occasion and so can be presumed to have been acting on the basis of conviction rather than faction; and 21 MPs who had previously opposed the annual grant now voted with the government, prepared, it would seem, to stand by Peel in the crisis.[58] Furthermore, Conservative rebels still commonly emphasized that their opposition to the government was exceptional.[59] Subsequently Inglis complained that some were 'drawing back from timidity; some from . . . self-interest'.[60]

Meanwhile, the Whig–Liberal opponents of the Bill, whom Inglis had not involved in the discussions among his Tory rebels, showed themselves generally to be adopting a very different kind of stance. Of the 31 Liberal rebels, 23 were acting on more or less Voluntaryist grounds, including those Scottish MPs, of whom Fox Maule was the most prominent, who linked opposition to the Maynooth grant with support for the Free Church.[61] Only one Liberal speaker on the second reading, P. M. Stewart, who represented Renfrewshire, opposed the Bill on exclusively 'Protestant' grounds.[62]

Early in 1845 leaders of the government had taken a gloomy view of the prospects for the Conservative party. In January Peel had believed that his proposals would 'very probably be fatal to the Government', and in April Graham thought: 'the Bill will pass, but our party is destroyed. The result will very probably resemble the consequences which ensued on the passing of the Relief Act.'[63] In the event, it was in

examined', *Historical Journal*, 18 (1975), 279–302. Fisher, however, sees the Maynooth crisis as marking the beginning of a more serious split. See also R. M. Stewart, *The Foundation of the Conservative Party 1830–1867* (1978), 187–95.

[58] 3 *Hansard*, lxxix. 1042, 18 Apr. 1845; Thelwall, *Anti-Maynooth Conference*, p. lxiii; *R*, 21 Apr. 1845; Machin, *Politics and the Churches*, p. 172; *PM*, 12 (1850), 30. Norman's figures for Conservative voting in this division (*Anti-Catholicism*, p. 42) are inaccurate: it appears that he has transposed the minority and the majority and miscounted by one. Stewart (*Foundation of the Conservative Party*, p. 193) confirms my calculation.

[59] See the statements of Plumptre (3 *Hansard*, lxxix. 88–9, 3 Apr. 1845), Law (ibid. 71, 3 Apr.), and Northland (ibid. 577, 11 Apr.).

[60] Inglis Diary, 25 Apr. 1845.

[61] Thelwall, *Anti-Maynooth Conference*, pp. lxxvii–lxxxv; 3 *Hansard*, lxxix. 603–12, 14 Apr. 1845, and *passim*. Fox Maule (1801–74) was MP for Perth from 1841 to 1852, when he succeeded as 2nd Baron Panmure. He was to be secretary at war under Russell and Palmerston (*DNB*, xxxvii. 85).

[62] 3 *Hansard*, lxxix. 722–7, 15 Apr. 1845.

[63] Stewart, *Foundation of the Conservative Party*, p. 192; Graham MSS, MS Films 120, Graham to Heytesbury, 12 Apr. 1845.

1846 not 1845, and on a different issue, that the Conservatives seemed to be reliving the trauma of 1829. Despite its noisiness, the resistance to Maynooth in 1845 was ultimately too fragmented—ideologically, institutionally, and socially—to disrupt the political fabric in a lasting fashion. It undoubtedly contributed to the resentments that exploded in 1846, but there was nothing inevitable about this sequel. On the other hand, though Protestant groups could not impose their will on Parliament as long as a strong government endured, they did possess a significant degree of support which was to enable them to exercise greater influence on the weaker political groupings that emerged after 1846.

The impression that a growth in Protestant influence in politics was a consequence rather than a major cause of the Conservative split in 1846 is confirmed by an examination of the early history of the National Club. The arrangements for a Protestant club had been begun in mid-May by Colquhoun, together with Sir Digby Mackworth,[64] and appear to have been loosely linked with Palmer's and Wordsworth's plans for an association in defence of the Church. An initial meeting was held on 17 June. This set up a committee consisting of fourteen peers, nineteen MPs, and twenty-three others, all laymen.[65] Of the MPs involved, fourteen had opposed the second reading of the Maynooth Bill and the other five had abstained.[66] The Duke of Manchester, who, as Viscount Mandeville, had presided over the formation of the Reformation Society eighteen years before, became chairman, and the ubiquitous James Lord initially served as secretary.[67]

Among the National Club's promoters had been some who wanted to commit the new body to explicit general opposition to the government, but in the event it stopped short of this, stating in its founding resolutions, with a vagueness that was probably intentional, merely 'that a Club be formed in support of the Protestant principles of

[64] Sir Digby Mackworth (1789–1852), 4th baronet, of Glen Uske, Monmouthshire, served in the Peninsular war, stood for Parliament but was never elected. Evangelical sympathies are suggested by the fact that he sent his son to St Edmund Hall (Boase, ii. 642; Bod. Lib., St Edmund Hall MS 67/17, John Hill Diary, 13 Oct. 1848, 10 May, 16 June 1849).

[65] Newcastle Diary, Ne2F7, 27 May 1845; Bod. Lib., NC Papers, Dep.d.756, f. 4, proof copy of resolutions of meeting of 17 June 1845; NC minutes, 2 Nov. 1852. On Colquhoun's contacts with Wordsworth, see Overton and Wordsworth, *Christopher Wordsworth*, pp. 115–17.

[66] 3 *Hansard*, lxxix. 1042–5, 18 Apr. 1845.

[67] NC Papers, Dep.d.756, f. 4, resolutions of meeting of 17 June 1845; see above, p. 36.

the Constitution, and for raising the moral and religious condition of the people'.[68] A circular from the Duke of Manchester explicitly confronted the many different strands of Protestantism evident in 1845:

We belive that, while we differ on some important public questions, the crisis in which we find ourselves, is such as to demand the suppression of many points of difference, and to require that we should pass by those differences and insist together on the vital truths to which we all give a hearty assent. It may be true that we shall, in many cases, work better by working separately . . . [69]

In its first general statement, issued in November 1845, the Club disclaimed any intention of entering into party cabals.[70] Clearly, Colquhoun and others had concluded that Protestantism on its own was an insufficiently strong basis for open rebellion against Peel, but believed that the formation of a pressure group would assist their cause. Ashley, however, believed that such an effort was likely to be worse than useless, simply demonstrating the weakness of Protestantism.[71] Others appeared tacitly to agree, and in its early days the Club found that the recruitment of members was a slow process. It immediately sought to draw in clergymen as well as active politicians.[72]

The chaotic state of the Conservative party after the repeal of the Corn Laws provided the Club with an environment in which it could recruit more extensively. By late 1846 membership was growing steadily, and in April 1847 Mackworth thought that very gratifying progress had been made.[73] By 1848 the Club had a total of 451 members, of whom no less than 254 were clergy. There were, however, 13 peers and 29 MPs among them, providing a secure, albeit limited, basis for exerting parliamentary influence.[74] Table 6 provides a list of their names and political allegiances. The membership of the National Club showed considerable continuity with the Protestant Association, but was more restricted socially and represented a broader Anglican ecclesiastical spectrum. Among laymen, the Club

---

[68] NC Papers, Dep.d.756, f. 4; Shaftesbury Diary, SHA/PD/3, 21 June 1845.

[69] NC Papers, Dep.d.756, f. 5.

[70] NC Papers, Dep.d.756, f. 7, *First General Statement* (1845), 9.

[71] Shaftesbury Diary, SHA/PD/3, 21 June 1845.

[72] Cambridgeshire County Record Office, Huntingdon, Manchester MSS, ddM/7, Colquhoun to Manchester, 24 June 1845.

[73] Manchester MSS, ddM53/7, Nugent to Manchester, 13 Oct. 1846; Mackworth to Manchester, 14 Apr. 1847.

[74] NC Papers, Dep.d.756, ff.180–3, *Alphabetical List of Members for the Year 1848* (1848).

TABLE 6. *Peer and MP members of the National Club, 1848*

PEERS

Duke of Manchester	Earl of Roden	Viscount Lorton
Earl of Cavan	Earl of Winchilsea	Viscount O'Neill
Earl of Egmont	Viscount Combermere	Lord Kenyon
Earl of Enniskillen	Viscount Hill	Lord Southampton
Earl of Mountcashel		

MPs

	Constituency	Party		Constituency	Party
Alexander, N.	Antrim	Pt.	Hamilton, G. A.	Dublin Univ.	Pt.
Bennet, P.	West Suffolk	Pt.	Hamilton, J. H.	Co. Dublin	Pt.
Viscount Bernard	Bandon Bridge	Pt.	Heald, J.	Stockport	Pe.
Marquess of Blandford	Woodstock	Pe.	Viscount Mandeville[a]	Bewdley	Pt.
Bruen, Col. H.	Co. Carlow	Pt.	Moody, C. A.	West Somerset	Pt.
Cabbell, B. B.	Boston	Pr.	Napier, J.[b]	Dublin Univ.	Pt.

Coles, H. B.	Andover	Pt.	Pugh, D.	Montgomery	Pe.
Duncuft, J.	Oldham	Pe.	Lord Rendlesham	East Suffolk	Pt.
Ffolliott, J.	Co. Sligo	Pt.	Shirley, E. J.	S. Warwickshire	Pt.
Fox, S. L.	Beverley	Pt.	Spooner, R.	N. Warwickshire	Pt.
Frewen, C. H.	East Sussex	Pt.	Tollemache, J.	South Cheshire	Pt.
Greenall, G.	Warrington	Pt.	Verner, Sir. W.	Co. Armagh	Pt.
Grogan, E.	Dublin City	Pt.			

Note: Party designations are as ascribed by Dod (*The Parliamentary Companion* (1832–60)): Pe., Peelite; Pt., Protectionist; Lib., 'Liberal'; Lib.Pt, 'Liberal Protectionist'.

[a] Returned at by-election in Apr. 1848.
[b] Returned at by-election in Feb. 1848.

Source: NC Papers, Dep.d. 756, ff. 180–3, *Alphabetical List of Members for the Year 1848* (1848).

attracted Evangelicals like Colquhoun and Plumptre, former Ultras such as Kenyon and Winchilsea, and leading Irish Protestants, including Røden and Hamilton, all of whom had previously been involved in different strands of the anti-Catholic movement but now came together in one organization. In addition, there were several men not previously active in Protestant societies who joined the National Club in the aftermath of the political events of 1845 and 1846. Richard Spooner (1783–1864), a banker, was MP for Birmingham from 1844 to 1847 and for North Warwickshire from 1849 until his death.[75] Two Protectionist whips were involved in the Club: Charles Newdegate (1816–87), Spooner's colleague in the representation of North Warwickshire,[76] and William Beresford (1798–1883), secretary at war in the 1852 Derby administration, who represented Harwich from 1841 to 1847 and subsequently North Essex.[77] Two prominent members of the committee who were not MPs themselves provided a link with leading politicians of the past: Dudley M. Perceval (1800–56) was a son of Spencer Perceval,[78] and Augustus Stapleton presented himself as an inheritor of the Canningite mantle.[79] Colquhoun, Hamilton, Mackworth, and Stapleton were the dominant figures in the Club, and by May 1848 they were all holding positions as deputy chairmen. Manchester was more than a figurehead, as he was kept fully informed of the details of business and was an occasional attender at committee meetings, but he was not the main driving force.[80] Lord was shortly succeeded as secretary by Richard Nugent, an otherwise obscure Irish country gentleman, who was himself replaced before 1848 by William Henry Bellamy.[81]

The clerical members included such leading Evangelicals as Edward and Robert Bickersteth, John Cumming, C. J. Goodhart, and Robert M'Ghee. Mortimer O'Sullivan was also a member, and there were several conservative High-Church clergy, notably Christopher Wordsworth, George Townsend, and Edward Ellerton (1770–1851), a fellow of Magdalen and Martin Routh's curate at Theale, who had at one time been a close friend of Pusey.[82] With the exception of Robert

[75] Boase, iii. 691.
[76] *DNB*, xl. 329; W. L. Arnstein, *Protestant versus Catholic in Mid-Victorian England* (Columbia, Mo., 1982).
[77] Boase, i. 252.
[78] Ibid. ii, 1461.
[79] See above, p. 129.
[80] NC, *3rd AR* (1848), 2; NC minutes, *passim*; Manchester MSS, *passim*.
[81] NC, *1st AR* (1846), 2; *3rd AR* (1848), 2.
[82] *DNB*, xvii. 244.

Daly (1783–1872), the Evangelical Bishop of Cashel,[83] the Club did not initially have any episcopal members. In contrast with the situation in other Protestant societies, clergy, despite their numerical prominence in the rank and file, did not take a consistently active role in leadership, but an exception was Dr George Edward Biber (1801–74), a German who became a naturalized Englishman in 1839. He was vicar of Roehampton from 1842 to 1872 and editor of the strongly Protestant *John Bull* newspaper between 1848 and 1856.[84]

In its ideology and objectives, as in its membership, the National Club represented a further convergence of the high Tory and establishmentarian Evangelical strands of anti-Catholicism. Colquhoun explained in 1846: 'We call our Club national, because it seeks to maintain the *national* principles and *national* institutions of England— the great national principle, that of Protestant truth—the great national institution, that of the Church of England.'[85] A speaker in May 1847 echoed Gladstone's recently abandoned position, stating that the Club's role was 'to teach the world that the State ought to have a conscience and politics a religion'.[86]

Despite the presence of prominent Protectionists among the membership, as an institution the Club saw Protestantism as its major concern. Indeed, Stapleton stated that he had favoured a relaxation in the Corn Laws, while Colquhoun maintained that free trade was not to be feared so much as the insidious workings of 'Liberalism', inimical to true liberty, undermining local independence through the exercise of arbitrary central power.[87] This was linked to his Protestant concerns by the claim that true dignity and freedom of conscience could only come through education in the principles of the Established Church. Deficient religious instruction was seen as a key root of lax morals, which engendered reckless politics with adverse economic effects. Support for the Church of England was to be linked with 'relief of the social wants of the poor', a vision which the Club did carry into some

---

[83] *DNB*, xiii. 440; H. Madden, *Memoir of the Late Right Rev. Robert Daly, DD, Lord Bishop of Cashel* (1875).

[84] Boase, i. 269.

[85] *A Report of Speeches Delivered at a Meeting of the Members and Friends of the NC Held at Willis's Rooms on Saturday 2 May 1846* (1846), 14.

[86] *A Report of the Speeches Delivered at the Dinner of the NC, May 12 1847*, 18.

[87] *Substance of the Speech of A. G. Stapleton, Esq. in the Anti-Corn-Law-League Hall at Manchester on the Occasion of the Meeting of the Protestant Association of that Town, 29 April 1847* (1847), 4–5; J. C. Colquhoun, *The Effects of Sir Robert Peel's Administration on the Political State and Prospects of England* (1847), *passim*.

practical effect in vigorous campaigns to raise money for the relief of famine victims in Ireland and the Highlands.[88]

The appeal of the National Club was limited by four factors. Firstly, the individuals involved were largely untried and distrusted politically, and men who might have given effective leadership did not join. Ashley, despite his superficial affinity with the Club's programme, held aloof because he doubted the discretion and integrity of its leaders. In common with Disraeli he appears to have thought that Colquhoun intended to use the Club as a power-base from which to launch a bid for the leadership of the party, and was determined not to give him any encouragement.[89] Sir Robert Inglis also, while he attended some meetings at the Club, did not join it. This was despite the fact that he had declined to join the Protectionists because he considered them unsatisfactory on Protestantism.[90] Thus the Club never fully gained even the support of its own natural constituency in Parliament. Furthermore, such leadership as the Club possessed proved to be of uncertain effectiveness: Colquhoun was dogged by ill health and retired from Parliament in 1847, and Mackworth, despite repeated efforts, failed to gain a parliamentary seat.[91]

Secondly, the Club's association with High-Churchmen was liable to be divisive and to alienate Evangelicals, particularly because it initially refused to take active steps against the Tractarians. The *Record* only gave it lukewarm support. Perceval recognized the problem, but thought that it was a necessary price to pay in order to secure a 'broad, just and liberal comprehension of all true Church opinions'.[92] With this end in view, extreme Evangelicals were viewed with almost as much distaste as Romanizers.[93] Although the committee did decide in late 1850 to send a circular to churchwardens urging action against ritualists, this provoked an angry reaction from High-Churchmen who feared interference with legitimate practices. There were a number of

[88] *Address of the NC to the Subscribers to the Relief of Distress in Ireland and the Highlands of Scotland, 15 Jan. 1847* (1847); NC minutes, 11 Apr. 1848.

[89] Shaftesbury Diary, SHA/PD/4, 17, 21 June 1845; Disraeli MSS, A/X/A13, memorandum on Colquhoun.

[90] Inglis Diary, 21 Apr., 5 May, 9 July 1846, 17 May 1850. Inglis continued to sit on the government benches until 1851 (Diary, 19 Jan. 1847, 4 Feb. 1851).

[91] *DNB*, xi. 403; Manchester MSS, ddM53/7, Mackworth to Manchester, 14 Apr. 1847.

[92] Manchester MSS, ddM53/7, Perceval to Manchester?, n.d. (late 1850 or early 1851); *R*, 13 July 1846.

[93] NC minutes, Dep.b.235, 12 Dec. 1848; *Meeting of the NC, 2 May 1846*, p. 15.

resignations from the Club and from the committee, which was forced to reaffirm neutrality between Church parties.[94]

Thirdly, while relations with Anglican Evangelicals were uneasy, those with all but the most moderate Dissenters were essentially hostile. The rules stated that members were required to 'profess the Protestant faith, as embodied in the Thirty-Nine Articles of the Church of England', a slightly ambiguous formula which appears to have been interpreted as excluding all non-Anglicans. The Club expressed a willingness to co-operate with those Dissenters who acknowledged 'the great and inestimable blessings' which the Church of England had conferred on the country, but not with those 'desirous of subverting the Established Church'.[95] Ashley believed that in thinking this a sound basis for Protestant action, the Club was misunderstanding the nature of the resistance to the Maynooth Bill in 1845: 'It displayed, doubtless, a great hatred of Popery, but it contained very little love of the Church of England—they had better take into their calculation that a large proportion of the Petitioners, on whom they rely for the "Protestant party", will not join them in making the Establishment a bulwark against the aggressions of Rome . . . '.[96]

Finally, the Club had an underlying distrust of popular agitation. It did issue a number of pamphlets and short *Addresses to the Protestants of the Empire* which appeared initially as broadsheets and were subsequently collected into pamphlets, but in May 1848 some potential members expressed concern that they might be compromised by these publications. The committee therefore decided to study them more carefully before publication, and also issued an explicit statement to the effect that members of the Club who were not on the committee were not responsible for the content of publications.[97] Thereafter the frequency of such addresses declined, reflecting a sense of impropriety at attempting to influence Parliament in this manner while it was sitting.[98]

The Club's initial statement had urged the formation of local associations, but in practice the committee did little or nothing actively

[94] NC minutes, Dep.b.235, 26 Nov., 10, 17, 31 Dec. 1850, 28 Jan. 1851.
[95] NC papers, Dep.d.756, f.40, General Rules, p. 1; NC minutes, Dep.b.235, 12 Dec. 1848.
[96] Shaftesbury Diary, SHA/PD/4, 21 June 1845.
[97] *Addresses to the Protestants of the Empire Issued by the Committee of the NC* (1846–52). The only extant set is in the Bodleian Libary. NC minutes, Dep.b.235, 30 May 1848.
[98] NC minutes, Dep.b.235, 26 Feb., 5 Mar., 19 Nov. 1850.

to promote such bodies, beyond sending out copies of its publications.[99] There were no official deputation tours,[100] primarily because the leaders were nervous about delegating responsibility to subordinates: Stapleton thought Nugent was unreliable, and when the committee did decide to look for a travelling secretary, they were unable to find anyone suitable.[101] They were reluctant to become too closely associated with popular Protestant societies: in November 1849 the Brighton Protestant Operative Association asked if they could prefix the names of the committee of the Club to their annual report, thereby implying a potentially useful connection, but this was declined as an 'obviously dangerous and inexpedient precedent'. The same meeting treated a request from the Islington Protestant Institute to provide a chairman for their annual meeting as a matter requiring careful consideration.[102] The Club's aloofness from the lower orders of society was perceived by an East End clergyman, who complained particularly about its political dinners and urged the development of deferential support:

[A dinner] draws together men already deeply interested in the Club and adds nothing to their feeling but feeling common to a world from which we must be separate, if we want to succeed, whilst it affronts and alienates those who are not deemed sufficiently honourable to mix with its elite, but men upon whom . . . the preservation of England now depends. Public meetings and local parochial meetings presided over by men of noble birth from the Club would do more . . . to win the affections of the people, to draw from them a sense of thankfulness, that men of noble rank interest themselves so much in their cause and condescend to mingle in their ranks and to lead them in this great struggle . . . [103]

Such limitations did not prevent the National Club from exerting a significant influence within the arena of high politics. It provided its members with all the normal facilities of a gentleman's club at premises initially in Old Palace Yard and subsequently in Whitehall Gardens. Unlike the Protestant Association, it was a natural centre for

---

[99] *Suggestions for the Formation of Local Associations in Defence of our National Institutions* (1845), 13–14.

[100] But note the visits to Manchester and Cambridge referred to in Manchester MSS, ddM53/7, Mackworth to Manchester, 8 July 1847; Stapleton to Manchester, 12 Nov. 1847; NC minutes, Dep.b.235, 23 Nov. 1847.

[101] Manchester MSS, ddM53/7, Stapleton to Manchester, 12 Nov. 1847; NC minutes, Dep.b.235, 7 Mar. 1849.

[102] NC minutes, Dep.b.235, 6 Nov. 1849.

[103] Manchester MSS, ddM53/7, J. E. Kearne to Manchester, 11 May 1847.

promoting direct parliamentary action. This was initially done on an informal basis, but could be quite effective: in April 1847 Mackworth reported to Manchester that for the vote on Watson's Roman Catholic Relief Bill they had 'pressed the attendance in the House of all our friends, and all others we could think of', thus helping to secure the defeat of the measure by a substantial majority.[104] In August 1848 whips were sent out on the Bill for diplomatic relations with Rome, and Spooner and others used the Club as a base from which to plan their opposition to the measure.[105] In early 1849 it was decided to arrange meetings of the Club's parliamentary members, and the secretary was authorized to send out whips at the request of one or more MPs.[106]

The Club also had substantial links with the Conservative press. In March 1849 the committee considered whether they should pay the *Morning Herald* to give full reports of debates in Parliament regarding matters of concern to the Club.[107] In January 1850 they decided to elect its proprietor, Charles Baldwin, an honorary member in return 'for his willingness at all times to forward [their] views and wishes'. Baldwin was also proprietor of the *Standard*, a newspaper similarly favoured by the Club. At the same time they also elected as honorary members Robert Knox, editor of the *Morning Herald* from 1846 to 1858, Stanley Lees Giffard, who had been editor of the *Standard* since 1827, and Samuel Phillips, who had owned and edited *John Bull* during 1845 and 1846, served as leader-writer on the *Morning Herald*, and contributed literary reviews to *The Times*.[108] Their most direct link was with *John Bull*, through Biber and Phillips, who acquired it again in 1848.[109]

Furthermore, if the National Club's activity is placed in a wider context, it becomes clear that anti-Catholicism as a whole was far from ineffective in the late 1840s. The Protestant Association was enjoying a revival in some towns, and the Evangelical Alliance, despite its divisions and limitations, served to focus some Dissenting anti-Catholicism.[110] Undoubtedly Protestantism was fragmented, but that very fragmentation gave it a certain pervasiveness. In this respect,

[104] Ibid. Mackworth to Manchester, 14 Apr. 1847.
[105] Ibid. W. H. Bellamy to Manchester, 16 Aug. 1848.
[106] NC minutes, Dep.b.235, 13, 26 Feb., 13 Mar. 1849.
[107] Ibid. 13 Mar. 1849.
[108] Ibid. 29 Jan. 1850; *DNB*, xxi. 296; xlv. 212; Boase, i. 140; ii. 263.
[109] NC minutes, Dep.b.235, 28 Mar. 1848, 19 Mar. 1850.
[110] See above, pp. 157–8.

moreover, it mirrored the confused political structure of the years after 1846: a weak government and enfeebled Protectionist party could not disregard pressure groups whose capacity for combined action, superficial and short-lived though it was, had been so dramatically demonstrated in 1845. In the remainder of this chapter we shall turn to consider the impact of anti-Catholicism on the politics of the later 1840s, considering first its relationship to elections, secondly its influence on government policy, and finally its role in the Protectionist party.

The threat that pro-Maynooth MPs would be called to account by their constituents at the next election had been widely made in 1845. Throughout the two years that preceded the 1847 general election the Protestant Association laid great stress on the need for action at the polls.[111] At Manchester a declaration was drawn up, the signatories to which declared 'our determination, on the occurrence of an election for Members of Parliament, to give our vote to no candidates, of whose solemn conviction that no further concessions to Rome should be made, we are not perfectly satisfied'.[112] A prospectus on behalf of an Edinburgh Protestant Association made explicit the need for continued vigilance and agitation: 'unless the opposition of the people be maintained and strengthened . . . the natural abatement of the excitement about Maynooth, which will take place after the thing is done, will . . . be held to be a relaxation of the anti-popish feeling of the people and the amalgamation of Popery with the Constitutional religion of the State will be then consummated'.[113]

Peel's record over Maynooth was a factor in by-elections,[114] but the Protestant Association and the National Club, reserving their main effort for the general election, were not directly involved in any contests, with the exception of those at Southwark in September 1845 and Derby in September 1846. In both cases, Dissenters declined to support an Anglican anti-Catholic candidate. At Southwark the local Operative Association pledged its support for Mr Jeremiah Pilcher after holding a meeting to hear his views on Maynooth, and linked his Protestant credentials with claims that he was 'the friend of the poor'. Pilcher had to contend with the rival candidacy of Edward Miall, who

---

[111] *PM*, 7 (1845), 367–8; 8 (1846), 1–8, 465–74, and *passim*.

[112] *PM*, 8 (1846), 244–5.

[113] Scottish Record Office, Edinburgh, Hope MSS, GD 253/29/2/44; see also 28/3/16, Hope to James Hope Wallace, 23 Apr. 1845; *Witness*, 14, 25 June 1845.

[114] G. A. Cahill, 'Irish Catholicism and English Toryism', Ph.D. thesis (Iowa, 1954), 297–304.

fought the election on Protestant Voluntaryist grounds, but the successful candidate, Sir William Molesworth, had taken a pro-Maynooth stand.[115] At Derby Mackworth, hoping to capitalize on the strong Protestant feeling of the town, stood on an anti-Maynooth platform. Strutt, the Radical candidate, had expressed his support for Maynooth, but still carried the Nonconformists with him. Ashley thus thought that Mackworth had been defeated 'principally by the backwardness or activity of the Dissenters', and considered it 'manifest that the Dissenters will ever prefer their political opinions to their religious principles'.[116]

As the general election approached, there was an increasing flow of anti-Catholic literature. A leaflet produced by the Protestant Association declared that the political and national destiny of the country would depend on the next election, and listed ten questions which electors were advised to put to candidates. These concerned the maintenance of Protestant institutions, particularly the Church of England and Ireland, opposition to all grants to the Roman Catholic Church, and the preservation of the civil and religious rights of both Protestants and Catholics. They went on to require exertions to exclude foreign influence over British legislation, to demand that Protestant truth be held superior to the claims of party, and to urge parliamentary enquiry into the tenets of the Church of Rome. Other allegiances, whether commitments on policy such as free trade or personal ties of party and family, should be held as secondary.[117] Meanwhile, Captain Gordon, enjoying a short-lived recovery of health, also entered the fray with a number of letters to the *Record*, subsequently published by the Protestant Association, calling on electors to demand from candidates a pledge to vote for the repeal of Emancipation.[118] The Christian Influence Society, an Evangelical body founded in 1832 and particularly concerned with the defence of the Established Church, also issued an address linking electoral resistance to concessions to Rome with the upholding of the authority of God in the land.[119]

[115] *PM*, 7 (1845), 418–19.

[116] Shaftesbury Diary, SHA/PD/4, 5 Sept. 1846; Cahill, 'Irish Catholicism and English Toryism', pp. 304–6.

[117] *Address of the Protestant Association to the Electors of Great Britain and Ireland. Duties of Protestant Electors. Questions to Candidates* (1846).

[118] J. E. Gordon, *British Protestantism: Its Present Position, Rights and Duties* (1847).

[119] Christian Influence Society, *To the Electors of the United Kingdom of Great Britain and Ireland* (1847); D. M. Lewis, *Lighten their Darkness* (Westport, Conn., 1986), 154.

The National Club wrote of a great crisis and break-up of parties. The questions of the establishment of 'Popery' and the nature of education would be settled during the next Parliament, and every candidate should be asked for his views on these issues. Local committees should be formed and should draw up a short declaration of adherence to Protestant principles; having obtained the signatures of electors, this should be sent to each candidate with a request that he should answer the questions.[120] On 16 July 1847 Nugent, correctly believing the dissolution to be imminent, dispatched a circular urging immediate action. The following day the committee published a list of all the present members of the Commons, giving their votes in recent divisions on matters of Protestant concern, together with a list of the former MPs who might be expected to stand. Hence electors would be able to verify their record at a glance.[121]

Before assessing whether the Protestant efforts in the general election of 1847 met with success or failure, we must first consider what they were intended to achieve. There is very little evidence that a new anti-Catholic political party was seriously contemplated. The *Record* noted that there was an absence of leadership and of suitable candidates.[122] The National Club seemed to be abdicating such a role when its committee, in accordance with Manchester's wishes, rejected a suggestion that they should raise money for electoral expenses, believing that this would entail 'great difficulties and great liability to abuse and misrepresentation'.[123] There was general unease about some of the necessary mechanics of exerting electoral pressure: the Protestant Association allowed one of its officers, probably James Lord, to set up a tri-weekly newspaper, the *Protestant Elector*, which appeared from late June until early October, but was careful to avoid becoming directly implicated in it.[124] Supporters were unhappy about demanding pledges from candidates, on the grounds that it reduced an MP to the status of a delegate. The *Protestant Elector*, however, while agreeing that this was undesirable, saw it as a necessary evil.[125]

---

[120] *Addresses to the Protestants of the Empire*, 1st series, 12 (1847), 30–2.
[121] NC Papers, Dep.d.756, f. 105, circular of 16 July 1847; ff.90–101, *List of the Present Members of the House of Commons* (1847).
[122] *R*, 6 May, 3, 21 June, 5 Aug. 1847.
[123] NC Papers, Dep.d.756, f. 103, committee minute, 8 June 1847; Manchester MSS, ddM53/7, Nugent to Manchester, 9 June 1847.
[124] *PM*, 10 (1848), 172.
[125] *Addresses to the Protestants of the Empire*, 1st series, 10 (1847), 24–7; *Protestant Elector*, 28 June 1847, pp. 1–2.

Therefore, to charge the Protestant movement with 'failure' because it did not secure the return of MPs standing on an exclusively anti-Catholic platform would be to misunderstand the nature of its ambitions. In reality, the aim was to ensure that Protestant views were prominently aired at the election in such a way as to ensure that the new Parliament would be more responsive to their wishes than the old one in 1845 had been. Above all, they wanted to ensure that the endowment of Maynooth could not be used as a precedent for a general endowment of the Catholic Church in Ireland. Viewed in these terms, their efforts enjoyed considerable success.

In some cases Protestant influence was evident in relation to the selection of candidates. At Manchester the Peelite Lord Lincoln, confronted with Stowell's determined opposition, decided that his pro-Catholic views would be such a liability that it would not be worth while for him to contest the seat.[126] At Liverpool the Conservatives withdrew their support from Viscount Sandon, who had represented them conscientiously for sixteen years, on account of his pro-Maynooth views.[127] Lord George Bentinck rejected a suggestion that he should stand for the town, believing that, because of his protectionism, his position would be even weaker than Sandon's:

so that I should lose the support of those who hold similar opinions to my own as regards the Roman Catholics because I was an Anti Freetrader and I should lose the support of the Tories and Protectionists because I take a different view from them of the true mode of advancing Protestantism and true Religion in the British Dominions.[128]

In the event, the Protectionist candidates were Sir Digby Mackworth and Lord John Manners. Mackworth publicly refused to engage in a joint canvass with Manners, who had supported the Maynooth Act, as this would have been a 'great and glaring' inconsistency in view of their differences on religious issues.[129] At the poll a Liberal and a Peelite were returned, but the nature of the electorate's views on the Catholic issue was evident in the fact that Mackworth obtained over 4,000 votes, while Manners trailed badly with 2,400. It was alleged that Mackworth's defeat had only been secured by the action of the

[126] Newcastle Diary, Ne2F7, 27 June 1846; *PM*, 9 (1847), 20, 63, 165.
[127] *R*, 7 June 1847; Dudley Ryder (1798–1882) succeeded his father as 2nd Earl of Harrowby in 1847 (*DNB*, l. 44).
[128] Disraeli MSS, B/XX/Be/94, Bentinck to Henry C. Chapman, 2 June 1847.
[129] NC Papers, Dep.d.756, f. 106, printed letter from Mackworth to Edmund Molyneux, 15 July 1847.

Catholics, who withheld their votes until the last minute and then divided them between his Liberal and Peelite opponents.[130]

The example of Lincoln City illustrates the manner in which the Catholic issue could dominate an election. At an adoption meeting for the Protectionist candidates, Sibthorp and Collett, the resolutions laid almost exclusive stress on the candidates' views on the religious question.[131] An address by 'a Protestant elector' declared:

I will not interfere with any of your predilictions for either Whiggery or Toryism; perhaps there never was a time when the two parties representing those antagonist principles were more broken up and merged than the present; but I will urge it upon you, by all means to secure men to represent you, who will not give their support to *any further concessions to Popery*.[132]

In the event, the Liberal candidates, Bulwer-Lytton and Seely, also pledged themselves against Catholic endowment, although the latter did so on Voluntaryist grounds.[133] As in the Southwark and Derby by-elections of the previous year, the divided character of the anti-Catholic vote was evident in Sibthorp and Seely's return.[134]

The force of Protestantism was also strongly apparent in Scotland, where a temporary alliance of the Free Church and the Voluntaries was forged in many constituencies. At Edinburgh Macaulay, who had beaten off a challenge from Eardley Smith at the by-election in July 1846 consequent upon his assuming office,[135] now succumbed to the anti-Catholic Liberal campaign of Charles Cowan. The middle-class basis of Protestant strength was very evident in this constituency.[136] At Greenock an election agent observed that if the Liberal Lord Melgund 'is sound on the question of non-endowment of the Roman Catholic clergy I have little fear of securing his election'.[137]

Liverpool was not the only constituency where a candidate with Protestant support, although defeated, made a strong showing. At Oxford University Gladstone had an uncomfortable campaign in the

---

[130] F. W. S. Craig, *British Parliamentary Election Results 1832–1885* (1977), 191; Machin, *Politics and the Churches*, pp. 188–9.

[131] Lincolnshire Archives Office, Election squibs collection, Hill 41/175.

[132] Ibid. Hill 41/195.

[133] Ibid. Hill 41/207, 208.

[134] Seely was subsequently unseated on petition.

[135] Macaulay's survival on this occasion was attributable to the manner in which the election was seen as a general judgement on the new ministry not a verdict on Macaulay as an individual (Williams, 'Edinburgh Politics', pp. 248–50).

[136] Ibid. 231–65; I. G. C. Hutchison, *A Political History of Scotland 1832–1924* (Edinburgh, 1986), 65–6.

[137] Minto MSS 12340, f. 6, James Turner to Captain Stewart, 16 Feb. 1847.

face of the challenge from Charles Gray Round.[138] In the City of London R. C. L. Bevan performed quite effectively against Russell, and the *Protestant Elector* felt that, although he was defeated, there was as much to cheer as to depress in the result. The political significance of such challenges lies in the impact that they had on successful candidates. In particular, Russell himself was forced to declare that he did not intend to bring forward any measure for Roman Catholic endowment.[139] His later consideration of the possibility suggests that he did not feel himself bound by this statement, but it certainly restricted his freedom of action and left him in no doubt that, if he were to give salaries to the Irish priests, he would be doing so in defiance of British public opinion.

A well-documented and important example of the manner in which Protestant pressure was brought to bear on an equivocating candidate is that of Disraeli in Buckinghamshire. Over eighty electors, led by D. B. Langley, the vicar of Olney, took a pledge only to support a candidate who could satisfy them of his anti-Catholicism.[140] In his election address Disraeli felt it necessary to dwell on his record on Protestant issues:

I thought it my duty to oppose in 1845, the Grant to the College of Maynooth, leading as it inevitably and avowedly did, to the endowment of the priesthood of another Church. I see no reason to regret the opposition which I offered to that measure, and I hold it to be quite consistent with an earnest desire to secure to our Roman Catholic fellow subjects, the civil and political equality to which they are entitled.[141]

Significantly, Disraeli chose to stress the Protestant grounds for his action rather than the criticism of the Peel ministry which had been the mainspring of his rhetoric at the time.

The statement, however, was too ambiguous to satisfy eagle-eyed Protestants among his constituents. William Jenner wrote from Tring to ask specifically whether Disraeli would resist any proposals for endowment of the Irish Catholic clergy, for diplomatic relations with Rome, or for unconditional grants to Roman Catholic education.[142] Although two electors wrote expressing their satisfaction, on Protestant grounds,

---

[138] Craig, *Election Results*, p. 614; Shaftesbury Diary, SHA/PD/4, 14 May 1847.

[139] Craig, *Election Results*, p. 4; *Protestant Elector*, 30 July 1847, p. 129.

[140] Disraeli MSS, B/I/C/33, R. J. Nott to Disraeli, 11 June 1847; cf. *R*, 14 June 1847.

[141] Disraeli MSS, B/I/C/192.

[142] Ibid. B/I/C/91, Jenner to Disraeli, 1 June 1847.

with Disraeli's address, several others still felt the need for further assurances.[143] Langley was concerned when Disraeli spoke of being opposed to the endowment of any priesthood—ambiguous language presumably intended to woo Dissenters, but alarming for Anglicans. Langley warned him that the Liberal candidate, the Hon. C. C. Cavendish, had gone some way towards satisfying him, and spoke of the possibility of a further Protestant Protectionist candidate.[144]

Disraeli therefore felt obliged to express himself more explicitly in a letter to Langley: 'First—I *have* hitherto opposed, and shall *still* oppose, the endowment of the Roman Catholic Church. Secondly—I am a *hearty* supporter of the union of Church and State. I can never admit that the *Church* of England *is* endowed by the *State* of England.'[145] He meant that the Church held its property by ancient right and not just by Act of Parliament.[146] It was sufficient to satisfy Langley, who published Disraeli's statement. The preoccupations of some of Disraeli's supporters were further indicated by printed cards circulating in the county, describing him and his Protectionist colleagues as, in large capitals, 'THE OPPONENTS OF POPERY', and only in much smaller type as 'The friends of agriculture'.[147]

In the event, Disraeli was returned unopposed, but, in a constituency not otherwise remarkable for strong 'No Popery' feeling, Protestant opinion had frightened him sufficiently to oblige him to make a more explicit commitment against Roman Catholic endowment than he might otherwise have wished. This appears to have been a common experience for candidates throughout England. The National Club examined the speeches and addresses of 428 MPs elected to the new House of Commons, and claimed that no fewer than 304 had given a pledge against Catholic endowment. An examination of *Dod's Parliamentary Companion* yields the more modest figure of 132, but to these can be added 10 listed by the *Protestant Magazine* and 10 members of the National Club not otherwise counted, giving a total of 152 individuals.[148] The discrepancy between this figure and the

---

[143] Disraeli MSS, B/I/C/33, Nott to Disraeli, 11 June 1847; B/I/C/39, Deane to Disraeli, 14 June 1847; B/I/C/86, Stone to Disraeli, 29 May 1847; B/I/C/145, Ramsey to Disraeli, 24 June 1847.

[144] Ibid. B/I/C/144, Langley to Disraeli, 26 June 1847.

[145] *The Church and State Gazette*, 2 July 1847, p. 420. It is not clear whether the italics are Disraeli's or Langley's.

[146] Disraeli had argued on these lines when opposing the Maynooth Bill in 1845 (3 *Hansard*, lxxix. 557, 11 Apr. 1845).

[147] Disraeli MSS, B/I/C/111a, 111b; Machin, *Politics and the Churches*, p. 189.

[148] NC, *Report of Speeches Delivered at the Annual Meeting, May 9 1848* (1848), 4; *Dod's*

National Club's calculation is best seen as representing the distinction between MPs who were against endowment from positive personal conviction, articulated in their contributions to *Dod* or in their association with the National Club and Protestant Association, and those who had merely given pledges under pressure from constitutents.[149]

Table 7 provides a breakdown of the 152 identifiable MPs opposed

TABLE 7. *MPs pledged against Catholic endowment, 1847*

MPs			Political Character	No. of MPs
	No.	% of total		
England	125	27	Protectionist	73
Scotland	12	23	Peelite	18
Wales	3	9	Liberal: Voluntaryist	27
Ireland	8	8	Protestant	28
Universities	4	67	Independent: Voluntaryist	2
			Protestant	4
OVERALL	152	23	TOTAL	152

to Catholic endowment.[150] While the backbone of opposition to endowment was among the Protectionists, it had a genuinely cross-party character. Among Liberals, although it came in part from the Voluntaryist lobby, it could also be found on Protestant grounds among the conservative Whigs who were the mainstay of Russell's

Parliamentary Companion (1847); *PM*, 11 (1849), 181; NC Papers, Dep.d.756, ff. 180–3, *Alphabetical List of Members for the Year 1848*. The 10 MPs named by the *Protestant Magazine* were Ashley, Beresford, G. A. Hamilton, J. H. Hamilton, Inglis, Law, Joseph Napier (who was returned for Dublin University at a by-election in Feb. 1848), Newdegate, Plumptre, and Verner.

[149] Cf. D. M. Lewis, 'The Evangelical Mission to the British Working Class', D.Phil. thesis (Oxford, 1981), 235, where it is emphasized that pledges exacted under duress could be lightly disregarded. Hope, discussing in 1846 the influence to be exerted on a prospective candidate, acknowledged that the latter might not positively agree with the Protestant lobby, but in that case 'he would not allow a difference on a point *he* would consider so insignificant to interfere with his representing the country' (Hope MSS 29/16/6, Hope to James Hope Wallace, 30 Apr. 1846).

[150] This table obscures a number of subtleties. Some MPs expressed views regarding the mode of Roman Catholic endowment, while Voluntaryists differed between those merely opposed to further religious endowments and those who campaigned also for the abolition of existing ones. All Peelite and Protectionist MPs who opposed Roman Catholic endowment did so on Protestant not Voluntaryist grounds. *Dod* (1847); *PM*, 11 (1849), 181; NC Papers, *Alphabetical List of Members for the Year 1848*; Craig, *Election Results*, p. 622.

administration. Classification of the 152 MPs on the basis of their constituencies is also revealing, indicating that Protestant feeling as represented in Parliament was centred on England and, to a lesser degree, Scotland, where 4 of the 12 MPs opposing endowment did so on Voluntaryist grounds. The small extent of avowed anti-Catholicism in Wales reflects the fact that the Protestant societies had not launched any significant agitation in the principality. In Ireland itself, outside Trinity College, Dublin, the prospect of Catholic endowment appears to have been viewed with relative apathy by Protestant and Catholic alike.

In reviewing the results of the election, Protestants found considerable cause for satisfaction. They bemoaned their continuing lack of leadership in Parliament, but felt that they had forced a very significant proportion of MPs to make some acknowledgement of their influence.[151] It can be noted that *Dod* listed only six MPs, including Bentinck but not Russell, who explicitly stated a willingness to endow the Catholic clergy. Even if others shared their views, they did not feel it prudent to admit to doing so.[152] Protestants derived further encouragement from evidence of the continuing influence of anti-Catholic feeling at by-elections. In the West Riding in December 1848 Fitzwilliam, a Liberal favourable to Catholic endowment, retired from the contest in the face of pressure from his own party, and E. B. Denison, who opposed endowment on religious principle, was returned.[153] The *Protestant Magazine* was similarly gratified at the result in South Devon, where a pro-Catholic candidate retired and the member elected, Sir Ralph Lopez, spoke of his 'unchanged and unchangeable' objections to Roman Catholic endowment.[154]

The main source of Protestant weakness was the continuing coolness of the Dissenters. The *Record* attributed Russell's victory in the City in part to his ability to retain Nonconformist support, while the *Protestant Elector* listed forty-four seats in the power of the Dissenters, it claimed, where a pro-Maynooth Liberal had been

---

[151] *R*, 26 Aug. 1847; *PM*, 9 (1847), 265–6; 10 (1848), 300.

[152] The other 5 avowed pro-endowment MPs were Sir Thomas Dyke Acland (Pt., North Devon), Viscount Courtenay (Pt., South Devon), James Heywood (Lib., North Lancs.), Hon C. W. G. Howard (Lib., East Cumberland), and the Earl of Lincoln (Pe., Falkirk Burghs). All except Lincoln had been returned unopposed, and thus had presumably felt secure enough to make their views known.

[153] *The Times*, 15, 24, 25 Nov., 2 Dec. 1848; *PM*, 11 (1849), 9. Cf. F. M. L. Thompson, 'Whigs and Liberals in the West Riding, 1830–1860', *English Historical Review*, 74 (1959), 236.

[154] *PM*, 11 (1849), 47.

returned.[155] The unreliability of the Dissenting vote was also evident in by-elections: at Derby in September 1848 James Lord of the Protestant Association fought the seat on Protestant principles but came bottom of the poll, and in the West Riding election of December 1848 Denison's opponent had been none other than Sir Culling Eardley Smith, the erstwhile chairman of the Anti-Maynooth Committee, who had stood on a radical Voluntaryist platform.[156] However, while such a contest indicated the divided nature of Protestantism, it also showed that opposition to the endowment of Roman Catholicism in Ireland was close to being a matter of consensus among candidates and electors alike.[157]

In turning to consider the impact of anti-Catholicism on legislation and government policy, it can at the outset be noted that both the prospect and retrospect of Protestant activity in the general election of 1847 had a substantial influence. In the two years after the Maynooth Act there was a general nervousness about the political potentialities of the 'No Popery' cry; after 1847, although Russell tried to pursue a policy of endowing Catholicism in Ireland and establishing diplomatic relations with Rome, knowledge of the force of Protestant resistance was a major factor which ultimately stayed the government's hand.

Shortly after Russell's accession to office, McNeile addressed an open letter to him which seemed almost to echo the language used by Gordon to Peel in not dissimilar circumstances a decade before, suggesting that he at least would be willing to follow anyone who might make a stand against Rome. McNeile recited the Protestant Association's usual arguments for the anti-social character of 'Popery', and went on to represent the question not as one of religious opinions but of 'safety from manifestly proved danger'.[158] He urged Russell: 'Contrast the miserable, crest-fallen, creedless Whig of 1846 . . . with the high, the noble, the patriotic, the Christian and Protestant Whig of 1688: and after your wanderings . . . amongst the mists and fogs of liberalism . . . your country [shall have] the safety of seeing your Lordship on the rock . . . of England's Scriptural Church.'[159] McNeile advised an appeal to the nation, whose 'slumbering protestantism'

[155] *R*, 2 Aug. 1847; *Protestant Elector*, 6 Aug. 1847, p. 154.
[156] *PM*, 10 (1848), 162–3; 11 (1849), 9; Craig, *Election Results*, pp. 104, 491.
[157] *The Times*, 2 Dec. 1848.
[158] H. McNeile, *The State in Danger: A Letter to the Rt. Hon. Lord John Russell, MP* (1846), 1–48.
[159] Ibid. 55–6.

would overcome 'factious voluntaryism and treacherous tractarianism'.[160]

Between 1845 and 1847 the Catholic question involved the two strands of penal legislation and education. In February 1845 William Henry Watson, Liberal MP for Kinsale, brought in a Bill to repeal obsolete penal statutes and the restrictive clauses of the Emancipation Act of 1829.[161] Opposition, although led by Inglis and Newdegate, was supported by the government, which wanted to wait for a report from the Criminal Law commissioners and was adamant that the 1829 Act was sacrosanct. The Bill was accordingly defeated in committee.[162] In February 1846 Lyndhurst, now armed with the commissioners' report, introduced a government measure, the Religious Opinions Relief Bill, in the Lords which aimed to repeal penal acts against a variety of religious groups but to leave the 1829 settlement intact. It did not concede as much to Catholics as Watson wanted. After protracted wrangling on technical matters, stirred by Phillpotts's fear that the measure would remove the legal basis of the royal supremacy, the Bill passed the Lords.[163] The incoming administration took it over, and Russell moved the second reading in the Commons on 6 August. Despite the vigorous protests of Sibthorp, Spooner, and others, the measure passed easily through the Commons.[164] However, it left the legal position of Catholics ambiguous: the penalties contained in the Act of Supremacy of 1559 had been repealed, but the offence of refusing the oath remained and could still technically be punished as a misdemeanour under the common law.[165]

Lyndhurst's Bill marked the limit of concession. Before it came down from the Lords, Watson reintroduced his own, more far-reaching, measure in the Lower House. Peel and Graham continued to stand by the 1829 Act, and, although they allowed the Bill to pass its second reading, it was again thrown out in committee.[166] Watson tried again in 1847, this time with the new government's qualified support. Bentinck spoke in favour of the Bill, and Peel was willing to support

[160] McNeile, *The State in Danger*, pp. 57–8.

[161] 3 *Hansard* lxxvii. 833–4, 20 Feb. 1845.

[162] Ibid. lxxix. 1440–2, 30 Apr. 1845; lxxx. 942–4, 28 May 1845; lxxxii. 279–91, 9 July 1845; Inglis Diary, 20 Feb. 1845.

[163] 3 *Hansard*, lxxxiii. 439–40, 3 Feb. 1846; lxxxv. 1252–87, 30 Apr. 1846; lxxxvi. 300–27, 581–612, 11, 15 May 1846; lxxxvii. 1378–9, 23 July 1846.

[164] Ibid. lxxxviii. 360–6, 630–8, 6, 12 Aug. 1846.

[165] Ibid. xc. 455–6, 24 Feb. 1847; Machin, *Politics and the Churches*, pp. 178–9.

[166] 3 *Hansard*, lxxxiv. 936–73, 11 Mar. 1846; lxxxvi. 141–66, 6 May 1846; lxxxvii. 917–37, 24 June 1846.

the second reading, but this was passed by such a narrow margin that Inglis felt himself justified in opposing the House going into committee.[167] Goulburn supported him on the grounds that the Act of 1829 was a solemn compact and that continued discussion of such issues acted as a stimulus to divisive religious feelings. He warned Watson that tampering with the Emancipation Act might encourage others to feel that it could be repealed altogether.[168] The result was a victory for Inglis, assisted by the National Club's efforts. Russell subsequently commented on how the strength of Protestant feeling could defeat a measure even when it had the limited support of his government.[169]

In April 1847 the Commons debated the increase in the education estimates necessitated by reforms contained in Privy Council minutes of the previous autumn, which provided particularly for improvements in the arrangements for the training of teachers. The Roman Catholics were still excluded from receiving state grants, and Russell, while hoping that government aid could be extended to them in due course, felt that, particularly in the light of the defeat of Watson's Bill, 'the state of [public] opinion on education is not yet ripe for such a proceeding'.[170] The Catholic Earl of Arundel and Surrey magnanimously decided, in the light of current popular feeling, not to oppose the plans or to insist on Catholics being included. Peel, too, regretted the exclusion of the Catholics, but feared that any efforts on their part might endanger the whole measure.[171] On 26 April Sir William Molesworth moved that the Roman Catholics be included in the grant, but his motion was defeated by a margin of 207 to 24, with Cabinet ministers voting in the majority.[172]

These parliamentary skirmishes were of particular significance in conjunction with the resurgence of vigorous Catholic nationalist agitation in Ireland, because they deterred Russell from taking any steps towards Catholic endowment.[173] He had openly stated his position on coming into office in 1846, believing in endowment as

[167] Ibid. lxxxix. 1059–61., 9 Feb. 1847; xc. 453–98, 24 Feb. 1847; xci. 753, 14 Apr. 1847; Inglis Diary, 9, 24 Feb. 1847.

[168] 3 *Hansard*, xci. 792–7, 14 Apr. 1847.

[169] Ibid. 1217, 22 Apr. 1847.

[170] Ibid. 819–21, 1217–20, 15, 22 Apr. 1847; Machin, *Politics and the Churches*, pp. 183–5.

[171] 3 *Hansard*, xci. 1055, 1230–3, 20, 22 Apr. 1847.

[172] Ibid. 1369–80, 26 Apr. 1847.

[173] The reactions of British public opinion to unrest in Ireland are discussed above, pp. 129–31.

'conducive to the welfare of Ireland, the maintenance of the Union and the peace of the United Kingdom'. 'But', he continued,

what do I find at this moment? I see, generally speaking, that the Church of England, that the Established Church of Scotland, that the Free Church of Scotland, that the Established Church of Ireland, that the Protestant Association in Ireland, and lastly, that the Roman Catholics of Ireland themselves, are all vehement in opposition to such a plan . . . I cannot see, then, that that is a measure which I am bound consistently with my duty, to bring under the consideration of the House, until I see some kind of more favourable disposition towards it on the part of the people.[174]

In July 1847 Clarendon, the Lord-Lieutenant of Ireland, wrote to Russell advocating the payment of priests as a means of freeing them from their dependence on the people. He thought that they would willingly accept such payment and that the Irish Protestants would consent to it, 'but upon this the bigotry of England and Scotland puts a veto now'.[175] Russell, preoccupied with his election contest in the City, replied that he had 'no thoughts of paying the priests' and bemoaned the difficulty of pleasing England, Scotland, and Ireland at the same time.[176]

In the months after the general election the government felt able to assume a less cautious stance on Catholic issues. In October 1847 Russell encouraged Clarendon to address the Irish Catholic bishops as 'Your Lordships', although fearing, correctly, that this would 'stir up the like of Inglis and Co.'.[177] On 18 December the committee of the Privy Council on education decided to extend government support to Catholic schools. However, the decision was not made public until August 1848, suggesting a continuing nervousness about the possible reaction both inside and outside Parliament.[178] Above all, the government now felt able to give serious consideration to far-reaching plans of establishing diplomatic relations with Rome and giving a state endowment to the Irish Catholic clergy, thus hoping to rule Ireland through Rome. Its confidence proved to be misplaced.

In the autumn of 1847 the government dispatched the Earl of Minto to Rome as part of an ambitious diplomatic strategy to stabilize the political situation in Italy and to win papal support for British policy in

---

[174] 3 *Hansard*, lxxxviii. 1180–1, 16 July 1846.
[175] Bod. Lib., Clarendon MSS, Letter-Book, i. 12 July 1847.
[176] Ibid. Box 43, 22 July, 2 Aug. 1847.
[177] Ibid. 15, 28 Oct. 1847; *PM*, 9 (1847), 387.
[178] NC, *Addresses to the Protestants of the Empire*, 3rd series, 1, 4 (1849).

Ireland.[179] Minto's subsequent correspondence with his Cabinet colleagues indicates the nervousness of the administration, caught between the twin fires of disorder in Ireland and strong anti-Catholicism at home. The latter, however, could prove a useful scapegoat in bringing diplomatic pressure to bear on Pius IX. Clarendon and Palmerston both thought the pope's pronouncement against the 'Godless Colleges' in October 1847 to be ill-judged and, in conjunction with continuing violence in which the priests were implicated, likely to inflame Protestant feelings.[180] By mid-November Palmerston observed to Minto that 'people are getting very angry with the Catholic Priesthood' and, apparently worried about the consequences for the government were the extent of its contacts with the Papacy to become public knowledge, added: 'I think all our communications on Irish matters had better be in private letters, even though there be no pressing danger of Premunire [*sic*].'[181] By 3 December his anxiety about public opinion had increased still further:

I begin to doubt whether it would be prudent at present to bring in our proposed Bill for legalizing diplomatic Intercourse with the Court of Rome: the sectarian Prejudices which under any circumstances would give much opposition to such a Bill, but in a better state of things we should be able to conquer, would find such sympathy in public opinion at present that our task would be more difficult. However we do not give up our intention, but must postpone its execution until after the Christmas Recess.[182]

In the event Lansdowne introduced legislation in the Lords on 7 February 1848.[183] The passing of a Coercion Act in December 1847 had brought calmer conditions to Ireland, done something to appease the Protestant lobby, and restored the government's nerve. Thus the Diplomatic Relations Bill did not include the provision, thought desirable by both Russell and Palmerston in the autumn, that any papal envoy to Britain should be a layman.[184] However, although anti-Catholicism in the Upper House was now less militant than in the Commons, the Bill did

---

[179] Machin, *Politics and the Churches*, pp. 211–12. For an account of subsequent events from the perspectives of the pope and the Irish Catholic bishops, see D. A. Kerr, 'England, Ireland and Rome, 1847–1848', *Studies in Church History*, 25 (1989), 259–77.

[180] Minto MSS 12073, ff. 16–19, Palmerston to Minto, 29 Oct. 1847; ff. 52–9, memorandum by Clarendon, 20 Nov. 1847. See above, Chap. 4, pp. 129–31.

[181] Ibid. ff. 30–4, Palmerston to Minto, 11 Nov. 1847.

[182] Ibid. ff. 49–51, Palmerston to Minto, 3 Dec. 1847.

[183] 3 *Hansard*, xcvi. 169 ff., 7 Feb. 1848.

[184] Minto MSS 12073, ff. 35–6, Palmerston to Minto, 17 Nov. 1847; f. 38, Russell to Minto, 17 Nov. 1847.

not pass unscathed. Newcastle's vehement opposition to the second reading was supported by the Bishops of Winchester and Exeter and the Duke of Richmond. They did not feel sufficiently strong to divide the House, but Stanley and Wellington professed themselves dissatisfied with the measure and looked for an opportunity to improve it.[185] An amendment in committee by the Earl of Eglinton provided that any papal ambassador to Britain must not be an ecclesiastic. This was supported by Aberdeen, Stanley, Harrowby, and Richmond, who feared that its rejection would offend the Protestant feeling of the country. It passed by 67 votes to 64, despite a warning from Shrewsbury that the pope would be unable to accept it.[186] Shrewsbury was furious with the government's weakness of purpose in accepting the clause.[187] Russell asked Minto to sound out the pope on how important the issue was to him, but was uncertain that the government would be able to remove the Eglinton clause even if, as proved to be the case, Pius did insist that it was a major obstacle.[188]

The Bill passed its third reading in the Lords on 28 February, but there was then a delay of nearly six months before it received its second reading in the Commons.[189] This is partially explained by Minto's departure from Rome, which removed any need for urgency, but also suggests that the government was nervous about raising a 'No Popery' cry. There had been a public meeting to oppose the Bill on 24 February, and the Protestant Association elicited petitions from 3,500 clergy.[190] When Palmerston ultimately moved the second reading on 17 August, he was greeted with allegations that the government had deliberately delayed proceedings until they could be sure of a majority. The Bill was opposed by a strange mixture of militant Protestants and Catholics led by Thomas Anstey.[191] When Anstey moved the deletion of the Eglinton clause, Palmerston, who privately thought the pope's objection wholly unrealistic, was willing to defend it as 'a proper deference to the feelings of a large class of the

[185] 3 *Hansard*, xcvi. 761–801, 17 Feb. 1848; Newcastle Diary, Ne2F8, 17 Feb. 1848.
[186] 3 *Hansard*, xcvi. 873–98, 18 Feb. 1848.
[187] Arundel Castle, Sussex, Norfolk MSS, correspondence of 14th duke, Shrews-bury to Arundel, 14 Mar. 1848.
[188] Minto MSS 12073, ff. 107–9, 111–12, Russell to Minto, 24, 28 Mar. 1848.
[189] 3 *Hansard*, xcvi. 1384, 28 Feb. 1848; ci. 201, 17 Aug. 1848.
[190] Machin, *Politics and the Churches*, p. 214; *PM*, 10 (1848), 69–75, 88–9, 101–5, 246–7.
[191] 3 *Hansard*, ci. 201–35, 17 Aug. 1848; Inglis Diary, 17 Aug. 1848. The Catholics were themselves divided on the matter: Arundel and Sheil were both in favour of the Bill (3 *Hansard*, ci. 235, 625–6, 17, 29 Aug. 1848). On Anstey, see *DNB*, ii. 40.

population', and, on the division, the minister present supported its retention. This was accordingly easily achieved by 79 votes to 22. As Shrewsbury had predicted, the result was that the Act could never be implemented.[192] The final nail in the coffin of Russell's Italian policy came with the pope's flight from Rome in November 1848.

Meanwhile, Catholic endowment was receiving active consideration from the government. Proposals from Clarendon were put to the Cabinet in February 1848, but, although it was willing to find the money, it was wary 'at the prospect of raising a new Maynooth question'.[193] Undeterred, Russell circulated further proposals to the Cabinet, but, due to the Chartist crisis, these were not discussed as planned in April. The matter was shelved until the autumn.[194]

During the summer there was a revealing conversation on the subject between Peel and Sheil which was reported to both Russell and Bentinck. Peel expressed his belief that the current extreme poverty of the Irish priests made the present time propitious for settling the question. He continued: 'I don't say but that any Government that attempted to settle the matter might be overthrown in the attempt but whatever might be the Government that succeeded to them that Government would find the impossibility of refusing to settle the question.' Evelyn Denison observed to Peel that the people of Britain would not allow payment to be made from the consolidated fund. Peel agreed that he was 'dispirited' by the strength of Protestant feeling, but believed that means would be found to overcome it. Bentinck himself thought that the Whigs would not venture to tackle the issue, but that Peel would. Writing to Disraeli, Lord George put forward his own scheme for raising the necessary money by a surcharge on the Irish poor-rate as likely to be more acceptable in Britain.[195]

Meanwhile, Russell visited Dublin and discussed the matter in detail with the Irish administration. On 24 October it was again considered by the Cabinet.[196] Lord John reaffirmed that the money

---

[192] 3 *Hansard*, ci. 487–514, 518–24, 615–28, 24, 25, 29 Aug. 1848; Minto MSS 12074, f. 12, Palmerston to Minto, 10 Aug. 1848; Machin, *Politics and the Churches*, pp. 214–15.

[193] Clarendon MSS, Box 43, Russell to Clarendon, 19 Feb. 1848.

[194] Ibid. Russell to Clarendon, 5, 6 Apr. 1848; G. P. Gooch (ed.), *The Later Correspondence of Lord John Russell 1840–1878*, 2 vols. (1925), i. 221–6.

[195] Disraeli MSS, B/XX/Be/66, Bentinck to Disraeli, 21 Sept. 1848; J. Prest, *Lord John Russell* (1972), 290–1.

[196] Clarendon MSS, Box 43, Russell to Clarendon, 6, 8 Oct. 1848; PRO, Russell MSS, PRO/30/22/7D, ff. 18–23, Russell to Redington, 6 Sept. 1848; ff. 30–48, Redington to Russell, 7 Sept. 1848; Prest, *Russell*, pp. 290–2.

required (£340,000 per annum) was to be raised by taxation in Ireland. The Cabinet was generally favourable: Minto noted that 'It is a formidable question which may try the stability of the government but which it is right to try.'[197] However, six weeks later, on 5 December, the Cabinet abandoned the idea. The immediate reason for this was the opposition of the Irish Catholic bishops and clergy, worried about the popular reaction were they to accept salaries from the government,[198] but awareness of Protestant feeling also played a significant part. Rumours of Russell's intentions had reached the committee of the National Club as early as 15 August, when its members set up a subcommittee 'to consider of the best mode of arousing the sense of the Country to the dangers which will result from the endowment of Romanism by the State'. The Club's contacts with the national and local press were exploited in order to ensure that the issue obtained wide publicity.[199] On 17 October three addresses were issued, together with a confidential memorandum containing the Club's plans for opposing the proposals. This was sent to every member of the Club. On 24 October it was decided to send copies of two of the addresses to current and former Cabinet ministers.[200]

Stanley knew of the government's intentions by 25 October and was concerned at the predicament in which he would be placed were Russell to fall over the issue. He and Hardinge were staying at Woburn during November 1848 and persuaded the Duke of Bedford that 'the question is surrounded by difficulties'. Bedford passed this opinion on to the prime minister. Hardinge thought that it 'would be a pity to raise a storm in this country', while Stanley believed that the opposition would come principally from Russell's own supporters, the Protestant Dissenters.[201] Greville noted on 7 November that the measure would be stillborn; it was impossible to attempt it with any chance of success, because 'Protestant bigotry and anti-Catholic rancour continue to flourish with undiminished intensity'. By 15 November both Sir Charles Wood and Sir George Grey had also become convinced that

[197] Russell MSS, PRO/30/22/7D, f. 176, Russell to the pope, 27 Oct. 1848; Minto MSS 11995, f. 7, diary entry for 24 Oct. 1848.
[198] Minto MSS 11995, ff. 17–18, entry for 5 Dec. 1848; Prest, *Russell*, p. 292.
[199] Manchester MSS, ddM53/7, Bellamy to Manchester, 16 Aug. 1848; NC minutes, Dep.b.235, 15, 22 Aug. 1848.
[200] NC minutes, Dep.b.235, 17, 24 Oct. 1848; *Addresses to the Protestants of the Empire*, 2nd series, 5, 6, 7 (1848), 17–25. The memorandum referred to in the minutes does not survive.
[201] Clarendon MSS, Box 43, Russell to Clarendon, 3, 4 Nov. 1848.

Parliament and the country would not be disposed to advance money in any shape for Irish purposes.[202] Russell had recognized from the outset that an unsuccessful attempt at endowment would be worse than useless, because it would give a stimulus to anti-Catholic feeling: he had been unwilling to propose it unless there was 'a very good prospect' that it could be carried. Accordingly he now found the difficulties overwhelming.[203]

The failure of Russell's Irish policy was attributable to a range of factors, notably the opposition of the Catholic bishops themselves and the unreliability of the pope in the face of revolution in Italy. However, the Protestant opposition at home was of key importance in the government's thinking, presenting it with the prospect of extensive resistance both inside and outside Parliament on at least the scale of the Maynooth agitation of 1845. This served as a strong deterrent for a weak administration. Thus, in a negative sense the Protestant agitation in the 1847 general election had achieved a major success, albeit assisted by an incongruous array of Dissenters and Roman Catholic bishops.

Protestant influence was also evident in the failure of renewed attempts to extend Roman Catholic Relief. In November 1847 Anstey reintroduced Watson's Bill, but the government, presumably anxious not to give hostages to fortune in the light of its Irish plans, was now cooler towards it. Inglis, supported by Newdegate, Goulburn, and Spencer Walpole, was as resolute as ever in his opposition. The Bill passed its second reading but became hopelessly bogged down in committee.[204] In the sessions of 1849 and 1850 Anstey was refused leave to bring in the Bill at all, and even Arundel thought that its discussion could serve no useful purpose. The government took little interest.[205] The strength of the anti-Catholic presence in the Commons was also demonstrated by the fact that additional grants to Maynooth to pay for repairs were contested in 1849 and 1850. In 1850 the grant was carried by only 68 votes to 55.[206]

[202] L. Strachey and R. Fulford (eds.), *The Greville Memoirs 1814–1860*, 8 vols. (1938), vi. 124–5.
[203] Russell MSS, PRO/30/22/7D, ff. 18–23, Russell to Redington, 6 Sept. 1848.
[204] 3 *Hansard*, xcv. 800–54, 8 Dec. 1847; xcvi. 701–60, 16 Feb. 1848; xcvii. 314–30, 8 Mar. 1848; xcix. 134–70, 1292–5, 31 May, 28 June 1848; c. 570–80, 19 July 1848; Inglis Diary, 25 Nov., 8 Dec. 1847.
[205] 3 *Hansard* cii. 370–2, 7 Feb. 1849; cviii. 530–3, 8 Feb. 1850; Inglis Diary, 6 Feb. 1849, 7 Feb. 1850.
[206] 3 *Hansard*, cv. 1043–4, 1 June 1849; cxi. 596–8, 3 June 1850.

A third approach to the evaluation of anti-Catholic political influence between 1846 and 1850 is provided by an examination of the Protestant role in the Protectionist opposition. In this connection, the period can be divided into two: the months leading up to Bentinck's death in September 1848, during which the Catholic issue was a serious cause of division within the party; and, secondly, the succeeding two years, when Disraeli skilfully used a tactical alliance with anti-Catholicism to assist him in gaining and maintaining a hold over the leadership.

Lord George Bentinck quickly found that his pro-Catholic views were a liability in the party. In June 1846 these were already causing doubts to be cast on his credentials as a leader, although the *Record* was, for the present, more concerned about his racing connections.[207] In the spring of 1847 Newcastle described himself as 'greatly displeased and intensely mortified' by Bentinck's continued support for Watson's Bill. Newdegate felt that the party was 'overthrown by Lord George's imprudence'.[208] Tension was increased by Bentinck's public advocacy of Catholic endowment during the election campaign. In general, the divided position of the Protectionists meant that the 'No Popery' cry at the polls did them more harm than good.[209] The *Record* was scathing in its denunciation of Bentinck, and in November Newcastle endeavoured to persuade him to abandon his support for 'Romanism', but to no avail.[210] The immediate cause of Bentinck's resignation in December 1847 was his support for Jewish Emancipation, but Bentinck himself attributed his problems as much to his views on Roman Catholicism as to his support for the Jews. He complained that 'the great Protectionist party' had 'degenerated into a "No Popery", "No Jew" League', and acknowledged that he was 'a most unnatural leader for a high Protestant Party'. He attributed this religious zeal to Beresford, Newdegate, and Phillips of the *Morning Herald*.[211]

Stanley's views were scarcely more congenial to Protestants. In April

---

[207] Warwickshire County Record Office, Diary of Maria Newdegate (Charles Newdegate's mother), CR 1841/36, 24 June 1846; *R*, 18 June 1846.

[208] Newcastle Diary, Ne2F8, 1 Mar. 1847; Newdegate Diary, CR 1841/36, 21 Apr. 1847.

[209] R. Stewart, *The Politics of Protection* (Cambridge, 1971), 109–11.

[210] *R*, 21 June 1847; Newcastle Diary, Ne2F8, 16 Nov. 1847.

[211] Disraeli MSS, B/XX/Be/95a, Chapman to Disraeli, 9 Oct. 1850; B/XX/Be/95c, Bentinck to Chapman, 28 Dec. 1847 (copy); Stewart, *Foundation of the Conservative Party*, pp. 231–2, 243 n. 53).

1847 Newdegate and Newcastle were both appalled to discover that he was willing to support Roman Catholic endowment in Ireland.[212] Further tension was evident in 1848 over the Diplomatic Relations Bill, which Stanley himself feared would be an additional 'apple of discord' among the party. He urged Newcastle not to oppose the second reading, but to join him in pressing for amendments in committee. The duke was not to be dissuaded from offering unqualified opposition to the Bill, but also feared that 'all these disagreements and dissentions [*sic*] must break up our party'.[213] He did, however, refrain from dividing the House when he realized his position was hopeless, a decision at which Stanley was 'greatly gratified'.[214] Newdegate also had cause to be displeased at the attitude of Stanley, who had expressed a hope that there would not be a strong division against the Bill in the Commons, and, as the summer wore on, left him powerless to stop potential supporters drifting away to the country.[215]

The most pressing difficulty for the Protectionists during the session of 1848 was their lack of a recognized leader in the Commons. Neither the diffident Marquis of Granby nor the aged J. C. Herries was willing to accept full responsibility. Newdegate suggested Ashley, thus displaying the relative strength of his Protestant and Protectionist views but also, like Beresford, cherished ambitions of his own.[216] The situation was still profoundly unsettled when the political world was stunned by Bentinck's sudden death on 21 September. Newcastle, respecting Bentinck's integrity despite their differences on the Catholic issue, mourned the passing of the 'only honest, fearless and unconquerable politician in public life', and even the *Record* acknowledged the honourable boldness of his career.[217] Bentinck's demise, however, cleared the way for a more manipulative use of the Catholic issue, and Disraeli seized his opportunity to establish an effective ascendancy over the party. He quickly received the adherence of Bentinck's former supporters and worked strenuously during the winter

---

[212] Newcastle Diary, Ne2F8, 25 Apr. 1847; Newdegate Diary, CR 1841/36, 24 Apr. 1847.

[213] Derby MSS 177/2, p. 270, Stanley to Newcastle, 8 Feb. 1848; Newcastle Diary, Ne2F8, 8, 10, 11 Feb. 1848.

[214] Newcastle Diary, Ne2F8, 17 Feb. 1848.

[215] Newdegate Diary, CR 1841/35, 24 July 1848.

[216] Ibid. CR 1841/36, 22 May 1847; CR 1841/35, 29 Jan., 23 Mar. 1848; Stewart, *Foundation of the Conservative Party*, pp. 232–3.

[217] Newcastle Diary, Ne2F8, 22 Sept. 1848; *R*, 2 Oct. 1848.

of 1848–9 to widen his power-base.[218] He was particularly anxious to win over the anti-Catholic lobby which had been Bentinck's undoing, and thus effectively to outflank any challenge for the leadership from Beresford or Newdegate.[219] He had already provided himself with a good basis for such a move: his opposition to Maynooth in 1845, his willingness to pledge himself in accordance with Protestant views in 1847, and his abstention from participation in debates on Catholic issues between 1846 and 1848 all ensured that, at worst, anti-Catholics would regard him as a friendly neutral and, at best, they would see his leadership as the most effective means of securing their ends. Minds were concentrated by the prospect of the government bringing forward Irish Catholic endowment in the session of 1849.

Newcastle was easily recruited through the agency of Lord Henry Bentinck, and Disraeli was at pains to consolidate his position in the duke's favour.[220] Disraeli's link with the National Club was Samuel Phillips, who engaged in intrigues which Disraeli regarded as of considerable importance, and by 16 October he had gained the adherence of Manchester's son, Viscount Mandeville. Mandeville was willing to assist Disraeli on the understanding that he would resist Roman Catholic endowment, and believed that several of his acquaintances would be prepared to offer their support on the same terms.[221] In January 1849 Phillips approached Inglis, who, although characteristically reserving his own independence, agreed to give Disraeli 'his hearty cooperation and support'.[222] The most valuable capture was Colquhoun, who, Phillips observed, had 'much influence with the Low Church party'. He expressed his willingness to co-operate in mid-November, and on 26 January he reported to Phillips: 'you [Disraeli] have a perfect right to demand the full confidence of the party and that as far as our protestant friends are concerned you shall have it'.[223]

By the end of January, in the light of a meeting at the National Club headed by Colquhoun and attended by Inglis (among others) which expressed 'unreserved confidence' in Disraeli, the latter believed that

---

[218] Stewart, *Foundation of the Conservative Party*, pp. 232–3; Disraeli MSS, A/I/243, Disraeli to his wife, 8 Jan. 1849.

[219] Stewart, *Foundation of the Conservative Party*, p. 233; W. F. Monypenny and G. E. Buckle, *The Life of Benjamin Disraeli, Earl of Beaconsfield*, 6 vols. (1910–20), iii. 135–6.

[220] Newcastle Diary, Ne2F8, 17 Nov. 1848, 6 Jan., 6 Feb. 1849; R. Blake, *Disraeli* (1966), 264–5.

[221] Disraeli MSS, B/XX/Be/138, Mandeville to Disraeli, 16 Oct. 1848; Monypenny and Buckle, *Disraeli*, iii. 117–18, 131, 134–5.

[222] Disraeli MSS, B/XXI/P/225, Phillips to Disraeli, 19 Jan. 1849.

[223] Ibid. B/XXI/P/223, 229, Phillips to Disraeli, 18 Nov. 1848, 27 Jan. 1849.

he had received 'the adhesion unqualified and complete of every shade of Church Party'.[224] Phillips was using the *Morning Herald* to further Disraeli's interests: tentative hints were dropped, especially on 1 February, when the leading article stressed Disraeli's abilities and industry and also his links with Lord George Bentinck.[225] Following references by Disraeli in the Commons on 1 February to the payment of the Catholic clergy, the National Club reaffirmed its full confidence in him and appointed Phillips as its official channel of communication with him. This, Phillips thought, would remove any possibility of a challenge from Beresford, who, he complained, 'continues to write me very indignant and ungrammatical letters'.[226] By this time Stanley, who had himself been unfavourable to Disraeli, realized that he had acquired such extensive support in the party that it was pointless to resist any longer.[227]

Disraeli's anxiety to reconcile the Bentinckite and Protestant elements in the party was still evident in 1851, when he published his life of Lord George. This work contains remarkably little allusion to the Catholic question, and thus, to the extent that it has been used as a primary source for the events of 1845 to 1848, has misled historians, because Disraeli clearly had pressing personal motives for suppressing Bentinck's views on the subject. In his only reference to Bentinck's support for endowment of the priests, Disraeli commented: 'this opinion might offend the religious sentiments of some, and might justly be looked upon by others as a scheme ill-suited to the character of an age adverse to any further religious endowments'. He pointed out that Bentinck had honestly avowed his views on the matter, but even the *Record* was willing to grant him that much.[228] Following an elaborate apologia for Bentinck's pro-Jewish views, Disraeli proceeded to stress that those who brought about his fall did not have any deliberate malice and were 'very respectable', 'sincere', and 'highly estimable'. He did not refer to Bentinck's view, of which he was fully aware, that he was a victim of religious bigotry.[229] Furthermore, in

[224] Disraeli to Lord John Manners, 29 Jan. 1849, printed in Monypenny and Buckle, *Disraeli*, iii. 134–5.

[225] *Morning Herald*, 1 Feb. 1849; Disraeli MSS, B/XXI/P/230, Phillips to Disraeli, 1 Feb. 1849.

[226] Disraeli MSS, B/XXI/P/232, Phillips to Disraeli, 4 Feb. 1849.

[227] Blake, *Disraeli*, p. 267.

[228] B. Disraeli, *Lord George Bentinck: A Political Biography* (1852), 510; *R*, 2 Oct. 1848.

[229] Disraeli, *Bentinck*, pp. 482–514. There is a copy in Disraeli's papers of a letter from Bentinck complaining bitterly at the religious prejudice of the party (B/XX/Be/98c, Bentinck to Chapman, 24 June 1847).

recounting the events preceding Bentinck's death, he simply referred to the letter Bentinck sent to him on the very day of his fatal heart attack as 'full of interesting details of men and things': it was, in fact, almost entirely a discussion of the Catholic endowment issue.[230]

Thus, from early 1849 onwards the Protectionists had moved to a broadly Protestant stance, albeit, in the case of the leadership, more from tactical considerations than from conviction. Stanley had stated his position in a letter to Disraeli in December 1848:

I do not share in the objections of principle entertained by a large body of our friends, who see *moral guilt* in the endowment; but as a measure of policy I am prepared to oppose it, as revolting the feelings of a great majority of English and Scotch people . . . with a very faint prospect of effecting the *real* object, that of diminishing the community of feeling between the R. C. Priest and his flock . . . [231]

He expressed the hope that Disraeli shared his views. In his speech on the address on 1 February 1849 Disraeli, in alluding to the endowment of the Irish Catholic clergy, was therefore not only seeking to reinforce his hold on Protestant support but was acting in accordance with what he knew to be Stanley's wishes:

I think I may congratulate the House, the country and the Government, that they have not brought forward a measure with respect to Ireland . . . which it was rumoured was to be introduced the moment Parliament assembled, the rumour assuming at one time all the colour of authenticity . . . I trust we shall hear no more of that project. Of this I am certain, that it will never bear discussion in this House, and that no Parliament will pass it that fairly represents the opinion of the people of these realms.[232]

Greville considered this speech to be 'an evident appeal to Protestant bigotry'.[233] In a letter to Newcastle Disraeli himself noted that he appeared to be giving general satisfaction to the Protestant lobby.[234] Stanley, too, showed a continuing concern to maintain his Protestant credentials, evident in his attack on the government early in 1850 for their dismissal of Lord Roden from the Commission of the Peace after his alleged partiality in relation to an armed sectarian scuffle at Dolly's

---

[230] Disraeli, *Bentinck*, p. 584; Disraeli MSS, B/XX/Be/66, 21 Sept. 1848 (printed in Monypenny and Buckle, *Disraeli*, iii. 573–5). See above, p. 235.

[231] Stanley to Disraeli, 21 Dec. 1848, printed in Monypenny and Buckle, *Disraeli*, iii. 123–4.

[232] 3 *Hansard*, cii. 91–2, 1 Feb. 1849.

[233] Strachey and Fulford, *The Greville Memoirs*, vi. 154.

[234] Newcastle MSS 5476, Disraeli to Newcastle, 23 Feb. 1849.

Brae in County Down on 12 July 1848. Stanley also opposed the extension of the Irish franchise, on the grounds that it would give reinforcement to Roman Catholic influence.[235]

It was fortunate for the Protectionist leaders that for much of 1849 and 1850, following the government's decision to drop its endowment plans, the Catholic issue receded somewhat into the background, enabling them to avoid any test of their lukewarm commitment while concentrating on the revival of the campaign for agricultural protection.[236] Nevertheless, by the spring of 1850 it was clear, in the light of the Gorham case, which brought the tensions in the Church of England between Tractarians and Evangelicals to the centre of affairs, that the lull was only a temporary one.[237] It ended dramatically in the autumn, when the pope created Nicholas Wiseman a cardinal and Archbishop of Westminster and set him at the head of a new episcopal hierarchy for England and Wales. Public reactions in Britain were initially somewhat muted, but were raised to fever pitch when Lord John Russell's letter to the Bishop of Durham protesting at the pope's action and expressing particular concern about the activities of crypto-Catholics in the Church of England was published on 7 November 1850.[238]

This chapter can be concluded by relating the events of the autumn of 1850 to the discussion of the Protestant impact on politics during the later 1840s. Russell's political career provides ample illustration of the extent to which he was subject to impulsive actions:[239] the writing of the Durham Letter was clearly a short-term, imperfectly considered tactical gesture rather than a reflection of any change in his general beliefs. Russell's earlier moves to endow the Roman Catholic Church reflected no warmth to it *per se*. On the contrary, he was motivated by a general commitment to religious toleration, and also by a sense that Catholicism represented a genuine danger to the stability of Ireland and the security of the British State. In this respect he was at one with his Tory and Protestant critics: he differed from them in believing that the challenge was better controlled than confronted, and in holding a doctrine of the constitutional relationship between Church and State

---

[235] Stewart, *Politics of Protection*, pp. 170–1.
[236] Ibid. 139–64.
[237] Disraeli wrote to Lady Londonderry on 20 April 1850 that the Church question 'pervades all classes' (Monypenny and Buckle, *Disraeli*, pp. 247–8).
[238] The text of the Durham Letter is printed in Norman, *Anti-Catholicism*, pp. 159–61, and Prest, *Russell*, pp. 429–30.
[239] Prest, *Russell*, pp. 72–81.

that made it possible for him to accommodate concurrent endowment.[240] In November 1850, even as he condemned the pope's current action, he emphasized his sympathy with Roman Catholic demands for civil rights, and his belief that the Roman Catholic Church served a useful function in ministering to Irish immigrants. His indignation was directed not against Catholics as a whole but a particular rash act by the pope.

Moreover, Russell had good reason to fear that if he did not outflank the Protectionists by seeming to beat the 'No Popery' drum himself, the opposition would have little scruple in playing the anti-Catholic card against him. Beresford's clear resentment of Lord John's stealing of his political clothes was evident when he commented to Disraeli that his action was that of 'a dirty little trickster'.[241] In this connection, Russell's attack on the Tractarians in the Durham Letter is especially significant. Disraeli wrote to his sister: 'I had no idea of Lord John's riding the high Protestant horse, and making the poor devils of Puseyites the scapegoats, when he, after all, is the greater culprit.'[242] Russell's onslaught on 'the unworthy sons of the Church of England' in part reflected his frustration at their resistance to his appointment of Hampden as Bishop of Hereford in 1847, his awareness of the activities of W. J. E. Bennett at St Barnabas, Pimlico, and, most recently, their involvement in the Gorham controversy.[243] However, his exaggerated view of their importance led him to see them as an ideal means of deflecting public attention from his own Irish and Italian policies: the whole thrust of the Durham Letter appears directed to that end.

Russell succeeded inasmuch as he was now robed in incongruous guise as a Protestant champion, but failed in his attempt to fasten the main burden of public indignation on the Tractarians. Although attacks on the 'Puseyites' were widespread in the public meetings that followed,[244] the core of the Protestant movement had been firing its artillery against Rome and Ireland rather than Oxford for too long to

---

[240] Cf. R. Brent, *Liberal Anglican Politics* (Oxford, 1987), 65–6, 88.

[241] Disraeli MSS, B/XX/Bd/39, Beresford to Disraeli, 29 Nov. 1850.

[242] Monypenny and Buckle, *Disraeli*, iii. 267. Maria Newdegate interpreted Russell's conduct in a similar way (Newdegate Diary, CR 1841/34, 15 Nov. 1850).

[243] J. Nikol, 'The Oxford Movement in Decline: Lord John Russell and the Tractarians, 1846–52', *Historical Magazine of the Protestant Episcopal Church*, 43 (1974), 341–57.

[244] D. G. Paz, 'Popular Anti-Catholicism in England, 1850–1', *Albion*, 11 (1979), 349, calculated that 30.77% of memorials to the queen on the 'Papal Aggression' complained about Romanizing practices in the Church of England.

engage in a complete redeployment now. The prime minister was thus faced with the irresistible pressure to legislate against the new bishops which was to cause him so much difficulty in the session of 1851. Disraeli, meanwhile, was content to bide his time. He recognized at once that if Russell did not take firm action against the pope, the Protectionists were likely to be the ultimate beneficiaries of the Protestant outcry, but that if he did, he would have to run the gauntlet of Irish Catholic outrage. He took care, however, to restrain 'our too eager friends of the Spooner school' from reposing too much trust in Russell, while strengthening his own Protestant credentials in extensive consultation with Inglis.[245]

Thus the pope's tactless action, together with the energetic Protestant activity of the preceding years, produced a situation in which, for a few months, politics seemed to hinge on the Catholic issue. The dominant part played in the parliamentary session of 1851 by the Ecclesiastical Titles Bill can be seen as having considerable political logic when set against the Protestant pressure brought to bear on this very House of Commons at the general election of 1847 in conjunction with the consciousness that another return to the polls could not now be all that far in the future. Although both the National Club and the Protestant Association were to a significant extent overtaken by events in 1850, and the former divided by Russell's attack on Tractarianism,[246] the legacy of earlier agitation was very strongly in evidence.

The events of the later 1840s thus indicate that, given the favourable pre-conditions of a fluid political situation and the issues of Catholic endowment, relations with Rome, and the hierarchy on which Anglican and Dissenting anti-Catholicism could reinforce each other, Protestantism could exercise considerable influence. This was achieved more through a generalized working on public opinion than by means of a structured agitation. Nevertheless, the amorphous character of anti-Catholicism was in many respects a strength: it obscured the internal divisions which would have been apparent if efforts to construct a more defined structure had been made, and ensured that political leaders, whether Whig or Protectionist, viewed it as an unknown quantity and hence were perhaps prone to overestimate its real influence. However, essential weaknesses were also in

---

[245] Disraeli to Stanley, 16 Nov., 7 Dec. 1850, printed in Monypenny and Buckle, *Disraeli*, iii. 268, 271–2.

[246] See above, pp. 216–17.

evidence: despite the success of the campaign against endowment in Ireland, ground was given over education, penal statutes, and Maynooth itself. Unable to generate a continuing positive programme, the Protestant societies appeared in general to be engaged in a negative holding operation. Their limitations were to become more apparent as the political landscape changed during the ensuing decade.

7

THE DECLINE OF THE EARLY VICTORIAN ANTI-CATHOLIC MOVEMENT

In February 1851, as the first excitement of reaction to the 'Papal Aggression' began to recede, Lord Ashley observed: 'I doubt the *solid* Protestantism of the country, not the sparkling but evanescent feeling. There is talk and profession, but no work done; a great deal of criticism but no self-denial.'[1] The decade that followed was to confirm the truth of this observation. The high pitch of anti-papal fervour reached briefly in 1850 and 1851 could not be sustained, despite the extended machinery of Protestant agitation emerging from it. Although the early 1850s were still years of considerable anti-Catholic activity and political influence, from the middle of the decade onwards decline was obvious. This was to be in some respects reversed by the anti-ritualist litigation, convent campaigns, and Murphy riots of the 1860s and 1870s. Trends culminating in these later developments were in evidence during the 1850s. It will nevertheless be argued that the character of this later period was significantly different from that of the 1830s, 1840s, and early 1850s, which forms the focus of this book. This is an issue that will be addressed in the concluding pages of this chapter, but the primary concern of the discussion that follows will be the reasons for the loss of anti-Catholic momentum in the mid-1850s. Consideration will initially be given to the structure of the Protestant movement itself; we shall then turn to an analysis of its political campaigns, and close with a review of those factors which, from 1855 onwards, caused problems evident earlier to the discerning eye to become more fully apparent.

The central problem for the Protestant movement was its own continuing lack of unity. In 1850 the 'Papal Aggression' led to widespread professions of the need for combined action. The *British Protestant* used verse to instruct its readers on their 'present duty':

---

[1] Southampton University Library, Shaftesbury MSS, Diary, SHA/PD/6, 19 Feb. 1851.

Ye Protestants of England,
A common faith who prize,
Cease warring with each other,
And to defend it rise . . .

By all that is momentous
Your common interest see,
Lest ye lament your blindness
When all too late 'twill be.[2]

However, the failure of a renewed attempt to establish that the Reformation Society's committee should consist of equal members of Dissenters and Churchmen suggests that the sincerity of these lines scarcely exceeded their literary quality.[3] Similarly, the Evangelical Alliance agreed in passing a resolution denouncing 'the mystery of iniquity' but alluded, almost in the same breath, to their differences 'with regard to some of the grounds on which Popery should be resisted, and perhaps still more in reference to the modes in which that resistance should be carried on'.[4] Later in 1851 William Cunningham, principal of the Free Church college in Edinburgh, read a paper on 'Popery' to the annual conference, but the resulting resolution spoke only in generalities, and amendments urging specific action were defeated.[5]

Even at the height of the outcry against the pope the divergent preoccupations of Dissent and Establishment were apparent. The Protestant movement gained an important new advocate in the person of John Campbell, a Scottish Congregationalist, supporter of the Anti-State Church Association and editor of the *Christian Witness and Church Members' Magazine*,[6] but Voluntaryists in general were more cautious, as was evident from the attitude of the *Nonconformist* and the *Eclectic Review*. In an article entitled 'The Rival Hierarchies and the Duties of Dissenters' the *Eclectic* claimed that Anglicans were not protesting against the hierarchy as an attack on religious truth but rather as an invasion of their spiritual prerogatives. Dissenters, it argued, should not call for state intervention in an ecclesiastical dispute.[7] Only 120 addresses calling for action, containing about

---

[2] *BP*, 7 (1851), 29.

[3] RS minutes, 26 May 1851.

[4] *Report of a Meeting Convened by the Evangelical Alliance . . . February 21 1851* (1851), 5.

[5] Evangelical Alliance, *5th Annual Conference* (1851), 8–9.

[6] D. M. Lewis, *Lighten their Darkness* (Westport, Conn., 1986), 194–5.

[7] *Eclectic Review*, 4th series, 18 (1850), 739–62; E. R. Norman, *Anti-Catholicism in Victorian England* (1968), 65–7; G. I. T. Machin, *Politics and the Churches in Great Britain 1832–1868* (Oxford, 1977), 221–2.

20,000 signatures, came from bodies of Dissenters, although obviously many individual Nonconformists must have signed memorials from public meetings. A substantial proportion of petitions in favour of making the Ecclesiastical Titles Bill more stringent came from Dissenters, but this was almost entirely accounted for by Wesleyans who, as usual, were the most conspicuously anti-Catholic group after Anglican Evangelicals.[8]

The two major new Protestant societies to emerge from the crisis of 1850 to 1851, the Scottish Reformation Society (SRS) and the Protestant Alliance, both need to be understood against this background of hopes of vigorous united action. These had been unfulfilled by the Evangelical Alliance in the face of continuing tensions between Churches and even within them, above all over the Establishment issue. The Scottish Reformation Society was the first to be founded, having been established in Edinburgh in December 1850 as an immediate product of the general indignation at the 'Papal Aggression'. This was all the more remarkable in view of the fact that the new hierarchy did not extend to Scotland. Protestant solidarity, however, was more apparent than real. The movement against Rome was headed initially by the 'General Committee of the Free Church of Scotland on Popery', which promoted public meetings and sermons, and this official body had close links with the SRS.[9] Church of Scotland ministers were absent from the initial meeting which led to the foundation of the SRS, probably because of their suspicion of the Free Church and the Voluntaryists.[10] Although the new society claimed that its constitution and membership was 'thoroughly Catholic, embracing Ministers and members of every Protestant Evangelical denomination', in practice only three of the sixteen clergy on the committee in 1852 were Church of Scotland. Of the others, four were Free Church, two were Congregational, and the United Presbyterians, Reformed Presbyterians, United Original Secession, Scottish Episcopalians, English Episcopalians, Wesleyans, and Baptists all had one member each.[11]

[8] D..G. Paz, 'Popular Anti-Catholicism in England, 1850–1', *Albion*, 11 (1979), 331–55.

[9] SRS Archives, Minute-Book of the General Committee of the Free Church of Scotland on Popery, 27 Nov., 3, 9 Dec. 1850.

[10] SRO, Hope MSS 226/9, p. 78, Hope to Cumming, 5 Dec. 1850.

[11] SRO, Acts of the General Assembly of the Church of Scotland, 1852, Memorial of the SRS to the General Assembly. There were also 17 laymen on the committee, but their denominational affiliations cannot readily be established.

In practice, the dominance of the Free Church was greater than mere numbers suggest. As we have seen, Begg and Wylie were the central figures in the Society, and they were supported on the committee by other leading Free Churchmen such as Robert Candlish and William Cunningham. The Church of Scotland men associated with the Society were not generally of the same stature, a factor evident, too, on the editorial board of the *Bulwark*, where the Kirk's solitary representative was clearly no match for Begg.[12] Hope, while eventually agreeing to join the committee of the SRS in 1852, was not prepared to give it more than lukewarm support, clearly fearing its intentions with regard to the Establishment, as well as resenting on personal grounds what he felt was its usurpation of the leadership of the Scottish anti-Catholic movement.[13] The Church of Scotland itself preferred to act independently, setting up an 'Anti-Popery Committee' at its General Assembly in 1851.[14]

Parallel suspicions were evident in England in relation to the Protestant Alliance. The initial initiative leading to its formation came from the Anglican London Committee for the Defence of the Protestant Faith (LCDPF), led by Lord Ashley and set up on 11 November 1850.[15] During March and April 1851 this body had a series of discussions with Dissenters, among whom Sir Culling Eardley was prominent.[16] Ashley was excited at the prospects for greater union among Protestants, but other supporters of the LCDPF were less enthusiastic. T. H. Croft Moody, a Southampton solicitor, thought that there were considerable risks in associating with Dissenters if the Tractarian issue were to be taken up: 'no public body . . . uniting with Dissenters for the purpose of redressing Church of England grievances would secure the confidence of any considerable portion even of rightly thinking men within the Church . . . we cannot call to our aid anyone without the establishment to remedy evils within

---

[12] *Bulwark*, 1 (1851–2), 1; T. Smith, *Memoirs of James Begg, DD* (Edinburgh, 1885), ii. 175–6; Hope MSS 37/2/35, notes by Robertson, Feb. 1855.

[13] Hope MSS 226/9, p. 143, 226/11, pp. 187–9, Hope to Lyon, 30 Dec. 1850, 25 June 1852; 34/3/51, notes by Hope, Mar. 1853.

[14] Acts of the General Assembly of the Church of Scotland, 26 May 1851, Session 4.

[15] Southampton City Record Office, Croft Moody MSS, D/PM/10/1/5, printed resolutions of the meeting of 11 Nov.; Shaftesbury Diary, SHA/PD/6, 11 Nov. 1850 (quoted in E. Hodder, *The Life and Work of the Seventh Earl of Shaftesbury, KG*, 3 vols. (1887), ii. 328).

[16] Shaftesbury Diary, SHA/PD/6, 21 Mar., 4, 9 Apr. 1851; Croft Moody MSS, D/PM/10/3/29, MacGregor to Croft Moody, 10 Mar. 1851; D/PM/10/3/37, Eardley to Palk, 5 Apr. 1851.

it without great danger'. He also thought that harmony and effectiveness would be better achieved through separate organizations for each denomination.[17] The Protestant Alliance frankly admitted that similar views were widespread. Nevertheless, they went ahead with an initial meeting in Freemasons' Tavern on 25 June 1851 chaired by Lord Shaftesbury.[18]

The Protestant Alliance was more successful than the Scottish Reformation Society in gaining general evangelical support. It was claimed that 'on the first General Committee of the Alliance there was enrolled almost every Evangelical of note in town and country'.[19] Even James Lord, chairman of the Protestant Association, rejoiced at the formation of the Alliance.[20] The breadth of its appeal stemmed in part from the nature of its leadership: Shaftesbury was a valuable source of prestige who, initially at least, was actively involved,[21] and MacGregor was cast in a more conciliatory and subtle mould than the majority of anti-Catholic officials. However, the key factor in maintaining at least the nominal loyalty of disparate supporters was the vagueness of the Alliance's programme. There was an explicit agreement to differ, and the resolutions of the initial meeting chiefly consisted of generalizations. Thus they called for an association to 'combine all classes of Protestants' to maintain 'against all the encroachments of Popery, the . . . doctrines of the Reformation and the principles of religious liberty'. There were some more specific commitments that could command general assent, notably calls for efforts to secure the discontinuation of state endowment of Roman Catholicism and to support foreign Christians 'suffering persecution for the cause of the Gospel'. However, no allusion was made to the potentially divisive issue of Tractarianism.[22] While there was general satisfaction with the amount

[17] Shaftesbury Diary, SHA/PD/6, 9 Apr. 1851; Croft Moody MSS, D/PM/10/3/38, Croft Moody to MacGregor, 10 Apr. 1851.

[18] PAll, *1st AR* (1852), 4; Croft Moody MSS, D/PM/10/5/4, PAll circular. Ashley had succeeded as 7th Earl of Shaftesbury on 2 June 1851.

[19] E. Hodder, *John MacGregor* (1894), 103–4. A list of the general committee printed in 1859 serves to confirm the substance of Hodder's claim. Members included Cumming, Finch, Harcourt, Lord, McNeile, and Stowell. There were, however, some notable absentees, including Blakeney and Robert Bickersteth, both of whom presumably felt too strongly on the Establishment question to associate themselves with the Alliance (*Monthly Letter*, 74 (1859)).

[20] *PM*, 18 (1856), 68.

[21] Shaftesbury Diary, SHA/PD/6, 25 Sept., 6 Nov., 1, 4, 19 Dec. 1851, 1, 28 Jan., 5 June 1852, and *passim*; *R*, 6 Feb. 1856.

[22] Croft Moody MSS, D/PM/10/5/4, PAll circular; D/PM/10/8/23, summary of PAll activities.

of Protestant union that had been achieved, the *Record* was still worried
that the question of state endowments would prove a distraction,
especially as members of the Alliance would be exposed to conflicting
external pressures from Anglican High-Churchmen and militant
Voluntaryists respectively.[23]

It would appear that the effect was to cause the Alliance to draw
support from Nonconformist clergy and Anglican laymen. Of seven
clergy on the committee, only one, Edward Auriol, was an Anglican.[24]
On the other hand, of sixteen MPs who were members of the
Protestant Alliance in 1853, only four were Liberals and only two
avowed Voluntaries.[25] Seven Anglican lay members of the committee
of the LCDPF joined that of the Protestant Alliance, and MacGregor
was secretary of both bodies.[26] Croft Moody joined the Alliance in
November 1851, although with continuing reservations, and the
Record, whose proprietor Alexander Haldane was a member of the
committee, gave its support.[27] On the Dissenting side, Charles Prest
and Sir Culling Eardley were prominent.[28] Table 8 represents an
analysis of the subscription list which suggests that a similar pattern
prevailed among the rank and file. When these figures are set against
those for the Protestant Association and the Reformation Society, it
seems probable that the higher proportion of clergy in the Alliance was
accounted for by the recruitment of Dissenting ministers, while its
social profile implies that Nonconformist laymen generally did not
join. The low proportion of women and the relatively high numbers of
the politically active élite suggest that the Alliance, unlike the
Reformation Society, was perceived as a political pressure group rather
than a philanthropic organization.

[23] *R*, 1 Dec. 1851, 17 May 1852; *Bulwark*, 1 (1851–2), 245–7.
[24] Croft Moody MSS, D/PM/10/8/23, summary of PAll activities. One of the 7,
the Revd. W. Chalmers, has been impossible to identify, but, as he does not appear in
the registers of Oxford, Cambridge, or Dublin Universities, it seems safe to conclude
that he was probably not an Anglican. Edward Auriol (?1805–80), was rector of St
Dunstan in the West, 1841–80 (Boase, i. 107).
[25] Protestant Alliance, *2nd AR* (1853), 18–35; M. Stenton, *Who's Who of British
Members of Parliament, 1832–1885* (1976), *passim*. It is probable that the 2 avowed
Voluntaries, Pellatt and Challis, were also Dissenters, but Machin (*Politics and the
Churches*, p. 248) warns against an automatic equation of Voluntaryism and Dissent. It is
further striking that none of the leaders of parliamentary Voluntaryism was a member of
the Alliance.
[26] Croft Moody MSS, D/PM/10/1/5, D/PM/10/8/23.
[27] Ibid. D/PM/10/5/1, Croft Moody to MacGregor, 21 Nov. 1851; *R*, 11 Aug.
1851.
[28] Croft Moody MSS, D/PM/10/5/6, D/PM/10/8/23, PAll circulars.

TABLE 8. *Protestant Alliance subscribers, 1853*

	No.	%
Peers	7	0.8
Other titled laymen	11	1.3
MPs	16	1.9
Clergy	316	37.9
Laymen styled 'Esq.'	382	45.8
Laymen styled 'Mr'	21	2.5
Women	57	6.8
Anonymous	24	2.8
TOTAL	834	

Source: Protestant Alliance, *2nd AR* (1853), 18–35.

In practice, neither the Scottish Reformation Society nor the Protestant Alliance could become a fully effective focus for general anti-Catholic activity. The SRS was too closely associated with the denominational interests of the Free Church, and the Protestant Alliance was so anxious to find common ground that it had difficulty in developing a coherent programme. The intention in creating new societies had been to unite the Protestant movement; their effect was the reverse, inasmuch as institutions were multiplied and existing bodies were not convinced that they could allow themselves to be subsumed in younger organizations.

The counter-productive consequences at a local level of the proliferation of societies can be illustrated by events in Southampton in the early months of 1852. A branch of the Protestant Alliance had been formed in January, but its local promoters were then disconcerted to see advertisements in early March for a meeting of the British Protestant League. It transpired that this had been arranged from London by men ignorant of the pre-existence of a Protestant Alliance branch. They professed their friendly intent but persisted with the meeting, which appears to have led to a local reaction against specifically anti-Catholic agitation, expressed in a Voluntary amendment which was carried overwhelmingly at the British Protestant League meeting in March.[29]

The new societies represented a significant change in the general

[29] Croft Moody MSS, D/PM/10/2/60–1, D/PM/10/5/44–51, 53–5, letters and posters relating to Southampton British Protestant League meeting.

profile of anti-Catholicism after 1850, from an agitation dominated by establishmentarian concerns to one in which a concern for religious liberty conceived on Nonconformist terms was very much in evidence. A number of efforts were made to involve the older Protestant societies in this general realignment. The first of these was centred on the National Club and was instigated by Wilbraham Taylor, a member of the committee of the Protestant Alliance. He attempted to restructure the parliamentary side of the Protestant movement on less exclusively Tory lines through the formation of a new body, the Conference Club.[30] This scheme did not come to anything, but in February 1854 the National Club itself approached Taylor and his associates. Extended discussion followed, during which the National Club played down the exclusiveness of its Anglicanism, emphasized its discretion in the issue of addresses, and thus persuaded the group to join.[31] However, the limited extent of the Club's capacity for co-operation was indicated in 1856, when the Taylor faction, now with a foothold on the committee, proposed the opening of membership to Dissenters and the election of Shaftesbury to the presidency vacated by the death of Manchester in August 1855. An extraordinary general meeting was held in February 1856, at which the rebels were heavily defeated by the rank-and-file clerical membership. The 1856 *Annual Report* reaffirmed that 'the National Club expects support only from actual members of the Established Church, or from those who, recognising its worth, are well content that it should be upheld by us as the great National Institution for the maintenance of God's law and Gospel light in the land'. Winchilsea was elected president, and eleven members of the vanquished faction either resigned or were expelled from the committee. Four of these were members of the managing committee of the Protestant Alliance.[32] Later in the year the death of Dudley Perceval removed one of the leading High-Church members of the committee and encouraged Colquhoun early in 1857 to make fresh efforts to broaden the basis of the Club. He wrote to the *Record* to deny the charge that it was Orange, Tory, and High Church, and stressed the extent to which it was supported by leading Evangelicals. He appears to have convinced few people.[33]

---

[30] NC minutes, Dep.b.235, 24 Feb., 2, 9, 16 Mar. 1852.

[31] Ibid. 28 Feb., 28 Mar. 1854.

[32] *R*, 23 June 1856; NC, *11th AR* (1856), 3, 5–6.

[33] The Evangelical Liberal Arthur Kinnaird was elected to membership of the Club, but declined to join. *R*, 16 Jan., 2 Feb. 1857.

The Protestant Association encountered similar pressures at around the same date, suggesting a concerted plan to reorientate the movement. In November 1855 it rejected a proposal to unite with the Protestant Alliance as inconsistent with its fundamental resolutions.[34] Then, early in 1856, the *Record*, presumably speaking for Haldane, who was also among the group attempting to gain control of the National Club, came out in favour of the proposed amalgamation. It acknowledged that the Association's principles were 'very sound and good', but maintained that it had failed to answer the anticipations with which it had been founded. It denied that Anglicans joining the Alliance would be sacrificing their principles, but claimed that, on the contrary, the Church would gain from the better relations thus achieved.[35] Lord was furious with the *Record*, especially when it refused to insert a rejoinder from him. He published his reply in the *Protestant Magazine*, quoting a letter from Sir Culling Eardley which questioned whether union was feasible at this stage. The Association hastily recruited a number of vice-presidents, contrived to stave off the challenge, and was still in existence at the end of the decade.[36]

In Scotland suspicions and rivalries associated with the Establishment problem remained an even more serious bar to united action than in England. Blakeney, who took a close interest in Scottish affairs, believed that 'Popery' was labouring to overthrow the Establishment because, if Church property were to be alienated, many parishes would have to be abandoned and the priests could then fill up the vacancies. Thus, he went on, 'Dr Hetherington, Candlish, Begg may be zealous against Popery, but still *they* are doing *the work of Popery more effectively* than Wiseman, Newman and Cahill because they, as Protestants have weight in their attacks upon the Church.' Blakeney felt that to co-operate with them against Rome would give greater prestige and influence to the campaign which he believed them to be waging against the Church of Scotland , and would therefore be worse than useless.[37]

Blakeney was passionately committed to the promotion of Establishment as well as Protestant principles, seeing it as essential that agents employed by missions with which he was associated should be able to engage effectively in argument with Voluntaryists as well as Roman

[34] *PM*, 18 (1856), 35–6, 91, 129–30.
[35] *R*, 6 Feb. 1856.
[36] *PM*, 18 (1856), 66–71; Hope MSS 39/2/142, 39/3/122, Lord to Hope, 20 Feb., 3 Mar. 1856.
[37] Hope MSS 35/3/71, Blakeney to Hope, 13 Mar. 1854.

Catholics.[38] His extreme views on the subject were obviously divisive, as was noted by a correspondent of Hope's in 1855, who described himself as 'appalled' by passages in *Popery in its Social Aspect* which linked 'Jesuitism' with 'Anti-State-Churchism'.[39] Blakeney himself saw conflict with Dissent as inevitable, and believed that the cause of Protestantism should be unequivocally linked with that of state Churches.[40] He came to see Hope's activities in conjunction with the official operations of the Church of Scotland's Anti-Popery Committee as a basis for a grandiose scheme to bring together the Reformation Society and the Kirk, aiming not only to evangelize the Irish poor in Scotland but also to 'present the two Churches [the Church of England and the Church of Scotland] as in unity against the common foe and this unity would strengthen the two churches against the enemies of Establishments also'.[41] In Scotland this strategy would outflank the efforts of the Free Churchmen and Voluntaries to monopolize the anti-Catholic campaign, and in England it would stiffen the Protestant character of the Church and strengthen the hands of Evangelicals in their efforts against Tractarianism.[42] Thus, in May 1854 the Anti-Popery Committee persuaded the General Assembly to endorse a scheme for full co-operation with the Reformation Society.[43]

Hope, meanwhile, had been cherishing his own scheme for nothing less than the repeal of Emancipation. During a protest meeting in December 1850 he had publicly disagreed with a speaker who had claimed that everyone at the meeting was in favour of the 1829 Act.[44] His extreme views on this point gained little ground in the Protestant movement, but were a further source of division. Cumming agreed that Emancipation had been a 'chief great blunder', but thought that its repeal could only be achieved as the culmination of a sustained campaign.[45] John Angell James, approached by Hope to write a pamphlet on the subject, thought that Catholics could not have political power taken from them 'without a convulsion that would shake England to the centre'.[46] The National Club's committee

[38] Hope MSS, 34/4/108, Turnbull to Hope, 24 Apr. 1853.
[39] Ibid. 38/3/80, James Buchanan to Hope, 22 Sept. 1855.
[40] Ibid. 34/11/93, Blakeney to Hope, 29 Nov. 1853.
[41] Ibid. 34/10/90, Blakeney to Hope, 27 Oct. 1853.
[42] Ibid. 34/6/34, 34/11/25, Blakeney to Hope, 8 June, 5 Nov. 1853.
[43] *BP*, 10 (1854), 182–3.
[44] Hope MSS 226/9, p. 76, Hope to Cumming, 5 Dec. 1850.
[45] Ibid. 32/1/7, Cumming to Hope, Jan. 1851.
[46] Ibid. 34/11/19, James to Hope, 2 Nov. 1853.

considered issuing an address on Emancipation in December 1853, but after much consideration it decided not to do so.[47] Hope wanted the Protestant Reformation Society to take up the issue, but, quite apart from Cumming's reservations, it still adhered to its general 'no politics' rule.[48] The SRS was even more unsatisfactory for Hope's purposes, with many of its Dissenting members naturally opposed to such a campaign.[49] In the face of these rebuffs, in 1854 Hope set up yet another society, the Scottish Protestant Association, which was exclusively Church of Scotland in its composition. It made some progress among those who had held aloof from the Scottish Reformation Society, but it did not present a strong challenge.[50]

In February 1855 the dominant Free Church faction in the Scottish Reformation Society moved to reduce the Church of Scotland representation on the committee.[51] Matters came to a head in May 1856, when the general committee refused to petition against the lord advocate's Education Bill which allowed Dissenters to become parochial schoolmasters. The Church of Scotland members resigned, arguing that silence implied support for the Bill and thus played into the hands of the Free Church. The committee denied this imputation: 'The Society, in terms of its constitution, "consists of all Evangelical Denominations", and therefore must, in the nature of the case, exclude all questions on which those denominations differ among themselves.'[52] The incident demonstrated the difficulty inherent in 'agreements to differ': they were bound to be shattered in those circumstances in which inaction could itself be construed as a partisan position.

South of the Border the Reformation Society's increasingly close association with the Church of Scotland was a development which some of its own supporters found uncongenial. In June 1853, led by Dr Armstrong of Bermondsey, they formed a new society, the English Church Missions to Roman Catholics.[53] Captain Gordon supported it against the Reformation Society, and an advertisement appeared on 18 July listing a committee headed by Lord Shaftesbury and evidently

[47] NC minutes, Dep.b.235, 6 Dec, 1853.
[48] Hope MSS 226/13, pp. 392–3, Hope to Blakeney, 4 Feb. 1854.
[49] Ibid. p. 41, Hope to Blakeney, 20 Nov. 1853.
[50] D. Jamie, *John Hope: Philanthropist and Reformer* (Edinburgh, 1900), 317–18; Hope MSS 38/4/136, Hetherington to Hope, 30 Oct. 1855; *PM*, 18 (1856), 63–4.
[51] Hope MSS 37/2/34, 35, Robertson to Hope, 7 Feb. 1855; SRS minutes, 2 Feb. 1855.
[52] *Bulwark*, 6 (1856–7), Aug. 1856, cover.
[53] Hope MSS 34/6/34, 34/12/68, Blakeney to Hope, 8 June, 27 Dec. 1853.

representing a significant body of Evangelical opinion. It announced that the new society would seek to work in a manner 'consistent with the order and discipline of the United Church of England and Ireland' and to engraft its agency on to the parochial system. The advertisement continued:

With all the respect due to the Reformation Society for its faithful witness to Protestant and Evangelical truth, it never can with its present mixed constitution, obtain from the clergy and bishops of the Church of England that amount of cooperation which is absolutely essential for a movement equal to the present crisis of Rome's aggression upon the civil and religious liberties of England.[54]

Anglican unease about the 'irregularity' of the Reformation Society's proceedings was further evident in January 1854, when the Revd John Roberts, a clergyman who had been employed by the Society, published a letter attacking it in a Roman Catholic newspaper. He complained about the Society's disregard of Anglican Church order, its subjection of Church of England clergymen to examination by Cumming, and its sending of men to preach on street corners 'after the manner of the most canting Dissenters'.[55]

The English Church Missions to Roman Catholics clearly hoped that, by dissociating themselves from such conduct, they would gain the support of non-Evangelical but still anti-Roman elements in the Church of England. In this they were unsuccessful, but their existence is an interesting demonstration of the presence of what can be termed 'High-Church' Evangelicalism, resting its defence of the Church of England on a conviction of the inherent value of its order. This was distinct from the argument for national Churches advanced by Blakeney, to whom precise forms of Church government were irrelevant provided that Establishments survived and made an uncompromising stand against Rome. In 1858, when the English Church Missions were failing, they approached the Reformation Society to suggest a merger, but even under these circumstances differences over Church government proved irreconcilable.[56]

The Protestant societies were thus dissipating substantial amounts of time, energy, and money in duplicating institutions and on infighting

[54] *R*, 16, 23, 27 June, 18 July 1853.
[55] *Catholic Standard*, 28 Jan., 11 Feb. 1854. Roberts also alleged that the agents of the Society were of 'vulgar' character. In this connection, see above, Chap. 5, pp. 181–3.
[56] S. Gilley, 'Protestant London, No-Popery and the Irish Poor, 1830–1860', *Recusant History*, 11 (1971), 28.

among themselves. This conclusion is of considerable importance in relation to their political efforts from 1850 onwards, to which we shall now turn. Given the obvious discontinuities in the politics of the 1850s, a broadly chronological analysis is advisable.

The public outcry against the establishment of the Roman Catholic hierarchy provides an interesting contrast with the agitation against Maynooth in 1845, inasmuch as the direct part played by centralized agitation was substantially smaller. The National Club had issued an address on 29 October 1850 calling on the English people to rouse themselves, but had only acted after 'many urgent applications . . . from Members and others anxious to know what the Club meant to do'.[57] The Protestant Association initially contented itself with expressing a somewhat plaintive hope that Protestants might be aroused to a sense of their dangers and duties. By 25 November it had mustered sufficient energy to hold a meeting in St Martin's Hall to protest against the papal Bull, but decided not to mount an agitation similar to that of 1845.[58]

The newly formed London Committee for the Defence of the Protestant Faith was more active, meeting daily in November and early December and concerning itself primarily with the Tractarian issue. On 5 December its members held a public meeting in Freemasons' Hall, adopting a lay address to the queen which it circulated to the provinces for signature, together with a similar address to the Archbishop of Canterbury to be signed by both clergy and laity.[59] Energetic and systematic efforts were made to obtain signatures, and by 26 February 1851 the address to the queen had been signed by 65 peers, 109 MPs, and 317,578 other laymen, while that to the primate had received 239,679 signatures.[60] Impressive though these figures are, they were small in comparison with the number of signatures to addresses obtained through purely local initiatives, and, although the LCDPF was associated with 55 local committees, it does not appear to have promoted other significant agitation.[61]

[57] NC minutes, Dep.b.235, 29 Oct. 1850; *Addresses to the Protestants of the Empire Issued by the Committee of the National Club*, 3rd series (1850), 5.

[58] *PM*, 12 (1850), 168, 183–8; 13 (1851), 171.

[59] Croft Moody MSS, D/PM/10/1/25, instructions on obtaining signatures for petitions; D/PM/10/2/30; Shaftesbury Diary, SHA/PD/6, 5, 6 Dec. 1850; Hodder, *Shaftesbury*, ii. 330–4; Hodder, *MacGregor*, pp. 98–100.

[60] Croft Moody MSS, D/PM/10/1/11, letters from Lord Henry Cholmondeley to Croft Moody, Dec. 1850, Jan. 1851; D/PM/10/3/21, Protestant Defence Committee circular.

[61] The Protestant Defence Committee's address appears to have been presented too late to be included in the parliamentary return, which yields the figure of about 1 million

Thus there was little direct connection between the Protestant societies and the tangled political developments of the spring of 1851: debates on the Ecclesiastical Titles Bill from 7 February onwards; the obstructive tactics of the Irish Catholics in Parliament; the government's resignation following its defeat on Locke King's motion to equalize the franchises, and its subsequent return with a watered-down version of the Bill which, after very lengthy discussion, eventually completed its passage through Parliament in July. However, a number of general points about the political significance of anti-Catholic agitation at this juncture can be made.

Not only, as was shown in the previous chapter, did the Protestant pressure of the previous five years contribute substantially to a general political climate in which Parliament could spend inordinate amounts of time on unenforceable legislation of purely symbolic significance, but it also heightened certain features of the crisis. Indeed, the abstract and ideological rather than pragmatic frame of mind in which the issue was addressed can itself be seen as reflecting a characteristic feature of extra-parliamentary anti-Catholicism. More specifically, the government's realization that it could not escape from advancing legislation which applied to Ireland as well as England was a natural consequence of the vigour with which the Catholic endowment issue had been agitated between 1845 and 1848 as a matter of concern to the whole United Kingdom. This was a serious difficulty for Russell's administration, both in relation to the short-term parliamentary problems presented by the Irish Catholics, and also in rendering still more hopeless its prospects for developing a coherent Irish policy in the future.[62]

On the other hand, the Protestant societies proved unable to press home their advantages. Failure to mount an agitation in 1850 and 1851 as sophisticated and widespread as that of 1845 can in part be attributed to a tacit feeling that, given the force of the public outcry stirred by the Durham Letter, further stimuli would be supererogatory. However, it also stemmed from the movement's own lack of cohesion in advancing a Protestant programme that went beyond a generalized antagonism to the new hierarchy. The inadequacy of this response became more apparent in early March 1851 in the face of the

signatures. Thus the total figure should be somewhat higher than this, although probably by no means as much as 1.3 million, as individuals were likely to have signed both the PDC address and a local one.

[62] National Library of Scotland, Minto MSS 11997, ff. 68, 70–1, 90–1, diary entries for 13, 26 Apr., 22 July 1851.

government's retreat from its earlier, more vigorously anti-papal, position. The National Club noted the uncertainty of Protestant MPs as to what course they should follow, while Ashley observed after attending a LCDPF meeting: 'Men's minds are in every state and of every hue; furious, doubtful, lukewarm; some for no bill, some for every bill—clauses without end are proposed; all is gabble, confusion, uncertainty, fear and trembling, where they think at all.'[63]

A key feature of the political uncertainty was the confused relationship between Protestantism and the Protectionists. Ashley noted that the tone of parliamentary anti-Catholicism was primarily political rather than religious, and felt that Evangelical agitation was regarded with suspicion because of its perceived aura of Dissent.[64] Certainly, Stanley and Disraeli were primarily concerned with party advantage. In the ministerial crisis of late February Stanley initially attempted a reconciliation with the Peelites despite their opposition to the Ecclesiastical Titles Bill, but he sought to balance this by a gesture to the Protestant lobby. The medium he chose was to offer the presidency of the India Board to Inglis, who, out of unease at Russell's fickleness it would seem, had recently shown a greater disposition to support the Protectionists. Inglis initially accepted but then withdrew, presenting a significant further check to Stanley's already failing hopes of forming an administration.[65]

By late March Stanley, still disappointed by his failure to woo the Peelites, appeared to have given them up as a lost cause, a conclusion reached largely on Protestant grounds. He was now optimistic about the possibility of winning over some conservative Whigs and even Dissenters by means of the religious question.[66] Protestants, though, remained suspicious: Newdegate informed Stanley that some members of the National Club feared that he was willing to allow the *de facto* acceptance of the Catholic hierarchy, while Ashley worried about his High-Church leanings.[67] These tensions became further apparent on

[63] NC minutes, Dep.b.235, 8 Mar. 1851; Shaftesbury Diary, SHA/PD/6, 11 Mar. 1851.

[64] Shaftesbury Diary, SH/PD/6, 15, 27 Jan. 1851.

[65] Derby MSS 133/2, Inglis to Derby, 27 Feb. 1851, 31 Aug. 1852; W. F. Monypenny and G. E. Buckle, *The Life of Benjamin Disraeli, Earl of Beaconsfield*, 6 vols. (1910–20), iii. 287–97; R. Stewart, *The Foundation of the Conservative Party 1830–1867* (1978), 248–51.

[66] University of Illinois at Urbana-Champaign, Croker MSS, x942.08 D44c, ff. 16–17, Stanley to Croker, 22 Mar. 1851.

[67] Derby MSS 148/1, Newdegate to Stanley, 14 Mar. 1851; Warwickshire County Record Office, Maria Newdegate Diary, CR 1841/34, 3 Apr. 1851; Shaftesbury Diary, SHA/PD/6, 8 May 1851.

9 May 1851, when Disraeli and Stanley, in the hope of carrying what amounted to a vote of censure against Russell, connived at a motion to the effect that the government was indirectly responsible for the establishment of the hierarchy. This proceeding annoyed Protestant Tories. Inglis, for whom the matter of which party was in office was secondary to his aim of passing the Ecclesiastical Titles Bill, opposed the amendment, distancing himself again from the Protectionists. Plumptre asserted that 'If the people believed that members of that House were acting more from party than from patriotic motives, the greatest offence would be given to, and the greatest distrust excited among the Protestant community.' Thus, although some National Club members, including Frewen, Hamilton, and Mandeville, voted with Disraeli, others abstained. Several Protestants, notably Ashley, Inglis, and Plumptre, supported the government.[68] The motion was lost by 280 votes to 201, and Disraeli believed that the Protestant revolt, partial though it was, had done 'incalculable mischief'. He made use of Phillips's assistance in seeking to secure the loyalty of the parliamentary members of the National Club, now forty-five in number, and Stanley assured them that he was anxious 'to cooperate with them sincerely and heartily'. The quarrel appears to have been patched up, but the Conservatives had received a painful reminder that Protestant support could not be taken for granted.[69]

Even as the storm of 1850–1 receded, it seemed to offer ample encouragement to continue the struggle. At the beginning of November 1851 the Protestant Alliance and the Scottish Reformation Society, apparently acting in concert, both took steps to concentrate their efforts against Maynooth, the issue chosen as most likely to command general Protestant support.[70] The campaign was launched at a public meeting on 27 November, and between late November and mid-March fifty-one towns held similar gatherings, the movement being pursued in tandem with the Protestant Alliance's efforts to form local branches.[71] The figures for petitioning contained in Table 9 show that, proportionately, there was much greater enthusiasm in Scotland than in Wales and England, and very little interest in

---

[68] Machin, *Politics and the Churches*, p. 224; 3 *Hansard*, cxvi. 807, 816, 834, 9 May 1851; Shaftesbury MSS, SHA/PC/89/2, Ashley to Russell, 22 May 1851.

[69] Bod. Lib., Disraeli MSS, B/XXI/P/252, 253, 254, Phillips to Disraeli, 16, 17, 21 May 1851.

[70] *Bulwark*, 1 (1851–2), 134–6; cf. F. Wallis, 'The Revival of the Anti-Maynooth Campaign in Britain', *Albion*, 19 (1987), 527–48.

[71] *R*, 1 Dec. 1851; *PM*, 14 (1852), 124–6; *Bulwark*, 1 (1851–2), 164–5.

TABLE 9. *Anti-Maynooth petitioning, 1851–1852*

	Petitions	Signatures	% of population
England and Wales	501	166,320	0.9
Scotland	375	148,542	5.1
Ireland	66	8,059	0.12
TOTAL	942	322,921	1.18

Source: Bulwark, 2 (1852–3), 49.

Ireland.[72] These figures also point to the limits of active support for the renewal of the anti-Maynooth campaign, which failed to attract militant Dissenters, who preferred only to attack Maynooth in the context of a general assault on all state endowment of religion.[73]

When the Conservatives came into office in February 1852, they were immediately faced with the problem that anti-Catholic back-benchers would expect the vague statements of sympathy given in opposition to be translated into positive action in government. Both Stanley (now Earl of Derby) and Disraeli were questioned as to their intentions over Maynooth, but they tried to avoid committing themselves.[74] Anxiety to reconcile the Protestant interest was also evident in Derby's conciliatory but non-committal response to exhortations from M'Ghee to adopt a vigorously anti-Catholic policy.[75] However, most active Protestant MPs had no desire to embarrass the government. Spooner reached a compromise with Disraeli whereby he agreed to move for an inquiry and not for outright abolition of the grant. The proposal, debated extensively in May and June, was also convenient for MPs facing the imminent prospect of a general election, because they could appease their anti-Catholic constituents by voting for inquiry, while avoiding taking any position with respect to abolition, an attitude which Disraeli recognized and to which he was willing to be indulgent.[76] It was not so favourably received by the Protestant

[72] The list covers petitions received up to 15 June 1852. Figures for population are derived from the 1851 census. If the proportion of protestants to Catholics in the Irish population is taken as 1:4 (cf. S. Connolly, *Religion and Society in Nineteenth-Century Ireland* (Dundalk, 1985), 3), then the petitioners made up only 0.6% of the protestants of Ireland.

[73] *Nonconformist*, 21 Apr. 1852, p. 297.

[74] Machin, *Politics and the Churches*, pp. 228, 230–1.

[75] Derby MSS 142/4, M'Ghee to Derby, 30 Mar. 1852.

[76] Monypenny and Buckle, *Disraeli*, iii. 373–4; Canterbury Cathedral Library, Inglis MSS, Diary, 11 May 1852; Machin, *Politics and the Churches*, pp. 221–2; Wallis, 'Anti-Maynooth Campaign', p. 532.

societies, who dissociated themselves from it, maintaining that there was no need for an inquiry to tell them what Maynooth was like. Thus, estrangement between parliamentary anti-Catholicism and out-of-doors agitation was again apparent.[77]

With the dissolution of Parliament in July, the scene of action shifted from the Commons to the hustings. The general burden of statements by anti-Catholics was that no political party could be trusted and that electors should judge individual candidates according to their declared views on Maynooth, irrespective of the colours under which they fought. The National Club's electoral address laid rather greater stress on the maintenance of the Established Church, and stopped short of making Maynooth the sole test of a candidate.[78] There was much Protestant nervousness about the outcome. Although anti-Catholic feelings were currently being stirred by the Achilli case and the royal proclamation against Catholic processions on 17 June, the *Record* feared that emotions had already fallen some way from the high pitch they had reached in 1851. Shaftesbury thought that 'the Elections will prove incontestably what I have always asserted, that the country is not Protestant at heart'. He believed that the anti-Catholic cry would prove powerless against normal political loyalties.[79]

There was even less specifically Protestant electoral machinery than there had been in 1847. The National Club had set up subcommittees in 1851 to consider matters relating to the election and to supply constituencies with information on the 'Protestant character' of candidates, but they do not appear to have been particularly active.[80] There was no publication analogous to the *Protestant Elector* of 1847, and little evidence for direction of anti-Catholic opinion at a local level. Even at Liverpool no anti-Maynooth candidate came forward, and McNeile appeared to compromise his Protestantism by advocating support for the Protectionist candidate despite the latter's unsoundness on the religious front.[81] An exception was at Manchester. Stowell made a determined and eventually successful search for candidates

---

[77] *R*, 24, 27 May, 10 June 1852; *PM*, 14 (1852), 161.

[78] J. Lord, *Foreign or Domestic Legislation? An Address to Electors* (1852); *Bulwark*, 1 (1851–2), 274–7; *General Election: Address of the Scottish Reformation Society to the Electors of Scotland* (Edinburgh, 1852); NC, *Address to the Protestant Electors of the Empire* (1852), 4th series, 5.

[79] *R*, 13 May 1852; Shaftesbury Diary, SHA/PD/6, 10 July 1852.

[80] NC minutes, Dep.b.235, 6, 13 May 1851.

[81] F. Neal, *Sectarian Violence: The Liverpool Experience, 1819–1914* (Manchester, 1988).

who were both Protestants and free traders.[82] He then issued an address specifically repudiating Protectionism and calling on electors to vote in accordance with Protestant principles.[83] A systematic canvass by an election committee in each ward produced between 5,000 and 6,000 pledges for Stowell's candidates, Lock and Denman, but at the poll they only secured about 4,000 votes, and Gibson and Bright coasted home with comfortable majorities.[84]

The Manchester result illustrated the continuing divergence between the Church of England and Dissent. Stowell, while praising the loyalty of the Wesleyans, attacked other Nonconformists for violating their pledges.[85] A similar tendency was evident at Stockport, where, despite the sentiments manifested in the riots, the Radical Unitarian John Benjamin Smith was returned in place of the sitting member, James Heald, an anti-Catholic Wesleyan Peelite. A Radical broadsheet exulted: 'Let us not be misunderstood—we are as sincerely Protestant as any in her Majesty's dominions. The Protestant Lion means Church of Englandism, and Tories or Dissenters for its support. The Electors saw through the dodge of protestantism, and have returned men who will vote against all State endowments in matters of religion.'[86]

In general the anti-Maynooth cry had a significant impact on elections, but only when Protestantism was associated with other political forces. In a number of English constituencies Conservatives who were no longer deeply committed to Protection used Maynooth as a convenient stick with which to beat the Peelites, leading to some notable victories such as those against Roundell Palmer at Plymouth and Edward Cardwell at Liverpool.[87] In Scotland anti-Catholicism took on a political colour, being vigorously used against the Whigs by Free Church and Voluntary candidates, with a considerable impact in seats such as Glasgow, Greenock, and Stirling, although it was not strong enough to prevent Macaulay regaining Edinburgh.[88] As in

[82] NC minutes, Dep.b.235, 11 May 1852; *R*, 20 May 1852.

[83] H. Stowell, *To the Protestant Electors of Manchester* (Manchester, 1852).

[84] *PM*, 14 (1852), 263–4; F. W. S. Craig, *British Parliamentary Election Results 1832–1885* (1977), 206.

[85] *PM*, 14 (1852), 263.

[86] *Extinguisher*, 16 July 1852 (Stockport Public Library, SF 32); Machin, *Politics and the Churches*, pp. 241, 246–8.

[87] *PM*, 14 (1852), 233–4; *Bulwark*, 2 (1852–3), 29–30; Stewart, *Foundation of the Conservative Party*, pp. 256–7.

[88] I. G. C. Hutchison, *A Political History of Scotland 1832–1924* (Edinburgh, 1986), 66–8.

1847, the most important consequence of Protestant pressure was not in determining the outcome of specific contests, but in giving many successful candidates the impression that significant proportions of their constituents were opposed to the Maynooth grant and that a statement against it might therefore be diplomatic. Lord Minto, commenting on his son Melgund's defeat at Greenock, praised his 'honest and uncompromising assertion of opinion [in favour of the Maynooth grant] opposed to the fanaticism of the day—to which too many have less honestly conformed to save their seats'.[89] Nevertheless, subsequent events were to show that some MPs did not feel obliged to hold firmly to pledges given under duress in elections, and that even those whose commitments were sincere had such divergent convictions in other respects that effective united action was to prove impossible.

The fall of the Derby government in December 1852, and the formation of the Aberdeen coalition, was, from a Protestant point of view, a change for the worse, especially as the new Cabinet included 'Puseyites' such as Gladstone and Newcastle[90] and there were even three Irish Catholics holding junior posts. Shaftesbury considered Aberdeen's appointment as proof that there was 'no reality in the stir against "Papal Aggression"'.[91] On the other hand, Spooner now felt free to pursue the Maynooth question more forcefully. His motion was preceded by Protestant efforts to gather signatures to petitions, and came forward on 22 February 1853.[92] In the division he was defeated by twenty votes, a bitter disappointment for those who had calculated Protestant prospects on the basis of pledges given at the general election. Nevertheless, 164 MPs had voted against Maynooth, suggesting that there was a large body of Protestant feeling in the Commons, although it was divided on the Establishment question.[93]

Anti-Maynooth pressure was also exerted by Winchilsea in the Lords. Despite Spooner's defeat, it was a sufficient irritant for the government to take action. In a shrewd move Aberdeen divided the Protestant movement by appointing a royal commission to investigate the College. For anti-Catholics who opposed the grant on constitu-

---

[89] Minto MSS 11998, f. 104, diary entry for 4 June 1852.

[90] Fifth duke, formerly styled Earl of Lincoln, who succeeded his father, the staunchly Protestant 4th duke, in 1851.

[91] *Bulwark*, 2 (1852–3), 197–9; Shaftesbury Diary, SHA/PD/6, 8 Jan. 1853.

[92] Machin, *Politics and the Churches*, p. 263; *Bulwark*, 2 (1852–3), 169.

[93] *PM*, 15 (1853), 172; *Bulwark*, 2 (1852–3), 273; 3 *Hansard*, cxxiv. 521–3, 23 Feb. 1853.

tional grounds, this was an irrelevance, but it did something to appease those primarily worried about the practical impact of the instruction at Maynooth. Accordingly it weakened Protestant support somewhat, and, by placing the matter *sub judice*, it curtailed the possibility of agitating an issue that was a valuable basis for common anti-Catholic action. The appointment of the Earl of Harrowby, a moderate pro-Maynooth Evangelical, as chairman confirms the impression that Aberdeen was not trying to reconcile the anti-Maynooth movement but to isolate it. Stowell claimed that the inquiry was useless and the character of Maynooth was as self-evident as that 'it is dark at midnight'. The Protestant Alliance dissociated itself from the commission, but they could do little but wait two years in growing frustration for Harrowby's report.[94]

The temporary eclipse of the anti-Maynooth movement coincided with, and reinforced, a shift in Protestant preoccupations away from Ireland towards the perceived threats to personal liberty presented by Catholic governments in Europe and the confinement of nuns in Britain. The most prominent victims of Rome abroad were felt to be Francesco and Rosa Madiai, condemned in Florence in August 1852 to fifty-six and forty-six months' imprisonment respectively for allegedly holding a Protestant religious meeting in their home. This blatant act of religious persecution, perpetrated by an authoritarian government subject to strong influence from the Roman Catholic Church, seemed to substantiate the worst Protestant perceptions of Rome. The Protestant Alliance organized vigorous efforts to secure their release, directed in part at the Tuscan government and in part intended to stimulate the British government to take up the case.[95] A deputation headed by the Earl of Roden and including representatives from a number of other European countries was sent to Florence in October 1852, but the grand duke refused to receive it. Roden was permitted to visit the prisoners, however, and sent back to England emotional reports of their patient and saintly suffering in adversity.[96] This further stirred activity at home, with a campaign of public meetings keeping up pressure on successive governments to intervene. The outcry went far beyond the usual boundaries of the Protestant movement, as illustrated by Prince Albert's observation to Shaftesbury:

[94] *PM*, 15 (1853), 190; *Bulwark*, 2 (1852–3), 307.
[95] J. MacGregor, *The Madiai Case* (1853), 5–7.
[96] Ibid. 8–23; Public Record Office of Northern Ireland, Belfast, Roden MSS, MIC 147/5, Lord Roden's letter-book, 25A–25P, Roden to his wife, Oct., Nov. 1852.

'This is the Church which calls *us intolerant* merely because we do not choose to be governed by it.'[97] Popular feeling was intensified during the winter of 1852–3 by reports, which turned out to be unfounded, that Francesco had died in prison. Ultimately Russell, in his capacity as foreign secretary, was needled into making direct approaches to the grand duke early in 1853.[98] Dispatches from Florence indicate that, in the short term, the outcry in Britain was counter-productive, in that the Tuscan government was anxious not to seem to surrender too readily to foreign pressure. The Madiai were ultimately released on 17 March 1853, but this was in immediate response to representations from the French government, who had hitherto not taken the matter up with the same vigour as the British. However, the British had themselves solicited Napoleon III's intervention, and it would seem that the Protestant outcry was influential in causing the grand duke to back down when he could do so without too much loss of face.[99]

This satisfactory conclusion to the Madiai case was one of the Protestant Alliance's most notable achievements, a success which they endeavoured to repeat whenever they heard of other instances of European Protestants suffering for their faith. Most Catholic countries were criticized for restricting religious liberty, including Austria, France, and Spain. However, Protestants abroad were generally handled with greater moderation or greater discretion than in Tuscany. Even when they were not, most continental governments were in a stronger position to resist diplomatic pressure than vulnerable Tuscany had been.[100] Furthermore, the Protestant Alliance's tendency to apply double standards, showing relatively little concern for the far from ideal position of Catholics in some Protestant countries, was noted by its critics.[101]

Meanwhile, the position of nuns, not dissimilar in Protestant eyes, was receiving increased attention. Some anti-Catholics wanted an outright prohibition of convents, but most felt that this was unrealistic.[102] It would in any case have been inconsistent with the claim that

[97] Shaftesbury MSS, SHA/PC/4, Prince Albert to Shaftesbury, 24 Sept. 1852 (printed in Hodder, *Shaftesbury*, ii. 389–90).
[98] MacGregor, *Madiai Case*, pp. 25–7, 30–1; Hodder, *Shaftesbury*, ii. 392.
[99] PRO, FO79/165/2, Erskine to Clarendon, 28 Mar. 1853.
[100] *R*, 17 Oct. 1856; SRS minutes, 22 Aug. 1854; Shaftesbury Diary, SHA/PD/6, 2 Sept. 1856.
[101] 3 *Hansard*, cxxiv. 208–21, 17 Feb. 1853; E. Lucas, *The Life of Frederick Lucas, MP*, 2 vols. (1886), ii. 15–16; MacGregor, *Madiai Case*, pp. 33–4.
[102] Hope MSS 226/11, p. 187, Hope to Lyon, 25 June 1852; 33/6/1, Lyon to Hope, 30 June 1852.

the campaign against them was predicated on the assertion of individual liberty. They aimed rather to secure inspection and regulation of nunneries, and the enactment of safeguards to prevent nuns being detained against their will. The anti-convent movement, in which the political energies of women were stirred and exploited, began in Edinburgh in the second half of 1851 with the issuing of an 'Address to British Protestant Females'. It was taken up by the Protestant Alliance, and petitions and memorials were adopted in a number of English and Scottish towns. However, London was relatively slow to move, and until 1853 the issue was overshadowed by Maynooth.[103] The convent campaign was fuelled by the revelations made in the Achilli case and also by another well-reported court action concerning a child who complained of ill-treatment while in the care of nuns at Norwood.[104] In March 1853 a female auxiliary to the Scottish Reformation Society was formed, laying particular emphasis on the convent issue.[105]

On 10 May 1853 Thomas Chambers moved a successful resolution in the Commons for the introduction of legislation for the inspection of nunneries. Table 10, which gives details of the Commons votes on

TABLE 10. *Commons votes on Maynooth and convents, 1853*

	Maynooth (23 Feb.)	Convents (10 May)
Conservative	121	83
Peelite	2	4
Liberal	29	43
Voluntaryist	12	10
Total anti-Catholic vote	164	140

Sources: 3 *Hansard*, cxxiv. 521–3, 23 Feb. 1853; cxxvii. 132–4, 10 May 1853; *Dod's Parliamentary Companion*, 1853.

the two issues, indicates that the convent campaign attracted greater support from Liberals and less from Conservatives than Maynooth did. If all the Conservatives who had opposed Maynooth had supported Chambers, the anti-convent movement would have assumed powerful proportions, but many stayed away, not experiencing

[103] *Bulwark*, 1 (1851–2), 148, 170, 313; 2 (1852–3), 105; *PM*, 13 (1851), 384–6.
[104] *Bulwark*, 2 (1852–3), 105, 139; *PM*, 14 (1852), 292–6, 373 ff.; Shaftesbury Diary, SHA/PD/6, 12 Aug. 1852.
[105] *Bulwark*, 2 (1852–3), 269, 284–5.

the same degree of pressure from their constituents on this issue and probably reluctant to support a motion proposed by a Liberal. Chambers met with strong opposition from Russell, for whom the dictates of personal liberty pointed in a different direction, and his measure made little further progress. On 20 June a deputation from the Protestant Alliance saw Palmerston, now home secretary, to ask for the unrestricted rights of British subjects to be accorded to nuns, but they received little encouragement.[106]

The government's effective stalemating of both the anti-Maynooth and anti-convent campaigns in 1853 showed clearly the limitations of Protestant parliamentary action, but the administration then proceeded to overplay its hand. It felt itself in a position to conciliate the Catholics by disowning Russell when he suggested that the Roman Church was aiming to subvert the political system. Subsequently, in December 1853 Palmerston expressed an intention to provide salaried Roman Catholic chaplains in prisons.[107] Such developments caused the Protestant societies to become worried about their own lack of unity and to conclude that they needed to take further steps towards co-operation to bring pressure to bear on Parliament and government. The Scottish Reformation Society was particularly concerned to mobilize public opinion against Catholic gaol chaplains, and held a Protestant conference in Edinburgh at the beginning of March 1854 with an attendance of 760, over half of whom were representatives of Churches and other organizations. However, the need for an 'agreement to differ' had been explicitly stated, and, although a wide range of issues was discussed, there was little substantive action.[108]

Following the Edinburgh conference, the SRS sent Begg and Drummond as a deputation to London. They presented Protestant views on various matters to members of the government, conferred with Protestant MPs, and promoted the idea of a Protestant conference in London.[109] This subsequently met at the National Club from 23 to 25 May 1854, with all the major Protestant societies being represented. It was agreed to petition Parliament about the continuing delay in the production of the Maynooth Commission's report and to

[106] *PM*, 15 (1853), 197–201, 210, 222; Machin, *Politics and the Churches*, p. 264.

[107] *PM*, 15 (1853), 261 ff.; *Bulwark*, 3 (1853–4), 1–3; Machin, *Politics and the Churches*, pp. 260–1; J. H. Whyte, *The Independent Irish Party 1850–9*, (Oxford, 1958), 99–100; SRS minutes, 30 Dec. 1853.

[108] SRS minutes, 2, 3, 6, 16 Jan., 2, 10, 19, 21 Feb., 19 Mar. 1854; *Bulwark*, 3 (1853–4), 234–5, 254–9.

[109] SRS minutes, 9, 17 Apr. 1854; NC minutes, Dep.b.235, 28 Mar., 11 Apr. 1854.

support a Bill for the inspection of convents. There was also a vague pledge regarding electoral activity, but otherwise the resolutions did not move beyond generalities. It was decided to set up a committee to facilitate co-operation between the different societies, but only 'on the distinct understanding that no desire is entertained to interfere with their particular mode of operation'. Despite its obvious limitations, the conference nevertheless gave a significant boost to Protestant morale.[110]

Partly as a consequence of these shows of strength, the government's attempts at liberalization during the 1854 session were unsuccessful. The scheme for state payment of Roman Catholic prison chaplains was defeated, as was Russell's Oaths Bill, which would have opened up Parliament to Jews and removed the safeguards contained in the oath taken by Roman Catholics.[111] On the other hand, when the anti-Catholic movement took the offensive, it was less successful. In February Chambers's motion for a select committee on conventual institutions was carried by the substantial margin of 186 votes to 117, but was then frustrated by the obstructive parliamentary tactics employed by Catholics, who themselves appealed to public chivalry, judging the proposed inquiry 'an insult to the fathers and brothers of the ladies . . . an offensive reflection on the whole Catholic body, and a gross outrage on the ladies themselves'.[112] Sympathetic critics thought that the convent campaign had been ill-judged in that it led to a wider reaction in public opinion in favour of 'poor, pretty, innocent, charitable nuns'.[113] At the end of the session Spooner revived the anti-Maynooth campaign by moving for the transference of the grant from the consolidated fund to the annual estimates, a step that would have smoothed the path for its abolition once the commission reported. He was defeated on 3 July, but only by 106 votes to 90, a division that moved Frederick Lucas to conclude that the grant was doomed. Accordingly he urged Catholics to ensure that the most satisfactory possible terms were obtained.[114]

The political position of anti-Catholicism during the Aberdeen ministry can constructively be compared with that under Russell in the

[110] SRS minutes, 1, 10 May, 6 June 1854; *PM*, 16 (1854), 198–202.
[111] *PM*, 16 (1854), 71–5, 203; SRS minutes, 21 Feb. 1854; Machin, *Politics and the Churches*, pp. 266–7.
[112] *PM*, 16 (1854), 146–9.
[113] Hope MSS 35/5/75, Henry Drummond to Hope, 9 May 1854; Disraeli MSS, B/XX/H/31, J. Napier to G. A. Hamilton, 23 Nov. 1854.
[114] *PM*, 16 (1854), 229–34, 266; *Bulwark*, 4 (1854–5), 39–40, 57; 3 *Hansard*, cxxxiv. 1041–53, 3 July 1854.

late 1840s. There were important parallels. In both cases, an administration with liberal inclinations was anxious to conciliate the Catholics, and in some respects succeeded in doing so, but found itself too weak wholly to resist Protestant pressure. Thus Russell's plans for diplomatic relations with Rome and endowment in Ireland were frustrated; Aberdeen's government set up the Maynooth Commission and was pressurized into taking diplomatic action over the Madiai. On the other hand, such successes were equivocal and were not achieved solely through organized Protestant activity, whose limitations, unchanged by the reaction to the 'Papal Aggression', remained very obvious.

There were, however, two important differences. Firstly, whereas in the later 1840s Protestants had been primarily maintaining a defensive stance, resisting actual and prospective government measures, by 1853 they were also on the offensive, proposing legislative changes of their own. In some respects this suggested a position of greater strength, or at least of greater self-confidence, but it also made more conspicuous the limitations of their support and hence in the longer term reduced their credibility. Secondly, whereas parliamentary Catholicism in the late 1840s had generally been moderate, epitomized by Arundel's anxiety to avoid reinforcing Protestant hostility, in the early 1850s a more militant tone was in evidence. This was associated with the development of the Independent Irish party, which was fully prepared to engage in vigorous opposition to Protestant measures.[115] A weakening of broad parliamentary and public sympathy for anti-Catholicism is suggested by the failure of the Protestant societies to mobilize a public outcry against such tactics, while the Catholic impact in frustrating Protestant legislative attempts was a further source of demoralization.

In relation to the opposition, a valid comparison can also be made not only with the position in between 1849 and 1851 but also with the years before 1841. The lack of scruple of the Conservative leadership in using the Protestant groups, especially the National Club, for their own ends, while recognizing that relations needed to be handled with care, emerges with particular force in the early 1850s. In November 1853 Derby confided to Disraeli that, in his view, the National Club was 'a mischievous body whose extreme pretensions and views must not be encouraged but which must be kept, as I think they may be kept, in good humour by civility, and by the negative means of avoiding in

[115] Cf. Whyte, *Independent Irish Party, passim.*

debate, or in meetings of the Party, language which may unnecessarily *froisser* their . . . views'.[116] Disraeli kept open a line of communication with the National Club by way of George Hamilton, who was willing to work whole-heartedly for party unity. Having approached Colquhoun and Stapleton in November 1853, Hamilton reported to Disraeli the strengthening of his opinion 'that the requirements of the Protestant party will not be found impracticable or unreasonable . . . tho' there is disaffection among them, yet they dislike the present Govmt so much that I think there will be no great difficulty in reconciling them'.[117]

The presence of strongly Protestant members on the Conservative back-benches did, however, raise questions that were more funda-mental than pragmatic matters of party management. In years which Robert Stewart has aptly termed 'the nadir of Conservatism',[118] the party, having abandoned Protection in 1852, badly needed a recogniz-able rallying-point. For some of its supporters, therefore, Protestant-ism seemed the answer to a political dilemma as well as to a spiritual need. As in the later 1840s, Disraeli readily perceived this. Encour-aged presumably by the relatively strong showing of the Protestants in the 1854 session, he made a gesture to them in a speech on Maynooth in August 1854. Disraeli expressed his conviction of the importance of the issues they were agitating, thereby also contriving to score a point against the government because of their evident coolness to Protestant concerns.[119] This speech earned him votes of thanks from Protestant societies and moved Hamilton and others to urge him further to link Protestantism with patriotism in an attack on the government, increasingly embarrassed in its conduct of the Crimean war.[120]

Thus, although there were considerable tensions between Protestant-ism and the Conservative party which seemed to reach breaking-point on a number of occasions, an underlying continuity of association can be discerned throughout the period from 1829 to 1854. By the 1850s the relationship, shaken by the events of the mid-1840s, was shaped somewhat more by political calculations and less by principle than it had been in the 1830s. However, despite Russell's Protestant posturing and the development of more Liberal strands in the anti-

[116] Derby MSS 182/1, Derby to Disraeli, 14 Nov. 1853 (the last clause of the extract quoted is almost illegible).
[117] Disraeli MSS, B/XX/H/19, Hamilton to Disraeli, 27 Nov. 1853.
[118] Stewart, *Foundation of the Conservative Party*, pp. 272 ff.
[119] 3 *Hansard*, cxxxv. 1269–73, 3 Aug. 1854; *PM*, 16 (1854), 266–8.
[120] *PM*, 16 (1854), 321–3, 372–3; Disraeli MSS, B/XX/H/26–42, Hamilton to Disraeli, *passim*.

Catholic movement, it still seemed that the Conservative party was the natural home for Protestants with political concerns.

Set in this perspective, the failure to form a Conservative government after Aberdeen's resignation on 30 January 1855 assumes a pivotal significance in the history both of the Conservative party and of the Protestant movement. The conduct of Derby and Disraeli in January and February 1855 contrasts interestingly with that of Wellington and Peel in the not wholly dissimilar circumstances of November and December 1834. On the earlier occasion Wellington had played the anti-Catholic card, thus restoring the broadly Protestant character of the party, shaken by the Emancipation Act and its aftermath.[121] In 1855, however, Derby at least had no stomach for such a platform, writing on 21 February: 'it appears to me that the present moment would be singularly inopportune for the agitation of any question connected with such a subject'.[122] In 1855, unlike 1851, he does not appear to have considered a prominent Protestant for the Cabinet: Inglis had retired by this time, but it was to be Palmerston, not Derby, who solicited Shaftesbury's support.[123] The difference between 1834 and 1855 lay, of course, in the fact that the perceived challenge to the nation came in the former case from Ireland and in the latter from the Crimean war. So, Derby's implicit judgement that, at that time, Protestantism could not be so effectively linked with patriotism would seem to have been a correct one. Nevertheless, while the explanations for Derby's actions lie in the immediate circumstances of 1855 rather than in any long-term strategic calculations, they did represent a significant rejection of the possibility that Conservatism and Protestantism could again become intimately related. Disraeli certainly retained his sense of the political potentialities of Protestantism, as indicated both in 1868 and 1874, but by this time the cynicism and superficiality of his commitment was apparent to an extent that it had not been in the 1840s and early 1850s.[124] Religious issues remained central to Conservatism in the 1860s, 1870s, and 1880s, but the focus shifted from Protestantism to the Establishment.[125] The corollary of this for the anti-Catholic move-

---

[121] See above, Chap. 3.

[122] Derby MSS 183/1, Derby to M'Ghee, 21 Feb. 1855.

[123] G. B. A. M. Finlayson, *The Seventh Earl of Shaftesbury 1801–1885* (1981), 373–5.

[124] R. Blake, *Disraeli* (1966), 506–11, 550–1.

[125] By 1854, even Newdegate seemed to think a broad stance in defence of the 'Christianity' of the State preferable to a narrow, purely Protestant position (Derby MSS 148/1, Newdegate to Derby, 17 Feb. 1854).

ment was a future in pressure-group rather than party politics. It was ill-equipped for this; the changing orientation of religious politics was liable to pull it apart along the fundamental fault-line between Church and Dissent. The abortive attempt to reorganize the movement in 1855 and 1856 can be seen as an early recognition of this problem.[126]

Although these trends were associated with the Conservative decision not to form an administration, they were not immediately apparent. In March 1855 Hamilton still thought in terms of using the Maynooth issue against Palmerston, and Croft Moody wrote to Disraeli in May arguing that Protestantism and Conservatism were fast becoming synonymous.[127] However, Palmerston's unexpected capacity to appeal to Protestants confirmed the anachronism of this claim. This superannuated rake who could not distinguish Moses from Sydney Smith[128] seemed initially unlikely to be able to offer them much, but three factors served to work in his favour. Firstly, the departure of the Peelites from his administration, Gladstone above all, transferred the suspicions associated with Tractarian 'crypto-Jesuits' from the government to the opposition, especially as Gladstone began to contemplate reunion with Derby.[129] Secondly, Palmerston, unlike the Aberdeen coalition, was successful in playing the patriotic card in relation to the Crimean war, thus appealing to an instinct generally possessed in good measure by anti-Catholics. Finally, Palmerston's close family and personal ties with Shaftesbury provided a significant link between the Protestant movement and Downing Street.[130] The extent of Shaftesbury's influence on Palmerston should not be exaggerated, although it was certainly important in relation to ecclesiastical patronage, with the elevation of Robert Bickersteth to the see of Ripon in 1856 giving particular satisfaction to Protestants. However, the connection also operated in the reverse direction, to muffle Protestant criticism of government policy, a tendency especially evident in the *Record*, where Shaftesbury's friendship with Haldane was clearly influential.[131]

[126] See above, pp. 253–5.
[127] Disraeli MSS, B/XX/H/49, Hamilton to Disraeli, 12 Mar. 1855; Croft Moody MSS, D/PM/10/6/33, Croft Moody to Disraeli, 2 May 1855.
[128] Finlayson, *Shaftesbury*, p. 378.
[129] Machin, *Politics and the Churches*, p. 271.
[130] Finlayson, *Shaftesbury*, pp. 373–85.
[131] J. L. Altholz, 'Alexander Haldane, the *Record* and Religious Journalism', *Victorian Periodicals Review*, 20 (1987), 28; B. E. Hardman, 'The Evangelical Party in the Church of England, 1855–1865', Ph.D. thesis (Cambridge, 1963), 15–83.

Nevertheless, Palmerston's impact was not so much in gaining a monopoly of Protestant support for himself, but in driving a larger wedge between extra-parliamentary and evangelical elements who generally were willing to give the government the benefit of the doubt, and those, such as Spooner, with more firmly rooted Tory principles who continued their Protestant campaign but in the face of increasing coldness from the Conservative leadership. Thus the convent issue was quietly dropped but the anti-Maynooth campaign continued. The report of the commission was published on 1 March 1855 and concluded that disloyalty was not taught at the College. The Protestant societies were very far from satisfied: Lord claimed that objections to the textbooks had not been sufficiently answered and that the commission had not called an adequate number of Protestant witnesses. It was also alleged that Archbishop Cullen and even the pope had made revisions to the draft and that Harrowby and his colleagues had been deceived by the managers of Maynooth.[132]

The vigorous revival of the anti-Maynooth campaign in 1855 and 1856 rested more on energetic agitation and less on public sympathy than had been the case earlier in the decade. A Protestant conference was held in London in early March 1855 to decide on the course of action to be taken. Initial doubts as to whether the agitation should be renewed in time of war were overcome and a unanimous decision for concentrated effort was made.[133] A committee was instructed to prepare for the introduction of a Bill and for electoral action. It promptly issued a circular calling for the immediate preparation of petitions, and the Scottish Reformation Society set up its own subcommittee to co-ordinate similar activities. A Protestant meeting in mid-April placed particular emphasis on the value of bringing constituency pressure to bear on MPs.[134] Table 11 demonstrates how the number of signatures to petitions was almost exactly the same as it had been in 1852 and that signing had increased in England and declined somewhat in Scotland, although it still remained proportionately greater there. However, while the total number of petitions presented had increased significantly, the aggregate number of signatures had scarcely changed at all, thus suggesting that declining

[132] *Bulwark*, 5 (1855–6), 277; *PM*, 17 (1855), 104–8, 113–14, 170; Machin, *Politics and the Churches*, p. 273.
[133] SRS minutes, 19 Feb., 8 Mar. 1855.
[134] Ibid. 12, 23, 26, 30 Mar. 1855; Croft Moody MSS, D/PM/10/6/6, Protestant conference circular.

TABLE 11. *Anti-Maynooth petitioning, 1855*

	Petitions	Signatures	% of population
England and Wales	1,275	211,243	1.2
Scotland	425	99,379	3.4
Ireland	8	6,594	0.1
TOTAL	1,708	317,216	1.16

Source: PM, 17 (1855), 264–5.

public enthusiasm was being compensated for by more widespread promotion of petitions. This impression is confirmed by Croft Moody's correspondence, which shows that the response in the Southampton area to his exhortations to promote petitions was a lukewarm one.[135]

The impact of this activity was inconclusive. Palmerston, ready to exploit anti-Catholicism but wary of being compromised by it, gave a forthright refusal to a request to receive a deputation from the April meeting: 'I can easily imagine what the deputation would have to say to me, and while, on the one hand I could not hope to change their opinion, I am quite sure they would not alter mine.'[136] Spooner introduced a motion for a select committee to consider withdrawal of the grant, seconded by A. M. Dunlop, a Scottish Voluntaryist, which gave an impression of increased Protestant unity but underlined the extent to which there was a movement away from identification with Toryism to a more autonomous anti-Catholicism exposed to Liberal influences, especially from north of the Border.[137] The Roman Catholics prevented any decision from being taken until 18 July, when Spooner was defeated by a majority of three, with government influence supporting the College.[138] Nevertheless, in the following year the campaign came within sight of success. Spooner's Bill proceeded to a favourable vote on the second reading by a majority of 174 to 168. Although Spooner subsequently abandoned his Bill, frustrated as usual by the 'talking out' tactics of the Irish Catholic MPs, his supporters confidently looked forward to success in 1857.[139]

[135] Croft Moody MSS, D/PM/10/6, *passim*.
[136] *PM*, 17 (1855), 152.
[137] Ibid. 161–3; Machin, *Politics and the Churches*, pp. 273–4.
[138] *PM*, 17 (1855), 231, 283; *Bulwark*, 5 (1855–6), 43; Machin, *Politics and the Churches*, p. 274.
[139] 3 *Hansard*, cxlii. 1962–5, 25 June 1856; *PM*, 18 (1856), 180–7; *Bulwark*, 6 (1856–7), 29.

In the event, the next year was not to see Protestant triumph but rather unmistakable decline. When Spooner reintroduced his motion in February 1857, he was defeated by 167 votes to 159, a perceptible weakening in his support over that of the previous year.[140] The general election in March and April resulted in a significant set-back in spite of the continuing prominence of Maynooth in election speeches. The Protestant movement entered the campaign with serious handicaps. Firstly, internal divisions were accentuated by the sympathy for Palmerston expressed by important elements within the movement, while most anti-Catholic MPs had supported Cobden in the vote of censure on 3 March which led to the dissolution.[141] The *Record*, suspicious of Derby and Gladstone, threw its weight behind the government. Colquhoun judged that a coalition of Conservatives and Peelites would have nothing to offer to Protestants.[142] Spooner and Newdegate, however, remained loyal to the Conservatives.[143] The Protestant societies endeavoured to transcend these differences by urging electors to vote in accordance with the views of individual candidates, but they could not eliminate them.[144] Secondly, in 1857, unlike 1847 and 1852, there was no recent Protestant crisis to concentrate the minds of the electorate. While the Maynooth issue was widely discussed, the contest centred on Palmerston's Chinese policy. Thirdly, there was evidence of a growing sense that an anti-Maynooth stance was too narrow in itself as an electoral position. J. Banks Stanhope, Conservative MP for North Lincolnshire, wrote of the need for a principled stand by his party in the election, but went on: 'By fixed "principles" I do not mean "Maynooth" or any peculiar line of "policy" which may be the "fixed principles" of myself or other individuals on any minor point of policy.'[145] A correspondent of Hope's affirmed his antagonism to Maynooth but his refusal to 'support every anti-Maynooth candidate—at all hazards'.[146]

A number of supporters of the anti-Catholic cause lost their seats in the elections, and MPs who were returned were not subjected to the same degree of pressure on Catholic issues as had been experienced

---

[140]   3 *Hansard*, cxliv. 919–22, 19 Feb. 1857; Machin, *Politics and the Churches*, p. 280.
[141]   Machin, *Politics and the Churches*, pp. 280–5.
[142]   *R*, 6, 13 Mar. 1857.
[143]   Machin, *Politics and the Churches*, p. 281.
[144]   *PM*, 19 (1857), 81; *Bulwark*, 6 (1856–7), 253–7.
[145]   Somerset County Record Office, Hylton MSS, DD/HY/18/5/75, Stanhope to Jolliffe, 9 Mar. 1857.
[146]   Hope MSS 41/4/34, William Graham to Hope, 6 Apr. 1857.

by those elected to the 1847 and 1852 Parliaments. Furthermore, with the election out of the way, MPs whose support for the anti-Maynooth movement depended more on fear of their constituents than their personal convictions could relax their efforts. In May 1857 Spooner again proposed his Maynooth motion, but found that the majority against him had increased from eight to thirty-four.[147]

The closing years of the decade saw continuing failure and growing disillusion. There were internal disagreements about the wisdom of continuing the anti-Maynooth campaign, which was felt by the *Bulwark* to be leading to boredom, allowing Catholics to make advances on other fronts and associating the movement too closely with the Tories.[148] On the other hand, Protestant dissatisfaction with Palmerston was increasingly evident, especially in Scotland, where Shaftesbury's influence was not as effective as in London.[149] However, Derby's second ministry, which held power from February 1858 to June 1859, met with even less approval. On 27 April 1858 a Protestant deputation saw the new prime minister to discuss Maynooth. Derby suggested that he would be pleased to see the commutation of the grant for a down payment, a hint which further divided anti-Catholics.[150] Eardley and the Evangelical Alliance were anxious to discuss Derby's plan, but there was general reluctance to retreat from the call for complete abolition, a difference of opinion which led to competing anti-Maynooth candidates at Leith in the 1859 general election.[151] Meanwhile, in 1858 Spooner's regular anti-Maynooth motion was defeated by an increased majority of fifty-five, having been strongly opposed by the home secretary, Spencer Walpole, who seemed to have retained little of the sympathy with anti-Catholicism which he had shown in the later 1840s.[152]

As the 1859 session approached, the *Bulwark* published figures on the amount of public money spent on propagating Roman Catholicism, through schools and military chaplains as well as at Maynooth, and complained that governments of every colour seemed equally willing to advance the interests of Rome.[153] Spooner was deprived of the

[147] *Bulwark*, 6 (1856–7), 288–9; 3 *Hansard*, cxlv. 668–9, 21 May 1857; *PM*, 20 (1858), 83.
[148] *Bulwark*, 6 (1856–7), 263; 7 (1857–8), 197–8.
[149] Ibid. 253.
[150] *PM*, 20 (1858), 59–64.
[151] Ibid. 166–9; 21 (1859), 14–16; *Bulwark*, 8 (1858–9), 321–4.
[152] *PM*. 20 (1858), 72 ff.; 3 *Hansard*, cxlix. 1999, 23 Feb. 1858; see above, Chap. 6, p. 237.
[153] *Bulwark*, 8 (1858–9), 92–5, 100–3, 169.

opportunity even to raise the Maynooth issue by Derby's decision to hold a general election at the end of May. The Protestant societies were again poorly prepared, and anti-Catholicism was only a relatively minor force in the election.[154] Derby and even Disraeli thought it more worth while to attempt to woo the Roman Catholic vote than to strive to appease the Protestants.[155] Palmerston's subsequent return to office scarcely brought any cause for rejoicing. Spooner succeeded in having a debate on Maynooth in 1860, only to be defeated by a majority of fifty-eight. Old, ill, and discouraged, he did not try again. The campaign was revived during the 1860s by G. H. Whalley, but never came near to success.[156]

So far, the argument of this chapter has concentrated on two major reasons for Protestant decline in the 1850s: the movement's own chronic lack of unity, and its gradual loss of political credibility, factors which in the second half of the decade increasingly reinforced each other. However, there were a number of other circumstances which further accentuated the trend.

Firstly, there was a failure of leadership. The generation that had stirred anti-Catholic feeling in the two decades after 1829 was passing. Edward Bickersteth died in 1850, Newcastle in 1851, Mackworth in 1852, Inglis, Kenyon, and Manchester in 1855, O'Sullivan and Winchilsea in 1858. Those who remained were ageing: in 1860 McNeile and Thelwall were 65, Stowell 61, Shaftesbury 59, and Colquhoun 57. Depletion was especially apparent on the Anglican side of the movement, and the Protestant Association found itself embarrassed by the steadily increasing age of its platform parties.[157] While the newer Protestant societies were able to gain support and leadership from a younger generation, these recruits generally lacked the qualities of leadership and oratorical ability which had characterized the older men in their prime. Furthermore, by 1860, even younger men such as Blakeney, Hope, and MacGregor seemed to be losing their initial drive and maintaining the structure of Protestant agitation without giving further significant impetus to it.

Secondly, the proliferation of Protestant societies in the 1850s

[154] *PM*, 21 (1859), 49.
[155] J. Altholz, 'The Political Behaviour of English Catholics, 1850–1867', *Journal of British Studies*, 4 (1964), 89–103; *Bulwark*, (1858–9), 324–6.
[156] Machin, *Politics and the Churches*, pp. 303–4. The grant was commuted in 1869, as part of the Irish disestablishment measure (P. M. H. Bell, *Disestablishment in Ireland and Wales* (1969), 135–6).
[157] *PM*, 17 (1855), 175–6.

rendered them more exposed to careerism and self-interest than they had been in the past. The case of James Mathison was discussed in an earlier chapter (Chapter 5, pp. 185–6), but the point can be further illustrated at a different social level by the activities of Edward Harper. He first made his mark in Protestant movements in Dublin, and began to exploit Irish anti-Catholicism to his own financial advantage by forming sham organizations whose income clearly went largely into his own pocket.[158] In August 1854 he approached Hope, stating his pretensions as a Protestant journalist and claiming an association with Disraeli. Persistent requests for employment in Edinburgh ultimately led to a post with the Scottish Protestant Association.[159] At the end of 1856 Harper then used this position as a basis from which to launch the Protestant Publication Society, which, according to Tresham Gregg, an Irish anti-Catholic leader, was simply 'Harper's Milch cow'. Gregg felt that such activities discredited Protestantism while diverting desperately needed funds from more reputable bodies.[160] Harper was an extreme if conspicuous case, but it is clear that other Protestant officials, such as Lord of the Protestant Association and Miller of the Reformation Society, although honest men committed to the cause, represented a strong, institutionally conservative, vested interest which absorbed financial resources and weighed against adaptation to changing circumstances.

Thirdly, the Crimean war had a serious impact on public support for anti-Catholicism. To some extent this was part of the general economic and psychological consequences of wartime conditions. MacGregor wrote in November 1854: 'high prices and war taxes prevent our enterprise being very daring as our funds must be less this year than with peace abroad and men's minds turned on Popery at home'.[161] The Protestant societies were especially vulnerable because of the circumstances of the war, which, despite an underlying patriotism, they regarded with a degree of unease. Catholic France and Muslim Turkey were in their eyes strange allies for Protestant England and Orthodox Russia not the most obvious of adversaries.[162] Shaftesbury presented an ingenious argument for the war on

[158] Hope MSS 42/6/100, Gregg to Hope, 11 Dec. 1857.
[159] Ibid. 36/2/59, 36/3/35, 36/6/69, 38/6/154, Harper to Hope, 29 Aug., 22 Sept., 14 Dec. 1854, 1 Dec. 1855.
[160] Ibid. 41/1/34, Gregg to Hope, 7 Jan. 1857.
[161] Ibid. 36/5/121, MacGregor to Hope, 18 Nov. 1854.
[162] *Bulwark*, 3 (1853–4), 240–2, 261–2; 4 (1854–5), 189–93; Hope MSS 38/4/36, 39/4/122, Blakeney to Hope, 8 Oct. 1855, 3 Apr. 1856.

Protestant grounds, but does not appear to have convinced all strands in the movement.[163] In addition, the needs of the army led to steps which anti-Catholics criticized but could not prevent, the payment of Roman Catholic military chaplains and the use of nuns and Sisters of Mercy in nursing. Such attitudes were liable to seem petty-minded and unpatriotic and thus weaken support further.[164] In the longer term, the Crimean war and the conflicts that followed it, notably the Canton incident and the Indian mutiny, brought to an end a period in which it was credible to view Rome as the major challenge to British power, and directed patriotic xenophobia in new directions.

Finally, as was indicated in Chapter 5, anti-Catholicism was a victim of its own success in the 1850s, inasmuch as it caused people initially neutral towards it to react adversely to its methods and to become opponents, while lukewarm supporters could palliate their Protestant consciences by nominal involvement in some organization. This is illustrated in a Scottish observer's comments on the Newcastle branch of the Protestant Alliance in July 1858:

From what I have been able to gather, it appears to be an association formed by some of the ministers of the town; who, like some others south of the Tweed, slumber 364 days 21 hours and then devote the three remaining hours of the year to the proposing of sundry resolutions, whose magical effect will cause the wall of old Babylon to topple to their fall.[165]

On a national level the Protestant Alliance even considered dissolving itself in November and December 1858.[166]

However, the declining fortunes of the Protestant societies in the 1850s need to be set in the wider context of evidence of continuing, strong, popular anti-Catholicism, which seemed in some measure to be gathering momentum in the 1850s and certainly remained a force well after 1860.[167] In part, as was seen in Chapter 5, this was a localized development, related to the presence of substantial bodies of Irish immigrants, but two national trends need some further exploration here. These were the continuing development of a strong link

[163] O. Anderson, 'The Reactions of Church and Dissent towards the Crimean War', *Journal of Ecclesiastical History*, 16 (1965), 211–12.

[164] *Bulwark*, 4 (1854–5), 113, 141–4, 175; *PM*, 17 (1855), 53–4; C. B. Woodham-Smith, *Florence Nightingale, 1820–1910* (1950), 183–5.

[165] Hope MSS 44/1/8, John Symington to Hope, 30 July 1858.

[166] SRS minutes, 27 Nov. 1858.

[167] On anti-Catholicism and anti-ritualism in the 1860s and 1870s, see W. L. Arnstein, *Protestant versus Catholic in Mid-Victorian England* (Columbia, Mo., 1982); J. Bentley, *Ritualism and Politics in Victorian Britain* (Oxford, 1978).

between anti-Catholicism and support for the cause of political and religious liberty, especially in Italy; and the growth of antagonism to ritualism.

The public outcry against the imprisonment of the Madiai in 1852–3 had reinforced the perception in Britain that the influence of the Roman Catholic Church in Italy, and the temporal power of the Papacy in particular, resulted in severe restriction on religious and political liberty. There was an overlap between the positions of political liberals and evangelical anti-Catholics, a broad basis of sympathy for attacks on Pius IX, and support for Piedmont, which was perceived as the heroic guardian of Italian political and religious liberty. Attacks on the Papacy by numerous itinerant speakers in Britain in the 1850s drew on a broad spectrum of arguments, ranging from evangelical theology to secular nationalism and anti-clericalism.[168] Lectures such as that of 'Madame Mario' at Preston in June 1858 which recounted the history of Italy and the Papacy, arguing that the latter had always been opposed to liberty, could accordingly tap extensive reservoirs of sympathy.[169] The Protestant societies contrived both to exploit and to stimulate further such attitudes. When King Victor Emmanuel visited Britain in 1855, he was presented with an address from representatives of religious societies, headed by Shaftesbury and the Archbishop of Canterbury. An address from the Protestant Association congratulated the king on his efforts to secure the rights and independence of Italy, and praised 'the course so successfully pursued by your Majesty as regards the interference of the See and Court of Rome in the internal affairs of your kingdom'. A public meeting in Edinburgh, called by the Evangelical Alliance assisted by the Scottish Reformation Society, produced a similar address.[170] In the late 1850s the Protestant societies also took up the case of Edgar Mortara, a Jewish boy who had been seized from his parents with the authority of the papal government on the grounds that he had been surreptitiously baptized by a Catholic servant.[171] Broad linkages between anti-Catholicism and liberal attitudes were maintained in the early 1860s in enthusiastic—

---

[168] C. T. McIntire, *England against the Papacy, 1858–1861* (Cambridge, 1983).
[169] *'The Papacy the Corner Stone of Tyranny': The Substance of a Lecture Delivered by Madame Mario (late Miss Jessie Merton White) in the Exchange Assembly Room Preston, June 28 1858* (1858).
[170] *PM*, 18 (1856), 3–9; *Bulwark*, 5 (1855–6), 221.
[171] *PM*, 20 (1858), 149–50, 161–2; 21 (1859), 1–2; *Bulwark*, 8 (1858–9), 144–6; 9 (1858–9), 144–6; 10 (1859–60), 209; E. R. Norman, *The English Catholic Church in the Nineteenth Century* (Oxford, 1984), 187.

indeed, at times riotous—support for Garibaldi, and in the longer term by the continuing activity of the Protestant Alliance and the Evangelical Alliance in relation to religious liberty abroad.[172] Further reinforcement of such connections from a different quarter came with the renewal of the anti-convent campaign in Britain, led by the Tory Newdegate but drawing significant support from Liberals who shared his perception that the liberties of the subject were at stake.[173]

During the 1850s the Protestant societies continued to be slow to promote opposition to ritualism. As late as the mid-1840s there had been a sense that, if it was left alone, the problem of Tractarianism would eventually go away; in the face of the reformed tradition of the Church of England and the good sense of the laity, the movement was felt to be too exotic to strike any deep roots. Meanwhile, it was better to concentrate energies on the Roman roots rather than the Oxonian branches.[174] In the later 1840s and early 1850s, conversions, the Gorham case, the Durham Letter, and the manner in which the growth of Anglo-Catholicism was giving useful arguments to the Dissenting opponents of the Church[175] all served to heighten concern. The issue accordingly became a significant factor in Protestant calculations; for example, in generating suspicion of the High-Church leanings of Derby and Gladstone, and in Blakeney's attempts to use association with the Church of Scotland to stiffen resistance to Romanizing in the Church of England. However, the divisions within the anti-Catholic movement meant that generalized antagonism was seldom translated into specific action.[176] The initiative taken by the London Committee for the Defence of the Protestant Faith in the autumn of 1850 seemed to run out of steam and to become subsumed in the broader anti-Catholic movement. The Protestant Alliance was precluded from tackling the problem by the very compromises which made its continued existence possible; the Scottish Reformation Society was not initially particularly concerned with what was primarily an English problem; the Reformation Society was preoccupied with urban missionary work, and the Protestant Association with political matters. Thus the brunt of this particular battle was borne by the small Church Protestant Defence Society and, more importantly, by

[172] S. Gilley, 'The Garibaldi Riots of 1862', *Historical Journal*, 16 (1973), 698–732; SRS minutes, 10 Dec. 1860, 30 Jan. 1862.

[173] Arnstein, *Protestant versus Catholic*, pp. 65, 127.

[174] See above, Chap. 4, pp. 117–18; *R*, 29 Mar. 1841.

[175] *Nonconformist*, 21 Apr. 1852, p. 297; 28 Apr. 1852, p. 317.

[176] See above, p. 251.

individuals who took the initiative against ritualizing clergy. It was not until the formation of the Church Association in 1864 that there was a major Evangelical society exclusively concerned with the question of ritualism.

The lack of Evangelical resolve for a general confrontation with the Tractarians was further evident in 1852, when the Duke of Wellington's death produced a vacancy in the chancellorship of Oxford University. Derby was the obvious candidate to succeed, but there were murmurings of discontent because of his High-Church leanings, and Shaftesbury was suggested as a possible alternative. Nevertheless, no serious attempt was made to promote the latter's candidacy, and Derby was quickly elected unopposed.[177] Similarly tentative was a meeting held in November 1852 to protest against auricular confession in the Church of England and the revival of Convocation: this appears to have been an isolated demonstration.[178]

The slow growth of organized resistance to ritualism should occasion no surprise in the light of G. W. Herring's recent conclusion that ritualism itself was not an immediate outcome of early Tractarianism but only developed extensively from the 1850s onwards. Indeed, ritualism, which owed more to the Gothic revival and the development of Eucharistic doctrine than to the direct impact of the Oxford tracts, marked a substantial discontinuity within Anglo-Catholicism and should not be allowed to obscure the moderation of the majority of Tractarians where ritual was concerned.[179] The origins of anti-ritualism are therefore best seen in a local rather than a national context, above all in the West of England, as responses to circumstances that were unusual rather than representative. There were surplice riots in Exeter as early as 1845, but these were as much a political protest against Bishop Phillpotts's Toryism and high-handed administration as a specifically religious movement: it is significant that the surplice had been used in the pulpit at St Sidwell's, Exeter for three years without serious trouble and it was only the bishop's intervention that provoked extensive street protest.[180] The Gorham case in 1850 made Phillpotts's name widely execrated by Evangelicals,

[177] Shaftesbury Diary, SHA/PD/6, 22, 24, 27, 29 Sept., 9 Oct. 1852.

[178] *PM*, 14 (1852), 392.

[179] G. W. Herring, 'Tractarianism to Ritualism: A Study of Some Aspects of Tractarianism outside Oxford from the Time of Newman's Conversion in 1845, until the First Ritual Commission in 1867', D.Phil. thesis (Oxford, 1984), pp. v–xiii, 274–83.

[180] G. C. B. Davies, *Henry Phillpotts, Bishop of Exeter, 1778–1869* (1954), 180–9. The *Western Times* in 1843 and 1844 made extensive political attacks on Phillpotts.

and the holding of a diocesan synod at Exeter in June 1851 was denounced by the *Bulwark* as 'Popery of the rankest kind'. At Plymouth strongly Evangelical local clergy confronted Priscilla Lydia Sellon's Devonport sisterhood and the ritualist incumbent of St Peter's, George Rundle Prynne.[181] In the neighbouring diocese of Bath and Wells episcopal tolerance similarly permitted ritualists to establish themselves, but was powerless to protect them from the outraged reaction of Evangelicals. In 1852 objection was raised to the institution of W. J. E. Bennett to the living of Frome, and in 1856 G. A. Denison, the Archdeacon of Taunton, was prosecuted in the Court of Arches by the vicar of a neighbouring parish and found to hold views inconsistent with the Thirty-nine Articles, although the verdict was reversed on appeal on a technicality.[182] Brighton was a further early centre of conflict, due to the combination of strong local Evangelicalism and provocative action by Tractarians which led to the formation of a Church Protestant Defence Association and the holding of a boisterous public meeting in January 1854. At nearby Lewes the funeral of a nun from J. M. Neale's community at East Grinstead gave rise to a riot in late 1857.[183] Anti-ritualism appears to have been more common in the South than in the North of England, and this probably reflected the distribution of ritualism itself. However, an early instance in the North was at Leeds, in response to Pusey's parochial experiment at St Saviour's.[184]

Only in London did anti-ritualist activity in the 1850s clearly have other than local roots, and even there it did not develop until late in the decade. Disturbances at St Barnabas's, Pimlico in 1850 were a result of the general hysteria following the 'Papal Aggression', and when this subsided and Bennett left the parish, his successor Robert Liddell, also a ritualist, does not appear to have experienced the same degree of disruption to worship, although he was confronted with legal action.[185] In 1858, however, allegations were brought against Arthur Poole, curate of St Barnabas's, that he had asked improper questions of

[181] J. R. Wolffe, 'Bishop Henry Phillpotts and the Administration of the Diocese of Exeter, 1830–1869', *Transactions of the Devonshire Association*, 114 (1982), 108–10; *Bulwark*, 1 (1851–2), 40.

[182] Machin, *Politics and the Churches*, pp. 236–7, 255–6; Hardman, 'The Evangelical Party in the Church of England', pp. 127–43.

[183] Shaftesbury Diary, SHA/PD/6, 7 Jan. 1854; Church Protestant Defence Society, *Address No. 3* (1853), 8; *Bulwark*, 7 (1857–8), 183–7.

[184] N. Yates, *The Oxford Movement and Parish Life: St Saviour's Leeds, 1839–1929* (Borthwick Papers 48; York, 1975), 12–16.

[185] L. E. Ellsworth, *Charles Lowder and the Ritualist Movement* (1982), 13–20.

women in the confessional. The women involved were themselves of dubious moral character, but Bishop Tait of London was persuaded to suspend Poole.[186] Penny pamplets were circulated, with lurid illustrations of a priest trying to rape a woman in front of a crucifix, and garbled versions of the Maria Monk story, an attempt to draw on a popular taste for pornography and sensation in promoting anti-ritualist antagonism.[187] When riots associated with the ritualist practices of Bryan King and Charles Lowder at St George in the East broke out in May 1859, they were linked to the continuing disreputable activities of Edward Harper. King wrote to the home secretary in November 1859:

I have every reason to believe that these riots are *organized* by two bodies—by the 'Anti-Puseyite League'—a society which seems to have been instituted in this neighbourhood for the express purpose, and by the 'National Protestant Society'—the Secretary of which Mr Edward Harper is in the habit of holding lectures in London, when he exhorts his hearers to join in making their first attack against 'Puseyism' at my Church and then in following up that, by attacking every other similar Church in London in turn.

These riots, which continued into 1860, were fuelled in part by generalized disorderliness rather than specific anti-ritualism: on one occasion in February 1860 a Wesleyan chapel was also attacked.[188]

In the late 1850s there were eventually signs that more organized and extensive opposition to ritualism was developing among the more reputable Protestant societies. In Scotland this took the form of concern about the 'popish' tendencies of the Episcopal Church, made all the more pressing by its efforts to achieve intercommunion with the Church of England, thus potentially compromising the reformed identity of the Establishment south of the Border.[189] D. T. K. Drummond, who, as an Anglican clergyman in Scotland, clearly felt the problem particularly acutely, delivered a vigorous call to action against Romanizing at the SRS annual meeting in February 1859.[190]

---

[186] O. Chadwick, *The Victorian Church*, 2 vols. (1966–70), i. 503.

[187] *Astounding Revelations of Puseyism in Belgravia* (1858); *Awful Disclosures of Miss Julia Gordon* (1858). It is not clear who was responsible for these publications, but the style is entirely different from that of the established Protestant societies, and it seems plausible that there was a link with those who subsequently promoted the riots at St George in the East.

[188] PRO, Ho45/6751/31, King to Cornewall Lewis, 9 Nov. 1859.

[189] Church Protestant Defence Society, *Addresses Nos. 10, 11* (1857); *Bulwark*, 9 (1859–60), 92–4; Hope MSS 40/6/102, Lord John Scott to Hope, 15 Dec. 1856; 41/1/138, Blakeney to Hope, 24 Jan. 1857.

[190] SRS minutes, 121 Feb. 1859.

In England in 1858 there were meetings in a number of towns to protest about the Tractarian use of the confessional, but in 1860 anti-ritualist movements still lacked coherent organization: a meeting convened at the National Club in that year to consider the present state of the Church of England came to the conclusion that united action was not yet possible.[191]

The largely spontaneous growth of resistance to ritualism contrasts with the declining capacity of opposition to Roman Catholicism to maintain its support. However, this paradox suggests another underlying reason for Protestant weakness in the later 1850s. Anti-ritualism was growing because the practices and values which provoked it were a new, objective, and verifiable challenge to the existing religious order. On the other hand, by 1860 Roman Catholicism seemed less of a threat than it had twenty years earlier. Irish immigrants were becoming more stable in their loyalty to the Church, and therefore the pastoral activity of priests could become more regularized and less likely to provoke Protestants. In the more stable political and social conditions of the 1850s prophetic expectation became less intense, and when it was stirred somewhat by the Crimean war, it was no longer focused primarily against Rome.[192] Meanwhile, the relative calm of Ireland weakened a major political and ideological influence which had both directly and indirectly done so much to inflame Protestant antagonism in the 1830s and 1840s.

The year 1860 is an appropriate point at which to terminate the period surveyed by this book, because the ultimate failure of Spooner's anti-Maynooth campaign can be seen as marking the end of the rearguard action in defence of exclusively Protestant constitutional norms which had been fought over the three decades since 1829. The original ideals of the Ultras had been redefined under Evangelical influence by the Protestant Association and the National Club: but these efforts retarded rather than reversed their slow slide into anachronism. In the 1850s it was becoming increasingly obvious that significant elements in the anti-Catholic movement itself no longer subscribed to this vision. At the same time there was a decisive weakening in the association between Evangelicalism and Conservat-

---

[191] *Bulwark*, 8 (1858–9), 161; 10 (1860–1), 12–13. The nature of early antagonism to ritualism would merit further exploration within frames of reference that fall outside the specific scope of this book, particularly the ecclesiological and constitutional dimensions of Anglican identity, and the development of popular anticlericalism.

[192] Anderson, 'Reactions of Church and Dissent towards the Crimean War', pp. 209–20.

ism which had been an important political factor since the mid-1830s. Nevertheless, although 1860 was the end of a phase in anti-Catholicism, and the movement seemed to have become stagnant and uncertain of its future course, Protestant societies still had many decades of active life ahead of them. The future lay not with the advocacy of abstract constitutional ideals but with the wider defence of the British Protestant tradition against the rival claims of the Anglo-Catholics; with urban missionary and education work and concern for associated social and moral problems; and with the promotion of Protestantism as a force for international brotherhood and liberty. Such aspirations pulled anti-Catholicism in divergent directions, further weakening whatever superficial coherence the movement had possessed in the 1850s. Ultimately the effect was to weaken the capacity of Protestantism to offer an integrated world-view, and hence its ability to inspire the intense commitment which it had received from its supporters in mid-century.

8

PROTESTANTISM AND VICTORIAN BRITAIN

IN this final chapter the central themes of the book will be recapitulated and the significance of anti-Catholicism for the broader understanding of the period will be explored. In doing this we shall move beyond the Protestant societies themselves to consider the nature and impact of wider public opinion. The argument will be built primarily on the evidence presented in the preceding chapters, but some further material will be introduced to set the discussion in context. In particular, just as the development of anti-Catholicism before 1829 was traced in Chapter 1, it is now desirable to give some account of developments after 1860. In addition, it is helpful to widen the geographical scope by comparing the British anti-Catholic societies with contemporary organizations in the United States.

Victorian anti-Catholicism, it has been contended in this book, reflected the contemporary context in important respects, and should not be seen as merely a continuation of the antagonism to 'Papists' which had been evident in earlier periods of British history. As in many other ways, however, the beginnings of Victorianism pre-dated the queen's accession in 1837. Factors of particular importance were the development of more militant Evangelicalism in both Britain and Ireland; the increase in the number of Catholics in Britain due to Irish immigration; the advance of more uncompromising clerical Ultra-montanism; the political crisis of Irish Protestantism in the late 1820s and early 1830s; and the need of the Conservative party for a focus for recovery after 1832.

In relation to these influences, the activity of the Reformation Society and the Protestant Association was an important catalyst. The public debates orchestrated by the Reformation Society in the late 1820s and early 1830s attracted considerable attention in a significant number of towns, and polarized positions to a greater extent than had hitherto been the case. Despite the Reformation Society's 'no politics' rule, individuals closely associated with the movement carried the confrontation into Parliament from 1831. In 1835 this impulse blended with some elements of resurgent Ultra-Toryism to produce a new platform for political anti-Catholicism in the form of the Protestant Association. The subsequent extensive campaign of public meetings disseminated a polemic against Irish Catholicism which formed a key part of Conservative rhetoric in the period up to 1841.

In the light of these developments, it is important to qualify the view that Catholic Emancipation destroyed conclusively the Protestant character of the kingdom.[1] Certainly, the admission of Roman Catholics to Parliament forced a reformulation of the case for viewing the constitution as fundamentally Protestant, but little sense can be made of the struggles over Ireland in the 1830s, over Maynooth in 1845, and the 'Papal Aggression' in 1850–1 if it is not recognized that the advocates of the anti-Catholic position still felt that there was everything to play for. The year 1829 saw a breach in the 'theoretical hegemony'[2] of the old order, but it did not topple overnight. It is worth emphasizing that, before the 1850s, the struggle between anti-Catholics and the perceived architects of mid-Victorian toleration was not at all a clash of generations. Lord Roden was the same age as Sir Robert Peel, and Hugh McNeile was three years younger than Lord John Russell. The readiness of both Peel and Russell to revert under pressure to Protestant positions suggests that the outcome was by no means a foregone conclusion. This impression is confirmed by recognizing the intensity of the struggle for the soul of the next generation, as represented in the tortured conscience of the young Gladstone.[3] Moreover, even after 1860, a parliamentary rearguard defence of a Protestant constitutional position was maintained for a further generation by Charles Newdegate.[4]

Having said this, the reasons for the undeniably substantial failure of anti-Catholics to achieve their ends must now be summarized. We shall then turn to consider how, nevertheless, their efforts influenced the course of the history of Victorian Britain. Most of the root causes of lack of direct success were indicated in Chapters 4 and 5, in the discussion of the ideology of anti-Catholicism and its impact on the public. Although movements such as the Protestant Association and

---

[1] Cf. J. C. D. Clark, *English Society 1688–1832* (Cambridge, 1985); G. I. T. Machin, *The Catholic Question in English Politics 1820–1830* (Oxford, 1964).

[2] Clark, *English Society*, p. 419.

[3] P. A. Butler, *Gladstone, Church, State and Tractarianism* (Oxford, 1982).

[4] W. L. Arnstein, *Protestant versus Catholic in Mid-Victorian England* (Columbia, Mo., 1982), *passim*.

the National Club proved able to reconstruct the case for a Protestant constitution in such a way as to accommodate the reality of Emancipation, their principles were never sufficiently comprehensive to incorporate the views of all those predisposed to adopt an anti-Catholic position. Above all, they failed to overcome, except superficially, the fundamental divide between Church and Dissent. Even within the Church of England, the antipathy of conservative High-Churchmen to the Protestant Association, and of some Evangelicals to the National Club, was a significant stumbling-block. An equally important fissure was between those who viewed Protestantism in intensely spiritual terms and those who saw it primarily in a political context.[5] Thus, while anti-Catholics might on occasion, as in 1845 and 1853, prove able to act together, in reality they were moved by such a variety of impulses that sustained united action was impossible. Appeals to 'common Protestantism' had a transient emotional allure, as they touched chords of loyalty to the Reformation heritage and aspirations to spiritual purity, but in practice these feelings were bound up closely with other elements of the world-view of individuals in a manner which inexorably pulled the different strands of anti-Catholicism apart.

The incapacity of the Protestant societies to speak with a united voice was naturally a serious initial handicap in their efforts to promote sympathetic public opinion. This difficulty was compounded by their own ambiguous attitudes to the machinery of popular agitation. The societies were happiest when they were holding spectacular public meetings and publishing a variety of literature, hoping that the income generated by these activities would be sufficient to maintain and expand them. Although they formed branches, some of which were quite successful in the local sphere, they lacked the capacity and the will to form a sustained agitational machine of the kind associated with the anti-slavery movement, the Anti-Corn Law League, or the Liberation Society. In so far as the Protestant societies were influenced after 1829 by the legacy of Ultra-Toryism, this failure reflected an inherited antipathy to the machinery of agitation. Given the primarily Evangelical composition of the movement, however, a more important factor appears to have been an enduring complacency regarding the potential of public opinion to assume a militantly anti-Catholic stance. The explanation for the apparent paradox of the evident anti-Catholic orientation of popular sentiment, and the failure of the Protestant

[5] PAss, *Occasional Papers*, 12 (Aug. 1870), 6.

societies to mobilize sustained support for their objectives, lies in the essentially passive and reactive nature of mass Protestantism, and the tendency of organized anti-Catholicism to alienate many potential sympathizers by its rhetoric and methods. A further problem was inherent in the programme of a movement which, in essence, sought to maintain the status quo: for the anti-Catholic societies, unlike 'progressive' reform movements, there was usually no definable objective until the agenda had been set by the government. This gap was filled to some extent in the 1850s by the campaign to repeal the Maynooth Act, but, as we have seen, there was great scope for confusion and division over the best means of achieving this end.

The difficulties of the Protestant movement in its relations with its popular base were reflected and compounded by its lack of direction in the arena of high politics. Broadly speaking, the two extremes of political strategy which might have been open were the formation of an independent Protestant party and the acceptance of a subordinate position as a lobby within a wider political grouping. A middle course, feasible in periods of loose party discipline, particularly after 1846, was that of pressure-group politics. During the course of the years in question one can discern experimentation along the whole spectrum, with the failure to pursue a consistent strategy meaning that the place of Protestantism in the political fabric remained unclear, making it difficult to sustain stable support. Embryonic Protestant parties can be discerned in the 'Recordite' parliamentary campaign of 1831–2 and in the National Club after 1845. In each case, there was both a failure of leadership, Gordon being too extreme and Colquhoun too lethargic, and an incapacity to provide an ideology and a programme that went beyond Protestantism. The 'Recordites' could offer only the apocalyptic social analysis of a Spencer Perceval,[6] and the National Club's paternalism was too hollow to buy the support of the future Lord Shaftesbury. Absorption as an interest group in a larger party was tried in relation to the Conservatives from 1834, the Protectionists from 1849, and, by some strands of anti-Catholicism, in support for the Palmerstonians after 1855. Such an approach had the obvious disadvantage that it could not but reinforce the divisions between Anglican and Nonconformist anti-Catholics. It also induced tensions between Protestant politicians on the one hand, and, on the other, clergy who felt that essential spiritual principles were being sacrificed.

[6] See above, Chap. 3, p. 72. Cf. B. Hilton, *The Age of Atonement* (Oxford, 1988), 214–15.

Moreover, experience was to show that loyalty to a half-trusted party leader *faute de mieux* gave hostages to fortune. The 'betrayal' of Protestantism by Peel in 1845 was the most spectacular and bitterly resented of such reversals, but in the long term the cynical manœuvres of Palmerston and Disraeli sapped Protestant credibility and compromised their objectives, while denying them the kind of pretext for an energizing confrontation which Sir Robert had granted them over Maynooth.

The most effective strategy was that of pressure-group activity, drawing together sympathetic MPs on matters of Protestant concern, but not attempting to claim their loyalty to a more wide-ranging programme. This was the course pursued in the late 1840s and early 1850s. In the long run the weaknesses of this, too, became apparent. In part this was because, from 1852, the anti-Maynooth campaign exposed the limits of Protestant support, whereas up to that time government and party leaders had been nervous about the potentialities of what had remained something of an unknown quantity. Fundamentally, however, this was a means of exerting Protestant influence which could only be successful in times of general party weakness and fluidity. While the anti-Catholic movement was strong enough to take advantage of such pre-conditions when they existed, it lacked sufficient force to sustain such a favourable environment for itself when other political currents began to set against it.

Nevertheless, even though the early Victorian anti-Catholic movement failed in its political objective of maintaining the constitutional predominance of Protestantism, its activity shaped Victorian politics and society in important ways. In terms of governmental policy options, it played a major role in stalemating the powerful forces which sought to resolve the problem of Irish disorder by forging closer links between the British State and the Roman Catholic Church. This was a policy which at times seemed close to being the consensus objective of the political élite. It was advocated by the Duke of Wellington in a memorandum of 1825,[7] and was felt to be presaged by Peel in his decision to enhance the Maynooth grant. Lord John Russell's position as a minister in the 1830s seemed clearly to point in this direction, and, leading his own government after 1847, he made a serious attempt to formulate a measure for Catholic endowment. The policy had the

---

[7] Second Duke of Wellington (ed.), *Despatches, Correspondence and Memoranda of Field Marshal Arthur Duke of Wellington, KG*, 8 vols. (1867–80), ii. 592–607.

enthusiastic support of Lord George Bentinck, and even Lord Stanley saw no objections of principle.[8] Nevertheless, it came to nothing.

The role of Protestant pressure in bringing about this outcome has been discussed above: but it is worth while now to consider the implications of this failure to pursue this line of policy. It should be noted in passing that the presupposition behind the strategy of endowing the Catholic Church was in general terms an anti-Catholic one: Wellington, Peel, and Russell were no friends of Rome, which they perceived as presenting a fundamental challenge to the integrity of the United Kingdom. They differed from the Protestant societies in thinking that it was ultimately better to tame the beast than to fight it, and that the pragmatic maintenance of good order was of more importance than the preservation of an elusive constitutional purity.

In the long term, Protestants were obliged to face the logic of their hostility to Catholic endowment in recognizing that the disestablishment of the Church of Ireland was inevitable. In July 1868 Viscount Sandon,[9] like his father before him, was standing as Conservative parliamentary candidate for the borough of Liverpool. He received a letter from William Clementson, formerly superintendent of the Reformation Society's Special Mission to Roman Catholics and now incumbent of St Michael's, Toxteth Park, who addressed him as follows:

You are aware that two opposite principles are advocated by politicians as desirable to be applied to religious institutions, these two principles being familiarly known as 'levelling *down*' and 'levelling up'. The great bulk of Protestant Churchmen are, if possible more determinately opposed to the latter than they are to the former. In fact, if the question now agitating the Nation were to be narrowed to this point:—shall the Irish branch of the United Church be disestablished and disendowed? or shall the church of Rome be endowed by the British Government?—I am bold to affirm that nine-tenths, at least of the Churchmen both of England and Ireland would prefer the former.[10]

Lord Harrowby, no doubt mindful of his own unhappy experience at

[8] R. Brent, *Liberal Anglican Politics* (Oxford, 1987), 88–9; W. F. Monypenny and G. E. Buckle, *The Life of Benjamin Disraeli, Earl of Beaconsfield*, 6 vols. (1910–20), iii. 123, Stanley to Disraeli, 21 Dec. 1848.

[9] Dudley Francis Stewart Ryder (1831–1900), MP for Lichfield, 1856–9 and Liverpool, 1868–82, held government office under Disraeli, 1874–80, succeeded as 3rd Earl of Harrowby in 1882 (*DNB, Supp.*, iii. 334).

[10] Sandon Hall, Stafford, Harrowby MSS, l. 71, Clementson to Sandon, 20 July 1868.

Liverpool in the election of 1847, had already written in despairing tones to his son, acknowledging the indefensibility of the Church of Ireland but seeing its 'destruction' as an 'unmitigated evil'. While the option of concurrent endowment was, of course, seriously explored in 1869, the Cabinet was in no doubt that it was impracticable.[11]

Moreover, as Harrowby recognized in his lament of 1868, the cause of Establishment in Britain as well was suffering a severe blow. It is a fine irony that the political associates of men who had been the key defenders of the Protestant constitution in the 1820s and 1830s were now coming to perceive disestablishment as a lesser evil than the alternatives. In 1832 the fourth Duke of Newcastle had given his electoral patronage at Newark to the young William Ewart Gladstone. At the time, the convictions of the two men had seemed similar, but Gladstone's support for Maynooth in 1845 had precipitated an irrevocable separation. Nevertheless, in 1869 Gladstone's profound personal antipathy to concurrent endowment was the ultimate logic of the uncompromising Protestantism of his erstwhile patron.[12] Similarly, behind Clementson one senses the shadow of McNeile, still living but now beginning to seem like a survivor from an earlier generation. Almost imperceptibly, Anglican anti-Catholics had been driven close to Nonconformist ground.

If the development of the relationship between Britain and Ireland is viewed in more general terms, it can be argued that Protestant agitation in Britain had a significant impact. In September 1834 Charles Boyton of the Dublin Conservative Society was planning the Irish Protestant appeal to Britain, but expressed reservations about it to Lord Roden: 'I am endeavouring to prepare our case for English ears and of this I am certain, a most tremendous case can be made, but one thing frets me and that is it makes the line of separation from the Catholics more decided and the hope of an Irish Party if it fails quite hopeless . . . '.[13] Aspirations towards a non-sectarian nationalism in Ireland still had some life in the later nineteenth century.[14] However,

[11] Harrowby MSS, lxv. 128–9, Harrowby to Sandon, 17 Apr. 1868; P. M. H. Bell, *Disestablishment in Ireland and Wales* (1969), 149–54 and *passim*.

[12] J. Brooke and M. Sorensen (eds.), *The Prime Ministers' Papers: W. E. Gladstone*, ii. *Autobiographical Memoranda, 1832–1845* (1972), 23–31; Nottingham University Library, Newcastle MSS, Diary, Ne2F7, 24 Dec. 1845; H. C. G. Matthew, *Gladstone 1809–1874* (Oxford, 1986), 193.

[13] Public Record Office of Northern Ireland, Belfast, Roden MSS, MIC 147/7, xiv. 389–94, Boyton to Roden, 27 Sept. 1834. See above, Chap. 3, pp. 77–82.

[14] J. Loughlin, *Gladstone, Home Rule and the Ulster Question* (Dublin, 1986), 5–34.

Protestant appeals to Britain on religious grounds inevitably weakened the basis of understanding and sympathy for a more secular approach to Ireland's political, social, and economic difficulties. The consequent one-dimensional view of the situation which was held by some was reinforced in 1868 by Disraeli's cynical attempt to rally Protestant opinion to the Conservatives in the disestablishment crisis. Subsequently, in July 1874 Disraeli presented the religious argument as the most compelling grounds for rejecting Butt's Home Rule motion.[15] For the Liberals, Protestant attitudes were a significant stumbling-block in the path of any movement towards Home Rule. After 1886 Gladstone was faced with the virtually unanimous hostility of Ulster Protestants, and on the British mainland suspicion of the Catholics affected both Anglican Evangelicals and a significant body of his own Nonconformist supporters, particularly Wesleyans and others with strong Irish ties.[16] His attempt to present Irish nationalism as essentially constitutional rather than sectarian in character thus stood little chance of commanding general assent.[17]

In connection with the development of the British party system, anti-Catholicism played an important role in the history of Conservatism. The nature of the relationship has been explored in detail above. It can be concluded that to view either Conservativism as intrinsically militantly anti-Catholic or Protestantism as the defining characteristic of a 'reactionary' faction within the party has some limited applicability to particular incidents and periods but is not sustainable as a general interpretation. A more subtle assessment has to start from the recognition that it is unsatisfactory to postulate a crude dichotomy between 'Protestant' and 'reformist' forces. Individuals did not perceive the situation in such terms; they expressed genuine tensions of conscience and naturally reacted in different ways in different political circumstances. This point can be applied not only to Peel, Wellington, Disraeli, and Derby, but also to all but a small core of supporters of the anti-Catholic societies themselves. In particular, it is clear that the party was more likely to be conspicuously anti-Catholic in opposition than in government, as was evident both between 1835 and 1841, and 1848 and 1852.

[15] R. Blake, *Disraeli* (1966), 508–15; 3 *Hansard*, ccxx. 961–3, 2 July 1874. I am indebted to Dr Allen Warren for the latter reference.
[16] J. P. Rossi, 'Home Rule and the Liverpool By-Election of 1880', *Irish Historical Studies*, 19 (1974–5), 156–8; D. W. Bebbington, *The Nonconformist Conscience* (1982), 89–93.
[17] Loughlin, *Gladstone*, pp. 191 ff., 289.

In the light of the arguments advanced in this book for viewing Victorian anti-Catholicism as a phenomenon with important contemporary causes, it follows that, to the limited extent that the Conservatives benefited from it electorally, this was part of their adaptation to the post-Reform Act system rather than a relic from the past. In this connection it is worth emphasizing the ways in which Protestant societies contributed, albeit in a limited and somewhat ambivalent fashion, to the strengthening of the popular base of Conservatism. In retrospect it would seem that they helped to point the way forward to the more positive acceptance of official party organization by the Conservatives in the years after the Reform Act of 1867 and in the Primrose League from the 1880s.[18] In this respect their impact can be seen as analogous to that of the more numerous and sophisticated pressure groups in the prehistory of the later nineteenth-century Liberal party.

Analysis of the relationship btween political decision-making and the Protestant movement also provides a basis for some reflection on the interaction between Parliament and extra-parliamentary politics.[19] It emerges clearly that anti-Catholics in Parliament were usually only indirectly associated with agitation outside Westminster. The actions of MPs at particular junctures were shaped largely by personal views and by 'inside' rather than 'outside' pressures. This was illustrated particularly in the Maynooth crisis. Nevertheless, the case should not be overstated: the force of Protestant public opinion was acknowledged, especially in the later 1830s and after 1845, and was a factor in ministerial and parliamentary calculations even when this did not imply a readiness to submit to it. Moreover, the persistent petitioning and lobbying by the anti-Catholic societies suggests an underlying faith that the system could be made responsive to them. Thus, Protestant agitation contributed to the growth of a consensus that MPs should respond to public opinion, all the more so as it tended to stimulate professions of such conviction in such surprising quarters as the Duke of Newcastle in April 1845.[20] Granted that Tory aristocrats would only make such superficially democratic professions when it suited them,

---

[18] E. J. Feuchtwanger, *Disraeli, Democracy and the Tory Party* (Oxford, 1968); J. P. Cornford, 'The Transformation of Conservatism in the Late Nineteenth Century', *Victorian Studies*, 7 (1963–4), 35–66; M. Pugh, *The Tories and the People 1880–1935* (Oxford, 1985).

[19] Cf. M. Bentley and J. Stevenson, *High and Low Politics in Modern Britain* (Oxford, 1983).

[20] Newcastle Diary, Ne2F7, 19 Apr. 1845.

the fact that extra-parliamentary anti-Catholicism encouraged them to do so on several occasions could only weaken their credibility when, in different circumstances, they might choose to emphasize the rights of MPs to independence from constituency pressure.

In assessing the relationship of anti-Catholicism to social class, a fairly complex picture emerges. This book has placed particular emphasis on the role of evangelicalism in forming anti-Catholic positions, while the work of other scholars has presented evangelicalism itself as a key element in the development of middle-class identity.[21] Accordingly, the inference can be drawn that, in its mid-nineteenth-century form, anti-Catholicism should be associated primarily with bourgeois values. This suggestion is helpful up to a point: it provides a not unconvincing context for the linkage of Protestantism with prosperity, progress, and propriety, as explored in Chapter 4. It correlates with the primarily urban focus of organized anti-Catholicism; with the perceptions of contemporaries such as Shaftesbury that anti-Catholicism was a middle-class movement;[22] and, to some extent, with what is known about the membership of the societies. It provides a social dimension to consideration of the limitations of anti-Catholic agitation, as, for example, in the failure of MPs to identify with the anti-Maynooth agitation of 1845, or, on a different front, in the inability of the societies to harness the force of popular Merseyside and Clydeside sectarianism in the 1850s to sustain their flagging fortunes.

Nevertheless, this interpretation is little more than a half-truth. The anti-Catholic societies, particularly in the early part of the period, were graced with a goodly array of titled vice-presidents. The family connections of members of the committees of the Reformation Society, the Protestant Association, and the National Club can be traced in the pages of *Burke* and *Debrett*. When aristocrats such as Roden, Manchester, and Shaftesbury chose actively to involve themselves in the movement, they were accorded not only prestige but also as much actual influence as they chose to exercise. Aristocratic links were strong even in less immediately apparent places: John Hope, solicitor in a city where the social prestige of lawyers was the highest of any in Britain, was connected with the landed branch of the Hope family.[23] Hugh McNeile can validly be seen as a leader of the

---

[21] L. Davidoff and C. Hall, *Family Fortunes: Men and Women of the English Middle Class 1780–1850* (1987).

[22] Shaftesbury Diary, SHA/PD/3, 23 May 1845.

[23] D. Jamie, *John Hope: Philanthropist and Reformer* (Edinburgh, 1900), 1–2.

Liverpool middle class, but he had his origins in a substantial County Antrim family and had served his first incumbency in a setting which comes close to providing a textbook example of village Anglicanism.[24]

Thus there were significant respects in which anti-Catholicism bridged social distinctions, although it certainly did not level them. It reflected the capacity of evangelicalism, by virtue of its strength within the Established Churches, to gain supporters, albeit a minority, among the aristocracy and, as a corollary, to be a channel of upward social mobility. This was recognized by George Eliot in the opening sentences of her famous attack on Dr Cumming: 'Given a man with moderate intellect, a moral standard not higher than the average, some rhetorical affluence and great glibness of speech, what is the career in which, without the aid of birth or money, he may most easily attain power and reputation in English society? . . . Let such a man become an evangelical preacher . . . '.[25] Cumming's church in Covent Garden was fashionable not only with the wealthy bourgeoisie but also with the aristocracy.[26]

Anti-Catholicism was especially significant as a medium of such social interaction because of the ideological convergence between Toryism and Evangelicalism which was particularly evident in the mid-1830s. Men like Roden, Shaftesbury, and McNeile had feet in both camps. Indeed, as we have seen, the Anglican Evangelicals proved in some respects to be the most credible political heirs of the pre-1829 Ultras, suggesting a further dimension to arguments about the acquiescence of the middle class in the 1832 settlement, and the permeation of 'aristocratic' values through the social system.[27] Of course, this applied much less to the Dissenting anti-Catholics, whose slowness to become involved in the movement clearly had social as well as religious roots, but even this divide was not impermeable, as was shown by the membership of the Protestant Alliance.[28] Nevertheless, it seems that the growth of Nonconformist involvement in anti-Catholicism after 1845 was associated with a gradual weakening of the aristocratic presence.

[24] J. A. Wardle, 'The Life and Times of the Rev. Dr Hugh M'Neile, DD, 1795–1875', MA thesis (Manchester, 1981), 1–9.

[25] George Eliot, 'Dr Cumming', in *Essays of George Eliot*, ed. T. Pinney (1963), 169.

[26] R. B. Knox, 'Dr John Cumming and Crown Court Church, London', *Records of the Scottish Church History Society*, 22 (1984), 59–61.

[27] F. M. L. Thompson, 'English Landed Society in the Nineteenth Century', in P. Thane, G. Crossick, and R. Floud, *The Power of the Past: Essays for Eric Hobsbawm* (Cambridge, 1984), 195–214.

[28] PAll, *2nd AR* (1853), 18–35.

Similarly, anti-Catholicism had the capacity to assimulate elements within the working class, as was indicated by Protestant Operative Associations, Protestant classes, and the activities of missionaries to the urban Catholics. There was an evident gap to be spanned, but popular sectarianism was likely to form a more receptive bed for anti-Catholic evangelicalism than a working-class culture where there was no Catholic presence to fuel hostility. For Protestants seeking to differentiate themelves from their poorer Catholic neighbours, evangelicalism could well become a logical extension of their aspirations to 'respectability'. In the medium term, middle-class and working-class forms of anti-Catholicism converged: this was evident in the support for the Protestant orator William Murphy in the 1860s. Murphy was sponsored by a new national anti-Catholic society, the Protestant Evangelical Mission and Electoral Union, which gave him a certain aura of middle-class respectability, but his lectures clearly had considerable appeal among the working class.[29] Thus, during the first half of Victoria's reign the social centre of gravity of organized anti-Catholicism moved downwards until it came to rest at that level of the lower middle and upper working class where it maintained an abiding hold until well into the twentieth century, particularly in areas with a substantial Irish Catholic presence. At the same time, anti-Catholicism provides an indication of the extent to which ideological and cultural influences moved across class boundaries.

Having considered the political and social implications of anti-Catholicism, we must now turn to consider its more specific relationship to the development of British religion. Some key points are implicit in what has been said above. In particular, the hostility of the Protestant movement to any extension of state endowment of the Roman Catholic Church in effect, though not, of course, in intent, reinforced the pressure from Dissent towards *de facto* secularization of the State. Meanwhile, the appeal of anti-Catholicism did something to prepare the ground for the impact of Anglican Evangelicalism in social milieux in which it was not otherwise particularly successful. Taking these pressures together, the result was a reinforcing of the impetus towards denominationalism.

This conclusion is confirmed by more directly religious considerations. As we have seen, early Victorian anti-Catholicism reflected and reinforced a polemical, dualistic mental framework which was further stimulated by the militancy of Ultramontane and Irish nationalist

[29] Arnstein, *Protestant versus Catholic*, pp. 88–107.

Catholicism. For many in the Catholic Church itself, the intensity of the attack on their faith naturally fostered a sense that there could be no compromise or meaningful dialogue with the attackers. The consequent Catholic militancy was more grist to the Protestant mill. At the extremes, the two other obvious religious conflicts of the period, those between Church and Dissent and Christianity and 'Infidelity', were both seen as rooted in the struggle of Protestant and Catholic. Thus there were instances in which the Protestant issue might lead to a suspension of hostilities on the Establishment front, rendering the formation of the Evangelical and Protestant Alliances feasible. For others, however, the Establishment issue was the primary one, and militant Dissenters as represented by the *Nonconformist* could see a common interest with Irish Catholicism in hostility to state Churches.[30] Conversely, government plans for concurrent endowment can be seen as Anglican attempts to gain the support of the Catholics against Nonconformity. All these alignments reflected a common feeling that there was a tangible ultimate enemy, whether Catholicism, Establishment, or disestablishment, an outlook which precluded the flexibility of analysis and response which would have been necessary for institutional Christianity to maintain its cultural ascendancy in the long term.

With the benefit of hindsight, it would seem a truism that Catholics and anti-Catholics had a common interest in resisting trends towards theological liberalism and the rejection of orthodox Christianity. The Protestant societies were innocent of any such perception, and their Catholic antagonists were generally equally resistant to such an idea. One notable exception to this was provided by the Earl of Arundel in a speech in the Commons in 1847: 'I look with pleasure and pride upon the deep religious feeling of the people of this country, and I delight in the idea that when they are most disturbed, it is religious feeling by which they are excited. I prefer the "iron sides" of Cromwell to the demons of the French Revolution.'[31] Arundel, speaking from the vantage-point of the English Catholic aristocracy, was close to uttering a cry in the wilderness. The contrary pressures were strong, arising not only from the feeling that 'Infidelity' was rooted in 'false' religion, but also from the sense that any acknowledgement that the opposing view could in any respect be legitimate Christianity implied the reduction of religious truth to the lowest common denominator. Constructive dialogue with a view to removing misconceptions would have been the

[30] *Nonconformist*, 28 May 1845, p. 386.
[31] 3 *Hansard*, xci. 1056–7, 20 Apr. 1847.

only route out of this dilemma: the early readiness of Roman Catholic clergy to participate in debates suggests a partial realization of this, but their subsequent reluctance to be involved in such events implies that they had come to the conclusion that it had proved impossible to move from negative polemics to a positive search for common ground.

In his study of mid-Victorian anti-Catholicism Walter Arnstein maintains that 'the more justifiable context is one of Protestant–Catholic rivalry rather than anti-Catholicism'.[32] This view has been broadly endorsed in this book. Anti-Catholicism was stirred by a variety of direct stimuli from Catholics, including pastoral competition in the slums, the political campaign of Daniel O'Connell, and the triumphalism of Cardinal Wiseman. However, two refinements of Arnstein's view need to be made. Firstly, one of his reviewers comments that he confuses Protestant perceptions with reality.[33] In Arnstein's defence, it should be stressed that the perception of irresistible Roman advance was one shared and articulated by many Catholics themselves. However, in order to understand the vigour of the Protestant response, it is necessary to give due attention to their own mental framework, which ensured that reaction to Catholic provocation was frequently disproportionate. Secondly, it is significant that the general anti-Catholic perception was of Catholic advance and Protestant retreat. This gloomy view was qualified by occasional euphoria at supposed missionary successes, but the dominant Protestant mood suggested a crisis of morale. To some extent this attitude reflected eschatological beliefs: the growth of Rome was a sign of the imminence of the catastrophes ushering in the pre-millennial advent; but in the long term such convictions served to endorse a growing defeatism, which in the end was likely to become self-fulfilling.

For evangelicalism the effects of anti-Catholicism were thus ambivalent. Antagonism to Rome was a central strand in the 'new' evangelicalism of the late 1820s and early 1830s which, in the short term, destroyed the relative unity that had underpinned the strong social and political influence of evangelicalism in the Wilberforce era. On the other hand, as the dust settled, it gave evangelicalism, particularly in its Anglican forms, important points of contact with key political and ideological forces in the early Victorian era, notably Irish Protestantism and the revived Conservative party. The effect was to reinforce a further period of strong cultural influence in the central

---

[32] Arnstein, *Protestant versus Catholic*, p. 212.
[33] J. L. Altholz, in *Victorian Studies*, 26 (1982–3), 363–4.

third of the century. Ultimately, however, anti-Catholicism, with its tendency to foster a general contentiousness, reinforced evangelical fragmentation. The extent to which it became ingrained in religious consciousness was an important factor in the subsequent failure of evangelicals to adapt to the further changes of the late 1850s and 1860s as effectively as they had to those of the previous generation. In part this was simply a consequence of the direction of theological endeavour: later Victorian evangelicals could draw on a large corpus of anti-Catholic writing, but they had relatively little on which to build in developing a response to liberalism and secularism. A deeper problem, however, was that, even when evangelical attentions were diverted from Rome, the polemical reflex was transferred, contributing to the 'all or nothing' arguments so evident in the response to Darwin, Colenso, and *Essays and Reviews*.[34] Well before the 1860s such a position was already alienating more subtle minds and leading to that reduction of the intellectual stock of evangelicalism which limited its credibility in later periods.[35]

In relation to the internal conflicts of the Church of England, this book has argued that the Evangelical reaction to Tractarianism was as much a consequence as a cause of more general anti-Catholicism. Indeed, the increasing propensity of Evangelicals to smell a popish rat under the most moderate High-Church arguments and practices itself weakened the credibility of the *via media* position and reinforced the eventual trend to Rome and advanced Anglo-Catholicism. On the other hand, there was an element of ambivalence in the attitude of anti-Catholics in the Church of England towards the Oxford Movement: however anxious they might be to purify the Church from Romish tendencies, they recognized that division in the Establishment would ultimately play into the hands of Dissenters, whose motives for attacking the Tractarians were more Voluntaryist than Protestant. Such considerations, combined with a degree of optimism that the problem might recede of itself, help to explain the lack of a sustained anti-ritualist campaign before the 1860s. Moreover, the counter-productive effect of the activity of the Church Association after 1865

---

[34] J. L. Altholz, 'The Mind of Victorian Orthodoxy: Anglican Responses to *Essays and Reviews*, 1860–1864', *Church History*, 57 (1982), 186–97.

[35] Eliot, 'Dr Cumming', *passim*. David Bebbington (*Evangelicalism in Modern Britain* (1989), 140–1) rightly points out that the potential intellectual resources of evangelicalism should not be underestimated. However, by the 1860s there was considerable dependence on older men whose best work had already been done and who were shortly to pass from the scene.

seems in retrospect to confirm the wisdom of the earlier, more cautious attitude. Although the Public Worship Regulation Act of 1874 appeared to constitute a parliamentary recognition of the Protestant position, the futile effort to enforce it only cast the Evangelicals in the light of persecutors, while the ritualists gained the aura of martyrdom. The long-term result was a loss of credibility for the Church as a whole and for Evangelicalism in particular.[36]

The history of anti-Catholic societies since 1860 has yet to be written, and it is impossible to anticipate that task here, other than in the broadest outline. The 1860s and 1870s saw numerous fresh stimuli, including the growth of ritualism, the activities of William Murphy, the Irish disestablishment crisis, not to mention the Syllabus of Errors of 1864 and the Vatican decrees of 1870. Against this background, most of the Protestant societies, strengthened no doubt by the maturing of the people who, in their formative years, had been influenced by the classes and missions of the 1850s, continued to enjoy a modest prosperity. The Scottish Reformation Society extended its operations to England in 1866, setting up Protestant classes in London. It was shortly to operate in a number of provincial centres also, and in 1872 the aggregate attendance at its classes was estimated to be 5,000. In 1887 it was claimed that 65,000 students had passed through the classes in the previous twenty years.[37] The late 1860s and early 1870s saw the mobilization of substantial support for Newdegate's anti-convent campaign in a manner reminiscent of the anti-Maynooth activity of two decades before.[38] As late as 1908 the prospect of a Catholic Eucharistic procession in London produced significant protest and a delicate political dilemma for the government.[39] New anti-Catholic societies continued to be formed, notably John Kensit's Protestant Truth Society in 1889. The 1933 edition of the *Protestant Dictionary* also listed the Calvinistic Protestant

---

[36] J. Bentley, *Ritualism and Politics in Victorian Britain* (Oxford, 1978); A. Bentley, 'The Transformation of the Evangelical Party in the later nineteenth century', Ph.D. thesis (Durham, 1971), 124–71.

[37] Protestant Educational Institute, *Proposed Erection of a Protestant Educational Institute in London* (1869); *Protestant Educational Classes in England: May Meeting and Distribution of Prizes in London 1869* (1869); *Transactions of the Protestant Educational Institute for the year ending 30th April 1872* (1872), 6; *Short Report of the Operations of the Protestant Educational Institute for the Year 1887* (1888), 2 ff.; cf. Arnstein, *Protestant versus Catholic*, pp. 83, 166.

[38] Arnstein, *Protestant versus Catholic*, pp. 129–35, 199.

[39] G. I. T. Machin, 'The Liberal Government and the Eucharistic Procession of 1908', *Journal of Ecclesiastical History*, 34 (1983), 559–83. On political anti-Catholicism, see G. I. T. Machin, *Politics and the Churches in Great Britain 1869–1921* (Oxford, 1987).

Union, the National Church League, and the Women's Protestant Union. In 1897 the London Council of United Protestant Societies (later the United Protestant Council) was formed to co-ordinate action on matters of common concern.⁴⁰ Meanwhile, in Scotland John Hope, who died in 1893, left the bulk of his very considerable fortune to promote anti-Catholicism there.⁴¹

Protestant decline, therefore, should neither be exaggerated nor pre-dated, especially not in Scotland. There were, however, some telling symptoms, including the demise of the Protestant Association. During the 1860s this body continued to suffer from declining income, but resisted pressure to amalgamate with the Protestant Alliance.⁴² It enjoyed a brief and limited revival in the face of the Irish Church crisis, only to be merged with the English arm of the Scottish Reformation Society in 1871, a graphic indication of the manner in which the ideals for which it had stood seemed to have received a decisive eclipse in the disestablishment of the Church of Ireland.⁴³ Another later indication was the degree of success achieved by John Hope's disappointed relatives when they contested his will, alleging that the testator had had delusions regarding the Roman Catholic Church which implied that he was not of sound mind. The House of Lords, on appeal from the Court of Session, agreed that there was a case to answer, and Hope's trustees made an out-of-court settlement. Hope himself had made his original bequest because he was aware of the contemporary unpopularity of the cause and was anxious to see it maintained.⁴⁴

By the turn of the century the Protestant societies were moving to what was a more moderate stance compared with the position adopted in the early Victorian period. This point is well supported by Edmund Gosse's spendidly ironical account of his childhood, written in 1907:

If there was one institution more than another which, at this early stage in my history, I loathed and feared, it was what we invariably spoke of as 'the so-called Church of Rome'. In later years, I have met with stout Protestants, gallant 'Down-with-the-Pope' men from County Antrim and ladies who see the hand of the Jesuits in every public and private misfortune. It is the habit of a loose and indifferent age to consider this dwindling body of enthusiasts with suspicion, and to regard their attitude towards Rome as illiberal. But my own

⁴⁰ C. S. Carter and G. E. A. Weeks, *The Protestant Dictionary* (new edn., 1933), 548–53.
⁴¹ Jamie, *Hope*, pp. 531–3.
⁴² PAss, *31st AR (1866)*, 15, 18.
⁴³ PAss, *Occasional Papers*, 9 (1869); 12 (1870); *Transactions of the Protestant Educational Institute for . . . 1872*, p. 3.
⁴⁴ Jamie, *Hope*, p. 566.

feeling is that they are all too mild, that their denunciations err on the side of the anodyne. I have no longer the slightest wish myself to denounce the Roman communion, but, if it is to be done, I have an idea that the latter-day Protestants do not know how to do it. In Lord Chesterfield's phrase, these anti-Pope men 'don't understand their own silly business'. They make concessions and allowances, they put on gloves to touch the accursed thing.[45]

This trend was confirmed as the twentieth century moved on. The impact of the Protestant societies was largely confined to a subcultural evangelicalism. In order even to maintain this, they have tended to broaden their positions, emphasizing the positive cause of promoting interest in Protestant history and mission rather than negative anti-Catholicism. In some cases, notably those of the Scottish Reformation Society and the Evangelical Alliance, this strategy has met with a significant degree of success. The Reformation Society has continued to have a role as a focus for Anglican Evangelical concern about Anglo-Catholicism, and the National Club has endured as a discreet political pressure group and social focus for Evangelical professionals in London. Even the Protestant Alliance, which has perhaps adhered more closely to its original programme and style than any of the other societies, has managed to cling on to life.[46]

The continued existence of the original anti-Catholic societies is a significant indication that, even though organized Protestantism changed its style in the twentieth century and declined into relative marginality, it was by no means a spent force. Its tenacity was especially evident at a regional level. The long ascendancy of the Conservative party in late nineteenth- and early twentieth-century Liverpool was closely associated with the sectarian base of local politics.[47] North of the Border, in the inter-war period, Protestant Action and the Scottish Protestant League made a considerable impact on local politics in Edinburgh and Glasgow respectively. The Orange Order, drawing continued life from the endless struggle of Ulster Protestantism, has continued to thrive in areas of Irish settlement in Britain.[48]

---

[45] Edmund Gosse, *Father and Son* (Penguin edn., 1979), 66.

[46] All the organizations mentioned in this paragraph are still in existence at the time of writing (Mar. 1989). The information given has been derived from correspondence and conversation with current officers. See also *Bulwark* (Scottish Reformation Society); *Reformer* (Protestant Alliance), and D. N. Samuel, *The Reformation and the Church of England Today* (Grimsby, 1973).

[47] P. J. Waller, *Democracy and Sectarianism: A Political and Social History of Liverpool 1868–1939* (Liverpool, 1981); F. Neal, *Sectarian Violence: The Liverpool Experience, 1819–1914* (Manchester, 1988).

[48] S. Bruce, *No Pope of Rome: Militant Protestantism in Modern Scotland* (Edinburgh,

The survival of such vigorous, if localized, anti-Catholicism throughout the twentieth century provides a further reminder, if one is needed, that, whatever its limitations, the early Victorian Protestant movement cannot be dismissed as merely an anomalous byway off the high road of reform and toleration. Certainly the long-run continuity evident on Merseyside and Clydeside and in Northern Ireland reflects wider pressures of the formation and defence of community groups which cannot by any means wholly be understood in terms of polemical religion. Nevertheless, in Ian Paisley's Ulster the force of continuing explicit anti-Catholicism remains very much in the open.

Moreover, a similar continuity can be seen, albeit of a much more diffuse kind, in relation to much of the United Kingdom, if one relates the impact of anti-Catholicism to the development of nationalism. Many Protestant arguments were couched in a patriotic framework, linked with a sense of Britain's providential mission to defend and propagate reformed Christianity. Indeed, Hugh McNeile was one of the earliest people to use the word 'nationalism' in Britain, when he addressed the Protestant Association in 1839.[49] Two further illustrations of intensely patriotic rhetoric are worthy of note here, particularly as they were both directed at an audience with a substantial lower-class element. In October 1840 a speaker at a meeting of the York Protestant Operative Association wound up his address by arguing that Britain had been raised to her present position in the world by her adherence to the Bible. This, he claimed, had made us 'the loveliest land on the face of the earth . . . While I have a voice . . . it shall be Britain for ever! Victoria, our lovely queen for ever! Protestantism for ever! Three times three for Protestantism!'[50] Ten years later, in the face of the 'Papal Aggression', Hugh McNeile, in a striking appropriation of traditional radical language, urged: 'Free-born Englishmen, be wise, be firm!'[51] The sometimes problematic distinc-

1985); T. Gallagher, *Edinburgh Divided: John Cormack and No Popery in the 1930s* (Edinburgh, 1987); id., *Glasgow The Uneasy Peace: Religious Tension in Modern Scotland* (Manchester, 1987).

[49] H. McNeile, *Nationalism in Religion* (1839), 2–3. The earliest occurrence of the word 'nationalism' recorded in the *Oxford English Dictionary* is in G. S. Faber's *Primitive Doctrine of Election* (1836). Faber used the word to denote the supposed 'election of certain whole nations into the pale of the visible Church Catholic' (see pp. ix–x, xii–xiii, 20–3, 27, 368).

[50] *Speech of the Rev. James Everett Delivered at the Adjourned Meeting of the York Operative Protestant Association in the Concert Room, York, on Tuesday, October 13th 1840* (York, 1840), 8.

[51] Quoted by Wardle, 'McNeile', p. 258.

tion between 'patriotism' and 'nationalism' can be conceptualized by holding that the latter contains an inherent conviction of objective national superiority. This implies a degree of cultural and institutional coherence (real or imagined) which is not intrinsic to patriotism. Within such a framework, it would seem that anti-Catholicism in the nineteenth century played a significant part in the transition from one to the other.[52]

If this hypothesis is to carry conviction, evangelical anti-Catholicism needs to be set in a wider context. In particular, due weight should be given to the strongly nationalistic tone of some Broad-Church Anglicanism, which had its ideological foundation in the work of S. T. Coleridge and Thomas Arnold and was popularized by men such as Charles Kingsley and Thomas Hughes.[53] Here, too, an anti-Catholic strand was frequently present, as, for example, in the writings and attitudes of Kingsley.[54] A similar point can be made somewhat more tentatively in relation to the adulation of the monarchy, which has been such a conspicuous feature of later nineteenth- and twentieth-century British nationalism: as in the York speech quoted above, loyalty to the queen was frequently linked with hostility to the pope. Victoria's accession in 1837 coincided with the reverberations of the supposedly morally corrupting influence of Dens's *Theologia*, and the young queen therefore provided a perfect example of the pure Protestant British maiden threatened by Roman impurity.[55] It does not seem unduly fanciful to suggest that, as she grew older, her perceived qualities of committed wifely loyalty and matriarchal virtue offered an appealing antithesis to Roman veneration of the Virgin Mary. At the time of the diamond jubilee 'A Woman's Tribute' included the following lines:

As Maiden, Wife and Mother thou hast shone
With radiance sweet
And every love-born grace hath clustered fair
Around thy feet;
And all true women of thy realm may claim
A sister's heart

[52] For recent discussion of the nature of nationalism, cf. J. Breuilly, *Nationalism and the State* (Manchester, 1982); B. Anderson, *Imagined Communities* (1983).
[53] D. Forbes, *The Liberal Anglican Idea of History* (Cambridge, 1952).
[54] F. Kingsley (ed.), *Charles Kingsley: His Letters and Memories of his Life*, 2 vols. (1877), i. 247–60.
[55] *Christian Lady's Magazine*, 8 (1837), pp. vi–vii; 9 (1838), 542–8. Cf. E. Trudgill, *Madonnas and Magdalens: The Origins and Development of Victorian Sexual Attitudes* (1976).

In thee, O Queen, for in thy sympathy
They have a part.[56]

Her immediate successors were precluded by gender from such a role, but the wider linkage of Protestantism with the monarch is evident in the continuing tendency of the Crown to be the focus of anti-Catholic rumblings, from controversy over the Coronation Oath at the beginning of the century to concern in 1980 that the current Prince of Wales might marry a Roman Catholic.[57]

In the light of this linkage between Protestantism and British identity, those anxious to affirm their place in the national community, while lacking part of the qualifications, tended to be more vigorous in their assertion of the ties which they did possess. This provides a framework for appreciating the anxiety of Anglo-Catholics to emphasize the 'Englishness' of their tradition, and the tendency of Roman Catholicism to take opportunities, especially at times of national crisis, to assert their loyalty.[58] Conversely, it is relevant to understanding the position of the majority community in Northern Ireland, with its Protestant declamations resounding across the Irish Sea in assertion of a shared essential 'Britishness'.

Clearly, such attitudes demonstrate an unresolved ambiguity between 'English' and 'British' identity.[59] In Scotland the tensions within the anti-Catholic movement reflected the respective pressures of 'Britishness' and 'Scottishness'. On the one hand, Protestantism, especially in the Church of Scotland, promoted a sense of common identity with England, reflected particularly in the links between the Reformation Society in London and the General Assembly of the Kirk, Scottish participation in the Protestant conferences of the 1850s; and the leading role played in the English Protestant movement by Scots such as Colquhoun and Gordon. On the other hand, the Free Church side of the Scottish movement manifested more distinctively

[56] *Go Forward: YWCA Monthly Journal for Secretaries and Workers*, 11 (1897), 228. Cf. W. L. Arnstein, 'Queen Victoria and Religion, in G. Malmgreen (ed.), *Religion in the Lives of English Women, 1760–1830* (1986), 88–128.

[57] *The Sovereign's Accession Declaration* (Protestant Reformation Society broadsheet, 1910, in the British Library); H. Varley, *The King's Declaration in the Light of Rome's Recent History* (1910); K. Robbins, 'Religion and Identity in Modern British History', *Studies in Church History*, 18 (1982), 465.

[58] A. Hastings, *A History of English Christianity* (1986), 393.

[59] Cf. Robbins, 'Religion and Identity'; D. W. Bebbington, 'Religion and National Identity in Nineteenth-Century Wales and Scotland', *Studies in Church History*, 18 (1982), 489–503; K. Robbins, *Nineteenth-Century Britain: Integration and Diversity* (Oxford, 1988).

Scottish tendencies, and James Begg had close links with the mid-century nationalist movement.[60] However, the net effect was, as in other areas of life, not any significant pull towards Scottish separation, but rather an assimulation of the Scots with the British movement on their own terms, as illustrated by the partial shift of gravity of anti-Catholicism from London to Edinburgh during the 1850s.

The almost total absence of organized anti-Catholicism in Wales[61] represents a striking contrast with Scotland. This probably stemmed in part from the absence of any significant Catholic presence in most parts of the principality, and in part from the relative weakness of the Anglican networks which were of such importance in the development of anti-Catholicism in England.[62] It may well be that the explanation of Wales's quietness was more organizational than cultural: in other words, the Protestant societies never troubled themselves with the principality and did not make any attempt to rise to the challenge of translating their material into Welsh. A root of the rather greater force of Welsh nationalism in a later period can be seen here: when religious rivalries did take on a political colour, it was in the ultimately successful struggle for disestablishment rather than in any anti-Roman movement which would have implied greater solidarity with England and Scotland.

Nevertheless, while the Welsh case was an important exception, the general connection between anti-Catholicism and nationalism in Britain was strong. This contention is the final strand in the argument for anti-Catholicism having had a considerable formative influence on Victorian life. Further ramifications might profitably be investigated, including, pre-eminently, the role of anti-Catholicism in literature. In its crudest form, the Protestant didactic novel was more propaganda than art, but in skilful hands the scheming Jesuit or tortured Catholic conscience could provide the basis for some not unsubtle characterization. This was evident even in Charlotte Elizabeth's work, but it was

[60] H. J. Hanham, 'Mid-Century Scottish Nationalism: Romantic and Radical', in R. Robson (ed.), *Ideas and Institutions of Victorian Britain* (1967), 143–79.

[61] This conclusion should be regarded as provisional, and may well have to be modified in the light of further more specific research on Wales. It does seem significant, however, that John Hickey, in his study of Catholics in Cardiff (J. Hickey, *Urban Catholics* (1967), 46–55), felt the need to swell the local material on antagonism to the immigrants with English material and that, when confrontation between Irish and Welsh did occur in the valleys, it was communal rather than religious in character (Cf. D. Williams, *A History of Modern Wales* (1950), 230).

[62] E. T. Davies, *Religion in the Industrial Revolution in South Wales* (Cardiff, 1965), 187–91.

more apparent in a late novel by Wilkie Collins, *The Black Robe* (1881).[63] In this context the Victorian Jesuit should be seen as in some respects the precursor of the twentieth-century German or Russian spy. Painting and architecture also drew on anti-Catholic influencs, as in the portrayal of nuns and the advocacy of a distinctively 'Protestant' Church architecture by Evangelicals such as Francis Close.[64] Such developments of the subject inevitably move beyond the scope of the present book.

Before concluding, it is worth drawing some comparisons between British anti-Catholicism and comparable movements in the United States. Indeed, Protestant societies in some form existed in other parts of the Anglo-Saxon world, notably in Canada, Australia, and New Zealand, but the American movement was the most developed at this time, and so offers the most natural ground for comparison. Several points will be made as illustrations of the ways in which American Protestantism shared in a number of features which have been presented above as fundamental features of nineteenth-century anti-Catholicism.[65]

Evangelicalism had a central role in bodies such as the American Protestant Society and the American and Foreign Christian Union, just as it did in their British counterparts. There was a similar interrelationship between antagonism to 'Popery' and the development of pure evangelical spirituality.[66] The geographical distribution of support for the American societies indicates the importance of Congregational and Presbyterian denominational networks. Although the presence of Irish Catholic immigrants in the East Coast cities clearly stimulated increased support for Protestantism, there was, as in Britain, no simple geographical correlation. Moreover, Protestant

[63] W. W. Collins, *The Black Robe* (1881); E. Jay, *The Religion of the Heart* (1979), 113–14, 129–30, 133–4; M. M. Maison, *Search Your Soul, Eustace: A Survey of the Religious Novel in the Victorian Age* (1961), *passim*.

[64] S. P. Casteras, 'Virgin Vows: The Early Victorian Artists' Portrayal of Nuns and Novices', *Victorian Studies*, 24 (1981–2), 157–84; F. Close, *Church Architecture Spiritually Considered from the Earliest Ages to the Present Time* (1844), extracts reprinted in E. Jay (ed.), *The Evangelical and Oxford Movements* (Cambridge, 1983), 54–64.

[65] The only general survey of American anti-Catholicism remains R. A. Billington, *The Protestant Crusade* (New York, 1938), which, although invaluable, begins to look somewhat outdated. See also M. Feldberg, *The Philadelphia Riots of 1844* (Westport, Conn., 1975), and R. Carwardine, 'The Know-Nothing Party, the Protestant Evangelical Community and American National Identity', *Studies in Church History*, 18 (1982), 449–63. On anti-Catholicism in Australia, Canada, and New Zealand, see the bibliography in J. H. Whyte, *Catholics in Western Democracies: A Study in Political Behaviour* (Dublin, 1981).

[66] G. B. Cheever, *The Religion of Experience and that of Imitation* (New York, 1843).

societies were active among French and German immigrants as well as
Irish ones, suggesting concerns that reflected religion more than a
specific racial antagonism. Above all, the degree to which membership
was dominated by the clergy in America—to a greater extent than in
Britain—underlines the conclusion that these societies were seen as
having a primarily spiritual and evangelistic function.[67]

In relation to the political dimension of anti-Catholicism, two
important differences of context must be underlined. Firstly, the lack
of formal links between Church and State in America meant that there
was no counterpart to the central strand in British anti-Catholicism
which reflected the pressures against the Church of England and
Ireland. Indeed, it is interesting that Episcopalians took little part in
the American movement, which, from the outset, was dominated by
Congregationalists and Presbyterians, who only came to prominence in
Britain after 1845. Secondly, the differences in social structure meant
that initially there was no obvious parallel to the involvement of
aristocrats in British anti-Catholicism. Moreover, the tendency of anti-
Catholicism to become linked with anti-slavery meant that southern
planters were not recruited.[68] A corollary of disestablishment in
America was a sense that it was inappropriate, particularly for
clergymen, to link religion with politics. Nevertheless, this did not
prevent the anti-Catholic campaign from assuming a political dimension, predicated on the assumption that Rome herself had political
objectives which must be met on that ground.[69]

The political strategies of Protestantism in the United States show
strong affinities with the position in Britain. In the earlier part of the
period the Whigs in America stood in a similar relationship to anti-
Catholicism as the Conservatives in Britain. This was seen particularly
in support for Clay and Freylinghusen, who was an evangelical, in the
presidential campaign of 1844.[70] On the face of it, the emergence of
nativist political parties, including the American Republicans in the

[67] American Protestant Society, *4th AR* (New York, 1847), 34–9.
[68] These observations are derived from a survey of a range of publications of
American anti-Catholic societies, including the *Annual Reports* of the American
Protestant Society and the American and Foreign Christian Union.
[69] *Priestcraft Exposed and Primitive Christianity Defended* (Lockport, 1828); *Priestcraft
Unmasked* (New York and Philadelphia, 1830), *Address to the People of the State of New
York by the General Executive Committee of the American Republican Party of the City of New
York* (New York, 1844), 5–6.
[70] T. W. Chambers, *Memoir of the Life and Character of the late Hon. Theo
Freylinghusen, LLD* (New York, 1863), 89–90, 177, 179; D. W. Howe, *The Political
Culture of the American Whigs* (Chicago, 1979), 164–5.

mid-1840s and the Know-Nothings in the mid-1850s, suggests that there was more scope for independent anti-Catholic organization. However, the programme of the directly political bodies was always substantially broader than that of the Protestant societies, and the success of the Know-Nothings, although dramatic, was short-lived.[71] It was the collapse of the Whigs in the early 1850s, like the British Conservative split of 1846, that offered the greatest potential for anti-Catholic influence in a fluid party-political situation, but the position of the Know-Nothings could not be sustained for long in the face of the rise of the Republican party, with its capacity for accommodating anti-Catholic impulses.[72]

The British tendency for anti-Catholicism to be linked with the rhetoric of 'liberty' was more pronounced in America. Protestants were passionate republicans, influenced particularly by Samuel F. B. Morse's *Foreign Conspiracy against the Liberties of the United States*, published in 1834 and alleging that there was a papal and Austrian conspiracy to subvert liberty in North America in order to outflank the challenges to absolutism in Europe. Ideologically, this represented a blending of the tradition derived from the Revolution with the contemporary impact of evangelicalism. The effect, as with the interaction of Toryism, Whiggery, and evangelicalism in Britain, was to transmit a modified version of past political positions to a new generation. Moreover, the anti-Catholicism mediated in the nativist movements implied a widening of the bounds of political participation among the American population, and a reformist social programme.[73]

In America, as in Britain, there was significant popular sectarianism, displayed most dramatically in the burning of the Ursuline convent at Charlestown, Massachusetts in 1834 and the savage riots in Philadelphia in 1844.[74] Such events had their own dynamics, but the greater fluidity of class structures was evident in somewhat more extensive interaction between working-class, middle-class, and clerical anti-Catholicism. Clergy generally held aloof from popular nativist

[71] *Proceedings of the Native American State Convention* (Newbury, Vermont, 1847); J. H. Lee, *The Origin and Progress of the American Party in Politics* (Philadelphia, 1855), 136–63; T. R. Whitney, *A Defence of the American Policy* (New York, 1856), 32–51, 124–87.
[72] W. L. Gienapp, *The Origins of the Republican Party 1852–1856* (New York, 1987), 21–8, 444–5.
[73] R. P. Formisano, *The Transformation of Political Culture: Massachusetts Parties 1790s–1840s* (New York, 1983), 329–43.
[74] Billington, *Protestant Crusade*, pp. 51–76; Feldberg, *Philadelphia Riots, passim.*

organizations,[75] but their preaching contributed to the pre-conditions which gave rise to cruder expressions of anti-Catholic hostility. Moreover, in the later 1830s clerical sanction was given to the circulation of such scurrilous works as *Maria Monk* and the periodical the *Downfall of Babylon*.[76]

The final and, in many respects, the most significant parallel to be drawn between Britain and America is in the formative role played by anti-Catholicism in the development of nationalism. As in Britain, Protestants in the United States perceived Rome as seeking to subvert their own incomparable institutions, and saw themselves as possessing the status of a 'chosen nation' in relation to the divine call to resist 'Popery'. Thus, in 1857 the annual meeting of the American and Foreign Christian Union resolved: 'That the happy experience of our country, whose resources have been so remarkably developed under the fostering influences of a pure and scriptural faith, gives to the American Churches a special mission to spread abroad the blessings and benefits of a pure Christianity in all parts of the Papal world.'[77] Protestantism was presented as a defining characteristic of Americans, and a source of cohesion in a national community in constant danger of being torn apart by the pressure of the slavery issue.

It might seem paradoxical that an impulse shared by Britons and Americans should have been instrumental in reinforcing their distinct national identities. However, the effect of Protestantism was to channel 'Americanism' into a direction which played down the confrontations of 1775 and 1812 and stressed the common ground possessed by the two nations. American evangelicals saw Britain as a Protestant power blessed by God to an extent only exceeded by themselves, and were particularly anxious that there should be no further wars between the two countries.[78] In 1846 the London conference of the Evangelical Alliance indicated the degree to which Protestant sympathies could bridge the Atlantic. Although American resentment at the apparent British dictation over the slavery issue suggested that historic antipathies could still readily be reawakened,

[75] Feldberg, *Philadelphia Riots*, pp. 59–60. Feldberg's observation that there was minimal active clerical involvement in nativism is confirmed by my own comparisons of membership lists.
[76] *Downfall of Babylon*, 17 Aug., 12 Nov. 1836; *Awful Exposure of the Atrocious Plot Formed . . . against the Clergy and Nuns of Lower Canada* (New York, 1836), 80.
[77] American and Foreign Christian Union, *8th AR* (New York, 1857), 11; R. L. Tuveson, *Redeemer Nation* (Chicago, 1968).
[78] *New York Observer*, 16 Oct., 25 Dec. 1841, 27 Dec. 1845.

this was in the medium term an issue which was to divide Americans from each other far more decisively than it was to separate them from the British.

International comparisons of anti-Catholicism could also be extended to continental Europe. It is a truism that the long-term political and cultural consequences of the Reformation were of crucial importance in the origins of the modern-nation state system. In the nineteenth century anti-Catholicism was a discernible strand in the ideological basis of Italian and German nationalism. To a considerable extent, of course, this merely reflected political antagonism to the Papacy and to Catholic Austria, combined with a secular liberalism stirred by reaction to Pius IX. However, especially in the German case, the impact of a more religiously based Protestantism should not be underestimated.[79] Moreover, in the *Kulturkampf* of the 1870s, which evoked significant interest in Britain, Bismarck seemed to endorse Treitschke's view of 1870 as a triumph of Protestantism. Bismarck's policy showed a considerable affinity with the use of anti-Catholicism by British politicians and was praised by the aged Earl Russell.[80]

In seeking a general understanding of anti-Catholicism, therefore, we must look for conditions prevalent throughout the North Atlantic world and present to some extent also in Europe. Relevant influences were the universal human tendency to prejudice and paranoia, the development of militant Ultramontanism, the Irish Catholic diaspora, and a pervasive sense of political and social crisis. However, the crucial factor linking these impulses together was evangelical Christianity. In a culture in which religious idioms were widespread even in those places where committed evangelicalism only had a limited appeal, the resulting ideology found receptive soil, especially in connection with patriotic and nationalist emotions. At the same time anti-Catholicism was a complex and internally divided movement: the force of different influences varied widely, and the terms on which evangelical motifs were assimilated could be set in very different ways.

Historical assessment of the consequences of anti-Catholicism must

[79] B. Hall, 'Alessandro Gavazzi: A Barnebite Friar and the Risorgimento', *Studies in Church History*, 12 (1975), 303–56; F. Hertz, *The German Public Mind in the Nineteenth Century* (1975), 182–3, 347; E. L. Evans, *The German Center Party 1870–1933* (Carbondale, 1981), 1–35; H-U. Wehler, *The German Empire, 1871–1918* (Leamington Spa, 1985), 113–18; F. Fischer, 'Der deutsche Protestantismus und die Politik im 19. Jahrhundert', *Historische Zeitschrift*, 171 (1951), 473–518. I am indebted to Dr Hans Koch for the last reference.

[80] G. R. Craig, *Germany 1866–1945* (Oxford, 1978), 71–2; Arnstein, *Protestant versus Catholic*, p. 188.

seek to transcend entrenched positions. On the one hand is a defensive and negative Protestantism which seeks to vindicate past positions by reiterating them; on the other is the anti-Protestant stance of some Roman Catholic and secular writers which reduces anti-Catholicism to prejudice and bigotry.[81] Both standpoints are inadequate bases for appreciating the formative role of anti-Catholicism in a variety of fields—in forming political positions, reinforcing contemporary ideologies of morality and progress, stimulating evangelistic, educational, and social involvement, and defining the boundaries of national communities. In all its passionate intensity and respectable vulgarity, it was, for better or for worse, an inescapable force in the history of the Victorian age.

[81] Cf. J. Kent, *The Unacceptable Face: The Modern Church in the Eyes of the Historian* (1987), esp. chap. 4.

APPENDIX: MID-NINETEENTH-CENTURY PROTESTANT SOCIETIES

Major Societies	Formed	Composition	Objectives	Leading supporters
Loyal Orange Institution	1795	Interdenominational in theory, largely Anglican and Presbyterian in practice	Defence of Irish Protestants, revival of Toryism, mutual support for members	Col. W. B. Fairman Duke of Cumberland 2nd Lord Kenyon
British (Protestant) Reformation Society	1827	Interdenominational in theory, but predominantly Anglican and Church of Scotland in practice	Religious Protestantism, including education, proselytism, and publication	J. E. Gordon J. Cumming R. P. Blakeney J. Hope
Protestant Association	1835/6	Interdenominational in theory, but almost exclusively Anglican and Church of Scotland in practice	Maintenance of the Protestant character of the State	J. E. Gordon H. M‘Neile R. J. M‘Ghee J. P. Plumptre
National Club	1845	Anglican	Focus for Protestant efforts in Parliament	J. C. Colquhoun Sir D. Mackworth 6th Duke of Manchester
Evangelical Alliance	1845/6	Interdenominational, but principally moderate Nonconformity	Evangelical harmony; anti-Catholicism as part of a broader spiritual and moral crusade	E. Bickersteth Sir C. Eardley T. Chalmers
Scottish Reformation Society	1850	Interdenominational, but dominated by Free Church	Raising of Scottish Protestant consciousness; political pressure group	J. Begg J. A. Wylie R. S. Candlish
Protestant Alliance	1851	Interdenominational	Political pressure group; Protestant	J. MacGregor 7th Earl of Shaftesbury

Protestant Union	1813–14	Resistance to Catholic Emancipation
Parker Society	1840–55	Republication of Reformation classics
Islington Protestant Institute	1846–	Protestant classes and missionary and educational work among Catholics
London Committee for the Defence of the Protestant Faith	1850–?	Anti-Tractarian and anti-Catholic agitation in response to the 'Papal Aggression'
Glasgow Protestant Laymen's Society	?1850–?	Controversial discussions and missions to Catholics
British Protestant League and Bible and Anti-Popery Mission	1852–?	Rival of the Protestant Alliance
Church Protestant Defence Society	1853–?	Small Anglican body, publishing anti-Tractarian pamphlets
English Church Missions to Roman Catholics	1853–8	Exclusively Anglican rival to the Reformation Society
Scottish Protestant Association	1854–?	Church of Scotland rival to the Scottish Reformation Society
North of England Protestant Organization	1855–?	Regional society centred on Manchester

Note: This table represents an attempt to list all the formally constituted Protestant societies in the period which made any impact on the historical record. I have omitted a number of shadowy organizations which probably only had a purely nominal existence, societies formed solely for Irish purposes, and local branches of national societies. It is probable, however, that further research in local sources would yield information on other independent local and regional bodies.

All the major societies were still in existence in 1860. The majority of minor societies only survived for relatively short periods, but they were prone to become dormant without formally dissolving themselves. Documentation of the ending of a society is only available for the Parker Society and the English Church Missions to Roman Catholics, but only the Islington Protestant Institute was definitely still in existence in 1860.

For references, see the Bibliography and the relevant portions of the text.

BIBLIOGRAPHY

Place of publication is London unless otherwise stated.

I. PRIMARY SOURCES

Manuscript

(i) Records of Protestant Societies

Brief notes are given on the privately owned records of the societies: the author would be pleased to answer enquiries.

Evangelical Alliance: extensive minute-books from a range of committees, regional committees, and subcommittees survive at the Alliance's London headquarters for the period from 1845 but did not prove to be of much value for the present work.

National Club: (deposited in the Bodleian Library, Oxford), minutes for 1847–54; printed circulars.

Protestant Alliance: it was not possible to obtain access to any records.

Protestant Association: no records have been traced.

British (Protestant) Reformation Society: an unbroken sequence of minute-books covering the whole period examined in this book survives in the custody of the present secretary.

Scottish Reformation Society: the following records were consulted at the Society's Edinburgh headquarters: minutes from 1853; minutes of the Anti-Popery Committee of the Free Church, 1850–4; Branches Associations Book.

(ii) Other Collections

Bembridge Journal, Manchester Central Library.
Beresford Papers, Public Record Office of Northern Ireland, Belfast.
Bickersteth Papers, Bodleian Library, Oxford.
Blackburn Papers, Dr Williams Library, London.
Blackwood Papers, National Library of Scotland, Edinburgh.
Burgess Papers, Bodleian Library, Oxford.
Chalmers Papers, New College Library, Edinburgh.
Clarendon Papers, Bodleian Library, Oxford.
Colquhoun Papers, Comrie, Perthshire.

Croft Moody Papers, Southampton City Record Office.
Croker Papers, University of Illinois at Urbana-Champaign, Illinois.
Derby Papers, consulted at the Queen's College, Oxford, by kind permission of Lord Blake.
Disraeli Papers, Bodleian Library, Oxford.
Downshire Papers, Public Record Office of Northern Ireland, Belfast.
Edinburgh, Free Presbytery of, minutes, Scottish Record Office, Edinburgh.
Finch Papers (transcripts shown to me by Mr G. S. Finch; the originals were either lost or unavailable). Ayston Hall, Rutland.
Foreign Office Papers, FO 79 (Tuscany), Public Record Office, Kew.
Giffard Papers, Bodleian Library, Oxford.
Giffard Papers, British Library, London.
Gladstone Papers, British Library, London.
Graham Papers (microfilm copy of originals at Netherby, Cumbria), Bodleian Library, Oxford.
Harrowby Papers, Sandon Hall, Stafford.
Hill (John) Diary, Bodleian Library, Oxford.
Home Office Papers, HO 45, Public Record Office, Kew.
Hope (John) Papers, Scottish Record Office, Edinburgh.
Hylton Papers, Somerset County Record Office, Taunton.
Inglis Papers, Canterbury Cathedral Library.
Jesus, Society of, English Province, Scrap-books and Correspondence, Farm Street, London.
Kenyon Papers, Gredington, Clywd.
Liverpool Papers, British Library, London.
Londonderry Papers, Durham County Record Office, Durham.
MacGregor Papers, Greater London Record Office.
Manchester Papers, Cambridgeshire County Record Office, Huntingdon.
Minto Papers, National Library of Scotland, Edinburgh.
Newdegate Papers (diary of Maria Newdegate and papers of Charles Newdegate), Warwickshire County Record Office, Warwick.
Newcastle Papers (4th duke), Nottingham University Library.
Norfolk Papers (correspondence of 14th duke), Arundel Castle, Sussex.
Palmerston (Broadlands) Papers, Southampton University Library.
Peel Papers, British Library, London.
Perceval (Dudley) Papers, British Library, London.
Roden Papers (microfilm copy of originals in the care of the present Earl of Roden), Public Record Office of Northern Ireland, Belfast.
Russell Papers, PRO 30/22, Public Record Office, Kew.
Scotland, Church of, acts and papers of the General Assembly, Scottish Record Office, Edinburgh.
Shaftesbury (Broadlands) Papers, Southampton University Library.
Wellington Papers, Southampton University Library.
Winchilsea Papers, Northamptonshire Record Office, Northampton.
Wordsworth (Christopher) Papers, Lambeth Palace Library, London.

Bibliography

Parliamentary Debates and Papers

Hansard's Parliamentary Debates, 2nd series, xii–xxv.
Hansard's Parliamentary Debates, 3rd series, i–cxliv.
Journals of the House of Commons.
Journals of the House of Lords.
Parliamentary Papers: 1831–2, xvi (677), Report from the Select Committee on the Immediate Causes of the Disturbances in Ireland and on the Efficiency of the Laws for the Suppression of Outrages against the Public Peace; 1835, viii (547), Report from the Select Committee on Bribery at Elections; 1835, xv (377), Report of the Select Committee appointed to Inquire into the Nature, Extent and Tendency of the Orange Lodges, Associations or Societies in Ireland; 1835, xvii (605), Report from the Select Committee on Orange Institutions in Great Britain and the Colonies.
Reports of the Select Committee on Public Petitions

Serial Publications

Achill Missionary Herald
Annual Register
Baptist Magazine
Blackwood's Edinburgh Magazine
British Protestant
Bulwark
Catholic Magazine
Catholic Standard
Christian Lady's Magazine
Christian Observer
Christian Guardian
Church and State Gazette
Congregational Magazine
Dublin Review
Eclectic Review
Edinburgh Review
Evangelical Christendom
Go Forward: YWCA Monthly Journal for Secretaries and Workers
London and Westminster Review
Month
Morning Herald
Nonconformist
Penny Protestant Operative
Protestant Advocate
Protestant Elector

Protestant Journal
Protestant Magazine
Protestant Watchman
Protestant Witness
Standard
Tablet
The Times
Wesleyan Methodist Magazine
Western Times
Witness
Yorkshire Gazette

United States Publications

Downfall of Babylon
New York Observer
Priestcraft Exposed and Primitive Christianity Defended
Priestcraft Unmasked

Contemporary Autobiographies, Biographies, and Memoirs

Arnot, W., *Life of James Hamilton, DD* (1870).
Balfour, C. L., *A Sketch of Charlotte Elizabeth* (1854).
'C.B.' [Charlotte Bickersteth], *Dawn and Sunrise: Brief Notes of the Life and Early Death of Barbara Sophia Gordon* (1860), daughter of J. E. Gordon.
Bickersteth, M. C., *A Sketch of the Life and Episcopate of the Rt. Rev. Robert Bickersteth, DD* (1887).
Birks, T. R., *Memoir of the Rev. Edward Bickersteth*, 2 vols. (1851).
Bridges, J., *Memoir of Sir Andrew Agnew of Locknaw, Bt.* (Edinburgh, 1849).
Brown, A. N., *Recollections of the Conversation Parties of the Revd Charles Simeon, MA* (1863).
Chambers, T. W., *Memoir of the Life and Character of the Late Hon. Theo Freylinghusen, LLD* (New York, 1863).
Colquhoun, J. C., *William Wilberforce: His Friends and his Times* (1866).
——*Memorials of H. M. C.* (1870).
Corsbie, A. H., *Alexander Haldane: A Biographical Sketch* (1882).
Dalton, W., *A Brief Memoir of a Beloved Wife* (Wolverhampton, 1862).
Disraeli, B., *Lord George Bentinck: A Political Biography* (1852).
Eardley, C. E., *A Brief Notice of the Life of the Rev. Edward Bickersteth* (1850).
Gosse, E., *Father and Son* (1907; Penguin edn., 1979).
Hanna, W., *Memoirs of the Life and Writings of Thomas Chalmers, DD*, 4 vols. (Edinburgh, 1849–52).
Hodder, E., *John MacGregor ('Rob Roy')* (1894).

Hodder, E., *The Life and Work of the Seventh Earl of Shaftesbury KG*, 3 vols. (1887).

Husenbeth, F. C., *Sermon Preached at the Funeral of the Very Rev. Thomas Michael McDonnell* (1869).

James, H., and Howe, E., *Two Sermons Preached in the Parish Church of Nonington, Kent, January 17 1864* (1864), on J. P. Plumptre.

Jamie, D., *John Hope: Philanthropist and Reformer* (Edinburgh, 1900).

Kingsley, F., *Charles Kingsley: His Letters and Memories of his Life*, 2 vols. (1877).

Lewis, A., *George Maxwell Gordon: The Pilgrim Missionary of the Punjab* (1889), son of J. E. Gordon.

Life, Letters and Lectures of the late Dr Cahill: Biographical Sketch (Dublin, 1880).

Lucas, E., *The Life of Frederick Lucas, MP*, 2 vols. (1886).

Madden, H., *Memoir of the Late Right Rev. Robert Daly, DD, Lord Bishop of Cashel* (1875).

Magee, W. C., *Remains of Edward Tottenham BD* (1855).

Marsden, J. B., *Memoirs of the Life and Labours of the Rev. Hugh Stowell, MA* (1868).

Memoir of Charlotte Elizabeth (Bristol, 1852).

Monypenny, W. F., and Buckle, G. E., *The Life of Benjamin Disraeli, Earl of Beaconsfield*, 6 vols. (1910–20).

Oliphant, M. O. W., *The Life of Edward Irving*, 2 vols. (1862).

Overton, J. H., and Wordsworth, E., *Christopher Wordsworth, Bishop of Lincoln, 1867–1883* (1888).

Primmer, J. B. (ed.), *Life of Jacob Primmer, Minister of the Church of Scotland* (Edinburgh, 1916).

Smith, T., *Memoirs of James Begg, DD* (Edinburgh, 1885).

Stewart, A. M., *The Life and Letters of Elizabeth, Last Duchess of Gordon*, 3rd edn. (1865).

Charlotte Elizabeth [Tonna], *Personal Reminiscences*, 4th edn. (1854).

Second Duke of Wellington (ed.), *Despatches, Correspondence and Memoranda of Field Marshal Arthur Duke of Wellington*, 8 vols. (1867–80).

Wilson, W., *Memorials of Robert Smith Candlish, DD* (Edinburgh, 1880).

Other Contemporary Printed Primary Sources

Achilli v. Newman: A Full and Authentic Report of the Above Prosecution for Libel (1852).

American and Foreign Christian Union, *8th Annual Report* (New York, 1857).

American Protestant Society, *4th Annual Report* (New York, 1847).

American Republican Party, *Address to the People of the State of New York by the General Executive Committee of the American Republican Party of the City of New York* (New York, 1844).

Arundel and Surrey, Earl of, *A Few Remarks on the Social and Political Condition of English Catholics* (1847).

—— *A Letter to J. P. Plumptre, Esq., MP, on the Bull 'In Coena Domini'* (1848).

Arthur, C. M., *Authenticated Report of the Controversial Discussion between the Rev. John Cumming, AM and Daniel French, Esq.* (1841).

Astounding Revelations of Puseyism in Belgravia (1858).

Awful Disclosures of Miss Julia Gordon (1858).

Awful Exposure of the Atrocious Plot Formed . . . against the Clergy and Nuns of Lower Canada (New York, 1836).

[Berington, J.], *The State and Behaviour of English Catholics, from the Reformation to the Year 1780, with a View of their Present Number, Wealth, Character &c.* (1780).

[Biber, G. E.], *The Bull 'In Coena Domini'* (1848).

—— *A Letter to the Earl of Arundel and Surrey on the Bull 'In Coena Domini'* (1849).

Bickersteth, E., *The Testimony of the Reformers* (1836).

—— *The Divine Warning to the Church* (1842).

Bickersteth, R., *Romanism in Relation to the Second Coming of Christ* (1854).

Blakeney, R. P., *A Manual of Romish Controversy* (Edinburgh, 1851).

—— *Popery in its Social Aspect* (Edinburgh 1852).

—— *Protestant Catechism* (1853).

British and Foreign Anti-Slavery Society, *1st Annual Report* (1840).

Butler, T., *Letter . . . Containing Strictures on the Rev. J. Baylee's Challenge to Dr Butler* (Liverpool, 1841).

Cahill, D. W., *Letters Addressed to Several Members of the British Cabinet; and Speeches on Various Subjects Delivered in Several Towns and Cities in England, Ireland and Scotland* (Dublin, 1856).

—— and Kinsella, W., *Letter on the Subject of the New Reformation* (Carlow, 1827).

Catholic Institute of Great Britain, *Declaration of the Catholic Bishops, the Vicars Apostolic and their Coadjutors in Great Britain* (1838).

—— *Tracts* (1838–41).

—— *1st–5th Annual Reports* (1839–43), Newberry Library, Chicago.

—— *A Short Account of the Catholic Institute of Great Britain* (1839).

—— *Interim Report* (1843).

Cheever, G. B., *The Religion of Experience and that of Imitation* (New York, 1843).

Chillingworth, W., *The Religion of Protestants: A Sure Way to Salvation* (Oxford, 1838; London, 1846).

Christian Influence Society, *To the Electors of the United Kingdom of Great Britain and Ireland* (1847).

Church Protestant Defence Society, *Addresses* (1853–7).

Collins, W. W., *The Black Robe* (1881).

Colquhoun, J. C., *The Effects of Sir Robert Peel's Administration on the Political State and Prospects of England* (1847).

Conference on Christian Union Held at Liverpool on Wednesday the 1st of October 1845 and Subsequent Days (Liverpool, 1845).

Conference on Christian Union: Narrative of the Proceedings of the Meeting Held in Liverpool, October 1845 (1845).

Croly, G., *England the Fortress of Christianity* (1839).

Cumming, J., *Apocalyptic Sketches*, 9th edn. (1849).

Cursory Remarks on a Late Fanatical Publication Entitled a Full Detection of Popery etc. (1783).

Dalton, E., *No Peace with Rome* (1841).

Dens, P., *Theologia Moralis et Dogmatica*, 8 vols. (Dublin, 1832).

Essays on Christian Union (1845).

Evangelical Alliance, British Organization: *Report of the Proceedings of the Conference of British Members Held at Manchester, from Nov. 4th to the 9th inclusive 1846* (1847).

—— *Report of the Proceedings of the Conference at Freemasons' Hall, London from August 19th to September 2nd inclusive* (1847).

—— *5th Annual Conference* (1851).

—— *Report of a Meeting Convened by the Evangelical Alliance but Open to All Christians Holding the Doctrines of the Protestant Reformation, February 21 1851* (1851).

Extinguisher (The), 16 July 1852 (broadsheet in Stockport Public Library).

Extracts from Peter Dens on the Nature of Confession and the Obligation of the Seal (Dublin, 1836).

Everett, J., *Speech of the Rev. James Everett Delivered at the Adjourned Meeting of the York Operative Protestant Association in the Concert Room, York, on Tuesday, October 13th 1840* (York, 1840).

Faber, G. S., *Primitive Doctrine of Election* (1836).

Finch, G., *A Sketch of the Romish Controversy*, (1830).

Foxe, J., *The Acts and Monuments of John Foxe*, ed. S. R. Cattley, 8 vols. (1837–41).

—— *The Acts and Monuments of the Church*, ed. M. H. Seymour, 2 vols. (1838).

—— *A History of Protestant Martyrdom* (1839).

Full Report of the Proceedings of a Public Meeting Held at the Wesleyan Chapel, Hartlepool (Sunderland, 1840).

Furlason, W. F., *Report on the Trial and Preliminary Proceedings in the Case of the Queen on the Prosecution of G. Achilli v. Dr Newman* (1852).

Gibson, E., *A Preservative against Popery . . . Collected by the Rt. Rev. Edmund Gibson, DD*, ed. J. Cumming, 18 vols. (1848–9).

—— *Supplement to Gibson's Preservative from Popery*, ed. R. P. Blakeney, J. Cumming, and M. W. Foye, 8 vols. (1849–50).

Gordon, J. E., *British Protestantism: Its Present Position, Rights and Duties* (1847).

Harcourt, F. E. V., *The Protestant Missionary's Catechism* (1853).

Hardy, P. D., *Achilli v. Newman: An Action for Libel* (Dublin, 1852).

Horne, T. H., *A Protestant Memorial for the Commemoration of the Fourth Day of October 1835* (1835).

Hymns Composed for the Use of the Stockport Sunday School (Manchester, 1848).

Inglis, R. H., *Church Extension: Substance of a Speech Delivered in the House of Commons, 30 June 1840* (1840).

Islington Protestant Institute, *1st, 2nd, 12th Annual Report* (1847, 1848, 1858).

Irving, E., *Babylon and Infidelity Foredoomed of God* (Glasgow, 1826).

Larkin, C., *A Vindication of the Catholic Religion* (Newcastle upon Tyne, 1831).

Lectures on the Points in Controversy between Romanists and Protestants (1828).

Lee, J. H., *The Origin and Progress of the American Party in Politics* (Philadelphia, 1855).

A Letter to the Inhabitants of Derby, by a Catholic (Wirksworth, 1830).

Lincolnshire Archives Office, Election Squibs Collection, Hill 41/175.

Lord, J., *Foreign or Domestic Legislation? An Address to Electors* (1852).

M'Ghee, R. J., *Truth and Error Contrasted* (1830).

J. M.[acgregor], *Popery in 1900* (1852).

—— *The Madiai Case* (1853).

McHugh, J., *The Real Character of the Rev. Robert M'Ghee* (Dublin, 1836).

McNeile, H., *Anti-Slavery and Anti-Popery: A Letter Addressed to Edward Cropper, Esq. and Thomas Berry Horsfall, Esq*, 2nd edn. (1838).

—— *Jezebel: Speech of the Rev. Hugh McNeile at Market Drayton, Salop* (1839).

—— *Nationalism in Religion* (1839).

—— *The State in Danger: A Letter to the Rt. Hon. Lord John Russell, MP* (1846).

—— *The Famine, the Rod of God* (1847).

—— *Slave Labor versus Free Labor Sugar* (1848).

Mario, Mme., *The Papacy, the Corner Stone of Tyranny: The Substance of a Lecture Delivered by Madame Mario (Late Miss Jessie Merton White) in the Exchange Assembly Room Preston, June 28 1858* (1858).

Massie, J. W., *The Evangelical Alliance: Its Origins and Development, Containing Personal Notices of its Distinguished Friends in Europe and America* (1847).

Merle d'Aubigné, J. H., *History of the Reformation*, trans. W. K. Kelly (1842?).

Milner, J., *The End of Religious Controversy, in a Friendly Controversy between a Religious Society of Protestants and a Roman Catholic Divine* (1819 edn.).

Mr O'Connell's Political Tour to Manchester, Newcastle, Edinburgh and Other Towns in the North of England and Scotland (Cork, 1835).

Monk, M., *The Awful Disclosures of Maria Monk* (1836, 1851).

Morse, S. F. B., *Foreign Conspiracy against the Liberties of the United States* (New York, 1835).

Murch, J., *The Trial of Maynooth* (Bath, 1838).

National Club, *First General Statement* (1845).

—— *Suggestions for the Formation of Local Associations in Defence of our National Institutions* (1845).

—— *Addresses to the Protestants of the Empire Issued by the Committee of the National Club* (1846–52); the only set traced is in the Bodleian Library, Oxford.

—— *1st–15th Annual Reports* (1846–60); no copies of the *Annual Reports* for 1851–4 and for 1856 were traced.

—— *A Report of Speeches Delivered at a Meeting of the Members and Friends of the National Club held at Willis's Rooms on Saturday May 2 1846* (1846).

—— *Address of the National Club to the Subscribers to the Relief of Distress in Ireland and the Highlands of Scotland, 15 Jan. 1847* (1847).

—— *A Report of the Speeches Delivered at the Dinner of the Members and Friends of the National Club, May 12 1847* (1847).

—— *Alphabetical List of Members for the Year 1848* (1848).

—— *Report of Speeches Delivered at the Annual Meeting, May 9 1848* (1848).

Newcastle, 4th Duke of, *An Address to all Classes and Conditions of Englishmen* (1832).

—— *Thoughts in Times Past, Tested by Subsequent Events* (1837).

Newman, J. H., 'The Second Spring', in *Sermons Preached on Various Occasions* (1857), 171–2.

—— *Lectures on the Present Position of Catholics in England* (1892 edn.).

O'Connell, D., *A Full Account of the . . . Great Meeting of the Catholics of London* (1839).

—— *Letter to the Ministers and Office Bearers of the Wesleyan Methodist Societies in Manchester* (1839).

O'Sullivan, M., and M'Ghee, R. J., *Romanism as it Rules in Ireland* (1840).

Phillpotts, H., *Letters to Charles Butler, Esq. on the Theological Parts of his Book of the Roman Catholic Church* (1825).

Proceedings of the Native American State Convention (Newbury, Vermont, 1847).

Protestant Alliance, *1st, 2nd, 9th Annual Reports* (1852, 1853, 1860); a number of lithographed Protestant Alliance circulars survive in the Croft Moody Papers.

Protestant Association, *Publications*, 1 (no more published).

—— *Statement of Views and Objects.*

—— *Glasgow Protestant Association Tracts* (Glasgow, 1835–6).

—— *1st–3rd, 16th, 31st Annual Reports*, (1837–9, 1852, 1866).

—— *Address of the Protestant Association to the Electors of Great Britain* (Bath, 1841).

—— *Address of the Protestant Association to the Electors of Great Britain and Ireland: Duties of Protestant Electors, Questions to Candidates* (1846).

—— *Occasional Papers*, 9 (1869), 12 (1870).

Protestant Educational Institute, *Proposed Erection of a Protestant Educational Institute in London* (1869).

—— *Protestant Educational Classes in England: May Meeting and Distribution of Prizes in London 1869.*

—— *Transactions of the Protestant Educational Institute for the Year Ending 30th April 1872.*

——*Short Report of the Operations of the Protestant Educational Institute for the Year 1887* (1888).

Protestant or Orange Associations, by an English Protestant (Hereford, 1835).

Protestant Union, *Papers I–II* (1813–14).

Random Recollections of Exeter Hall in 1834–1837, by one of the Protestant party (1838).

Reformation Society, *Quarterly Extracts*.

——*1st–16th Annual Reports* (1828–44): The first *Annual Report* survives in significantly different versions, one in the Bodleian Library and the other in the British Library. Reports for 1837 and 1843–7 do not survive; those from 1848 onwards were published in the *British Protestant*.

——*Report of the Proceedings of the Auxiliary Reformation Society for St Giles* (1828).

——*Report of the Proceedings of the Aberdeen Auxiliary Reformation Society* (Aberdeen, 1831).

Report of the Proceedings of the Midland Catholic Association at their Annual Meeting (1826).

Report of the Proceedings of Three Public Meetings in the City of Cork (Dublin, 1825).

Report of a Public Discussion Held at Eastbrook Chapel in Bradford (Bradford, 1829).

Scotland, Church of, *Annual Report to the General Assembly by the Committee on Popery* (1859).

Scottish Reformation Society, *Annual Report* (1858).

——*General Election: Address of the Scottish Reformation Society to the Electors of Scotland* (Edinburgh, 1852).

Smyth, G. H., *Maynooth College: Justification of the Term 'Beastly', as Applied to the Instruction Authorized at Maynooth College*, 2nd edn. (Colchester, 1845).

The Sovereign's Accession Declaration (Protestant Reformation Society, 1910; broadsheet in British Library).

Stapleton, A. G., *Substance of the Speech of A. G. Stapleton, Esq. in the Anti-Corn Law League Hall at Manchester on the Occasion of the Meeting of the Protestant Association of that Town, 29 April 1847* (1847).

——*Suggestions for a Conservative and Popular Reform in the Commons House of Parliament* (1850).

The *Stockport Letter Bag*, 30 April 1852 (broadsheet in Stockport Public Library).

Stone, W. L., *Maria Monk and the Nunnery of the Hôtel Dieu* (New York, 1836).

Stowell, H., *A Letter to the Protestant Electors of Great Britain on their Duty at the Present Crisis*, 2nd edn. (Manchester, 1841).

——*To the Protestant Electors of Manchester* (Manchester, 1852).

Thelwall, A. S., *Proceedings of the Anti-Maynooth Conference* (1845).

[Todd, J. H.], *Sanctissimi Domini Nostra Gregorii Papae XVI Epistola ad Archiepiscopos et Episcopos Hiberniae . . . Translated from the Original Latin and now First Published* (1836).
[Tonna, C. E.], *The Rockite: An Irish Story* (1829).
Trevelyan, C. E., *The No Popery Agitation*, 4th edn. (1840).
Varley, H., *The King's Declaration in the Light of Rome's Recent History* (1910).
Whitney, T. R., *A Defence of the American Policy* (New York, 1856).
Willet, A., *Synopsis Papismi*, ed. J. Cumming (1852).
Wiseman, N., *Lectures on the Principal Doctrines and Practices of the Catholic Church* (1836).
[Wordsworth, C.], *Maynooth: The Crown and the Country* (1845).

Modern Editions of Sources

Burke, E., *Reflections on the Revolution in France*, ed. C. C. O'Brien (1969).
Dickens, C., *Barnaby Rudge: A Tale of the Riots of 'Eighty*, ed. K. Tillotson (1954).
Essays of George Eliot, ed. T. Pinney (1963).
G. P. Gooch (ed.), *The Later Correspondence of Lord John Russell, 1840–1878*, 2 vols. (1925).
The Prime Ministers' Papers: W. E. Gladstone, ii. *Autobiographical Memoranda 1832–1845*, ed. J. Brooke and M. Sorensen (1972).
The Greville Memoirs 1814–1860, 8 vols., ed. L. Strachey and R. Fulford (1938).
Jay, E. (ed.), *The Evangelical and Oxford Movements* (Cambridge, 1983).
Locke, J., *A Letter Concerning Toleration*, ed. C. L. Sherman (New York, 1979).
The Letters and Diaries of John Henry Newman, iv., ed. I. Ker and T. Gornall (1980).
R. Southey, *Letters from England*, ed. J. Simmonds (1984).
Wellington Political Correspondence, i (1975), ed. J. Brooke and J. Gandy; ii (1986), ed. R. J. Olney and J. Melvin.

II. SECONDARY SOURCES

Unpublished

Acheson, A. R., 'The Evangelicals in the Church of Ireland, 1784–1859', Ph.D. thesis (Belfast, 1967).
Adams, P. A., 'Converts to the Roman Catholic Church in England, c.1830–1870', B.Litt. thesis (Oxford, 1977).
Baker, W. J., 'The Attitudes of English Churchmen, 1800–1850, towards the Reformation', Ph.D. thesis (Cambridge, 1966).

Bentley, A., 'The Transformation of the Evangelical Party in the Later Nineteenth Century', Ph.D. thesis (Durham, 1971).

Bradfield, B. T., 'Sir Richard Vyvyan and Tory Politics', Ph.D. thesis (London, 1965).

Bradley, I. C., 'The Politics of Godliness: Evangelicals in Parliament 1784–1832', D.Phil. thesis (Oxford, 1974).

Cahill, G. A., 'Irish Catholicism and English Toryism', Ph.D. thesis (Iowa, 1954).

Champ. J., 'Assimilation and Separation: The Catholic Revival in Birmingham, *c.* 1650–1850', Ph.D. thesis (Birmingham, 1985).

Close, D. H., 'The General Elections of 1835 and 1837 in England and Wales', D.Phil. thesis (Oxford, 1966).

Ervine, W. J. C., 'Doctrine and Diplomacy: Some Aspects of the Life and Thought of the Anglican Evangelical Clergy, 1797–1837', Ph.D. thesis (Cambridge, 1979).

Haydon, C., 'Anti-Catholicism in Eighteenth-Century England *c.*1714–1780', D.Phil. thesis (Oxford, 1985).

Hardman, B. E., 'The Evangelical Party in the Church of England 1855–65', Ph.D. thesis (Cambridge, 1963).

Herring, G. W., 'Tractarianism to Ritualism: A Study of Some Aspects of Tractarianism outside Oxford from the Time of Newman's Conversion in 1845, until the First Ritual Commission in 1867', D.Phil. thesis (Oxford, 1984).

Hill, M., 'Evangelicalism and the Churches in Ulster Society, 1770–1850', Ph.D. thesis (Belfast, 1987).

Holland, V., 'Anti-Catholic Riot in Stockport 1852', unpublished paper (Stockport Public Library).

Lesourd, J. A., 'Les Catholiques dans la société anglaise, 1765–1865', Ph.D. thesis (Lille, 1973).

Lewis, D. M., 'The Evangelical Mission to the British Working Class', D.Phil. thesis (Oxford, 1981).

Lowe, W. J., 'Irish in Lancashire, 1846–71', Ph.D. thesis (Dublin, 1974).

Milne, J. M., 'The Politics of *Blackwood's*, 1817–1846', Ph.D. thesis (Newcastle upon Tyne, 1984).

Murray, N. U., 'The Influence of the French Revolution on the Church of England and its Rivals, 1789–1802', D.Phil. thesis (Oxford, 1975).

Nockles, P. B., 'Continuity and Change in Anglican High Churchmanship in Britain, 1792–1850', D.Phil. thesis (Oxford, 1982).

Orchard, S. C., 'English Evangelical Eschatology, 1790–1850', Ph.D. thesis (Cambridge, 1968).

Rennie, I. S., 'Evangelicalism and English Public Life', Ph.D. thesis (Toronto, 1962).

Simes, D. G. S., 'The Ultra Tories in British Politics, 1824–1834', D.Phil. thesis (Oxford, 1975).

Stanley, B., 'Home Support for Overseas Missions in Victorian England', Ph.D. thesis (Cambridge, 1979).

Walters, J. D., 'The Impact of Anglican Evangelicalism on the Religious Life of Wolverhampton and its Locality', M.Phil. thesis (CNAA, Wolverhampton Polytechnic, 1983).

Wardle, J. A., 'The Life and Times of the Rev. Dr Hugh M'Neile, DD, 1795–1875', MA thesis (Manchester, 1981).

Williams, J. C., 'Edinburgh Politics, 1832–1852', Ph.D. thesis (Edinburgh, 1972).

Willmer, H., 'Evangelicalism, 1785–1835', Hulsean prize essay (Cambridge, 1962).

Wolffe, J. R., 'Protestant Societies and Anti-Catholic Agitation in Great Britain, 1829–1860', D.Phil. thesis (Oxford, 1984).

Published

Anon., *Guide to the Monument, with an Account of the Great Fire of London of 1666 which it Commemorates* (1957).

Allport, G. W., *The Nature of Prejudice* (Reading, Mass., 1954).

Altholz, J. L., 'The Political Behaviour of English Catholics, 1850–1867', *Journal of British Studies*, 4 (1964), 89–103.

—— 'The Mind of Victorian Orthodoxy: Anglican Responses to *Essays and Reviews*, 1860–1864', *Church History*, 57 (1982), 186–97.

—— 'Alexander Haldane, the *Record* and Religious Journalism', *Victorian Periodicals Review*, 20 (1987), 23–31.

Anderson, B., *Imagined Communities* (1983).

Anderson, O., 'The Reactions of Church and Dissent towards the Crimean War', *Journal of Ecclesiastical History*, 16 (1965), 209–20.

Arnstein, W. L., *Protestant versus Catholic in Mid-Victorian England* (Columbia, Mo., 1982).

—— 'Queen Victoria and Religion', in G. Malmgreen (ed.), *Religion in the Lives of English Women, 1760–1830* (1986), 88–128.

Balleine, G. R., *A History of the Evangelical Party in the Church of England* (1908).

Bebbington, D. W., 'The Life of Baptist Noel', *Baptist Quarterly*, 24 (1972), 390–401.

—— *The Nonconformist Conscience* (1982).

—— 'Religion and National Identity in Nineteenth-Century Wales and Scotland', in S. Mews (ed.), *Religion and National Identity* (Studies in Church History, 18; 1982), 489–503.

—— *Evangelicalism in Modern Britain: A History from the 1730s to the 1980s* (1989).

Beckett, J. C., *The Making of Modern Ireland 1603–1923* (1966).

Bell, P. M. H., *Disestablishment in Ireland and Wales* (1969).

Bellenger, D., 'The Émigré Clergy and the English Church, 1789–1815', *Journal of Ecclesiastical History*, 34 (1983), 392–410.

Bentley, J., *Ritualism and Politics in Victorian Britain* (Oxford, 1978).

Bentley, M., and Stevenson, J., *High and Low Politics in Modern Britain* (Oxford, 1983).

Best, G. F. A., 'The Protestant Constitution and its Supporters, 1800–29', *Transactions of the Royal Historical Society*, 5th series, 8 (1958), 105–27.

—— *Shaftesbury* (1964).

—— 'Popular Protestantism in Victorian Britain', in R. Robson (ed.), *Ideas and Institutions of Victorian Britain* (1967), 115–42.

—— 'Evangelicalism and the Victorians', in A. Symondson (ed.), *The Victorian Crisis of Faith* (1970).

Billington, R. A., *The Protestant Crusade* (New York, 1938).

Blackey, R., 'A War of Words: The Significance of the Propaganda Conflict between English Catholics and Protestants, 1715–1745', *Catholic Historical Review*, 58 (1972–3), 535–55.

Blake, R., *Disraeli* (1966).

Booth, A., 'Popular Loyalism and Public Violence in the North-West of England, 1790–1800', *Social History*, 8 (1983), 295–313.

Bossy, J., *The English Catholic Community 1570–1850* (1975).

Bowen, D., *The Idea of the Victorian Church* (1968).

—— 'Alexander R. C. Dallas: The Warrior Saint', in P. T. Phillips (ed.), *The View from the Pulpit* (Toronto, 1978), 17–44.

—— *The Protestant Crusade in Ireland* (Dublin, 1978).

Bradfield, B. T., 'Sir Richard Vyvyan and the Country Gentlemen', *English Historical Review*, 83 (1968), 729–43.

Bradley, I., *The Call to Seriousness: The Evangelical Impact on the Victorians* (1976).

Brent, R., *Liberal Anglican Politics* (Oxford, 1987).

Breuilly, J., *Nationalism and the State* (Manchester, 1982).

Briggs, A., *William Cobbett* (Oxford, 1967).

Brock, M. G., *The Great Reform Act* (1973).

Brown, S. J., *Thomas Chalmers* (Oxford, 1982).

Bruce, S., *No Pope of Rome: Militant Protestantism in Modern Scotland* (Edinburgh, 1985).

Butler, P. A., *Gladstone, Church, State and Tractarianism* (Oxford, 1982).

Cahill, G. A., 'Irish Catholicism and English Toryism', *Review of Politics*, 19 (1956), 62–76.

—— 'The Protestant Association and the Anti-Maynooth Agitation of 1845', *Catholic Historical Review*, 43 (1957), 273–308.

Cameron, C. G., *The Scots Kirk in London* (Oxford, 1979).

Campbell, A. B., *The Lanarkshire Miners* (Edinburgh, 1979).

Carwardine, R., 'The Know-Nothing Party, the Protestant Evangelical Community and American National Identity', in S. Mews (ed.), *Religion and National Identity* (Studies in Church History, 18; 1982), 449–63.

Casteras, S. P., 'Virgin Vows: The Early Victorian Artists' Portrayal of Nuns and Novices', *Victorian Studies*, 24 (1981–2), 157–84.

Chadwick, O., *The Victorian Church*, 2 vols. (1966–70).

Champ, J., 'Priesthood and Politics in the Nineteenth Century: The Turbulent Career of Thomas McDonnell', *Recusant History*, 18 (1987), 289–303.

Checkland, O., *Philanthropy in Victorian Scotland* (Edinburgh, 1980).

Clark, J. C. D., *English Society 1688–1832* (Cambridge, 1985).

Clifton, R., 'The Popular Fear of Catholics during the English Revolution', *Past and Present*, 52 (1971), 23–55.

Cole, G. D. H., *The Life of William Cobbett* (1924).

Colley, L., 'Radical Patriotism in Eighteenth-Century England', in R. Samuel (ed.), *Patriotism: The Making and Unmaking of British National Identity*, i. *History and Politics* (1989), 169–87.

Connolly, G., 'The Transubstantiation of Myth: Towards a New Popular History of Roman Catholicism in England', *Journal of Ecclesiastical History*, 30 (1984), 78–104.

Connolly, S. J., *Priests and People in Pre-Famine Ireland* (Dublin, 1982).

—— *Religion and Society in Nineteenth-Century Ireland* (Dundalk, 1985).

Cornford, J. P., 'The Transformation of Conservatism in the Late Nineteenth Century', *Victorian Studies*, 7 (1963–4), 35–66.

Cowie, C. W., 'Exeter Hall', *History Today*, 18 (1968), 390–7.

Craig, G. R., *Germany 1866–1945* (Oxford, 1978).

Cunningham, H., 'The Language of Patriotism'. *History Workshop Journal*, 12 (1981), 8–33.

Curtis, L. P., *Anglo-Saxons and Celts* (Bridgeport, 1968).

Davidoff, L., and Hall, C., *Family Fortunes: Men and Women of the English Middle Class 1780–1850* (1987).

Davies, E. T., *Religion in the Industrial Revolution in South Wales* (Cardiff, 1965).

Davies, G. C. B., *Henry Phillpotts, Bishop of Exeter, 1778–1869* (1954).

Davies, K. M., 'Continuity and Change in Literary Advice on Marriage', in R. B. Outhwaite (ed.), *Marriage and Society: Studies in the Social History of Marriage* (1981), 58–80.

Davis, D. B., 'Some Themes of Counter Subversion', *Missisippi Valley Historical Review*, 47 (1966), 205–24.

Davis, R. W., 'Toryism to Tamworth: The Triumph of Reform, 1827–1835', *Albion*, 12 (1980), 132–46.

Donnelly, J. S., 'Pastorini and Captain Rock: Millenarianism and Sectarianism in the Rockite Movement of 1821–4', in S. Clark and J. S. Donnelly (eds.),

Irish Peasants, Violence and Political Unrest 1780–1914 (Manchester, 1983), 102–39.

Donovan, R. K., 'Voices of Distrust: The Expression of Anti-Catholic Feeling in Scotland, 1778–1781', *Innes Review*, 30 (1979), 62–75.

Droz, J., *Europe between Revolutions* (1967).

Drummond, A. L., *Edward Irving and his Circle* (1937).

—— and Bulloch, J., *The Church in Victorian Scotland, 1843–1874* (Edinburgh, 1975).

Eccleshall, R., *British Liberalism* (New York, 1986).

Ellsworth, L. E., *Charles Lowder and the Ritualist Movement* (1982).

Evans, E. L., *The German Center Party 1870–1933* (Carbondale, 1981).

Feldberg, M., *The Philadelphia Riots of 1844* (Westport, 1975).

Feuchtwanger, E. J., *Disraeli, Democracy and the Tory Party* (Oxford, 1968).

Finlayson, G. B. A. M., *The Seventh Earl of Shaftesbury 1801–1885* (1981).

Fischer, F., 'Der deutsche Protestantismus und die Politik im 19. Jahrhundert', *Historische Zeitschrift*, 171 (1951), 473–518.

Fisher, D. R., 'Peel and the Conservative Party: The Sugar Crisis of 1844 Re-examined', *Historical Journal*, 18 (1975), 279–302.

Forbes, D., *The Liberal Anglican Idea of History* (Cambridge, 1952).

Formisano, R. P., *The Transformation of Political Culture: Massachusetts Parties 1790s–1840s* (New York, 1983).

Foskett, R., 'The Drummond Controversy, 1842', *Records of the Scottish Church History Society*, 16 (1968), 99–109.

Furley, O. W., 'The Pope-Burning Processions of the Late-Seventeenth Century', *History*, 45 (1959), 16–23.

Gallagher, T., *Edinburgh Divided: John Cormack and No Popery in the 1930s* (Edinburgh, 1987).

—— *Glasgow, the Uneasy Peace: Religious Tension in Modern Scotland* (Manchester, 1987).

Gash, N., *Mr Secretary Peel* (1961).

—— *Reaction and Reconstruction in English Politics, 1832–1852* (Oxford, 1966).

—— *Sir Robert Peel* (1972).

Gienapp, W. L., *The Origins of the Republican Party 1852–1856* (New York, 1987).

Gilbert, A. D., *Religion and Society in Industrial England: Church, Chapel and Social Change* (1976).

Gill, J. C., *Parson Bull of Byerley* (1963).

Gilley, S., 'Protestant London, No-Popery and the Irish Poor, 1830–1860', *Recusant History*, 10 (1970), 210–21; 11 (1971), 21–38.

—— 'The Garibaldi Riots of 1862', *Historical Journal*, 16 (1973), 698–732.

—— 'English Attitudes to the Irish in England, 1780–1900', in C. Holmes and K. Lunn (eds.), *Hosts, Immigrants and Minorities* (1980).

—— 'Nationality and Liberty, Protestant and Catholic: Robert Southey's *Book of the Church*, in S. Mews (ed.), *Religion and National Identity* (Studies in Church History, 18; 1982), 409–32.

—— 'Newman and Prophecy, Evangelical and Catholic', *Journal of the United Reformed Church History Society*, 3 (1985), 160–88.

Golby, J., 'A Great Electioneer and his Motives: The Fourth Duke of Newcastle', *Historical Journal*, 8 (1965), 210–18.

Goodway, D., *London Chartism 1838–1848* (Cambridge, 1982).

Gray, D., *Spencer Perceval: The Evangelical Prime Minister 1762–1812* (Manchester, 1963).

Gray, R. Q., *The Labour Aristocracy in Victorian Edinburgh* (Oxford, 1976).

Gywnn, D., *Cardinal Wiseman* (Dublin, 1950).

Hall, B., 'Alessandro Gavazzi: A Barnebite Friar and the Risorgimento', in D. Baker (ed.), *Church, Society and Politics* (Studies in Church History, 12; 1975), 303–56.

Haller, W., *Foxe's Book of Martyrs and the Elect Nation* (1963).

Handley, J. E., *The Irish in Modern Scotland* (Cork, 1947).

Hanham, H. J., 'Mid-Century Scottish Nationalism: Romantic and Radical', in R. Robson (ed.), *Ideas and Institutions of Victorian Britain* (1967), 143–79.

Harris, R., *Prejudice and Tolerance in Ulster* (Manchester, 1972).

Harrison, J. F. C., *The Second Coming: Popular Millenarianism 1780–1850* (1979).

Hastings, A., *A History of English Christianity 1920–1985* (1986).

Hempton, D. N., 'Evangelicalism and Eschatology', *Journal of Ecclesiastical History*, 31 (1980), 179–94.

—— 'The Methodist Crusade in Ireland, 1795–1845', *Irish Historical Studies*, 22 (1980–1), 33–48.

—— 'Bickersteth, Bishop of Ripon: The Episcopate of a Mid-Victorian Evangelical', *Northern History*, 17 (1981), 183–202.

—— *Methodism and Politics in British Society 1750–1850* (1984).

—— 'Methodism in Irish Society, 1770–1830', *Transactions of the Royal Historical Society*, 5th series, 36 (1986), 117–42.

Hennell, M., *Sons of the Prophets: Evangelical Leaders of the Victorian Church* (1979).

Hertz, F., *The German Public Mind in the Nineteenth Century* (1975).

Hexter, J. H., 'The Protestant Revival and the Catholic Question in England, 1778–1829', *Journal of Modern History*, 8 (1936), 297–319.

Hickey, J., *Urban Catholics* (1967).

Higham, J., 'Another Look at Nativism', *Catholic Historical Review*, 44 (1958), 147–58.

—— *Strangers in the Land* (New Brunswick, 1958).

Hill, M., *The Religious Order* (1973).

Hilton, B., 'Peel: A Reappraisal', *Historical Journal*, 22 (1979), 585–614.

—— 'The Role of Providence in Evangelical Social Thought', in D. Beales and G. F. A. Best (eds.), *History, Society and the Churches* (Cambridge, 1985), 215–33.

—— *The Age of Atonement* (Oxford, 1988).

Holmes, F., *Henry Cooke* (Belfast, 1981).

Holmes, J. D., *More Roman than Rome: English Catholicism in the Nineteenth Century* (1978).

Hoppen, K. T., *Elections, Politics and Society in Ireland, 1832–1885* (Oxford, 1984).

Howe, D. W., *The Political Culture of the American Whigs* (Chicago, 1979).

Howse, E. M., *Saints in Politics* (1953).

Hurwitz, E. F., *Politics and the Public Conscience* (1973).

Hutchison, I. G. C., *A Political History of Scotland 1832–1924* (Edinburgh, 1986).

Jackson, J. A., *The Irish in Britain* (1963).

Jay, E., *The Religion of the Heart* (Oxford, 1979).

Johnson, C., *Developments in the Roman Catholic Church in Scotland 1789–1829* (Edinburgh, 1983).

Jordan, P. D., *The Evangelical Alliance for the United States of America 1847–1900* (New York, 1983).

Joyce, P., *Work, Society and Politics* (1980).

Kent, J., *The Unacceptable Face: The Modern Church in the Eyes of the Historian* (1987).

Kenyon, J. P., *The Popish Plot* (1972).

Kerr, D. A., *Peel, Priests and Politics* (Oxford, 1982).

—— 'England, Ireland and Rome, 1847–1848', W. J. Sheils and D. Wood (eds.), *The Churches, Ireland and the Irish* (Studies in Church History, 25; 1989), 259–77.

Kessler, J. B. A., *A Study of the Evangelical Alliance in Great Britain* (Goes, Netherlands, 1968).

Knox, R. B., 'Dr John Cumming and Crown Court Church, London', *Records of the Scottish Church History Society*, 22 (1984), 57–84.

Lees, L. H., *Exiles of Erin: Irish Migrants in Victorian London* (Manchester, 1979).

Lesourd, J. A., *Sociologie du catholicisme anglais 1767–1851* (Nancy, 1981).

Lewis, D. M., *Lighten Their Darkness; The Evangelical Mission to Working Class London 1828–1860* (Westport, Conn., 1986).

Loughlin, J., *Gladstone, Home Rule and the Ulster Question* (Dublin, 1986).

McCord, N., *The Anti-Corn Law League 1838–1846* (1958).

Machin, G. I. T., *The Catholic Question in English Politics 1820 to 1830* (Oxford, 1964).

—— *Politics and the Churches in Great Britain, 1832–1868* (Oxford 1977).

—— 'The Liberal Government and the Eucharistic Procession of 1908', *Journal of Ecclesiastical History*, 34 (1983), 559–83.

Machin, G. I. T., *Politics and the Churches in Great Britain, 1869–1921* (Oxford, 1987).

McIntire, C. T., *England against the Papacy 1858–1861* (Cambridge, 1983).

McRoberts, D. (ed.), *Modern Scottish Catholicism 1878–1978* (Glasgow, 1979).

Maison, M. M., *Search your Soul, Eustace: A Survey of the Religious Novel in the Victorian Age* (1961).

Marcus, S., *The Other Victorians* (1966).

Martin, R. H., *Evangelicals United: Ecumenical Stirrings in Pre-Victorian Britain, 1795–1830* (Metuchen, NJ, 1983).

Martineau, J., *The Life of Henry Pelham, Fifth Duke of Newcastle* (1908).

Matthew, H. C. G., *Gladstone 1809–1874* (Oxford, 1986).

Moberg, D. O., *The Church as a Social Institution* (Englewood Cliffs, 1962).

Morgan, G., 'The Guildford Guy Riots (1842–1865)', *Surrey Archaeological Collections*, 76 (1985), 61–8.

Moore, D. C., 'The Other Face of Reform', *Victorian Studies*, 5 (1961), 7–34.

Moule, H. C. G., *Charles Simeon* (1965 edn.).

Muirhead, I. A., 'Catholic Emancipation: Scottish Reactions in 1829'. *Innes Review*, 24 (1973), 26–42.

—— 'Catholic Emancipation in Scotland: The Debate and the Aftermath', *Innes Review*, 24 (1973), 103–20.

Munsell, F. D., *The Unfortunate Duke: Henry Pelham, Fifth Duke of Newcastle 1811–1864* (1985).

Murphy, J., *The Religious Problem in English Education* (Liverpool, 1959).

Neal, F., *Sectarian Violence: The Liverpool Experience, 1819–1914* (Manchester, 1988).

Newbould, I. D. C., 'Sir Robert Peel and the Conservative Party 1832–1841: A Study in Failure', *English Historical Review*, 98 (1983), 529–51.

Newsome, D., *The Parting of Friends* (1966).

Nikol, J., 'The Oxford Movement in Decline: Lord John Russell and the Tractarians, 1846–52,' *Historical Magazine of the Protestant Episcopal Church*, 43 (1974), 341–57.

Norman, E. R., *Anti-Catholicism in Victorian England* (1968).

—— *The English Catholic Church in the Nineteenth Century* (Oxford, 1984).

—— *Roman Catholicism in England* (Oxford, 1985).

O'Donaghue, P., 'Causes of the Opposition to Tithes, 1830–8', *Studia Hibernica*, 5 (1965), 7–29.

—— 'Opposition to Tithe Payment in 1830–1', *Studia Hibernica*, 6 (1966), 69–99.

O'Ferrall, F., *Catholic Emancipation: Daniel O'Connell and the Birth of Irish Democracy* (Dublin, 1985).

Oliver, W. H., *Prophets and Millennialists* (Auckland, 1978).

Parsons, G., and Moore, J. (eds.), *Religion in Victorian Britain*, 4 vols. (Manchester, 1988).

Paz, D. G. 'Popular Anti-Catholicism in England, 1850–1', *Albion*, 11 (1979), 331–55.

Phillips, P. T., *The Sectarian Spirit: Sectarianism, Society and Politics in Victorian Cotton Towns* (Toronto, 1982).

Porter, R., and Teich, M. (eds.), *The Enlightenment in National Context* (Cambridge, 1981).

Prest, J., *Lord John Russell* (1972).

Pugh, M., *The Tories and the People 1880–1935* (Oxford, 1985).

Ralls, W., 'The Papal Aggression of 1850: A Study in Victorian Anti-Catholicism', *Church History*, 43 (1974), 242–56.

Reynolds, J. S., *The Evangelicals at Oxford 1735–1871* (Oxford, 1953).

Robbins, K., 'Religion and Identity in Modern British History', in S. Mews (ed.), *Religion and National Identity* (Studies in Church History, 18; 1982), 465–88.

——*Nineteenth-Century Britain: Integration and Diversity* (Oxford, 1988).

Rosman, D., *Evangelicals and Culture* (1984).

Rossi, J. P., 'Home Rule and the Liverpool By-Election of 1880', *Irish Historical Studies*, 19 (1974–5), 156–8.

Rudé, G. F. E., 'The Gordon Riots: A Study of the Rioters and their Victims', *Transactions of the Royal Historical Society*, 5th series, 6 (1956), 93–113.

Samuel, D. N., *The Reformation and the Church of England Today* (Grimsby, 1973).

Sandeen, E. R., *The Roots of Fundamentalism* (Chicago, 1970).

Senior, H., *Orangeism in Ireland and Britain 1795–1836* (1966).

Shaw, P. E., *The Catholic Apostolic Church* (New York, 1946).

Sher, R. B., *Church and University in the Scottish Enlightenment* (Edinburgh, 1985).

[Sibbett, S. M.], *Orangeism in Ireland and throughout the Empire*, 2 vols. (1929).

Smyth, C., 'The Evangelical Movement in Perspective', *Cambridge Historical Journal*, 7 (1943), 160–74.

Stengers, J., 'Les Pratiques anti-conceptionelles dans le mariage au XIXe et au XXe siècle: Problèmes humains et attitudes religeuses'. *Revue belge de philologie et d'histoire*, 49 (1971), 403–81.

Stevenson, J., *Popular Disturbances in England 1700–1870* (1979).

Stewart, R., *The Politics of Protection* (Cambridge, 1971).

——*The Foundation of the Conservative Party 1830–1867* (1978)

Storch, R. D., 'Please to Remember the Fifth of November', in R. D. Storch (ed.), *Popular Culture and Custom in Nineteenth-Century Britain* (1982), 71–99.

Stunt, T., 'John Henry Newman and the Evangelicals', *Journal of Ecclesiastical History*, 21 (1970), 65–74.

——'Geneva and British Evangelicals in the Early Nineteenth Century', *Journal of Ecclesiastical History*, 32 (1981), 35–46.

Strachan, C. G., *The Pentecostal Theology of Edward Irving* (1973).

Swift, R., 'Guy Fawkes Celebrations in Victorian Exeter', *History Today*, 31 (1981), 5–9.

—— and Gilley, S. (eds.), *The Irish in the Victorian City* (1985).

Thompson, D., *The Chartists* (1984).

Thompson, F. M. L., 'Whigs and Liberals in the West Riding, 1830–1860', *English Historical Review*, 74 (1959), 214–39.

—— 'English Landed Society in the Nineteenth Century', in P. Thane, G. Crossick, and R. Floud (eds.), *The Power of the Past: Essays for Eric Hobsbawm* (Cambridge, 1984), 195–214.

Toon, P., *Evangelical Theology 1833–1856* (1979).

Trudgill, E., *Madonnas and Magdalens: The Origins and Development of Victorian Sexual Attitudes* (1976).

Tuveson, R. L., *Redeemer Nation* (Chicago, 1968).

Usherwood, S., 'No Popery under Queen Victoria', *History Today*, 23 (1973), 274–9.

Waller, P. J., *Democracy and Sectarianism: A Political and Social History of Liverpool 1868–1939* (Liverpool, 1981).

Wallis, F., 'The Revival of the Anti-Maynooth Campaign in Britain', *Albion*, 19 (1987), 527–48.

Walsh, J. D., 'Joseph Milner's Evangelical Church History', *Journal of Ecclesiastical History*, 10 (1959), 174–87.

Ward, B., *The Eve of Catholic Emancipation*, 3 vols. (1912).

—— *The Sequel to Catholic Emancipation*, 2 vols. (1915).

Ward, W. R., *The Life and Times of Cardinal Wiseman* (1897).

Wehler, H-U., *The German Empire, 1871–1918* (Leamington Spa, 1985).

Whyte, J. H., *The Independent Irish Party, 1850–9* (Oxford, 1958).

—— *Catholics in Western Democracies: A Study in Political Behaviour* (Dublin, 1981).

Wiener, C. Z., 'The Beleaguered Isle: A Study of Elizabethan and Early Jacobean Anticatholicism', *Past and Present*, 51 (1971), 27–62.

Williams, D., *A History of Modern Wales* (1950).

Wolffe, J. R., 'Bishop Henry Phillpotts and the Administration of the Diocese of Exeter, 1830–1869', *Transactions of the Devonshire Association*, 114 (1982), 99-113.

—— 'The Evangelical Alliance in the 1840s', in W. J. Sheils and D. Wood (eds.), *Voluntary Religion* (Studies in Church History, 23; 1986), 333–46.

—— 'Evangelicalism in Mid-Nineteenth-Century England', in R. Samuel (ed.), *Patriotism: The Making and Unmaking of British National Identity*, i. *History and Politics* (1989), 169–87.

Wooden, W. W., *John Foxe* (Boston, Mass., 1983).

Woodham-Smith, C. B., *Florence Nightingale, 1820–1910* (1950).

Yates, N., *The Oxford Movement and Parish Life: St Saviour's, Leeds, 1839–1929* (Borthwick Papers, 48; York, 1975).

Yeo, E., 'Christianity in Chartist Struggle, 1838–1842', *Past and Present*, 91 (1981), 109–39.

Reference

Anon., *New Edinburgh Almanac* (Edinburgh, 1845)

Addison, W. L., *A Roll of Graduates of the University of Glasgow* (Glasgow, 1898).

Altholz, J. L., *Victorian England 1837–1901* (Cambridge, 1970), bibliographical handbook.

Boase, F., *Modern English Biography: Containing Many Thousand Concise Memoirs of Persons who have Died since the Year 1850*, 6 vols. (Truro, 1892–1921).

Brown, L. M., and Christie, I. R., *Bibliography of British History 1789–1851* (Oxford, 1977).

Burke, J., *et al.*, *A Genealogical and Heraldic Dictionary of the Peerage and Baronetage of the British Empire*, various edns. (1826–).

——*A Genealogical and Heraldic Dictionary of the Landed Gentry of Great Britain and Ireland*, various edns. (1833–).

Burtchaell, G. D., and Sadleir, T. U., *Alumni Dublinenes: A Register of Students, Graduates, Professors and Provosts of Trinity College, in the University of Dublin* (Dublin, 1924).

Carter, C. S., and Weeks, G. E. A., *The Protestant Dictionary*, new edn. (1933).

Craig, F. W. S., *British Parliamentary Election Results 1832–1885* (1977).

Cross, F. L. (ed.), *Oxford Dictionary of the Christian Church* (Oxford, 1957).

Dod, C. R. P., *The Parliamentary Companion* (1832–60).

Foster, J., *Alumni Oxonienses: The Members of the University of Oxford, 1715–1886*, 4 vols. (1887–8).

Gillow, J., *A Literary and Biographical History of the English Catholics, from the Breach with Rome in 1534 to the Present Time*, 5 vols. (1885–1903).

Hanham, H. J., *Bibliography of British History, 1815–1914* (Oxford, 1976).

O'Byrne, W. R., *A Naval Biographical Dictionary* (1849).

Powicke, F. M., and Fryde, F. B. (eds.), *Handbook of British Chronology* (1961).

Royal Commission on Historical Manuscripts, *Papers of British Cabinet Ministers 1782–1900* (1982).

——*Papers of British Churchmen 1780–1940* (1987).

Scott, H., *Fasti Ecclesiae Scoticanae: The Succession of Ministers in the Church of Scotland from the Reformation*, 8 vols. (Edinburgh, 1914–50).

Stephens, L., and Lee, S., *The Dictionary of National Biography*, 65 vols. (1885–1900); *Supplement*, 3 vols. (1901).

Stenton, M., *Who's Who of British Members of Parliament, 1832–1885* (1976).

Venn, J., and J. A., *Alumni Cantabrigienses: A Biographical List of All Known Students, Graduates and Holders of Office at the University of Cambridge from the Earliest Times to 1900*, ii. *1752–1900*, 6 vols. (1951).

INDEX

Langdale, Charles 168
Langley, Daniel Baxter 225–6
Lansdowne, Henry Petty-Fitzmaurice,
    third Marquis of 233
Latchford 153
Latimer, Thomas 58
Latin 174, 182, 183
Laud, William, Archbishop of
    Canterbury 112
Launceston 50, 51, 153
Law, George Henry, Bishop of Bath and
    Wells 81
Lawyers, involvement of in anti-
    Catholicism 131 n., 138, 149, 299
Leamington 153
Leeds 153
    St Saviour's Church 286
Lefroy, Thomas 71
Leicester 51, 60, 81, 151, 153
Leinster 18, 19
Leith 161, 279
    Anti-Popery Class in 178, 182
Letter Concerning Toleration 11
Lewes 286
Lewis, Sir George Cornewall 287
Liberal Party 7, 284, 297, 298
Liberalism 7, 63, 69, 70, 215, 229, 302,
    304, 316
Liberals 226, 227, 252, 269, 277, 283
Liberation Society 292
Liberty, concepts of 107, 282–3, 314
    civil 58, 120, 143, 258
    political 120, 121, 127–31, 174
    physical 126, 267, 268–9
    religious 21, 46, 58, 68, 120, 127, 136,
        251, 254, 258, 267
Libraries, Protestant literature 157–8,
    161
Lichfield House compact 85
Lichfield, Bishop of, *see* Ryder
Liddell, Robert 286
Limerick, Bishop of, *see* Jebb
Lincoln 101 n., 224
Lincoln, Earl of (later fifth Duke of
    Newcastle) 90, 223, 228 n., 266
Lincolnshire 213, 278
Littlemore 3
Liverpool 101 n., 166, 181, 183, 299–
    300, 307, 308
    educational dispute at 98–9, 102
    elections in 25, 104, 192, 223–4, 264,
        265, 295
    Protestant meetings in 52, 53, 81, 84,
        90–1, 92, 140, 142, 184

Protestant missions in 187, 191
Protestant Operative Association
    in 171–2, 175
Protestant societies in 51, 150, 151,
    152, 153, 154, 157
sectarian violence in 192, 195–6
see also Toxteth, Wavertree
Liverpool, Robert Banks Jenkinson,
    second Earl of 23, 33, 67
Lock, George 265
Locke King, motion on franchise
    (1851) 260
Locke, John 11
London 2, 13, 152, 168, 177, 269, 279,
    305, 311
    anti-ritualism in 286–7
    Bishop of, *see* Tait
    Irish presence in 2, 13, 16, 18, 19, 191
    missions to RCs in 180, 187, 188, 190,
        191
    Orangeism in 27
    Protestant meetings in 57, 137, 140;
        see also Exeter Hall; Freemasons
        Hall; and *specific organizations*
    Protestant Operative societies in 171,
        172, 173, 174, 175
    Protestant societies in 52, 150, 151,
        153
    sectarian violence in 13, 195
    see also specific districts
London and Westminster Review 93
London, City of 151, 225, 232
London City Mission 180
London Committee for the Defence of
    the Protestant Faith 250, 252, 259,
    261, 284, 319
London Council of United Protestant
    Societies 306
London District, RC 1
London, Great Fire of 9
London Hibernian Society 33, 36
London, St George in the East 287
Londonderry 39
Londonderry, Charles Stewart, third
    Marquis of 73
Londonderry, Frances Anne,
    Marchioness of 243 n.
Long Acre Episcopal Chapel 42, 51
Lopez, Sir Ralph 228
Lord, James 149, 159, 201, 210, 214,
    222, 229, 251, 255, 276, 281
Lorton, Robert King, first Viscount 73,
    102, 212
Loughborough 151, 153

Roman Catholics (*Cont.*)
meetings 38–9, 41, 89–90, 97, 184
changing nature of community 17–19,
21, 27, 116, 147–8, 288
community identity of 188, 191
condition in eighteenth century 10–17,
21
conversions to Protestantism 39, 42,
122, 166, 171, 181–2, 186, 188,
189–90, 191
discussions with, in Britain 42, 46–8,
52–4, 60, 109, 110, 148, 156, 169,
178, 184–5, 186, 189, 290–1, 303
distinguished from Roman
Catholicism 115, 139
distribution 16–18, 146, 154
and education 168, 190, 231, 232
legal position of 10, 23, 230, 244
numbers 16–18, 290
perceptions of Protestantism 52–3, 54,
167–8, 169, 258, 302, 317
political activity of 34, 46, 70–1, 86,
130, 167–9, 223–4, 234, 260, 266,
270, 271, 272, 277
Protestant proslytism among, *see*
Missionary activity among RCs
religious practice 17, 19–21, 187–91
responses to anti-Catholicism 3–5, 21,
23, 46, 48–9, 57, 60, 62, 64, 91, 95,
106, 130, 145, 167–9
tensions among 21, 26, 147, 168–9,
185, 234 n.
see also Anti-Catholicism; Catholic;
Roman Catholic Church
Romanticism, impact of 30
Rome, city of 116, 235
Rome, diplomatic relations with: see
Diplomatic Relations with Rome Bill
Roscoe, William 25
Ross and Cromarty, county of 89
Rothesay 51
Round, Charles Gray 224–5
Routh, Martin 214
Royal prerogative 22, 25
Rugby 153
Russell, Lord John (later first Earl
Russell) 169, 273, 291, 316
attitudes to Catholicism 270, 291, 295
and convents 270
and diplomatic relations with
Rome 233, 234
and education 136
and general election (1847) 225, 232

and Madiai 268
and Maynooth Bill (1845) 199, 200,
203
and Papal Aggression 242–4, 261, 262
and Peel government (1835) 84, 86
as prime minister (1846–52) 198, 220,
227, 231, 235–6, 237, 260, 271–2
and proposed RC endowment 225,
228, 229, 231–2, 235–7, 294–5
and repeal of penal statutes 230, 231
and South Devon by-election 86–7
Russia 166–7, 281, 312
Rutland, John Henry Manners, fifth Duke
of 99
Ryde 153
Ryder, Granville D. 43, 66, 69, 71
Ryder, Henry, Bishop of Lichfield 43, 52
Ryder, Richard 66

St Andrews 69
University of 166
St Edmund Hall, Oxford 50, 210 n.
St Giles (London district) 18, 41, 51,
108, 153, 184, 187
St Helens 151
St John's Wood 153, 173 n.
St Keverne 146
St Sulpice, RC seminary in Montreal 103
'Saints' 43, 45
Saints, veneration of 24, 46, 47, 110, 113
Salford 17, 21, 88 n., 151, 153, 172
Salisbury 153
Sandon, Viscount (later third Earl of
Harrowby) 295
Sandon, Viscount, *see* Harrowby, second
Earl of
Scotland 1, 10, 11, 12–13, 58, 75, 103,
121, 166
Act of Union with 10
anti-Catholicism in (general
references) 12, 77, 90, 108, 132–3,
142, 146, 150, 154, 177, 197, 209,
227–8, 232, 242, 248–9, 262–3, 265,
276–7, 279, 306
Church of, *see* Church of Scotland
denominational rivalries in 138, 249–
51
Establishment question in 57, 87, 90;
see also Disruption
Free Church of, *see* Free Church of
Scotland
missions to RCs in 180, 181
national identity 310–11